Poverty: Its Degrees, Its Causes and Its Relief – a Multidisciplinary Approach to an Urgent Problem

Mareike Hansen and Thomas Riis (eds)

Themengruppe:
Die Gesellschaft – Gruppen und Erscheinungen

ESF exploratory workshop on
Poverty: Its Degrees, Its Causes and Its Relief

Solivagus-Verlag
Kiel 2008

Poverty: Its Degrees, Its Causes and Its Relief – a Multidisciplinary Approach to an Urgent Problem

Mareike Hansen and Thomas Riis (eds)

Solivagus-Verlag
Kiel 2008

Bibliographische Information der Deutschen Nationalbibliothek
Diese Publikation ist von der Deutschen Nationalbibliothek verzeichnet.
Ihre bibliographischen Daten sind im Internet unter der Adresse http://
www.d-nb.de abzurufen.

Gefördert von European Science Foundation (ESF)

SETTING SCIENCE AGENDAS FOR EUROPE

Einbandgestaltung unter Verwendung des Bildes: „Stange halten" von
Sascha Kayser, Kiel
www.saschakayser.de
Die von Sascha Kayser ins Bild gesetzte Armut ist weiblich, alleinstehend,
alt und oftmals ein Ergebnis von Krieg, Naturkatastrophen und technis-
chem Wandel.

Satz: Kirstin Houser
Gedruckt auf säurefreiem und alterungsbeständigem Papier
978-3-9812101-1-8
© Solivagus-Verlag Kiel 2008

Printed in the European Union

Table of Contents

Poor Relief and Perceptions of Poverty

Poor Relief

Perceptions of Poverty

Preface

Since the early 1990s, poverty research has been abandoned by most historians,[1] however, numerous studies in various European countries give a satisfactory descriptive image.[2] Unfortunately, one must also consider the almost total neglect of the historical dimension as far as research into contemporary poverty is concerned. Nevertheless, recent studies have shown that physical poverty (e.g. a famine) is only the final and critical phase of a long development[3] and that poverty can be transmitted from one generation to another.[4] In both cases, the importance of the historical dimension is obvious. In this respect, the "Sonderforschungsbereich" of the University of Treves, is focussing on historical aspects of poverty.

As poverty is a relative phenomenon, the lack of a proper definition of the term "poverty" is a major obstacle for comparative interdisciplinary research into the subject. Contemporary studies apply two definitions, identifying the poor with the receivers of social aid or with those whose income does not exceed 50% or 60% of the average

---

1 The Sonderforschungsbereich at the University of Treves financed by the German Research Council is an exception.
2 E.g. JEAN-PIERRE GUTTON, *La société et les pauvres. L'exemple de la généralité de Lyon 1534–1789*, Paris 1971; MICHEL MOLLAT, *Études sur l'histoire de la pauvreté*, 2 vol., Paris 1974; PAUL SLACK, *The English Poor Law, 1531–1782*, London 1990; BRONISLAW GEREMEK, *La Potence ou la pitié: l'Europe et les pauvres du Moyen Age à nos jours*, Paris 1987; ROBERT JÜTTE, *Poverty and Deviance in Early Modern Europe*, Cambridge ²1999 [New approaches to European history 4]; OLE PETER GRELL/ANDREW CUNNINGHAM (ed.), *Health Care and Poor Relief in Protestant Europe 1500–1700*, London-New York 1997; OLE PETER GRELL / ANDREW CUNNINGHAM / ROBERT JÜTTE (ed.), *Health Care and Poor Relief in 18ᵗʰ and 19ᵗʰ Century Northern Europe*, Aldershot 2002.
3 A. RANGASAMI, "The Masking of Famine: The Role of the Bureaucracy," in: *Famine and Society*, ed. JEAN FLOUD & AMRITA RANGASAMI, New Delhi 1993, pp. 53–64.
4 TORSTEN FISCHER, *Y-a-t-il une fatalité d'hérédité dans la pauvreté ? Dans l'Europe moderne : les cas d'Aberdeen et de Lyon*, Kiel 2003 (thesis), published under the same title as Beiheft 187 of the Vierteljahrschrift für Sozial- und Wirtschaftsgeschichte, Stuttgart 2006.

income in a given society. Both definitions are based on official statistics, and do not consider the various forms of poverty. Hence, the former definition does not deal with the complete spectrum of parameters influencing the economical and social development of a poor individual or a poor family. For instance, the "hidden poverty" (economic poverty hidden by social wealth, refusing public aid) has hardly been systematically investigated until now.[5] The latter definition of "poverty" is more appropriate, but does not consider the importance of victuals in kind in the individual household (or more precisely: how valuable is the contribution of the vegetables and fruits grown by the poor family itself?).

Finally, contemporary sociological definitions leave out the historical dimensions of poverty, and consequently, the process leading into poverty is not taken into account. Accordingly, poor relief often treats the symptoms, not the evil itself, as its causes mainly remain unknown.

For the reasons mentioned it seemed useful to bring together leading scholars and to invite them to discuss the possibilities of an interdisciplinary approach to poverty and its relief, taking into account both the hereditary nature of poverty and the definition of famine as the last stage of malnutrition. By encouraging this kind of collaboration the coordinators Prof. René Leboutte, Luxembourg (formerly Aberdeen) and myself hoped to develop a medium-term initiative of cross-national and interdisciplinary poverty research.

Generously, the European Science Foundation declared itself ready to sponsor an interdisciplinary workshop on poverty, which took place at Kiel in November 2005. The objectives of the workshop can be divided in short term, medium term and longer-term aims.

In a short term, the workshop participants should examine the different degrees of poverty and identify its causes. In addition, the different forms of present and past poor relief were to be considered in order to gauge their efficiency. Here, the workshop participants

---

5 With one notable exception: GIOVANNI RICCI, *Povertà, vergogna, superbia. I declassati fra Medioevo e Età moderna*, Bologna 1996.

could rely on research already done. This approach would hopefully lead to fruitful discussions about contemporary concepts of poverty.

In a medium term perspective, the workshop intended to map out further collaborative, interdisciplinary research projects and to set an agenda for future academic efforts in this field. Finally, the workshop should be an impulse for the determination of research leading to a strategy for the fight against poverty. In this way, the workshop organisers hoped to initiate a common approach to academic impact on social and economic policy. To meet its objectives, the workshop comprised four interrelated thematic sessions.

The first theme should consider one of the key problems within poverty research, which is the measurement of "poverty" and its degrees. The scope was not only to treat results of past research, but also to link European poverty research with problems coming out of sociological field research in India, where successful fighting against poverty is a most urgent desideratum. The second session would then discuss the causes of poverty in the perspective of different disciplines. The parameters measured and defined in the two first sessions could then form the basis of a debate on medium term aims, which is to say the poor relief systems, once again focussing on past and present approaches in different countries. Finally, the last session would concentrate on the perception of poverty, trying to distinguish the problem circles of a multi-disciplinary approach.

For several reasons, scholars have not only neglected the historical dimension in their efforts to find remedies against poverty, but they have also denied the usefulness of diachronic statistical research for the analysis of the economic and social situation of lower social categories. They argue that it is methodologically impossible to compare facts given in different countries or societies in a long run. However, comparative approaches to other historical topics have been extremely productive for many years. In addition, the possibilities of collecting and analysing large data sets have led to more representative studies not only in contemporary history, economy and sociology, but also in modern history.[6] In addition, the results of historical investigations can well be the starting point for interdisciplinary research.

Hence, the workshop wanted to bring together – for the first time ever – researchers from different disciplines working with different methods to get new answers on the urgent problem of poverty. At least, it seemed possible to formulate new questions to be investigated in a mid-term perspective.

Besides to the sponsor, the European Science Foundation, my gratitude is due to my collaborators, Mrs Ursula Kunze, Miss Mareike Hansen who undertook a great deal of the editorial work, Dr Jan Schlürmann, Mr Philipp Schmidt and Mr Alexandre Karwaski, M.A. who translated part of the summaries and two of the contributions into French; without their friendly and competent work the workshop could not have been held.

Kiel, February 2008   Thomas Riis

---

6 As basis for his thesis quoted in note 4 Torsten Fischer collected 15,000 names of poor members of the society in Early Modern Lyons and Aberdeen.

Communication : La définition de la pauvreté
Thomas Riis

S'il n'est aucunement impossible de décrire la pauvreté et l'assistance aux pauvres, il en est autrement pour les causes de la pauvreté et pour la définition de la pauvreté. Évidemment, nous pouvons calculer le minimum d'existence en termes absolus, tandis que le minimum d'existence social est relatif. La possibilité de manger du pain blanc en faisait partie à Florence au XVᵉ siècle,[1] et aujourd'hui, en Europe occidentale, qui peut s'imaginer une famille sans auto ? Or, vers 1950, rares étaient les familles qui en possédaient, seulement des médecins, des hommes d'affaires ou ceux qui en avaient déjà avant la guerre. Par ailleurs, la société change, et quand la population en moyenne devient plus riche, le seuil de la pauvreté va se situer à un niveau plus élevé.[2]

En 1953, les Nations Unies ont constitué une commission avec la tâche de trouver une définition du niveau de vie ainsi que des méthodes d'évaluation valides à l'échelle internationale. Le rapport de la commission (de 1954) identifia douze facteurs à considérer :[3]

1) la santé et ses conditions démographiques, 2) l'alimentation, 3) éducation et alphabétisation, 4) les conditions de travail, 5) les conditions d'emploi, 6) consommation et économies, 7) transport, 8) l'habitat et son équipement, 9) les vêtements, 10) les loisirs, 11) la sécurité sociale et 12) les droits de l'homme, les libertés.

C'est évident que ces douze critères permettent la description du niveau de vie d'une population donnée dans toute sa complexité,

---

1 Amleto Spicciani, « The « Poveri Vergognosi » dans Fifteenth-Century Florence », dans : Thomas Riis éd., *Aspects of Poverty in Early Modern Europe* (I), Stuttgart 1981, pp. 130–136.
2 Wilfried Beckerman, « The Measurement of Poverty », dans : *Aspects of Poverty* I (comme note 1), p. 53.
3 Poul Thestrup, *The Standard of Living in Copenhagen 1730–1800. Some methods of measurement*, Copenhague 1971, p. 12.

pourvu qu'on trouve assez de sources. Le catalogue des critères est utile seulement si l'on peut comparer les réponses à une mesure extérieure, par exemple le niveau de vie moyen d'une population donnée.

On voit tout de suite que le catalogue des critères est aussi celui des privations – est-ce que le pauvre peut se permettre une bonne nourriture, donner à ses enfants une éducation qui correspond à leurs capacités intellectuelles, jouir des libertés en théorie à la portée de tout citoyen ? En outre, le catalogue de critères se réfère avant tout à la situation contemporaine et s'applique seulement avec difficulté aux sociétés du passé.

D'autres définitions contemporaines placent le seuil de la pauvreté à 50 % ou 60 % du revenu moyen. C'est une définition juste, mais vague, qui ne considère pas les revenus en nature, ni la valeur du travail manuel de la famille ; par contre, une autre, allemande, tranche : pauvre est celui qui reçoit l'assistance sociale.[4] Malgré toute sa clarté, elle n'est pas satisfaisante, car elle exclut les pauvres honteux ou, dans le passé, les mendiants valides, qui très souvent ne reçurent pas d'aide, parce que leur sous-emploi n'était pas reconnu comme une cause de la pauvreté.[5] Donc, les définitions contemporaines ne nous aident guère à trouver des définitions utiles dans le passé comme au présent.

En 1974, Richard Gascon publia un article sur la pauvreté à Lyon aux XVIe et XVIIe siècles, dans lequel il essaie de définir le seuil de la pauvreté. A base de la comptabilité de la construction du pont sur le Rhône en 1501–1502, il trouve la limite de la pauvreté franchie quand les dépenses pour le pain constituent plus de la moitié du revenu journalier.

---

4 *Lebenslagen in Deutschland – Der erste Armuts- und Reichtumsbericht der Bundesregierung*, Berlin 2001, p. 8 (http://www.bundesregierung.de/dokumente/Artikel/ix_36654_1388.htm).
5 En Allemagne, aux années 1980, on estimait le taux des pauvres honteux à 35 % du nombre total des pauvres, *Bericht über die Entwicklung der Armut in Kiel*, Kiel 1998, p. 1.

Le seuil de la pauvreté : Lyon 1501–1502

R(evenu) j(ournalier) disponible = S(alaire) j(ournalier) x (7/10 x 5/7) = Sj/2

7/10 = 30 % nécessaires pour d'autres dépenses que le pain

5/7 = cinq jours de travail par semaine

Seuil de la pauvreté : 50 % du revenu journalier dépensés pour le pain (Rj = Sj/2)

Source : RICHARD GASCON, « Économie et pauvreté aux XVIᵉ et XVIIᵉ siècles : Lyon, ville exemplaire et prophétique », dans : M. MOLLAT éd., *Études sur l'histoire de la pauvreté* II, Paris 1974, p. 749.

La documentation allemande nous apprend qu'entre 1771 et 1860 un compagnon des métiers de construction ne pouvait que rarement se permettre de fonder une famille :

Minimum d'existence d'une famille urbaine de cinq personnes, Allemagne 1771–1860

	Besoin annuel en Taler	Salaire annuel d'un compagnon dans les métiers de construction en Taler
1771–1780	85-105	60-120
1791–1799	130-150	70-130
1821–1830	105-120	90-130
1851–1860	140-160	100-155

Source : DIEDRICH SAALFELD, « Lebensstandard in Deutschland. Einkommensverhältnisse und Lebenshaltungskosten städtischer Populationen in der Übergangsperiode zum Industriezeitalter », dans : *Wirtschaftliche und soziale Strukturen im saekularen Wandel. Festschrift für Wilhelm Abel zum 70. Geburtstag* II, hrsg. INGOMAR BOG u.a., Hanovre 1974, pp. 417–443, ici p. 428.

Vers la fin du XVIIIᵉ siècle et de nouveau vers 1850, une famille ouvrière allemande devait dépenser deux tiers, voire trois quarts des revenus pour des vivres, dont deux tiers (ou 40 % des revenus totaux) pour le pain ou des substituts comme les petits pois ou les pommes de terre.[6]

En Angleterre, vers la fin du XVIIIᵉ siècle, une famille de Berkshire de sept personnes dépensait 56 % des revenus pour le pain et la farine ; même si les deux époux travaillaient, le résultat de chaque

---

6 SAALFELD, « Lebensstandard », p. 423.

semaine était un déficit. Aussi l'assistance de la paroisse ne pouvait pas empêcher le cumul de dettes.[7]

En 1831, pour une famille pauvre de la ville de Bath, à peu près deux tiers des dépenses se référaient aux vivres comme nous en montre l'aperçu suivant.

Dépenses hebdomadaires d'une famille pauvre de quatre personnes, Bath 1831 (pence)

Vivres	93	64,6 %
Bière	8	5,6 %
Vêtements, chaussures	16	11,1 %
Lessive, savon, bougies	3	2,1 %
Chauffage	6	4,2 %
Loyer	18	12,5 %
Total	144	

Source : R. S. Neale, « The Standard of Living 1780–1844 : a Regional and Class Study », *Economic History Review*, 2nd Series XIX, 1966, p. 598.

Dans une autre famille anglaise de sept membres, cette fois-ci de Suffolk en 1843, le pain comptait pour 65,5 % des dépenses ménagères. La famille paraît n'avoir jamais mangé de la viande, seulement de petites quantités de beurre et de fromage.[8]

Les documentations allemande et anglaise des XVIIIe–XIXe siècles paraissent confirmer la définition de Richard Gascon. Nous proposons une légère modification, c'est à dire : pauvre est celui qui dépense plus que la moitié du revenu pour le pain et les vivres le remplaçant (riz, pommes de terre, fèves, nouilles).

Aussi dans le domaine de l'habitat nous trouvons un seuil de la pauvreté. Si l'on définit la taille d'un adulte couché comme deux mètres, il en résulte que quatre mètres carrés constituent le minimum de superficie qui doit être à la disposition de chaque adulte. En effet, quatre m² étaient le minimum employé par l'administration britan-

---

7 John Burnett, *A History of the Cost of Living*, Harmondsworth 1969, p. 167.
8 *Ibid.*, pp. 262–263.

nique en Allemagne du Nord ainsi que par la municipalité de Kiel après 1945.[9] Ici, il faut pourtant se rappeler que des villes comme Hambourg ou Kiel avaient été largement détruites pendant la guerre. A Copenhague, en 1889, on avait défini la superficie minimale d'une pièce d'appartement comme six m²,[10] et aujourd'hui, l'Organisation mondiale de la santé considère 12 m² comme le minimum.

La définition du minimum de logement comme quatre mètres carrés par adulte paraît donc justifiée.

Nos réflexions nous ont ainsi permis d'identifier deux définitions de la pauvreté qui paraissent valides pour l'époque contemporaine comme pour le passé. En ce qui concerne l'habitat, le seuil de la pauvreté est franchie, si la famille dispose de moins de quatre mètres carrés par adulte, et quant aux revenus, il est dépassé, quand le pain et ses substituts exigent plus que la moitié des dépenses. La question reste, si une famille pauvre était jamais rassasiée ? Pour les ouvriers agricoles de la région autour d' Eckernförde (Schleswig-Holstein) on a pu reconstituer un budget de famille pour les deux dernières décennies du XIXe siècle.[11] Même si le rôle du pain et de ses substituts reste inférieur à la moitié des dépenses globales, la famille n'était pas suffisamment nourrie. Par personne, on a eu 1420 calories par jour, tandis qu'un adulte en a besoin de 2650 ou presque le double selon les normes des Nations Unies.[12]

Ce fait – qui n'était pas causé par des événements spéciaux – montre le bien-fondé de la nouvelle vue de la famine proposée par Madame Rangasami. Autrefois, on se l'est représentée comme l'effet d'une catastrophe. Aujourd'hui on sait, et le cas de notre famille d'Eckernförde le confirme, que la famine est seulement la dernière phase d'une longue évolution qui commence avec la sous-alimentation des pauvres et finit par le coup de grâce d'une mauvaise récolte.[13]

---

9 TIMM ERHARDT, « Lebenshaltungskosten und Einkünfte von Arbeitnehmern 1945–1948 », *Zeitschrift der Gesellschaft für Schleswig-Holsteinische Geschichte* CXXIV, 1999, p. 182.

10 RICHARD WILLERSLEV, « Arbejdernes boligforhold på det københavnske Vesterbro omkring år 1900 », *Erhvervshistorisk Årbog* XXVI, 1975 (=1976), pp. 7–30, p. 18.

11 HERMANN SCHLÜTER, « Die wirtschaftliche Lage der Landarbeiter im Kreise Eckernförde zwischen 1880 und 1900 », *Jahrbuch Heimatgemeinschaft Eckernförde* XLI, 1983, pp. 225–242.

12 *Ibid.*, p. 236.

13 AMRITA RANGASAMI, « The Masking of Famine: The Role of the Bureaucracy », dans : *Famine and Society,* » éd. JEAN FLOUD and AMRITA RANGASAMI, New Delhi 1993, pp. 55–57.

Size of Families: Are Children Poor People's Riches ?
Sølvi Sogner

Chacun portera son fardeau. Il est bien rude à pauvres gens chassés dehors par les épaules. Les enfants, c'est la richesse des pauvres.[1]

French prayerbook, 17th century

In the paper I look at the size of families in rural society, primarily in the early modern period. Focus is on Norwegian conditions, but comparisons are made with similar data from Denmark, Sweden and Germany. I will describe the composition of poor families (age of the adults, number and age of the children, and presence of grandparents in the household). The problem under discussion is: Can a huge number of children be regarded as social security?

Children are important to families

The desire to have children of one's own seems innate and a universal historical constant. "Who has no children, does not know what life is about," says a Danish proverb. In today's society, considerable resources go to remedy cases of childlessness. Historically, childlessness has been regarded as a malediction.[2] Within Christian society, impotence – if existing prior to the marriage and kept secret – was a legal ground for annulment or divorce. Inability to conceive was usually blamed on the wife – an infertile woman was called *óbyrja* in Old Norse. However, this relatively rare condition – some 3 per cent of married women are infertile at the age of 25 – did not have the same dire legal consequences; in principle it could not be known before marriage.[3]

---

1 In English: Every one has his burden to carry. It is very hard on poor people who are scornfully driven out. Children are poor people's riches.
2 SOGNER 1987.
3 Crulai about 1700; 3,4 % Rendalen 1733–80. These figures are comparable to present day figures.

Bridal pregnancy has been very common in historic Scandinavian peasant societies. Norwegian parish data show that half or even up to two thirds of all brides were pregnant, even though pre-nuptial sex was regarded as a sin by the Church and fined as a criminal offence by the State. Possibly, the importance of securing a fertile marriage may be a reasonable explanation. In medieval Norse inheritance law, if no child was born, property brought into the marriage by the wife would revert to her family of origin at the couple's death.[4]

Securing property through the continuation of the family line would, however, be a concern of the well-to-do rather than of the poor. Still, in a household based family economy, such as we find it in the early modern period, children as potential workers might be of interest to both rich and poor alike. For those who could afford it, like the farmers, hired labour might meet the need. For the poor this was not an option. Are children then poor people's riches in the sense that they represent potential future contributors to the family's needs?

In contrast to the farmers, whose farm was the unit of production and consumption, residence and workplace; non-property owning families would have to live by their wits and by their labour. By joint family effort, however, a sort of living could be pinched together, as the ethnologist Orvar Löfgren has shown.[5] Richard Wall uses the term adaptive family economy for the case when families "attempt to maximize their economic well-being by diversifying the employments of family members", taking "due account of the wide range of employment on offer and the varied responses of the persons who had to survive on the proceeds of their labour".[6] In the old society, before occupations became more specified, this boiled down more or less to sending your children out into service.

Children during their tender years must needs, however, be receivers of, rather than contributors to, the common family resources. It takes years before children become "productive" and parents can expect "dividends" of their "investments" in childrearing. And if it does work out, and the child contributes to the family economy ac-

---

4 To this day, a newborn baby is called an *arving*, an "inheritor".
5 LÖFGREN 1974, 1978.
6 WALL 1986, p. 265.

cording to theory, how substantial is the child's contribution? And for how long will it last? At what age is the child allowed to look out for its own future, and save for a nest-egg of its own?

Which poor families are to be discussed?

Leaving the few elite households aside, we find two main types of families in the peasant society – farmers and cottars.[7] The bulk of the rural population fits into one or the other category. The former is the solid, more affluent household, based upon ownership or rental of a farm. The latter is clearly underprivileged, the cottar family's existence contract bound at the discretion of the farmer on whose land the cottage is situated.

In this paper cottars are defined as "the poor". Poor they certainly were, clinging by the skin of their teeth to the next but last bottom wrung of the social ladder. Vulnerable, they easily slid all the way to the bottom and became beggars, drop-outs, regular paupers. Thus it is evidenced that 60 percent of the "poorest poor" in one parish were of cottar stock in the 18th century.[8] But these, the most destitute poor and their families – if they had any – mostly escape the historian's net. Also, they were beyond having much control of their own destiny. They are also exceedingly few – less than 2 per cent – as listed in Norway's first nominal census of 1801. The cottars on the other hand lend themselves to the analysis, as they had some potential for controlling their present and their future.

Farmer and cottar families c. 1800

To understand the situation of families within the traditional, pre-industrial household economy, we have to look at the family within the household context. For the sake of comparison the household components discussed here are roughly reduced to three main categories. (1) Nuclear family = parents and children. As a rule, parents are registered with a value close to 2, so to get the number of children,

---

7 The *innerst* (= lodger) is included in the cottar group, because of comparable precarious living conditions: forming a family and a separate household of sorts, and earning his living through labour.
8 Assev 1990, p. 185.

subtract 2 from the value given for the "nuclear family"! (2) Kin and others: grandparents, other relatives of the nuclear family, lodgers, fosterchildren. (3) Servants.

The distribution of persons according to categories in farmer and cottar households in the Scandinavian and German examples presented here, is quite similar, but each component of the household was smaller in the cottar household – fewer resident children, fewer resident kin and lodgers, and above all, hardly if any servants:

Table 1. Family household structure in the rural parishes of Dala, Sweden (1780), Krønge, Denmark (1787), Rendalen, Norway (1801), Belm in Osnabrück, Germany (1772). Three resident groups registered for comparison: (1) nuclear family, (2) resident kin and lodgers, (3) servants. Farmers and cottars.

	Nuclear family	Kin and lodgers	Servants	Total
FARMERS				
Dala, S	4,5	0,2	0,8	5,5
Krønge, DK	3,9	0,4	0,9	5,2
Rendalen, N	4,8	1,4	1,4	7,6
Belm, D small	4,2	0,5	0,3	5,0
Belm, D big	5,2	0,7	2,5	8,4

	Nuclear family	Kin and lodgers	Servants	Total
COTTARS				
Dala, S	2,9	0,1	0,1	3,1
Krønge, DK	3,1	0,3	0,2	3,6
Rendalen, N	3,3	0,4	-	3,7
Belm, D	3,8	0,2	0,1	4,0

Source: WINBERG 1977, p. 300; SOGNER 1979, p. 291; JOHANSEN 1976, p. 139; SCHLUMBOHM [1994] 1997, p. 201.

The nuclear family household of farmers comprises 5–8 persons: where the nuclear family counts for 4–5 persons, kin and lodgers range from hardly any to 1,5, servants from 1 to 2,5.

For cottars the family household totals 3–4 persons, of which the nuclear family counts 3–4, kin and lodgers 0–0,5, and servants are practically non-existant.

The only striking difference between the three Scandinavian parishes and the German parish is the elevated number of servants in the big farm households in Germany (*Grossbauern*). I believe this may be due to the difference in the size of the farms. The vast undulating fertile North German plains are suited for large scale agriculture, whereas the Scandinavian topography rarely allows that kind of activity, and certainly not the parishes under scrutiny. The Scandinavian topography actually lends itself more to the search for supplementary income outside of farming.

Our interest here focuses on the presence of children. Why are there fewer children in the cottars' households than in the farmers' households? Possibly, this may be caused by differences in fertility, mortality, or mobility. Were fewer children born in cottar families? Did the cottar children have higher mortality? Did the cottar children move out from home at an earlier age than farmers' children?

In the following, I shall concentrate the discussion on the Norwegian rural parish of Rendalen, which I know best. Rendalen was a vast and sparsely populated parish of more than 4,000 km², situated in south-eastern Norway, close to the border of Sweden. The population was about 1,000 people in 1733 and some 3,500 in 1900. The main industries were agriculture, animal husbandry, and forestry. The parish is situated in a highland area, with farms located at 250–540 metres above sea level in the mountain valley, and summer pastures up to 940 metres. The settlement pattern is characterized by separate farmsteads, and the majority of the farmers were freeholders. As the population increased, farms were divided up and new settlements sprang up in outlying areas. The number of farms nearly tripled from 112 in 1762 to 300 in 1900. In the eighteenth-century there was a rise of a semi-landless group called *husmenn* (cottars). They rented a small piece of land on the premises of a farm. The lease period was usually for life and as part of the payment of the lease the cottar and his family was often obliged to work on the farm. This provided a stable workforce for many of the farmers during the most labour intensive periods of the year. The number of cottars declined in the nineteenth-century and many of the oldest cottages were sold and turned into small farms.

Is differential fertility an explanation?

Can a difference in fertility between farmers and cottars go some way towards explaining the fewer children observed in cottar households as compared to farmer households? Were fewer children born to poorer parents?

Women, living through 25 years of unbroken marriage from age 20 to age 44 would in theory bear 8–9 children. Farmer wives, however, have consistently more children than cottar wives, during each five year period, for women of the same age, as evidenced in several Norwegian family reconstitution studies.[9] In actual practice, however, fertility was much lower. Women married later and spouses died prematurely. Actual observed sibling groups are therefore not as numerous as the theoretical figures would lead us to believe:

Farmer families generally had more time at their disposal, because they married earlier. Median age at marriage was for farmer brides about 25 (24.5 in the period 1733–1780, and 25.6 1781–1828). This was 5 years earlier than for cottar brides (median age in these periods: 30.5 and 30.1). Also, age at last birth decreased with about two years for both social groups after 1780, for farmer wives from 41.8 to 39.4, and for cottars' wives from 40 to 38.3. Cottars' wives thus had fewer years of exposure to pregnancy, as well as lower fertility rates during exposure than was the case for farmers' wives. Looking only at couples who lived in unbroken marriages through their childbearing years (endpoint set at age 45 for the wife), we find the following number of children actually born 1733–1828 to farmer and cottar couples respectively.

---

9 Age specific fertility rates for married women aged 20–44 years. Births per annum per woman in five year age groups. Rendalen, Norway, 1733–1828. Farmers and cottars.

parish	period	20–24	25–29	30–34	35–39	40–44	Total births
Farmer wives	1733–1828	.497	.414	.350	.310	.185	8.780
Cottar wives	1733–1828	.593	.335	.258	.217	.111	7.570

Source: SOGNER 1979, pp. 345, 350.

Table 2. Number of children born in complete families (unbroken marriage till wife's age 45), according to marriage age of wife. Farmers and cottars. Parish of Rendalen, Norway. 1733–1828.

Wife's marriage age	15-19	20-24	25-29	30-34	35-39	all ages
No. of farmer families	12	75	48	26	16	177
No. of farmer children	100	562	271	116	47	1096
No. of cottar families	1	11	29	36	31	108
No. of cottar children	4	58	101	101	53	317
Farmers' total no. of children	8,3	7,5	5,6	4,5	2,9	6,2
Cottars' total no. of children	4	5,3	3,5	2,8	1,7	2,9

Source: SOGNER 1979, p. 375.

Even if children actually were the riches of the poor, these same poor hesitated to bring forth too many! Did they intentionally try to limit their families, as best they could, in order not to increase the burden of their family responsibilities? Were children a burden rather than a resource to the poor cottar parents?

Differential infant and child mortality?

Recent studies of infant mortality in Scandinavia has repeatedly come up with the conclusion that the lower social strata had as good or even better survival chances when compared to their better offs.[10] The need for the poor to rely on breastfeeding in infant feeding practices, and the benevolent effect this had on infant mortality has been offered as a plausible explanation of this astounding finding.

For Rendalen 1733–1828 infant mortality is 125 per 1000 for farmers' infants, but no more than 135 per 1000 for cottars' infants. Otherwise expressed: of 1000 farmer babies 875 survive till their one year birthday, as against 865 cottar babies. Mortality is thus very similar. Cottar children, however, have got a higher mortality from age 1–9.

---

10 LØKKE 1998.

Between ages 10 and 15 the gap closes. By age 15, out of 1000 farmer newborn babies 755 have survived as against 691 cottar babies.

Table 3. Rendalen 1733–1828. Infant and child mortality. Farmers and cottars.

	FARMERS	COTTARS
infant mortality	125	135
death ratio 1-4	72	108
death ratio 5-9	44	80
death ratio 10-15	27	27

Source: SOGNER 1979, pp. 388–390.

The discrepancy in mortality between the two social groups cannot, in my view, explain the difference in the size of the sibling groups.

Domestic service and differential mobility of farmer and cottar children

What do we know about the prospects of cottars' children in life? In order to answer that question, we have to look at our knowledge about age at leaving home.

A constitutive element in the demographer John Hajnal's model for the European pre-industrial household formation system is the circulation of servants between households.[11] In his widely accepted model these servants are young unmarried people, who serve during a certain phase of their life cycle, before marrying and setting up a household of their own.

From the middle ages people of restricted means were by law obliged to take service.[12] The laws were reinforced subsequently at intervals all through the eighteenth century. The obligation applied

11 HAJNAL 1983.
12 SOGNER 2005.

to all unmarried men and women who did not possess an acceptable alternative – such as running a farm or using an important trade or craft. In 1754 a decree even laid down that farmers were no longer allowed to have more unmarried children above the age of 18 at home than were needed for running the farm. Cottars were only allowed to keep at home one son and one daughter above the age of 16. All others were obliged to enter service for at least a year. We have evidence that the law was at least occasionally enforced with rigour.

Also, the same decree of 1754 forbade the increase of wages above the traditional – very low – level. Servants' wages consisted of food, clothing, and a very small money payment. It took long years of service and a strong determination to save a nest-egg.

Not until the 19th century were these very restrictive laws repealed. Service was in principle compulsory until 1854, after having been enforced during half a millennium. By then society was undergoing a serious transition.

Could poor parents expect their children to contribute to the family budget?

The poorer the family, the harder it must have been to make both ends meet and keep the children at home long enough for them to cope in the world at large. Children worked for their living from an early age, at home or in other people's households. "Seven years old, old enough to earn her keep," to quote a seventeenth century judge giving sentence in a case involving a little servant girl.[13]

The age at which a child would be sent out in service is a strong indicator of the economic status of their parents. A little child may hardly be expected to earn enough to supplement the parents' income, but the formula "earn its own keep" may go a long way towards explaining why the child is sent away from home and into service. Poor parents had problems supporting their own children. At the first nominative census in Norway, in 1801, when one third of the population was less than fifteen years old, it was quite normal that children of tender ages were working in other people's households. 90 percent

---

13 *Tingbok for Finnmark* (1987), 28/3 1629.

of the children aged nine were still in their parental home, but by the age of ten they began to leave in a steady and regular stream, and 55 percent of all young boys and girls aged 19 were servants in other people's homes.[14] It is a fair assumption, that the poorer the household, the younger the child was sent out into service. In 1835, in a parish adjacent to the capital, nine out of ten child servants were recruited from the lower social classes.[15]

While small children certainly did their bit, it would be unrealistic to assume that this amounted to very much more than keeping alive. But by the age of fifteen – about the time for their confirmation – it was normal to go into service. This was the case for children in farmer families as well as in cottar families. In the parish of Rendalen, this age seems to be the normal age for children in general to go out into service. In 1801 only some three per cent are servants under the age of 14. The cottars just as well as the farmers keep their small children at home, but once serviceable age – as they see it – is reached, cottar children are much more liable to leave home than farmer children. Looking at children's ages, below and above age 15 in 1801, 15 % are still at home as against 30 % of farmer children.[16]

The crucial question – and one which I cannot answer – is whether or not children in service did contribute towards their parents' family budget? We do not know. Servants' money wages were quite low. As servants they had board, lodging and clothing so they might in principle be able to put something aside. We know that it was customary in many places that foster children, after confirmation, often served their foster parents some years without pay, thus paying back what they had received.[17] Taking in foster children was not necessarily a charitable act, but a cheap way for farmers to secure labour, at the lowest possible cost for the parish poor relief. However, it did not preclude the possibility of affectionate relations and feelings of gratitude developing between foster parents and foster children. Was this modelled on similar behaviour among children towards their real parents?

---

14 OLDERVOLL 1980.
15 BRYHN DAHL 1986.
16 SOGNER 1979, p. 289.
17 HOLMSEN 1977, pp. 25–31.

The decree of 1754 postulated that children working as servants for their parents were to receive regular wages. Did they indeed? Or was this a threat for the parents that it would cost them to keep their children at home, out of the labour market? Internal family relations are hard to look into. It is nevertheless fair to assume that, although not formalized nor evidenced, it is most likely that parents and children have had a common interest in reciprocal help. However, when the young people themselves were about to found their own family, their ability to assist their parents – in whatever fashion – would be greatly reduced.

Old age and poverty

The question then is whether or not it might be a help for poor parents in their old age to have a substantial number of children. To tackle this question we may again take a look at the household structure. Cohabitation may be one answer to this question. Do we find cohabitation among the older and the younger generation? Even if we do, the answer is not necessarily obvious. Having one child might indeed be sufficient for this purpose, having several is not necessarily helpful!

Parents have always been prime care givers and responsible for the support of their children. Who were responsible for the old? In medieval law paupers had the right to be supported by those next of kin who should have inherited them in case they had died in affluence in stead of in poverty. Negligence might be fined. If private support was unavailable, the local community would be responsible and the pauper would receive help according to a rotation system, *legd*. In the course of the 18th century – starting in 1741 – a public poor relief system was formally organized in the countryside, region by region.[18] Some correction houses were set up in towns, to deal with the "unjust poor", those undeserving poor, the vagrants, unwilling to work. The deserving poor, on the other hand, should be taken care of, each in his or her parish. Here a "poverty commission", consisting of the local vicar and some farmers, administered the poor relief. At their

---

18 Sogner 1984, pp. 115–120; Dørum 1995.

disposal the commission had on the one hand a small fund, based on a tiny annual tax – 8 s for men, 4 s for women – levied on the group of potentially needy, i.e. cottars, "servants and farmers' children". The fund made possible a small monetary contribution extended to poor people in their own home. The bulk of the poor relief, however, was based on the old rotation system from medieval time: Poor people were freighted around the parish and given the basics to keep them alive, spending some two weeks on each farm belonging to that particular rotation circle.[19]

The parish that I have studied in depth, Rendalen, had in 1801 in a population of 1685 persons; what is the situation for the really destitute?[20] We find 7 old paupers being freighted around from farm to farm, "on the parish", all women, aged 65 to 87. For one of them information is lacking, but three are widowed and three single. Three households and three individual persons receive public poor relief in their homes – they are all widowed or handicapped, above 60 and of cottar stock.[21]

We heard that public support did not enter the equation until family support had been exhausted. What then about family and kin support? In the tables presented Norwegian farmer households tend to have a relatively high number of members as compared to other farmer households. This is due to the presence of relatives. In almost half of all farmer households, we find them present, but only in 12 % of cottar households.[22]

I have looked at people aged 60 and more to see how old people of the cottar class fared in old age. At sixty and above eighteen farmers were still active, whereas 23 had retired. Cottars above sixty, however, still clung to their old living: twentyfive cottars were still ac-

---

19 Children were not supposed to take part in the rotation system, as it was not considered beneficial for them. They were instead placed in fostering, paid for by the parish; a so called licitation system developed, a kind of inverted auction, where poor children were auctioned out to the lowest bidder.

20 29 children are foster children – these are not necessarily poor but may be orphans, in need of care and without family and kin to help.

21 In one case, the husband (44) is probably insane and his wife is heading the household, as "widow".

22 Types 4 and 5 of the LASLETT/HAMMEL scheme combined.

tive, only two had retired. In all of these cases (but one), the cottar's wife is younger or of the same age as the husband.[23] A spouse of good working capacity was necessary to keep the household going. In addition, in five of these cases an adult son or daughter was also present in the household. The future prospect of taking over the lease for the cottage may be an attraction for the adult children to stay with the parents.

No widower heads a cottar household, but six widows do – three are in their fifties, three are aged 60 and above. And in all cases but one – the youngest widow, aged 53 – adult children are present in the household, without any doubt ready to take over.

In some cases the takeover has already taken place. One grandparent couple, one grandfather as well as eight grandmothers (all but one aged above 60) stay in their adult child's cottar household.[24]

The old contribute towards their support. Twelve relatives of the nuclear family present in cottar households are (all but one) aged above 60. Five of eight grandmothers staying with their adult children in the latter's cottar households have a retirement contract (føderåd), two do handiwork for a living. They all have a place to live, but they make a personal contribution towards their support!

By way of conclusion

For poor people, many children were not equivalent to a possibility of increasing the family income. Nor did they indeed have many children. The problem was basic sustenance. Children must earn their own keep, to quote the judge. If the parents were unable to provide for their own children, even very small children were sent into service. By 1900, child servants were becoming obsolete. The time spent by children in the parental home before going into service was considerably extended. The age when 25 percent – or one in four – had moved out was for girls in 1801 12,5 years, boys three months older, whereas a hundred years later one of four girls left home three

---

23 Of the 11 cases of husband 60–69, 8 of the wives are under 60; in the 6 cases where the husband is 70–79, the same is true in 5 cases.

24 One elderly couple (64–62) is related to the household heads, has got a private pension.

years later, about fifteen years old, and boys similarly were four years older, about seventeen.[25]

The children of poor people were certainly not in an economic sense their parents' riches, rather they were the potential riches of better-off people, who could afford to employ them cheaply and make use of their labour capacity. I will modify the adage quoted at the beginning of this paper to say that one possible conclusion may be that poor people's children are other people's riches.

But it is hard to poor people when their children are driven out to serve their "betters", with no prospect of improving their own condition. So there may be another possible conclusion as well. The cottar family household was indeed vulnerable enough to deserve the epithet "poor". Exposed to too much stress, it might very well collapse. And it did. In fact, the system as such was dismantled gradually in the course of the nineteenth and into the twentieth century, and it no longer exists.

Industrialization, urbanization, emigration, family limitation opened up new life careers for cottars. The small cottar family proved its adaptability to the new situation. In fact, it is arguable that the poor cottar family household is the real forerunner of today's small, afflu-ent family, and that children – in limited numbers – are the riches of their parents, be they poor or rich.

Bibliography

PER ASSEV 1990, *Rangspersoner, bønder og husmenn. Befolkningsutvikling i Luster på 1700-tallet.* MA-thesis in history, University of Oslo.

FRØYDIS BRYHN DAHL 1986, *Barnetjenere, fosterbarn og legdebarn. En un-dersøkelse av omsorgstrengende barn i Asker prestegjeld 1801–1835 med utgangspunkt i barns plassering i husstanden.* MA-thesis in history, University of Oslo.

C. M. CIPOLLA [1976] 1993, *Before the Industrial Revolution. European Soci-ety and Economy 1000–1700.* Third edition. London.

STÅLE DYRVIK 1972, "Historical Demography in Norway 1660–1801: A Short Survey", in *Scandinavian Economic History Review* XX, pp. 27–44.

---

25 SOLLI 2003, pp. 76, 243.

KNUT DØRUM 1995, "Fattigdommen på landsbygda på 1700-tallet", *Heimen* 32, pp. 73–83.

MARIANNE JARNÆS ERIKSTAD, *Husstandsstrukturen i Nord-Norge etter folketellinga i 1801*. MA-thesis in history, University of Bergen.

JOHN HAJNAL 1983, "Two kinds of pre-industrial household formation systems", in RICHARD WALL with JEAN ROBIN and PETER LASLETT (eds) 1983, *Family forms in historic Europe*. Cambridge.

LISBETH HIGLEY, *Husholdningsstruktur i Ullensaker i 1801 og 1865*. MA-thesis in history. University of Oslo. 1976.

RIGMOR FRIMANNSLUND HOLMSEN 1977, "Fosterbarn", *Dugnad* 1/1977.

TORE IVERSEN 1994, *Trelldommen: norsk slaveri i middelaldere*. Bergen.

HANS CHR. JOHANSEN 1976, *Studier i dansk befolkningshistorie*. Odense.

ORVAR LÖFGREN 1978, "The Potato People", in SUNE ÅKERMAN et al. (eds), *Chance and Change. Social and Economic Studies in Historical Demography in the Baltic Area*. Odense, pp. 95–106.

ORVAR LÖFGREN 1974, "Family and Household among Scandinavian Peasants", *Ethnologica Scandinavica*.

ANNE LØKKE 1998, *Døden i barndommen. Spædbørnsdødelighed og moderniseringsprocesser i Danmark 1800–1920*. København.

JAN OLDERVOLL 1980, "Det store oppbruddet", in SIVERT LANGHOLM og FRANCIS SEJERSTED (red.), *Vandringer*. Oslo, pp. 91-107.

JÜRGEN SCHLUMBOHM [1994] 1997, *Lebensläufe, Familien, Höfe*. Göttingen.

SØLVI SOGNER 2005, "The Legal Status of Service in Norway from the Seventeenth to the Twentieth Century", in A. FAUVE-CHAMOUX (ed.), *Domestic Service and the Formation of European Identity. Understanding the Globalization of Domestic Work, 16th to 21st Centuries*. Bern, pp. 175–188.

SØLVI SOGNER 1987, "Før den teknologiske tidsalder – barnløshet i det gamle samfunn", *Nytt om kvinneforskning* 1–87, pp. 8–17.

SØLVI SOGNER 1984, "Barna – familiens ansvar?", in BJARNE HODNE and SØLVI SOGNER (eds), *Barn av sin tid. Fra norske barns historie*. Oslo, pp. 115–122.

SØLVI SOGNER 1979, *Folkevekst og flytting. En historisk-demografisk studie i 1700-årenes Øst-Norge.* Oslo.

SØLVI SOGNER 1977, "Historisk demografi i Norge – en forskningsorientering med særlig vekt på fruktbarhet", in *Nordisk Demografi* 1977, pp. 50–68.

ARNE SOLLI 2003, *Livsløp – familie – samfunn: Endring av familiestrukturar i Noreg på 1800-talet.* Ph.D.-dissertation. Bergen.

POUL THESTRUP 1972, "Methodological Problems of a Family Reconstitution Study", in *Scandinavian Economic History Review* XX, pp. 1–26.

RICHARD WALL 1986, "Work, Welfare and the Family: An Illustration of the Adaptive Family Economy", in LLOYD BONFIELD et al. (eds), *The World We Have Gained. Histories of Population and Social Structure.* Oxford.

CHRISTER WINBERG 1977, *Folkökning och proletarisering.* Lund.

Des hommes pauvres et des femmes qui le sont encore davantage. Vivre avec le minimum vital*
———— Marion Kobelt-Groch ————

Quiconque aborde le problème de l'histoire de la pauvreté est rapidement confronté à des obstacles. La question de savoir en quoi consiste la pauvreté et comment celle-ci est mesurable constitue un premier obstacle. De même, la tentative d'appréhender le phénomène de façon individuelle, c'est-à-dire de prendre en compte les exemples précis d'existences d'hommes et de femmes vivant dans la pauvreté, n'est pas tâche facile. Qui était pauvre ? Ou plutôt : qui parmi les personnes intéressées se serait prétendue pauvre ? Et, le cas échéant, quel état de manque et éventuellement quelle indigence se cache-t-elle derrière cette auto-évaluation ? Il est vrai que les textes relatifs à la pauvreté en Europe, surtout au Moyen Âge et aux Temps modernes, ne manquent pas ;[1] les tentatives, de plusieurs pages parfois, de définition du sujet de cette recherche, aux contours flous, aux transitions fluides et aux perspectives changeantes sont éloquentes. Non seulement la vérité, mais aussi la pauvreté ont conservé au fil des siècles leur aspect vivant. Certains l'aimaient au nom de Dieu, d'autres la méprisaient parce qu'elle sentait la misère, les immondices et la mort. L'écrivain autrichien Christine Lavant, deux fois lauréate du prix Georg Trakl, décrit dans sa nouvelle « La Belle et la robe de pavot » la façon dont elle peignit un cœur à l'intérieur duquel elle in-

---

*Traduit de l'Allemand par Alexandre Karwaski, M.A.

1 Parmi les textes les plus récents, citons par exemple: WOLFGANG VON HIPPEL, *Armut, Unterschichten, Randgruppen in der Frühen Neuzeit*, Munich 1995 ; ROBERT JÜTTE, *Arme, Bettler, Beutelschneider. Eine Sozialgeschichte der Armut in der Frühen Neuzeit*. Traduit de l'anglais par RAINER VON SAVIGNY, Weimar 2000 ; MARTIN RHEINHEIMER, *Arme, Bettler und Vaganten. Überleben in der Not 1450–1850*, Francfort-sur-le-Main 2000 ; HELMUT BRÄUER (Éd.), *Arme – ohne Chance ?* Protokoll der internationalen Tagung « Kommunale Armut und Armutsbekämpfung vom Spätmittelalter bis zur Gegenwart » du 23 au 25 octobre 2003 à Leipzig, Leipzig 2004 ; OTTO GERHARD OEXLE (Éd.), *Armut im Mittelalter*, Ostfildern 2004 ; CHRISTOPH KÜHBERGER, CLEMENS SEDMAK (Éd.), *Aktuelle Tendenzen der historischen Armutforschung*, Vienne 2005.

scrivit en grand et d'une écriture droite les mots « Pour la Pauvreté » : « Si l'on examine ce mot », poursuit-elle, « et combien de fois l'ai-je fait ! alors on tire une multitude de conclusions, justes ou audacieuses. Il m'arrivait quelquefois de penser que justement ceux qui étaient pauvres en courage, étaient touchés par la pauvreté (de l'allemand/ *Armut*/-/pauvreté/ décomposé en /*arm*/-/pauvre/ et /*Mut*/-/courage/). Dépourvus de tout courage. Mais lorsque je repense à ma mère, qui lors des périodes de dénuement les plus acerbes, où elle ne parvenait même plus à retenir ses larmes devant nous, ses enfants, avait malgré tout cette lueur indescriptible de courage dans les prunelles de ses yeux, dès lors j'écarte une fois pour toutes cette théorie… peut-être serait-il plus juste de supposer que pauvreté signifie « le bras de la mère » (de l'allemand/*Arm*/-/bras/ et /*Mutter*/-/mère/). Car la pauvreté enserre, unit intimement et reste fidèle dans toute circonstance, aucune faute ne saurait l'éloigner, elle châtie et console, couche et réveille, au fond elle met tout en œuvre afin que rien d'étranger ne puisse porter atteinte à ses enfants. »[2]

Née en 1915 neuvième enfant d'une famille de mineurs et gagnant sa vie jusqu'au mariage en effectuant des travaux de tricotage, Christine Lavant vivait dans la pauvreté sans pour autant sombrer dans le désespoir. Peut-être ne menaçait-elle pas son existence suffisamment pour que notre auteur ne la haïsse complètement. Cette dernière décrit la pauvreté comme une compagne fidèle et maternelle, rassemblant et réchauffant les siens sans jamais les décourager. Elle est donc bien loin de cette pauvreté meurtrière qui, en laissant les gens mourir de faim, ne coûte pas que des larmes mais aussi la vie. Ce désert de misère, ne connaissant que des frontières individuelles et non universelles, s'étend entre courage et désespoir, entre faim et famine. Même s'il n'existe pour la pauvreté aucun critère objectif et intemporel, aucune définition précise de la notion même de pauvreté, on entrevoit quand même un dénominateur, consistant en le fait de se prémunir au moins du minimum vital, avant que celui-ci n'échappe ou ne vienne à manquer complètement. « La pauvreté désigne en premier lieu

---

2 CHRISTINE LAVANT, *Die Schöne im Mohnkleid. Erzählung.* Pour le compte du Brenner-Archiv (Innsbruck) édité et postface par ANNETTE STEINSIEK, 2e Ed., Salzbourg/Vienne 1996, pp. 10–11.

la privation de ressources matérielles, qui, en comparaison à d'autres conditions de vie, sont considérées comme un minimum vital et sont même requises en vue de certains objectifs sociaux […] »[3] Voici une approche thématique et méthodique sensée esquisser les contours de cet état de manque soumis à des changements perpétuels. Christoph Kühberger et Clemens Sedmak ont récemment souligné à nouveau qu'une réflexion épistémologique sérieuse sur la pauvreté nécessite un équilibre des facteurs « chauds » et « froids » : « Les facteurs froids et solides des méthodes quantitatives avec leurs indications numériques, leurs statistiques et leurs généralisations doivent être mis au même niveau que les facteurs chauds et flexibles de la recherche qualitative, comme les émotions ou les expériences individuelles de la vie. »[4] Une impulsion qui n'est pas nouvelle mais qui nous rappelle sans cesse que la pauvreté n'est pas uniquement une situation généralisante, à définir de façon statistique, mais surtout une expérience de vie humaine marquée par des émotions et des sentiments individuels.

La difficulté d'établir l'équilibre souhaité n'est pas uniquement due au fait que les déclarations et résultats généralisants soient encore considérés, par-delà les destins individuels, comme véritable valeur de la recherche historique, mais elle est également due à l'insuffisance des sources. Les pauvres des siècles derniers ne sont concevables que de façon fragmentaire, faisant de courtes apparitions historiques n'éclaircissant que partiellement leur existence sans jamais nous rendre possible de l'examiner plus en détail. Les indices dont nous disposons ne nous permettent que de deviner les raisons matérielles pour lesquelles des hommes et des femmes se sentaient pauvres et comment ils parvenaient à ne pas descendre au-dessous du minimum vital. Dans ce travail, incluant les critères de pauvreté propres à un sexe n'ayant jusqu'à présent pas été suffisamment pris en considération, il est tant question d'hommes que de femmes pauvres. Une histoire sexuée de la pauvreté en Europe demeure une revendication de la recherche, même si la sensibilité pour une recherche nuancée incluant hommes et femmes gagne du terrain.

---

3 Ernst-Ulrich Huster, *Armut in Europa*, Opladen 1996, p. 23.
4 Christoph Kühberger, Clemens Sednak (Éd.), *Aktuelle Tendenzen* (cf. note 1), p. 5.

Les pensées de Christine Lavant s'appuyant directement sur une expérience personnelle concrète, alors l'introduction littéraire à cette recherche sur la pauvreté n'apparaît pas trop poétique. La mère sanglotante et la fille tricotant des chaussettes. « La pauvreté est féminine » est le titre de l'étude de Ruth Köppens parue en 1985,[5] qui veut démontrer entre 1880 et le début du XXe siècle ce qui est encore valable et est sensé l'avoir toujours été. Les femmes semblent avoir été constamment plus touchées par la pauvreté que les hommes. Relevons ainsi dans le « bulletin d'informations du Réseau européen de lutte contre la pauvreté » en 2004, sous le titre « La pauvreté des femmes en Autriche : légende et vérité », un règlement de compte résolu avec les représentations oniriques de justice sociale. Plus de 200.000 femmes vivent dans un état de pauvreté aiguë, certaines seraient « en secret » sans-logis, les plus touchées étant les femmes élevant seules leurs enfants, mais aussi les étrangères ne profitant guère des aides de l'Etat ; soulignons par ailleurs que les femmes gagnent en moyenne presque 40% de moins que les hommes.[6] La pauvreté féminine ne se limite malheureusement pas à cela. Ce bilan inquiétant nous confronte à des aspects supplémentaires, donnant un aperçu des problèmes sociaux en Autriche. L'Autriche ne fait nullement office d'exception. À titre d'exemple, le taux de chômage de nombreux pays européens en 1994 faisait ressortir que les femmes étaient majoritairement touchées. Ce phénomène est particulièrement frappant en Espagne avec un rapport de 30 à 19, en Italie de 17 à 8 et en Grèce de 13 à 5, même si les différences ne sont pas partout aussi marquantes. On note néanmoins pour l'Union Européenne une distinction notoire avec un rapport de 13 à 9.[7] Si l'on peut dire de la pauvreté qu'elle est féminine, à l'instar du titre de Ruth Köppen, il semble que les chiffres témoignent pour le moins de la dite féminisation de la pauvreté, sensée éclaircir dans plusieurs ouvrages les difficultés propres à chaque sexe. Chaque regard en arrière semble surtout saisir une misère féminine. Au début

---

5 Ruth Köppen, *Die Armut ist weiblich*, Berlin 1985.

6 Réseau européen de lutte contre la pauvreté, *Bulletin d'information* N° 107, Juillet-Août 2004, p. 8.

7 Ernst-Ulrich Huster : *Armut in Europa* (cf. note 3), p. 65 (tableau : taux de chômage par sexe en 1985, 1992 et en mai 1994).

du XVe siècle la partie la plus pauvre de la population de Bâle était composée de 66% de femmes, celles-ci étaient également largement représentées parmi les mendiants des autres villes. Dans le protocole des pauvres de Strasbourg en 1523 on aurait compté 69% de femmes, en 1558 dans certaines paroisses de Tolède 73% et Lucerne atteignit même 85%.[8] Ces données ne constituent aucunement des exceptions : « Cette proportion considérable de femmes ne changea pas durant les Temps modernes. Encore dans la première moitié du XIXe siècle les femmes représentaient à Schaffhausen 75% des nécessiteux ».[9] Ce sont des destinées individuelles, qui ne sont guère ou que partiellement perceptibles, que masquent ces chiffres, d'autant plus que les femmes ne sont qu'ajoutées à cette vision masculine de l'histoire sans jamais y être intégrées à niveau égal. Robert Jütte critique ainsi à juste titre le fait que les femmes, ainsi que leur détresse particulière, ne font pas l'objet de la même considération que les hommes dans la vaste bibliographie de la pauvreté et de l'aide aux pauvres, et sont mentionnées en passant ou examinées à part, à quelques exceptions près.[10]

Mais retournons à Christine Lavant qui aborde un autre aspect qui me préoccupa lors de mon approche de la pauvreté. Elle parle du courage et de l'espoir que sa mère ait eu et de cette faculté de la pauvreté d'unir étroitement. Elle fait ici plus précisément allusion aux stratégies personnelles de survie, combinées aux notions indispensables de donner et de recevoir qui contribuèrent de tout temps à la survie des hommes. Souvent employé mais également controversé, le terme moderne « *social network* » caractérise cette forme d'aide collective pour la maîtrise de la pauvreté. Hormis le fait que « *social network* » est devenu un mot passe-partout, on le trouve surtout dans le discours

---

8 Martin Rheinheimer : *Arme, Bettler und Vaganten* (cf. note 1), p. 57.

9 *Ibid.*

10 Robert Jütte : « Dutzbetterinnen und Sündfegerinnen. Kriminelle Bettelpraktiken von Frauen in der Frühen Neuzeit », dans : Otto Ulbricht (Éd.): *Von Huren und Rabenmüttern. Weibliche Kriminalität in der Frühen Neuzeit*, Cologne/Weimar/Vienne 1995, p. 117 ; cf. à ce sujet les réflexions de Dietlind Hüchtker: « *Elende Mütter » und « liederliche Weibspersonen ». Geschlechterverhältnisse und Armenpolitik in Berlin (1770–1850)*, Münster 1999, p. 19 : « Trotz einer längeren Tradition der Studien zur Sozialgeschichte der Armut sind Forschungen, die nach Geschlechtern differenzieren, nach wie vor äußerst selten. Das historische Interesse an ,den armen Frauen' ist bis heute marginal. »

politologique moderne. Ce terme de réseau social décrit, à propos des stratégies de survie, la plupart du temps l'entraide dans des situations difficiles. Qui veillait à la stabilité des pauvres dans un tel réseau relationnel ? Robert Jütte nous renseigne dans son « Histoire sociale de la pauvreté » sur l'effort personnel et plus précisément sur « la signification des aides sociales ».[11] « L'organisation de réseaux d'aides structurés dans l'Europe des Temps modernes », ainsi que le décrit Jütte, comprenait outre le ménage, le bailleur, les voisins, la famille, les collègues de travail et les employeurs, les amis et les parrains ainsi que les œuvres de bienfaisance à caractère bénévole.[12] Si les réflexions de Jütte sont d'un côté convaincantes, il n'en demeure pas moins de questions sans réponses. L'entière construction n'est-elle pas trop lisse et rectiligne, pas assez souple ? Soit une assistance spontanée et limitée pouvait provenir d'une personne ou d'une institution extérieure à un réseau dont on puisse saisir la portée, soit l'aide pouvait ne pas arriver. Des parents décevant les espoirs placés en eux, des voisins dénonciateurs et des parrains ne se souciant guère de satisfaire à leur devoir. Qui se penche sur des destinées personnelles constate que les stratégies de survie, combinées à l'utilisation et l'organisation de toute aide, sont individuelles et ne se laissent pas placer dans un schéma idéal. Qu'en est-il de l'assistance des autorités ? Ne pourrait-elle pas être également considérée comme une partie du réseau social ? Il est généralement admis que les personnes touchées se préservent de la pauvreté en s'entraidant. La question se pose de savoir si cette distinction avec les autorités est judicieuse, car les mesures des autorités ont également contribué à garantir la survie. L'entraide reflète en réalité une certaine indigence à laquelle il faut remédier. Les mendiants et mendiantes des *Pauper letters* anglaises, qui firent fréquemment recopier leurs pétitions par des parents, faisaient partie d'un réseau social comprenant une aide autant familiale que communale. Les « *pauper letters* » dont Thomas Sokoll a fait l'étude, renseignent par ce

---

11 ROBERT JÜTTE : *Arme, Bettler, Beutelschneider* (cf. note 1), pp. 106–130.
12 *Ibid.*, p. 109.

biais sur la relation entre les pauvres, leurs familles et l'aide locale.[13] Ce n'est que la représentation exhaustive de réseaux sociaux conçus individuellement, comportant des possibilités d'aide et d'assistance diverses et les combinant entre elles en cas de besoin, qui lève le voile sur le caractère individuel de la pauvreté. Cela implique que certains facteurs d'aide perdent de leur signification voire leur entière fonction à partir du moment où un individu se décidait ou dut se décider pour une certaine forme d'intégration sociale en fonction de son existence. Dans son étude sur la politique relative à la pauvreté à Saint-Gall en Suisse vers la fin du XVIIIe siècle, Marcel Mayer déclare par exemple, que « l'approvisionnement des établissements » détruisit des communautés sociales existantes en isolant et en séparant les individus de leurs attaches préexistantes.[14] Cette forme constituait une possibilité de réduire ou de détruire entièrement des liens sociaux. Il existait cependant d'autres formes. En période d'extrême pénurie, lorsque la faim fauchait des vies humaines en grand nombre, qu'il n'y avait plus rien à distribuer ou que la peste commença ses ravages, les hommes ainsi que leurs réseaux, lorsque ces derniers n'étaient pas suffisamment étendus, moururent.[15]

De mon intention de ne pas me consacrer à une pauvreté masculine ou féminine mais plutôt aux stratégies de survie d'hommes et de femmes pauvres se dégage la nécessité de travailler avec des exemples n'évoquant que modestement d'autres concepts de vie et des développements généraux.

---

13 THOMAS SOKOLL, « Old Age in Poverty: The Record of Essex Pauper Letters, 1780–1834, » dans : *Chronicling Poverty. The voices and Strategies of the English Poor, 1640–1840*, Éd. par TIM HITCHCOCK, PETER KING et PAMELA SHARPE, Houndmills/Basingstoke/Hampshire/Londres 1997, pp. 127–154.

14 MARCEL MAYER, « Zur Armenpolitik der Stadt St. Gallen im späteren 18. Jahrhundert », dans : ANNE-LISE HEAD, BRIGITTE SCHNEGG (Éd.), *Armut in der Schweiz (17.–20.Jh.). La pauvreté en Suisse (17e–20e s.)*, Zurich 1989, p. 121.

15 PIERO CAMPORESI : *Das Brot der Träume. Hunger und Halluzinationen im vorindustriellen Europa.* Traduit de l'italien par KARL F. HAUBER, Francfort/New York 1990, p. 110; BRONISLAW GEREMEK : *Geschichte der Armut. Elend und Barmherzigkeit in Europa.* Traduit du polonais par FRIEDRICH GRIESE, Munich 1991, p. 86.

I. Des hommes morts ou absents :

Des femmes chef de famille

Le fait qu'au fil des siècles des femmes aient été chef de famille constituait une solution de fortune, une solution possible soit, mais un phénomène nullement désiré, bouleversant et menaçant l'ordre hiérarchique traditionnel des sexes. Jusqu'au XXᵉ siècle l'homme seul était admis en tant chef de l'union conjugale et de la famille. « L'homme est le chef de l'union conjugale et son jugement est décisif dans les affaires concernant la communauté matrimoniale » lit-on dans la deuxième partie du Code général des Etats prussiens de 1794[16] et le Code Civil de 1804 statue dans son article 213 : « Le mari doit protection à sa femme, la femme obéissance à son mari».[17] Cette stipulation juridique concorde tout à fait avec le message biblique. Si l'homme mourait, la femme se retrouvait non seulement dépourvue de tête et de voix, mais elle encourait également le danger de perdre le contrôle et de se retrouver dans le besoin. Que faire si le « chef » venait, mort, à manquer complètement ou alors à s'absenter un certain temps, comme c'est fréquemment le cas en temps de guerre ? Dans de telles circonstances la femme était contrainte d'une part à faire ses preuves au «*Heimatfront*» en approvisionnant le front et d'autre part à faire ses preuves en tant que nourricière et chef de famille responsable. Dans le film « Le miracle de Bern »[18] de Sönke Wortmann sorti en salle en 2003, il est bien entendu surtout question de la victoire des Allemands lors de la Coupe du Monde de football de 1954 mais il y est aussi question de la situation des familles dans l'Allemagne d'après-guerre. On y raconte comment une mère, à l'image de tant d'autres, parvient à s'en sortir avec ses enfants, sans le chef de famille toujours prisonnier de guerre en Russie. Lorsque le mari et père de famille refait son apparition dans leur vie après des années d'absence, il est alors devenu superflu, pour

---

16 Cit. d'après Barbara Dölemeyer, « Frau und Familie im Privatrecht des 19. Jahrhunderts, » dans : *Frauen in der Geschichte des Rechts. Von der Frühen Neuzeit bis zur Gegenwart*, ed. par Ute Gerhard, Munich 1997, p. 641.

17 *Ibid.*

18 *Le miracle de Bern*, Allemagne 2003 (sortie en salle : 16.10.2003) ; Mise en scène : Sönke Wortmann.

les enfants un inconnu et pour la femme une menace de l'existence qu'elle s'est péniblement et toute seule construite sous la forme d'un café. C'est peut-être là le point le plus important. Il est difficile à cet homme, traumatisé et souffrant des expériences vécues pendant la guerre et sa captivité, d'admettre et de reconnaître que sa femme est devenue indépendante économiquement et ce, uniquement du fait de son absence. Le fait que cette mère de trois enfants ait précisément réussi à s'établir dans l'univers masculin de la gastronomie renforce l'impression de force et de compétence féminine, outrepassant les frontières des sexes. Dans le désarroi du mari détrôné ne se reflète pas uniquement sa confusion personnelle, mais aussi le combat séculaire des sociétés européennes dominées par les hommes qui, armées de la Bible et d'un recueil de lois, veulent réduire la partie féminine de l'humanité à son caractère physique.

Du Moyen Âge aux Temps modernes, la situation des veuves qui durent soudainement prendre le rôle de chef de famille après la mort de leur mari, n'aura apporté aucun progrès d'ordre matériel, bien que contrairement au stéréotype de « la pauvre veuve », les veuves n'étaient pas nécessairement dans le besoin ou la misère.[19] Si les enfants et leur mères étaient issus d'un milieu économiquement faible, il était vraisemblable que ces dernières seraient dans l'incapacité de nourrir seules leurs enfants, alors que deux personnes y seraient peut-être parvenues. Sans aide extérieure cela semble n'avoir que rarement fonctionné. Dans de tels cas d'urgence les stratégies de survie personnelles ne sont guère détachables d'un «réseau social» qui complétait ou auquel cas remplaçait entièrement les efforts personnels de survie par des mesures d'aide de toutes sortes. Pour obtenir un maximum de revenus de survie, il importait de combiner tous les facteurs disponibles de la manière optimale ; cela constituait une grande nécessité en vue de cette alliance abstruse entre stratégie personnelle et assistance accordée par des personnes et des institutions. L'exemple de la femme

---

19 Cf. à ce sujet « *Widowhood dans Medieval and Early Modern Europe* », Éd. par SANDRA CAVALLO et LYNDAN WARNER, New York 1999 ; INGA WIEDEMANN, *Die Schriften für Witwen in der Frühen Neuzeit*, Berlin 2001 ; GESA INGENDAHL, « Elend und Wollust. Witwenschaft in kulturellen Bildern der Frühen Neuzeit, » dans : *Witwenschaft in der Frühen Neuzeit. Fürstliche und adlige Witwen zwischen Fremd- und Selbstbestimmung*, Leipzig 2003, pp. 265–279.

de Thomas Müntzer illustre bien le fait que ce n'était pas si facile. Cette dernière menait déjà du vivant de son mari tristement célèbre une vie de misère, et se retrouva après l'exécution de ce dernier le 27 mai 1525 enceinte et parfaitement démunie avec un petit enfant. Alors que Müntzer compte parmi les figures de proue les plus marquantes et les plus radicales de la Réforme,[20] auteur de divers écrits, on sait peu de chose sur Ottilie von Gersen.[21] Il est avéré qu'elle avait quitté le couvent afin d'épouser Thomas Müntzer en 1523,[22] qui venait d'être nommé pasteur de l'église Saint-Jean (la *Johanniskirche*) à Allstedt. Qu'elle ait été au fait de la pensée de Müntzer et partagé son anticléricalisme et sa volonté réformatrice est probable, voire incontestable dans certains cas. Par contre on méconnaît la façon dont elle surmonta l'absence de son mari qui dut quitter Allstedt début août 1524. Elle donna naissance à son fils le 27 mars de la même année et donna des soins à son beau-père jusqu'à sa mort. Alors que Thomas Müntzer était parti dans les régions paysannes insurgées, sa femme menait une vie de misère bien que Müntzer s'était efforcé d'améliorer sa situation. À la fin de sa lettre aux habitants d'Allstedt, Müntzer les conjure d'accorder du soutien à sa femme,[23] ce qui nous permet d'en déduire que cette dernière ne l'avait pas accompagnée à Mühlhausen. Démunie et continuellement sous la surveillance soupçonneuse des autori-

---

20 HANS-JÜRGEN GOERTZ, Thomas Müntzer. *Mystiker-Apokalyptiker-Revolutionär*, Munich 1989 ; pour l'état actuel de la recherche voir : « Müntzerforschung nach der Wende, » dans : *Theologische Literaturzeitung*, 128e année, numéro 9 (septembre 2003), pp. 972–987 ; GÜNTER VOGLER, *Thomas Müntzer und die Gesellschaft seiner Zeit*, Mühlhausen 2003.
21 JORDAN, « Thomas Münzers Witwe, » dans : *Zur Geschichte der Stadt Mühlhausen in Thüringen*, numéro 2, supplément du rapport annuel des lycées de Mühlhausen en Thüringen, Mühlhausen 1902, pp. 27–31; MANFRED BENSING, « Die Frau an der Seite Müntzers, » dans : *Eichsfelder Heimathefte*, 15e année (1975), p. 124 ; JULIANE BOBROWSKI, « Wege zu Ottilie, » dans : *Prediger für eine gerechte Welt*. A l'occasion du 500e anniversaire de Thomas Müntzer. Éd. par le secrétariat général de l'Union chrétienne démocrate d'Allemagne, Berlin 1989, pp. 72–83 ; MARION KOBELT-GROCH : « « So waren sie in meiner Erinnerung, die Frauen der Bauern. » Eine literarische und historische Spurensuche nach dem weiblichen Teil des « gemeinen Mannes » », dans : GÜNTER VOGLER (Éd.) : *Bauernkrieg zwischen Harz und Thüringer Wald 1525* (en cours de publication).
22 *Sources relatives à Thomas Müntzer*, remaniées par WIELAND HELD (†) et SIEGFRIED HOYER, Kritische Gesamtausgabe, T. 3, ed. par HELMAR JUNGHANS, Leipzig 2003, p.123.
23 THOMAS MÜNTZER, *Schriften, Liturgische Texte, Briefe*. Choisis et traduits en allemand moderne, édités par RUDOLF BENTZINGER et SIEGFRIED HOYER, Berlin 1990, p. 207.

tés, elle menait après l'exécution de Müntzer une vie de vagabonde, la conduisant les mois à venir vers Nordhausen, Mühlhausen et Erfurt. Dans sa lettre du 19 août 1525 au duc Georges elle ne décrit pas seulement son Odyssée de femme enceinte, mais elle y fait également part de sa déception face au Conseil de Mühlhausen qui accaparait ses biens.[24] La lettre de Müntzer du 17 mai 1525, adressée quelques jours avant sa mort aux habitants de Mühlhausen, révèle de quels biens il s'agissait. Il demande « …que vous fassiez parvenir à mon épouse les biens dont je dispose (livres, vêtements et autres objets de ce genre) et que vous ne lui fassiez rien payer, pour l'amour de Dieu. »[25] Sa demande ne fut pas entendue. Un retour au couvent, tel qu'il fut de toute évidence suggéré par les autorités, aurait-il été une solution adéquate pour la future mère de deux enfants ? Ottilie Müntzer, compte tenu de son dénuement, n'était probablement pas opposée aux souhaits du duc dans la lettre du 19 août. Mais peut-être s'agit-il là d'une remarque ironique. Le duc aurait certainement été plus rassuré de savoir la veuve de Müntzer derrière les murs du couvent. On ne saurait dire avec exactitude si ce fut le cas, de même que l'on méconnaît le reste de la vie d'Ottilie von Gersen et de ses deux enfants.

Même si au premier abord ce destin de veuve ne semble pas particulièrement bien documenté, il n'en demeure pas moins tout à fait approprié pour une comparaison. Que reliait et différenciait Ottilie Müntzer à d'autres veuves ?

1. Comme Müntzer, réaliste, reconnaissait que son absence ou sa mort compliquerait la vie de sa femme et de ses enfants, il chercha à prendre les dispositions nécessaires, à l'instar d'autres maris d'ailleurs. De fait, ses appels aux habitants d'Allstedt et plus tard à ceux de Mühlhausen nous éclairent sur les liens sociaux qu'il considérait comme stables et auxquels il accordait tant d'importance. Il ne demande d'aide ni à des parents ni à des amis choisis mais aux frères de croyance de la communauté spirituelle en laquelle il avait fondé désormais tous ses espoirs déçus. Si quelqu'un a satisfait à sa requête reste incertain. Plus tard sa femme tenta à plusieurs reprises de parve-

---

24 JORDAN : « Thomas Münzers Witwe » (cf. note 21), pp. 29–30.
25 THOMAS MÜNTZER, *Schriften, Liturgische Texte* (cf. note 23), p. 224.

nir à des objets dont elle aurait eu grand besoin dans son malheur. Les biens matériels, aussi modestes soient-ils, étaient d'une grande importance du fait qu'ils pouvaient être utilisés, vendus voire prêtés, comme des vêtements ou même un lit, constituant par exemple les biens dérisoires d'une veuve bordelaise.[26] L'attention que porte Müntzer envers sa femme et ses enfants témoigne du fait que les milieux aisés n'étaient pas seuls à prendre des dispositions en cas de veuvage, mais aussi les miséreux ayant peu de choses à léguer, la plupart du temps sous forme de testaments ou de contrats de mariage. C'est ainsi que Robert Salmon, un travailleur sans terre d'East Anglia, tentait à sa manière de régler judicieusement les finances en léguant à sa fille la maison à charge, ce qui était censé préserver sa femme de la pauvreté.[27] La femme de Müntzer ne pouvait espérer que la levée de la réquisition de quelques biens modestes. Bien que contrairement à d'autres femmes de pasteurs, dont les idées théologiques étaient moins contestées, elle était tombée en discrédit du fait des idées révolutionnaires de son mari, son destin illustre quand même la vie des veuves de pasteurs. Alors que de nombreuses jeunes veuves de pasteurs se remariaient, il était envisageable pour les plus âgées d'entre elles ou pour une de leurs filles d'épouser le successeur au poste de pasteur. On commençait néanmoins dès le XVIe siècle à « assurer selon leur rang les moyens d'existence des veuves de pasteurs à travers des caisses d'aide aux veuves ».[28] La situation financière d'Ottilie Müntzer aurait été probablement meilleure si elle avait eu le droit, en tant que veuve d'artisan, de poursuivre l'activité de l'entreprise, telle Kunigonde, la femme de l'imprimeur de Leipzig Hans Hergot, qui avait été décapité à Leipzig le 20 mai 1527. Jusqu'à sa mort en 1527 elle maintenait l'activité de l'imprimerie avec son deuxième mari, qu'elle avait épousé en décembre 1527, quelques

---

26 Martin Dinges, *Stadtarmut in Bordeaux, 1525–1675. Alltag, Politik, Mentalitäten*, Bonn 1988, p. 71.

27 Olwen Hufton, *Frauenleben. Eine europäische Geschichte 1500–1800*. Traduit de l'anglais par Holger Fliessbach et Rena Passenthien, Francfort-sur-le-Main 1998, p. 320.

28 Heide Wunder : « *Er ist die Sonn', sie ist der Mond* ». *Frauen in der Frühen Neuzeit*, Munich 1992, p. 184.

mois après la mort d'Hergot.[29] Le fait que des femmes poursuivaient l'activité de l'entreprise de leur mari et se préservaient ainsi de la misère, dépendait des possibilités locales dont elles étaient en mesure de profiter. Alors qu'à Lyon une grande partie des veuves tombait dans la pauvreté du fait qu'elles ne pouvaient pas poursuivre l'activité d'une entreprise qu'avait dirigé le mari,[30] on note plus tard une amélioration en Autriche notamment. Ici l'autorisation de diriger une entreprise, certes liée fondamentalement à la personne du propriétaire, fut reconnue dans le code de législation commerciale et du travail de 1859 comme partie de l'héritage, ainsi les veuves et les descendants mineurs ayant droit à la succession avaient exceptionnellement la liberté de poursuivre l'activité de l'entreprise.[31]

2. Du fait qu'Ottilie Müntzer ne disposait d'aucune ressource financière sur laquelle elle pouvait compter en tant que femme « pauvre, miséreuse et ayant été quittée » il fallut faire appel à des considérations plus vastes. On ignore cependant si elle trouva un travail ou dut mendier. Il est théoriquement tout à fait possible qu'elle dût payer l'hébergement chez des amis par quelques services, mais nous n'en avons pas la certitude. Enceinte et avec un enfant en bas âge, ses chances de trouver un travail étaient faibles de toute façon. Il est des veuves qui parvinrent à survivre grâce à des travaux artisanaux, telle Anna Margarethe Delfs du Dithmarschen, qui tricotait des chaussettes aux soldats au XIXe siècle pour subvenir à ses besoins ainsi qu'à ceux de ses sept enfants.[32] L'oraison funèbre du 7 janvier 1826 d'une veuve décédée à l'âge de 62 ans confirme le fait qu'elle ait été une femme véritablement pauvre, « qui dût au cours de sa vie chrétienne gagner son pain avec grand peine. Son travail habituel consistait à habiller les

---

29 Max Steinmetz, « Introduction, » dans : *Hans Hergot und die Flugschrift « Von der newen wandlung eynes christlichen Lebens »*. Faksimilewiedergabe mit Umschrift, Leipzig 1977, pp. 31–32.

30 Martin Dinges : *Stadtarmut in Bordeaux* (cf. note 26), p. 54 ; Dinges se réfère à l'étude de J.-P. Gutton sur Lyon entre 1534 et 1789 publiée en 1970.

31 Josef Ehmer, « Zünfte in Österreich in der frühen Neuzeit, » dans : Heinz-Gerhard Haupt, *Das Ende der Zünfte. Ein europäischer Vergleich*, Göttingen 2002, p. 119.

32 Kai Detlev Sievers : *Leben in Armut. Zeugnisse der Armutskultur aus Lübeck und Schleswig-Holstein vom Mittelalter bis ins 20. Jahrhundert*, Heide 1991, p. 90.

morts et à soigner les malades. »[33] Une autre alternative consistait en le fait soit d'envoyer ses enfants mendier, soit de se débarrasser d'eux complètement ou partiellement, une solution qui ne fut pas pratiquée uniquement par des femmes quittées par leur mari ou par des veuves, mais aussi par des mères mariées débordées par leurs enfants et le travail supplémentaire. Teresa Quaresi, une femme de trente ans dont le mari la quitta après avoir rejoint l'armée, confia son troisième enfant à l'hospice de Brescia. Le cas de la veuve Maria Giovanni C. démontre qu'une telle solution ne témoigne pas nécessairement d'un manque d'amour envers ses enfants ; cette dernière confia d'abord ses enfants à l'hospice et les récupéra ensuite.[34] Lorsqu'ils étaient disponibles, les hospices des enfants trouvés, les crèches et les orphelinats incarnent des éléments possibles d'un réseau social. Leur utilisation dépendait d'une part de la stratégie individuelle de vie, déterminée par les offres d'assistance sociale, d'autre part cette stratégie était, du fait du dénuement existant, également à l'origine de ces mêmes possibilités.

3. On peut raisonnablement affirmer que le Duc Georges aurait aimé que la veuve de Müntzer retourne au couvent. De cette façon, il aurait fait d'une pierre deux coups. D'un côté, on se serait occupé d'elle, et de l'autre elle aurait été sous contrôle. Même s'il s'agit là d'un cas précis, on retrouve une propension à un isolement englobant, dans cette politique monastique d'aide aux pauvres, tel qu'on a pu le constater dans les maisons de réclusions des XVIIe et XVIIIe siècles qui furent de véritables initiatrices. Nous touchons là aussi au problème de la discipline à l'intérieur de l'ordre social. Ordinairement les cloîtres étaient sous certaines réserves un asile pour femmes pauvres, en particulier pour les veuves. On penserait plutôt ici aux couvents de Béguines qui remplissaient le même rôle social. Si leur composition sociale était ordinairement très hétérogène, ils offraient un refuge aux femmes pauvres. À cela s'ajoutait la possibilité d'être nourrie, en exerçant un travail manuel ou une activité caritative dans le cadre d'une communauté. Même si le célibat n'était pas un critère d'admission

---

33 JOHANN JACOB BROMM : *Der Prediger am Grabe. Entwürfe zu Leichenreden aus einer zwanzigjährigen practischen Amtserfahrung. Dritter Teil : Greisenalter*, Mannheim 1832, p. 11.
34 VOLKER HUNECKE : *Die Findelkinder von Mailand. Kindsaussetzung und aussetzende Eltern vom 17. bis zum 19. Jahrhundert*, Stuttgart 1987, p. 148.

dans la plupart des couvents, il arrivait cependant, comme au couvent Monheimer près de Cologne, qu'aucune veuve ne soit admise.[35] Dans ce contexte, il faut évoquer les tentatives de rapprochements en Allemagne de diverses communautés de femmes avec les Béguines médiévales.[36] Cela avait souvent lieu de façon non critique. Au-delà de ces formes institutionnalisées de vie en communauté, les veuves avaient la possibilité de se joindre à des communautés basées sur la vie et le travail en commun. D'après Olwen Hufton, Rome était une ville très importante pour l'accueil des veuves, car on y trouvait, après la Contre-Réforme, beaucoup d'établissements d'assistance publique. Les veuves vivaient ensemble dans de petits appartements, s'occupaient de faire le ménage et travaillaient comme vendeuses, notamment à des petits stands de boissons, du reste très appréciés. En fait, elles vivotaient : « laver, nettoyer, garder les enfants, coudre, cuisiner pour les voisines qui travaillent et, quand tout va de travers, mendier et faire appel à l'aide sociale, étaient les possibilités qu'avaient les veuves de survivre », et pas seulement dans les riches villes du bord de la Méditerranée.[37] Apparemment, cette combinaison alliant le travail, voire la mendicité et les aides sociales semble avoir fait ses preuves. Cette alliance fut particulièrement secourable pour les veuves âgées, lesquelles n'avaient plus d'enfants à élever. Dans les villages du Pays de Velay, beaucoup de veuves vivaient de la dentellerie qui cependant ne leur permettait de vivre qu'à la limite du minimum vital.[38]

Rien n'indique que la veuve de Müntzer ait trouvé un logis « fixe ». Il semble plutôt qu'elle ait mené une vie instable qui s'apparentait au vagabondage. Les connaissances et les amis lui permirent de repartir à zéro. Rien n'indique non plus qu'elle ait songé à se remarier. D'un

---

35 Frank-Michael Reichstein : *Das Beginenwesen in Deutschland. Studien und Katalog*, Berlin 2001, p. 153.

36 Cf. à ce sujet : *Beginen – mehr als Mittelalter. Modelle für gemeinsames Leben.* Académie évangélique de Bad Boll, protocole du congrès du 16 au 18 novembre 2001 ; Marion Kobelt-Groch : « « Sind wir von gestern… oder morgen ? » Beginen : Gedächtniskultur als Sozialexperiment heute, » dans : Bea Lundt, Michael Salewski en collaboration avec Heiner Timmermann (Éd.) : *Frauen in Europa. Mythos und Realität*, Münster 2005, pp. 445–460.

37 Olwen Hufton : *Frauenleben* (cf. note 27), pp. 344–345.

38 *Ibid.*, p. 329.

point de vue économique, il eût été préférable qu'elle saute le pas, même si elle ne pouvait pas espérer, comme d'autres veuves de pasteur avant elle, que le nouveau titulaire du poste l'épousât. En Angleterre, à une époque plus tardive, elle aurait peut-être eu la chance de devenir gouvernante ou directrice d'une école pour les pauvres. Comme tant d'autres veuves, Ottilie Müntzer semble avoir été dépendante du bon vouloir des autres qui, en l'occurrence, n'étaient pas des membres de la famille, comme c'était l'habitude, mais des amis. Compte tenu de son passé, Ottilie Müntzer ne correspondait pas vraiment à l'image typique de la veuve, pauvre et indigente.

On peut supposer que la bouillie sucrée, celle qui dans le conte justement, déborde chez une pauvre jeune fille pieuse et sa mère, ne se serait pas répandue dans la pièce qu'occupait Ottilie Müntzer.[39] Elle n'était pas une veuve exemplaire, mais plutôt une femme que les autorités considéraient comme devant être soumise à un certain contrôle. Sa réputation se serait assombrie si elle avait opté, à une époque de bouleversement sur le plan social et religieux, pour une vie errante et versatile. Ainsi l'image radieuse de la veuve pauvre, ayant besoin de secours, offrait un contraste saisissant à celle de la femme errante, qui semblait tenter d'échapper à tout contrôle et que l'on pouvait soupçonner de pratiques criminelles.

II. Les vagabondes de la vie : les femmes non mariées

Rosina Ebner fut une de ces femmes. Elle n'avait ni domicile fixe, ni emploi stable et vagabondait vers 1700 en Styrie avec sa mère veuve. Dans les registres, elle est qualifiée de « putain » de l'huissier.[40] Elle avait probablement vu le jour à la fin de 1682, voire au début de 1683. Elle était née en France, en plein milieu d'un champ, alors que le régiment de son père faisait mouvement. Après que ce dernier fut

---

39 « La bouillie sucrée » (titre original « Der süße Brei ») dans : *Contes pour les enfants et les parents réunis par les frères Grimm*, illustrés par OTTO UBBELOHDE et préfacés par INGEBORG WEBER-KELLERMANN, t. 2, Francfort-sur-le-Main 1974, pp. 203–204.

40 HELFRIED VALENTINITSCH, « Frauen unterwegs. Eine Fallstudie zur Mobilität von Frauen in der Steiermark um 1700, » dans : *Weiber, Menschen, Frauenzimmer. Frauen in der ländlichen Gesellschaft, 1500–1800*, éd. par HEIDE WUNDER et CHRISTINA VANJA, Göttingen 1996, pp. 223–236.

mort, sans doute lors du deuxième siège de Vienne, une vie instable d'errance commença pour la veuve et ses enfants, qui les conduisit à travers la Styrie, l'archevêché de Salzbourg et le Tyrol. Pendant que ses frères et sœurs gagnaient leur vie, Rosina resta auprès de sa mère et mena cette vie errante jusqu'à ses vingt ans, c'est-à-dire jusqu'en 1703 ou 1704.[41] Au cours de leur voyage, elles rencontrèrent l'huissier Paul Zellinger. Celui-ci modifia dès cet instant cette relation mère-fille, dans la mesure où il tomba amoureux de Rosina, abandonna son travail et quitta son épouse pour vagabonder avec sa maîtresse et la mère de celle-ci. De temps à autres, d'autres personnes vinrent se joindre à eux. Ce fut le cas pour la mère et la sœur de Paul Zellinger, ainsi que pour des amis et connaissances de l'ancien huissier. Parmi eux, on vit aussi des voleurs et des escrocs.[42] Rosina vécut maritalement avec Zellinger, et, au fil des années, elle donna naissance à de nombreux enfants. Cela réduisait les possibilités pour Rosina Ebner de trouver un travail.[43] Aucun de ceux qui faisaient partie de ce groupe errant, n'avait de revenus fixes. Ils mendiaient, tentaient en hiver de se faire héberger par des paysans ou des artisans vivant à la campagne, en échange de travaux occasionnels. C'est ainsi qu'ils passèrent une semaine à l'hospice de Pernegg à fabriquer des brosses. Lorsque Rosina tomba malade pendant trois semaines, une paysanne carinthienne, prise de pitié, l'emmena chez le barbier-chirurgien le plus proche. Paul Zellinger régla la facture avec l'argent mendié.[44]

La vie en communauté de cette petite troupe de vagabonds procure un aperçu des qualités possédées par un réseau social. Il ne s'agit pas seulement ici de l'étrange solidarité interne, voire familiale, mais aussi de l'environnement, de tous ces gens qui leur firent l'aumône, les employèrent et les hébergèrent.

À l'exception d'un court séjour à l'hospice de Pernegg,[45] il semble qu'il n'y ait pas eu de contact avec une aide venant de l'autorité publique. Il semble au contraire que le mode de vie itinérant, lié à des

---

41 *Ibid.*, p. 227.
42 *Ibid.*, pp. 230–231.
43 *Ibid.*, p. 232.
44 *Loc.cit.*
45 *Ibid.*, p. 231.

activités criminelles, oblige justement à laisser complètement de côté ce facteur comme un possible élément d'interconnexion sociale. Zellinger fut arrêté plusieurs fois. Il fut entre autres choses accusé d'avoir assommé un paysan. Mais revenons à Rosina Ebner ; une question se pose à son endroit : peut-on la considérer comme une personne pour qui la dénomination de seule, au sens de sans soutien, s'applique ?

1. Si Rosina Ebner est assortie de la douteuse étiquette de « putain », cette caractéristique péjorative se rapporte tout d'abord à la liaison déréglée voire même punissable, du point de vue juridique, avec son concubin et père de ses enfants. Rosina Ebner et Paul Zellinger n'étaient pas mariés, ce qui ne les dérangeait absolument pas, à l'instar d'autres couples. On rencontrait par exemple des liaisons de cette sorte dans le milieu des brigands.[46] Mais on les découvre aussi dans d'autres contextes.[47] Beaucoup de personnes issues des classes populaires ne pouvaient se marier pour des raisons économiques, sans vouloir renoncer à une certaine forme de communauté matrimoniale. Dans le Paris du XIXe siècle, nombre de couples vivaient sous un même toit, bien avant le mariage.[48] L'appellation de « putain » ne peut être comprise que dans la perspective d'une morale et d'une politique d'ordre publique de l'autorité. Cette perspective ne rendait admissible aucune alternative à un mariage en bonne et due forme. Les femmes errantes, qui n'étaient soumises à aucun chef de famille, étaient qualifiées en bloc de putain. C'est le cas par exemple dans l'ordre mendiant de Soleure au XVIe siècle. Dans la langue du XIXe siècle, on parle de

---

46 MONIKA MACHNICKI, « « Sie trug stets das Brecheisen unter dem Rock » – aber hat sie es auch benutzt ? Zur Rolle der Frauen in den Räuberbanden des 18. und 19. Jahrhunderts, » dans : *Schurke oder Held ? Historische Räuber und Räuberbanden*, Éd. par HARALD SIEBENMORGEN, Sigmaringen 1995 (catalogue d'exposition), pp. 146–147.

47 EVA SUTTER qualifie par exemple ces liaisons non conjugales et relations de concubinage donnant naissance à des enfants illégitimes, en particulier dans la Suisse du début du XIXe siècle, de « Schutz- und Trutzbündnisse » contre les contraintes morales et sociales ainsi que contre la situation économique difficile. (EVA SUTTER, « Illegitimität und Armut im 19. Jahrhundert. Ledige Mütter zwischen Not und Norm, » dans : ANNE-LISE HEAD, BRIGITTE SCHNEGG [Éd.]: *Armut in der Schweiz* [cf. note 14], p. 52.).

48 MAREIKE KÖNIG, « Brüche als gestaltendes Element : Die Deutschen in Paris im 19. Jahrhundert, » dans : *Deutsche Handwerker, Arbeiter und Dienstmädchen in Paris. Eine vergessene Migration im 19. Jahrhundert*, éd. par MAREIKE KÖNIG, Munich 2003, p. 18.

« concubin » et de « concubine ».[49] Avec la dénomination de « putain », on partait donc d'un côté en campagne contre la stratégie de l'entraide propre au concubinage, qui représentait une alternative sociale au mariage légal, que l'on peut sans doute qualifier de populaire.

2. D'un autre côté, la dénomination de « putain » est plus vaste, puisqu'elle associe les enfants illégitimes à la critique. Particulier au sexe féminin, ce jugement unilatéral, verbal, duquel les femmes, dans tous les pays européens, ont plus ou moins dû souffrir, s'esquisse ici. Comme l'a constaté Michael Mitterauer, les sanctions appliquées par la société contre la sexualité prématrimoniale et la procréation illégale dans la vieille Europe touchaient en premier lieu la mère.[50] Cela ne signifie pas que l'illégitimité apparut partout en Europe dans les mêmes proportions, et qu'elle fut condamnée partout de la même façon. À l'instar de Rosina Ebner et de ses enfants, qui étaient dans la communauté des vagabonds entre de bonnes mains, beaucoup d'enfants illégitimes trouvaient un gîte dans un ménage paysan. D'autant plus que des enfants se laissaient tôt engager pour rendre des services, tels que la surveillance du bétail.[51] Le personnel féminin d'un ménage citadin ne pouvait par contre guère compter sur une telle solution. La plupart du temps une grossesse signifiait la fin de la relation professionnelle. À travers cela, ce n'était pas seulement le décisif aspect momentané de sécurité, sur le plan social, qui était détruit, mais aussi toutes les stratégies personnelles de planification de vie et d'avenir qui perdaient leur valeur. Certes, en cas de grossesse non désirée, ajoutée à des conditions de vie difficiles, un avortement pouvait être pris en considération. Il reste à savoir si ce dernier réglait les problèmes déjà existants, ou s'il en créait d'autres ; cela dépendait des cas respectifs.

3. Si Rosina Ebner devait se faire qualifier de « putain », cela annonce, au-delà du cas isolé, un changement d'attitude vis-à-vis de la prostitution entre le XIVe et le XVIe siècle qui est dû à de nombreuses

---

49 Thomas Meier, Rolf Wolfensberger, « Nichtsesshaftigkeit und geschlechtsspezifische Ausprägung von Armut, » dans : Anne-Lise Head, Brigitte Schnegg (Éd.) : *Armut in der Schweiz* (cf. note 14), p. 37 note 11.

50 Michael Mitterauer : *Ledige Mütter. Zur Geschichte unehelicher Geburten in Europa*, Munich 1983, p. 71.

51 *Ibid.*

causes, allant de la peste à la Réforme en passant par la Syphilis. La prostitution offrait en priorité pour les femmes seules la possibilité d'acquérir de l'argent. Il faut seulement préciser ici qu'elle n'était qu'un gagne-pain pendant une certaine période et non une activité à vie. La prostitution était pour beaucoup une solution transitoire entre deux emplois de domestique. D'autres femmes combinaient prostitution avec mendicité et menus larcins, ce qui leur permettait de subsister, ou bien exerçaient en plus l'activité d'entremetteuse. La prostitution put détruire le réseau social existant lorsque cette profession fut stigmatisée, car considéré comme suspecte. On peut ainsi voir clairement dans les dossiers judiciaires de Nantes, Paris et Marseille que des voisins se sentirent habilités à surveiller le comportement de femmes célibataires et de les dénoncer, le cas échéant.[52] Cet exemple montre que la solidarité souvent affirmée dans le voisinage et le quartier n'était pas toujours à l'ordre du jour. Les prostituées devaient aussi craindre des mesures disciplinaires qui d'un côté portaient scandaleusement atteinte à leur vie privée, mais qui, d'un autre côté, leur offraient les bases d'une vie digne. Nous évoquons ici ces petits cloîtres et ces institutions que les catholiques fondèrent aux XVIe et XVIIe siècles en France, en Espagne et en Italie pour rééduquer des prostituées.[53] Les prostituées les plus âgées, qui n'étaient pas parvenues à gagner leur vie d'une autre façon, s'apprêtaient à connaître d'extrêmes problèmes existentiels. Toutes les femmes ne restaient pas toute leur vie des prostituées. Certaines se mariaient. Cependant l'élévation sociale qui leur faisait obtenir l'honorabilité ne les protégeait pas de la pauvreté.[54] L'important était la garantie sociale. Celle qui gagnait de l'argent grâce à la prostitution, pour une courte période ou occasionnellement, ne devait pas nécessairement abandonner tout lien social déjà existant, puisqu'elle ne voulait pas être ancrée dans le milieu de la prostitution. Il en était tout autrement des femmes qui l'exerçaient

---

52 KATHRYN NORBERG : « Prostitution, » dans : GEORGES DUBY, MICHELLE PERROT (Éd.) : *Histoire des femmes en Occident*, T. 3 : 16e–18e siècle, Éd. par ARLETTE FARGE et NATHALIE ZEMON DAVIS, Francfort/New York 1994, p. 484.

53 *Ibid.*

54 BEATE SCHUSTER : *Die freien Frauen. Dirnen und Frauenhäuser im 15. und 16. Jahrhundert*, Francfort/New York 1995, p. 203.

pendant une longue période et qui voulaient s'établir comme prostituée. À cela était liée la fondation de foyers pour femmes ou bien l'utilisation de maisons de rapport. Les activités évoluèrent au fil du temps de façons très différentes. La première édition de « Der Pranger. Organ der Hamburg Altonaer Kontrollmädchen » parut le 9 février 1920. Son but était de s'opposer à la fermeture des bordels hambourgeois.[55] D'autres actions de ce genre à Dijon, à Paris et Grenoble, entre autres, suivirent l'occupation de l'église St-Nizier à Lyon le 2 juin 1975, qui marqua le début du soi-disant « mouvement des putains », une initiative contre la discrimination et la criminalisation des prostituées, qui porta ses fruits aussi en Allemagne, où le 1er janvier 2002 la « loi réglementant la situation juridique des prostituées » est entrée en vigueur. Un développement semblable a eu lieu également dans d'autres pays. En 1999 le Danemark autorisa officiellement la prostitution ; aux Pays-Bas elle est considérée depuis le 1er octobre 2000 comme une profession légale.[56]

4. Mais revenons à Rosina Ebner. Sa vie errante ne lui permit pas d'accéder à un emploi à long terme. C'est pour cette raison que sa biographie ne présente pas d'états de service en tant que servante. Telle l'embauche ultérieure comme domestique dans un ménage citadin, ces emplois souvent temporaires permettaient de s'approprier la base matérielle nécessaire au mariage. Pour cela les jeunes filles devaient prendre beaucoup sur elles. Il y avait parmi elles des Allemandes, des Luxembourgeoises, des Autrichiennes et des Suissesses, qui se rendirent à Paris au XIXe siècle pour entrer en charge.[57] Face à celles qui bénéficiaient déjà de relations sur place, et qui s'informaient réciproquement de façon épistolaire, il y avait celles qui, sur la base d'informations générales, émigraient avec la certitude de trouver du

---

55 Cf. à ce sujet FRIEDERIKE KÜCHLIN, « Der Streit um die Bordellaufhebung in Hamburg – « Hermann Abels Nachtpost », » dans : *Zeitschrift für Sozialgeschichte des 20. und 21. Jahrhunderts*, N° 1/92 (1999), pp. 12–33 ; un grand remerciement à SABINE TODT (Hambourg), qui attira mon attention sur ce titre et sur la revue « *Der Pranger* ».

56 ROMINA SCHMITTER, *Prostitution – Das älteste Gewerbe der Welt ? Fragen der Gegenwart an die Geschichte.* Éd. par le Musée de la femme de Brême, Oldenbourg 2004, pp. 75–88 (6. Prostitution – Laster oder Beruf ? Der Umweg zum Prostitutionsgesetz [2002]).

57 MAREIKE KÖNIG: « « Bonnes à tout faire ». Deutsche Dienstmädchen in Paris um 1900, » dans : *Deutsche Handwerker, Arbeiter* (cf. note 48), p. 71.

travail. Sur place, la situation se révélait être plus difficile que prévue, surtout quand les jeunes femmes venaient seules, et non pas accompagnées d'une sœur ou d'une amie. On peut ajouter à cela de mauvaises conditions de travail, la difficulté de trouver un emploi et le problème de l'isolation. Alors, que faire ?

Tout d'abord utiliser les contacts déjà existants. De plus, les églises catholiques et protestantes pouvaient venir en aide. En échange d'indemnités, elles laissaient des logements à disposition et, de surcroît, offraient une certaine sollicitude.[58]

En outre, quelques jeunes filles prirent elles-mêmes des initiatives : elles s'associèrent pour louer ensemble un logement, ou bien aussi pour organiser des rencontres. En cas de besoin, la prostitution fit aussi partie d'une stratégie de survie. Mareike König considère qu'au XIXe siècle 50% des prostituées à Berlin et à Paris étaient d'anciennes domestiques.[59] L'accent est ici porté sur le fait qu'il s'agissait de cas isolés. Il y eut également des états de service qui duraient des décennies et témoignaient d'une certaine solidarité.[60] Tout du moins, les employés de maisons avaient la chance, lors du décès des maîtres, d'hériter de vêtements, tel le cas d'une femme de chambre bordelaise à qui on attribuait, par testament une « cotte de drap violet ».[61]

III. Veufs, soldats et anciens esclaves : destins d'hommes

Il était possible, pour une femme, de tenter sa chance à Paris ou en Amérique, voire, déguisée en matelot, de partir pour l'Inde orientale. L'une ou l'autre femme se glissait dans des vêtements d'hommes pour assurer ses arrières. Lorsqu' au tribunal d'Amsterdam on demanda en 1653 à Anna Alders pourquoi elle portait des vêtements d'homme, elle répondit : « Par pauvreté ».[62] Une femme soldat danoise s'est comportée de la même façon. Manquant de moyens de subsi-

---

58 *Ibid.*, surtout pp. 86–89.

59 *Ibid.*, p. 85.

60 Cf. quelques exemples chez RENATE DÜRR : *Mägde in der Stadt. Das Beispiel Schwäbisch-Hall in der Frühen Neuzeit*, Francfort/New York 1995, pp. 176–177.

61 MARTIN DINGES : *Stadtarmut in Bordeaux* (cf. note 26), p. 223.

62 RUDOLF DECKER, LOTTE VAN DE POL : *Frauen in Männerkleidern. Weibliche Transvestiten und ihre Geschichte.* Avec une préface de PETER BURKE. Traduit du néerlandais par MARIA-THERESIA LEUKER, Berlin 1989, p. 48 ; cf. aussi p. 42.

stance, elle s'engagea en 1670. Ce cas particulier semble confirmer ce que Ruth Köppens fit savoir : La pauvreté est féminine. Les choses ne sont pas si simples ; on trouve partout des pauvres des deux sexes dans l'histoire, dans tous les pays européens et dans toutes les villes. À Paris il n'y avait absolument pas que des femmes de chambre pauvres. Il y avait aussi des ouvriers étrangers, des journaliers, des chiffonniers, des balayeurs, des manœuvres qui vivotaient misérablement. Même la vie militaire qui attirait tant le femmes était tout sauf rose. Le chemin qui conduisait vers le monde des mercenaires et des soldats permettait rarement de sortir de la misère, ou alors pour une courte période. Dans son étude sur les « mercenaires dans le Nord-Ouest de l'Allemagne aux XVIᵉ et XVIIᵉ siècles », Peter Burschel décrit quel genre d'hommes, vivants à la marge de la société urbaine, se faisait enrôler. À Lubeck par exemple le réservoir en hommes était « si grand que les avis du Conseil municipal – comme en 1570 – pouvaient se limiter à la ville même ».[63] Ces hommes voyaient en la guerre une façon d'assurer leur existence, de gagner leur vie, une alternative au salaire habituel dans l'artisanat, au salaire journalier, au travail occasionnel et au chômage. Nous n'avons pas évoqué ici tous ceux qui ont tenté leur chance en tant que mercenaire, et qui, à cause de leur solde, faisaient les rêves les plus beaux. Les couches basses et moyennes de la paysannerie en faisaient partie, ainsi que les criminels, ceux qui erraient et ceux qui étaient rejetés. Certains de ces hommes étaient célibataires, d'autres étaient mariés, ce qui leur permettait de laisser leur femme, voire leur famille, derrière eux, pour quelque temps ou pour toujours. S'éclipser ou disparaître, il s'agit là de plus que d'une façon populaire de divorcer. C'est aussi une stratégie pour se sortir de situations problématiques, mettant en jeu la vie et la survie, et qui ouvrait des perspectives d'avenir à ceux qui étaient concernés. Celui qui prenait ainsi ses distances avec son milieu social, aspirait à changer radicalement sa vie, du moins à l'améliorer, sans ménagement. Il n'y a pas que des époux ou des épouses qui fuirent, il y avait aussi des prostituées qui voulaient échapper aux griffes d'un souteneur. Ainsi en 1507 deux

---

63 PETER BURSCHEL : *Söldner im Nordwestdeutschland des 16. und 17. Jahrhunderts. Sozialgeschichtliche Studien*, Göttingen 1994, p. 61.

gaillards de Constance tramèrent un complot pour permettre à deux prostituées de s'enfuir.[64] Des soldats désertèrent et des hommes de couleurs échappèrent à leurs maîtres. Des Africains, amenés comme esclaves en Europe, ne sont pas seulement des laissés pour compte de l'Utopie, mais aussi de la recherche dans le domaine de la pauvreté. Dans des études sur le sujet on évoque les Tziganes et les Juifs, mais pas les individus de couleurs, comme par exemple Joseph Knight. Né en Jamaïque, il a été acheminé en Écosse à l'âge de douze ans par John Wedderburn. En 1788 il s'enfuit. La tentative de ramener l'esclave enfui dans son état de dépendance échoua : « …the Scots courts decided in the case of Joseph Knight that in Scotland no man is by right the property of another. »[65] Joseph Knight se maria et obtint le droit de rester en Écosse, car les Esclaves ne pouvaient être forcés ni à quitter l'Écosse, ni à servir un maître à vie – « thus practically, if not in theory, slavery was abolished in Scotland ».[66]

Même si il y eut des recrutements de force et que, de cette façon, beaucoup entrèrent en contact, contre leur volonté, avec le monde de la guerre et des batailles, la condition de mercenaire était pour beaucoup d'hommes très attirante, pas seulement pour des raisons économiques mais aussi sociales. En fin de compte, une telle vie aventureuse promettait, dans le réseau social resserré de la camaraderie et de la troupe, une certaine sécurité. Le journal intime d'un mercenaire[67] à l'époque de la guerre de Trente Ans offre un aperçu concret de ce monde. Ses notes débutent en 1625 dans la ville de Brescia, située au nord de l'Italie. Il était entré au service des Vénitiens. Les dernières lignes de ce journal ont été écrites en 1649. À partir de cette date on perd sa trace. Les années de guerre situées entre ces deux dates sont

---

64 BEATE SCHUSTER : *Die freien Frauen* (cf. note 54), p. 138.

65 HANS WERNER DEBRUNNER, *Presence and Prestige : Africans in Europe. A History of Africans in Europe before 1918*, Bâle 1979, p. 162 ; cf. aussi GRETCHEN GERZINA, *Black England. Life before Emancipation,* Londres 1995.

66 HANS WERNER DEBRUNNER : *Presence and Prestige* (cf. note 65), p. 162.

67 *Ein Söldnerleben im Dreißigjährigen Krieg. Eine Quelle zur Sozialgeschichte*, éd. et remanié par JAN PETERS, Berlin 1993 ; le secret autour de l'identité du mercenaire inconnu semble entre-temps être levé. MARCO VON MÜLLER a dans son mémoire de Magister à la FU Berlin, dont JAN PETERS et A. E. IMHOF étaient les tuteurs, confirmé la thèse de PETERS, comme quoi il s'agirait d'un certain Peter Hagendorf.

caractérisées par une fortune fluctuante. Il change de camp, offre ses services aux Bavarois puis aux Suédois, gagne des « sommes rondelettes » en travaillant de temps à autres comme artisan avant de devoir à nouveau mendier. Il en va de même pour la nourriture : Aux périodes d'abondance succède la disette. Il connaît toutes les épreuves : « … frôler la mort, constamment avec la douleur et la faim, l'humidité, subir le froid et la chaleur, camper en plein champ, dans une pièce extrêmement réduite, dans des cahutes misérables et surmonter des marches forcées de nuit. »[68] Les observations géographiques et militaires contenues dans ce journal intime permettent de conclure que son auteur s'identifiait à son existence de mercenaire, y compris à la brutalité quotidienne, inhérente à ce métier, que l'on retrouvait sous la forme de graves blessures, de rixes et de cruautés de toutes sortes. Il relate par exemple qu'en 1636 il régnait dans l'armée une telle famine que les chevaux n'étaient pas à l'abri des domestiques, même dans les écuries : « *haben dem pferdt, das messer, In die brust getoghen, vnd sindt davon gegangen, Also hat sich das pferdt must zu todt//bluten; darnach haben sie es gefressen, dis hat aber nicht lange wehret, sonder nur .5.tage* ».[69] Lorsqu'une ville venait d'être prise, la violence n'en était pas moins présente. Pillages, vols, meurtres, viols appartenaient à l'ordre du jour. En 1634 une « *huebsses medelein* »[70] échut à l'auteur tel un butin. L'évènement lance un trait de lumière sur les besoins sexuels qui, d'une façon ou d'une autre, devaient être assouvis. Cela fait allusion aux relations entre les sexes qui, sans pour autant être placées au premier plan, n'en étaient pas moins liées à la vie du mercenaire.

1. L'auteur, inconnu, n'est pas seulement mercenaire ; il a été aussi un mari, même si il ne l'a pas été dès le début. Il était tout à fait possible à un mercenaire d'être marié. Non seulement les femmes, mais des familles entières voyageaient avec le cortège qui accompagnait les mercenaires. Dans le cas présent, le chemin nous conduit du célibataire au mercenaire veuf, en passant par l'homme marié qui se mariera d'ailleurs une seconde fois. Il semble que les deux mariages aient été motivés par l'intérêt commun, marqués par une dépendance

---

68 *Ein Söldnerleben* (cf. note 67), p. 228.
69 *Ibid.*, pp. 69–70.
70 *Ibid.*, p. 59.

réciproque et une aide en cas de nécessité. Jan Peters, l'éditeur du journal intime parle justement d'un couple voué au « butin et à la production »[71] qui gère le ménage en commun. Les enfants morts en bas âge sont confiés aux bons soins de Dieu, sans perte de temps et sans peines excessives, puis le couple passe à autre chose.[72] Il semble que l'auteur n'a pas vécu la période de deux ans séparant la mort de la première femme et le remariage comme une période de veuvage. Tout du moins, rien n'indique que quoique ce soit ait pu changer dans la façon de vivre de cet homme après la mort de sa femme. Il ne devint pas veuf, il resta mercenaire, ce qui n'est en aucun cas étonnant. Par principe, les veufs semblent avoir été relativement rares, du moins du point de vue de la perception et de la désignation. Pendant que dans le dictionnaire des frères Grimm l'exposé sur les veuves remplit plusieurs pages, tout ce qu'il faut savoir sur les veufs tient en une seule page. Margaret Pelling, qui est allée à la recherche de veufs dans les villes anglaises avant 1700, constate qu'il est difficile de trouver des veufs. Bien que le concept exista déjà, ce dernier a été à peine utilisé, en tant que concept identificatoire, dans l'Angleterre du début des Temps modernes.[73] Ce phénomène ne se limite pas à l'Angleterre. Les « *poor relief records* » de Florence ne contiennent pour le XIVe siècle aucune appellation de « veuf ».[74] Une possible explication tient dans le fait que les hommes concernés se remariaient sans délai, si bien que leur veuvage était trop court pour être pris en compte. Dans les prédications pour les morts, dans lesquels les mœurs pieuses ont un rôle à jouer, la veuve mais aussi le pauvre veuf, qui ne figure pas dans le journal intime, sont enterrés. Reste à savoir si le fait d'être marié, célibataire ou veuf sont des critères normatifs décisifs d'une vie se limitant au minimum vital. Les mercenaires, les soldats mais aussi les brigands étaient liés entre eux par une camaraderie plus ou moins criminelle qui se plaçait au-dessus du mariage et de la famille,

---

71 *Ibid.*, p. 226.

72 *Ibid.*, entre autres pp. 43, 53.

73 Margret Pelling, « Finding widowers : men without women in English towns before 1700, » dans : *Widowhood in Medieval and Early Modern Europe* (cf. note 19), pp. 37–54.

74 *Ibid.*, p. 42.

et qui faisait d'eux les membres d'un système social de sécurité. À l'intérieur de celui-ci, les relations entre les deux sexes avaient lieu sous la forme d'un réseau intégré qui, sans pour autant être dominant, avait d'importantes fonctions.

Lorsqu'une femme venait à mourir, elle était remplacée dans un avenir proche. Les jeunes filles capturées et les cantinières assuraient, quant à elles, la transition.

2. Si on essaye de se mettre à la place de ce mercenaire dans son combat quotidien pour la survie, on peut se demander si cet homme pouvait développer une stratégie afin d'échapper à la misère. Il bénéficiait certainement d'une plus grande éducation que la plupart de ses camarades. Il est tout à fait possible à l'origine qu'il se destinait à être autre chose qu'un mercenaire. C'est ainsi que, contre sa volonté, Ulrich Bräker, Suisse originaire du Trockenburg, devint soldat.[75] Le récit de sa vie permet de constater que le fait d'être allé à l'école et d'y avoir reçu une certaine éducation, constituait un critère essentiel qui l'autorisait à espérer un destin autre que celui qu'il connut.[76] Lorsque, enthousiaste, il quitta la maison paternelle, il ne pouvait pas deviner que beaucoup de choses iraient de travers, et que son utopique rêve de jeunesse, un rêve de bonheur sur terre s'évanouirait en vue du régime pain-eau.[77] On peut difficilement partir du principe que ce mercenaire, à l'époque de la guerre de Trente Ans, qui acceptait la vie dans toute sa dureté et toute sa brutalité, nourrissait des espoirs qui allaient au-delà des butins, du pain, de la viande et d'une modeste carrière au sein de la hiérarchie militaire. La seule véritable tentative d'échapper à la misère concernait plutôt ses propres enfants, pour lesquels il espérait rendre possible un avenir meilleur. Il ne lui était resté aucun enfant de son premier mariage. Ils étaient tous les quatre morts en bas âge. Du second mariage il y eut cependant une fille et un fils sur lequel reposaient apparemment tous les espoirs du père. En février 1647 il confia son fils à Melchert Christoff, maître d'école à Altenheim. Il restera deux ans chez lui. Par la suite, le fils, âgé entre-temps de six ans, ira à

---

75 ULRICH BRÄKER : *Lebensgeschichte und natürliche Abenteuer des Armen Mannes im Tockenburg.* Avec une postface éd. par WERNER GÜNTHER, Stuttgart 1999, pp. 102–108.
76 *Ibid.*, p. 72.
77 *Ibid.*, p. 94.

l'école à Memmingen. Nous n'avons aucune information sur ce que ce dernier et sa sœur devinrent par la suite.

Pour les enfants des pauvres, qu'ils soient sédentaires ou errants, les chances de quitter ce milieu étaient extrêmement faibles. Beaucoup devaient très tôt travailler ou mendier. Il n'était pas question d'aller à l'école, et pour cette raison, il n'était pas rare que les parents entrent en conflit avec les autorités. C'est ainsi que Jacob Gülich, travailleur journalier né en 1805 dans une famille pauvre, se vit contraint, par dénuement, « d'envoyer ses enfants travailler et parfois mendier ».[78] Cela alarma l'Assistance Publique qui lui retira son fils aîné et le confia à une famille d'accueil. Une telle méthode était accablante car elle démoralisait les parents et désespérait les enfants concernés. De plus, le fond de lutte contre la pauvreté employait autant que possible des familles d'accueil « bon marché » par mesure d'économie. Dans ce cas précis, on constate qu'un réseau social ne peut pas toujours fonctionner sans désordre. D'un côté, Jacob Gülich était dépendant d'assistances de toutes sortes, d'un autre côté, il ne pouvait lui-même en fixer les limites et décider de garder son fils chez lui. Contrairement aux enfants de son frère Andreas qui tentèrent d'échapper à la « malchance sociale »[79], les enfants de Jacob Gülich ne parvinrent pas à grimper l'échelle sociale : Un fils devint domestique, les deux autres fils journaliers ; les deux filles épousèrent des journaliers. La tentative de faire sortir les enfants de la misère et de pouvoir faire vivre ainsi toute la famille, échouait souvent à cause du manque de moyens matériels et de l'impossibilité d'échapper à une situation désespérée grâce à l'école ou à l'apprentissage. C'était particulièrement le cas pour les filles. On se reportera à nouveau à l'interprétation de Christine Lavant, qui rappelle l'absence de courage empêchant les pauvres d'échapper à la misère. Enfin, les pauvres, dès la prime enfance, apprenaient à survivre par l'intermédiaire d'activités de toutes natures. Ulrich Bräker, pour citer son exemple, ne fut pas seulement soldat, il travailla comme son père le salpêtre, fit du commerce de toiles, il peignit le coton et tissait. Malgré tout, il eut certainement l'espoir d'atteindre des objectifs allant au delà de la maxime « peu est mieux que rien ».[80]

---

78 Martin Rheinheimer: *Arme, Bettler und Vaganten* (cf. note 1), p. 119.

79 *Loc. cit.*

80 Ulrich Bräker : *Lebensgeschichte* (cf. note 75), p. 161.

3. Le voyage au Pays de Cocagne faisait constamment partie des grands rêves des pauvres, dans ce paradis de la débauche, dans lequel la faim n'existe pas.[81] Le mercenaire inconnu le pénétrait lorsque le repas était abondant et qu'il pouvait se vautrer dans des montagnes de viande. Ces moments de bonheur, cependant, ne conduisaient nulle part. Ils enrichissaient la vie quotidienne sans pour autant faire quitter la voie sans issue de la pauvreté. Cela n'arrivait que lorsqu'une perspective concrète se présentait et que l'on agissait en ce sens : Le rêve, ici, ne suffisait pas. La tentative de Gerrard Winstanley par exemple, fait partie des expérimentations sociales pour combattre la pauvreté.[82] Celle-ci, dans le cadre de la révolution anglaise, devait établir la communauté des biens et une façon de vivre du point de vue social et religieux prêchée par les Baptistes.[83] C'était surtout à cause de la pauvreté que beaucoup d'hommes, de femmes et de couples, avec ou sans enfants, se rendaient en Moravie dans le but de vivre en communauté, une communauté dans laquelle il n'y aurait ni pauvres, ni riches, mais seulement des frères et des sœurs. La Moravie ou l'empire Baptiste de Münster[84] étaient aussi peu paradisiaques que n'importe quelle colline du comté de Surrey, à partir de laquelle le nouvel ordre du monde devait partir, mais c'est là une autre histoire. Il faut souligner une chose :

---

81 Cf. entre autres : A. L. Morton : *Die englische Utopia.* Traduit de l'anglais par Marianne Schmidt, Berlin 1958, pp. 11–41 ; Dieter Richter, *Schlaraffenland. Geschichte einer populären Phantasie,* Francfort-sur-le-Main 1989 ; Herman Pleij, *Der Traum vom Schlaraffenland. Mittelalterliche Phantasien vom vollkommenen Leben.* Traduit du néerlandais par Rainer Kersten, Francfort-sur-le-Main 2000 ; cf. aussi les indications chez Piero Camporesi : *Das Brot der Träume* (cf. note 15), en outre pp. 100–101 et Martin Dinges : *Stadtarmut in Bordeaux* (cf. note 26), p. 285.

82 Gerrard Winstanley, *Gleichheit im Reiche der Freiheit. Sozialphilosophische Pamphlete und Traktate. Auswahl.* Éd. par Hermann Klenner. Traduit de l'anglais par Klaus Udo Szudra, Francfort-sur-le-Main 1988.

83 Cf. Hans-Dieter Plümper, *Die Gütergemeinschaft bei den Täufern des 16. Jahrhunderts,* Göppingen 1972 ; Hans-Jürgen Görtz, *Die Täufer. Geschichte und Deutung,* 2ᵉ édition améliorée et complétée, Munich 1988 ; Werner O. Packull, *Die Hutterer in Tirol. Frühes Täufertum in der Schweiz, Tirol und Mähren.* Traduit de l'anglais par Astrid von Schlachta, Innsbruck 2000.

84 Ralf Klötzer : *Die Täuferherrschaft von Münster. Stadtreformation und Welterneuerung,* Münster 1992 ; *Das Königreich der Täufer. Reformation und Herrschaft der Täufer in Münster,* t.2, Stadtmuseum Münster 2000.

La pauvreté rendait les hommes et les femmes non seulement léthargiques, mais elle faisait d'eux des rebelles d'une façon ou d'une autre.

En guise de conclusion :

L'approche de ce thème fit apparaître les problèmes méthodiques et conceptuels suivants :

1. Appréhender la pauvreté dans son ensemble, et la concevoir sur les bases de la notion de minimum vital.

2. Choisir certains parcours de vie qui, pour la plupart, ne nous sont parvenus que de façon fragmentaire et qui ne témoignent que sous réserve d'une pauvreté vécue de façon continue.

3. Ces parcours choisis d'hommes et de femmes laissent apercevoir une multitude de réseaux sociaux, différents selon les cas et ne permettant pas de généralisation. Reste à savoir si jusqu'à présent, l'image du « réseau social » n'a pas été trop catégorique. En effet, elle s'oriente trop peu vers les stratégies de survie des personnes concernées, qui ne se laissent guère systématiser. Ceci implique que certaines parties de ce réseau ne fonctionnaient pas, se concurrençaient entre elles, ou bien, qu'en fonction des besoins de chacun, elles étaient reliées les unes aux autres de façon individuelle.

4. Dans le cadre d'une étude se basant sur des cas individuels, la question se pose de savoir si le terme de « réseau social » est approprié pour décrire ce réseau social de relations et de survie, dont hommes et femmes pauvres avaient besoin pour pouvoir exister. Ce terme n'est-il pas, dans son objectivité, sans vie et déshumanisé ?

5. Il reste à réfléchir à la question de savoir s'il est effectivement justifié de parler d'une féminisation de la pauvreté. Si tel est le cas, pourquoi les femmes étaient-elles particulièrement touchées ? À cela il existe une foule de raisons variées : elles n'avaient aucune formation ; elles ne disposaient d'aucun droit politique, elles devaient s'occuper des enfants et traditionnellement être soumises. La recherche aurait pour tâche future d'écrire une histoire de la pauvreté incluant les deux sexes.

Les pauvres honteux, ou l'anomalie légalisée
—————— Giovanni Ricci ——————

En France, à l'époque du Second Empire, un écrivain s'occupa dans de nombreux ouvrages du thème des « déclassés ». C'était Frédéric Béchard, dont la bibliographie comprend des comédies et des essais sous forme de roman. Dans tous ces ouvrages le mot clef, déclassé, apparaît continuellement. La société avait désormais acquis des valeurs libérales et libéralistes qui étaient le fruit de multiples révolutions ; et les débâcles individuelles étaient à l'ordre du jour. Néanmoins, on continuait à s'inquiéter vis-à-vis des pertes de richesse et de statut. A tel point que Béchard donna un titre exemplaire – Au pays d'Anomalie – à l'un des chapitres de son livre le plus fameux.[1] Sans doute, de la mauvaise littérature sillonne les pages réservées à la géographie d'Anomalie. Mais il ne s'agissait pas seulement de littérature. Le mot « anomalie » (et son synonyme moderne, « déviance ») devenait alors l'axe d'une nouvelle science positiviste, l'anthropologie criminelle.[2] Voilà donc que grâce à un écrivain romantique, l'historien social d'aujourd'hui se retrouve à manier un outil de travail non fortuit : l'anomalie. Ma relation suivra ces suggestions, dans le but d'esquisser un tableau interprétatif des traits généraux du déclassement, depuis la fin du Moyen Age jusqu'aux pleins Temps modernes.

La mobilité sociale entre droit et morale

Depuis un siècle et demi, depuis l'époque de Béchard, on parle couramment de déclassement. Ce terme désigne la condition d'une personne riche qui est devenue pauvre, tout en continuant à posséder

---

1 F. BÉCHARD, *Les déclassés*, Nouvelle édition, Paris 1880, pp. 251–281; la première édition est de 1860, en 1863 on était déjà à la cinquième. Voilà d'autres ouvrages de BÉCHARD à ce sujet : *Les déclassés, comédie en quatre actes*, Paris 1856 ; *L'échappé de Paris, nouvelle série des existences déclassées*, Paris 1862.

2 Cf. C. GINZBURG, Pillages rituels au Moyen Age et au début des temps modernes, dans *Normes et déviances*, Neuchâtel 1988, en part. pp. 312–313.

ou à revendiquer certains privilèges sociaux-juridiques. C'étaient des privilèges propres aux sociétés fondées ouvertement sur l'inégalité telles que les sociétés d'« ordres », au sein desquelles il ne manquait toutefois pas de forces de nature économique qui contrastaient, vers le haut et vers le bas, avec la prescription juridique. Par contre les hommes d'un passé plus lointain suivaient des approches attentives aux implications morales et psychologiques de la question. Au Moyen Age il y eut une élaboration doctrinale du thème à travers des commentaires de la Bible, des sermons, des sommes théologiques et juridiques, des vies de saints, des œuvres littéraires. Mais les textes aussi qui sortirent du cercle exégétique pour accompagner les premières apparitions concrètes des pauvres honteux se placèrent sur cette ligne intimiste : c'est le cas à Liège en 1042, à Lille en 1158, à Plaisance en 1192, à Modène en 1248.[3] Ces quatre lieux nous permettent de dessiner tout de suite une polarité entre les deux aires les plus avancées et urbanisées de l'Europe de l'époque, les Flandres et l'Italie du centre et du nord.

Après quoi le langage ne change plus pendant des siècles.[4] Le statut de l'Œuvre des Pauvres Honteux de Bologne, rédigé au début de 1507, qui définissait le domaine d'activités de cet organisme, ébauchait de la façon suivante le portrait des assistés : « très honnêtement on pourvoit aux pauvres, pour lesquels il est honteux de mendier parce qu'ils sont tombés dans la pauvreté par disgrâce de leur état et de leur condition ». Dans les textes normatifs comme celui-ci, les causes matérielles de déclassement restent toujours mystérieuses : « tombés dans la pauvreté par disgrâce ». En compensation, le privilège d'assistance est déclaré : « très honnêtement on pourvoit » ; et la souffrance subjective est reconnue : « il est honteux mendier ». Une vision partielle et inadéquate, sans aucun doute, mais qui peut aussi enseigner quelque chose à l'interprète d'aujourd'hui : à savoir que le dynamisme socio-économique – l'appauvrissement – est inséparable du vécu individuel – de l'aire des affections et des sentiments. Y compris les affections et

---

3 Cf. G. RICCI, *Povertà, vergogna, superbia. I declassati fra Medioevo e Età moderna*, Bologna 1996 (1998²). Dorénavant toutes les références historiographiques et de documentation qui ne sont pas autrement spécifiées sont tirées de ce volume.
4 Cf. A. SERRANO GONZÁLEZ, *Como lobo entre ovejas. Soberanos y marginados en Bodin, Shakespeare, Vives*, Madrid 1992, pp. 29–33.

les sentiments des bienfaiteurs, qui dans l'action envers les déchus exprimaient leur anxiété d'identification corporative. Erasme lui-même n'avait-il pas confirmé que la charité doit être sélective, et plus abondante, envers ceux qui nous sont plus proches, comme nos parents, nos amis et nos semblables ?[5] Comme on peut le voir, à travers cette voie l'histoire de la charité s'enrichit d'une importante connexion avec la phénoménologie du don.[6]

L'ombre de l'histoire économique et les causes du déclassement

On voit se profiler les nombreuses implications de l'histoire de l' « anomalie » incarnée par les pauvres honteux. Le problème de la mobilité sociale descendante est avant tout mis en évidence. Mais, sur un plan idéologique plus large, une autre question se pose : quelle acceptation réserve-t-on à chaque type de mobilité sociale ? L'image globale qu'a une société d'elle-même peut se dévoiler depuis l'observatoire de la pauvreté honteuse. En outre, certains sentiments (la honte, certes, mais aussi l'orgueil) perdent leur caractère fumeux pour se présenter à l'historien avec une face sociale concrète. Les conceptions et les pratiques de l'honneur et du déshonneur sont à leur tour appelées en cause.

Sur le terrain de l'histoire proprement économique, la courbe de la pauvreté honteuse calque de façon spectaculaire la courbe des rentes nobiliaires face à l'avancement de l'investissement productif. Dans tout cela, les cycles macro-économiques jouent sûrement leur rôle. Cependant les comportements biologiques et les contraintes culturelles comptent tout autant : natalité élevée, mortalité élevée, morbidité élevée, dépenses de rang, poids des dots, etc.. Ainsi on envisage un thème qui, même s'il est usé par la culture des manuels, n'en est pas moins important, comme la conquête du monde par la bourgeoisie.

---

5 Cf. N. Z. DAVIS, *The Gift in Sixteenth Century France*, Oxford 2000, pp. 23–29.
6 Cf. M. MAUSS, *Essai sur le don*, Paris 1950 ; G. TODESCHINI, *I mercanti e il tempio. La società cristiana e il circolo virtuoso della ricchezza fra Medioevo ed Età moderna*, Bologna 2002, pp. 187–211, 283–304.

Un travail pour les pauvres honteux /honteuses ?

Le thème reste sous-jacent. Tout dérive d'une idéologie sociale selon laquelle le travail, présent ou passé, n'est pas la condition qui institue des droits, mais bien au contraire qui les annule. Il est plus facile donc pour les nobles pauvres d'avoir recours à des raccourcis : par exemple, voler les couverts en argent chez leurs collègues plus fortunés. D'après les dires de monsieur de Brantôme c'est ce que faisaient à Rome certains Français, des chevaliers de Malte qui « n'ont que l'épée et la cappe et leur croix » [7] – donc leurs symboles de statut et rien d'autre.

Puis pour les femmes il y avait une autre solution – ou un autre danger, selon les points de vue. Derrière toute la documentation se profile le fantôme de la prostitution, désignant un conflit évident entre l'honneur social et l'honneur sexuel.[8] Dans la littérature hagiographique aussi, la femme pauvre honteuse est surprise au moment du choix entre ces deux types d'honneur, différents et complémentaires. Et l'intervention du saint réussit toujours à les sauvegarder tous les deux. Mais la réalité est moins réconfortante que la littérature dévote ; c'est pourquoi on continue à craindre. Le conseil civique de Vérone fait allusions aux « dangers non moins spirituels que temporels », quand il décide en 1538 de s'occuper des honteux ; à cette même époque on parle de « malhonnêteté et manquements » à Ferrare, de « déshonneur du monde et perdition de l'âme » à Crémone. D'autre part, les juristes de l'époque savent bien de quoi il s'agit. En 1562 le célèbre Cornelio Benincasa – dans le sillage de Baldo degli Uberti – décrète qu'une jeune fille noble dépourvue d'une dot suffisante doit être considérée comme pauvre, même s'il ne lui manque pas le nécessaire pour vivre. Pauvreté relative à l'ordre social, une fois encore. Il n'est pas étonnant, donc, que l'on préfère assister les jeunes filles belles – les plus exposées au travail de la prostitution.[9] A vrai dire, les hommes aussi y ont recours, même si cela est plus difficile à documenter. A Venise, déjà

---

7 BRANTÔME, *Œuvres complètes*, par P. MÉRIMÉE, L. LACOUR, III, Paris 1859, p. 193.

8 Cf. I. CHABOT, M. FORNASARI, *L'economia della carità. Le doti del Monte di Pietà di Bologna (secoli XVI–XX)*, Bologna 1997, pp. 35–41.

9 Cf. par exemple D. MONTANARI, S. ONGER (a cura di), *I ricoveri della città. Storia delle istituzioni di assistenza e beneficenza a Brescia*, Brescia 2002, p. 83.

ville de tourisme et de plaisir, en 1784 un espion du Sénat dénonce le très jeune Antonio Corner. Malgré ce nom illustre – nom de doges – Corner n'a que très peu de moyens de subsistance. Ce dernier, donc, « se porte le soir sous les vieilles Procuraties et use de la sodomie dans le rôle passif, en en tirant profit ».

A part les vols et la prostitution, il reste le travail plus banal. Pour la catégorie basse des honteux il n'avait jamais été exclu. Par catégorie basse j'entends les artisans ou les respectables salariés de la manufacture urbaine, que des circonstances défavorables avaient placé dans un état de besoin plus ou moins définitif. Le travail était leur dimension d'origine, sauf que maintenant il était complété par des subsides. Cette intégration au revenu était particulièrement fréquente dans les grands centres de la manufacture préindustrielle : Florence au XIVe siècle, Venise au XVe, Lyon au XVIe. Le travail était par contre décidément exclu pour la catégorie élevée des honteux, ceux qui pour la plupart sont concernés par les traités doctrinaux : les nobles déchus. Ici pour trouver des affirmations décidées et cohérentes il faut attendre l'époque du despotisme éclairé.

Un exemple de solution du problème bien typique du siècle des Lumières était arrivé d'une expérience mise en scène à Munich, en Bavière. Là-bas, sur volonté du prince Electeur Charles Théodore, le ministre de police, le comte de Rumford – alias le chimiste et physicien américain Benjamin Thompson – avait installé une Maison d'Industrie. La haine envers les pauvres imprégnait la fondation. Dans ce climat, même les honteux n'étaient pas tout à fait saufs, et pour eux aussi le travail se profila : « Grand nombre de personnes de naissance distinguée, et en particulier des veuves et des vieilles filles peu fortunées, envoient fréquemment chercher en secret dans cette Maison d'Industrie des matériaux bruts à travailler, comme le lin et la laine qu'elles filent et restituent […] Beaucoup d'autres se trouvant dans le besoin d'assistance vaincront, j'espère, avec le temps leur honte et profiteront de ces avantages ».[10] Prise de position importante, parce qu'elle introduit l'obligation du travail manuel même dans l'espace

---

10 B. Thompson (comte de Rumford), *Détails sur un établissement formé à Munich en faveur des pauvres*, Paris, Agasse, An VII (1798).

protégé des honteux. Les « avantages » vantés constituent dans le fait que, face à l'épuisement du privilège d'assistance, face à l'avancée de l'obligation universelle de travail, les honteux gardent le privilège de travailler « en secret ». Langages anciens et modernes se confondent dans un texte qui, traduit dans de nombreuses langues, connaîtra un grand succès en Europe, suscitant même des imitations de la Maison d'Industrie bavaroise.

La recherche historique contre la résistance des sources

Il reste beaucoup à faire aujourd'hui, surtout sur le front de l'histoire sociale et économique. A la différence de l'histoire culturelle et des mentalités, elle se fragmente plus facilement en des niches et en des chronologies spécifiques. En fait, en termes théoriques le déclassement est l'objet d'un discours infini, mais les termes individuels du phénomène tendent à nous échapper. Comment capturer des personnes aussi obscures, qui ont évité le plus possible de laisser des traces déchiffrables d'elles-mêmes ? Leur angoisse était précisément celle de se transformer en pauvres « publics », comme on disait. Des circonstances particulières, des obligations administratives, des lapsus individuels ou sociaux, tout cela a pourtant produit une documentation adéquate. Mais l'idée que ceci est un sujet à tenir loin des yeux indiscrets s'insinue à tout moment, et dans certains cas forme de véritables murs contre lesquels on se heurte. Violer la volonté de se cacher, rendre public celui qui a cherché à ne pas le devenir, reste le but principal de la recherche historique dans ce domaine.

L'expérience enseignait combien était difficile la gestion du déclassement. Durant le Moyen Age et les Temps Modernes, des statuts d'œuvres pieuses, des traités, des testaments regorgeaient d'invitations à la circonspection. Le problème était toujours le même : concilier le secret avec les contrôles de mérite et la rigueur administrative. Ici le dossier s'enrichit surtout ? – mais pas seulement – de contributions provenant d'Italie : cette Italie qui, faisait remarquer B. Geremek, expérimentait les formes les plus innovantes de gestion de la pauvreté. La compagnie florentine d'Orsanmichele n'enregistrait pas les noms des « nobles dames honteuses » qui recevaient des subsides, à condition que les Capitaines les approuvaient oralement. Mais cette mesure se révéla vite insuffisante et en 1333 la procédure changea : « Ecrire clairement à qui on donne et pourquoi. Et il ne suffit pas d'écrire : « à une famille pauvre ou honteuse » ou « à qui disent les capitaines' ou des mots similaires ». En fait, ces aumônes, couvertes par le secret, pouvaient être détournées vers des consanguins. Elles contribuaient ainsi à la conservation des patrimoines familiers, diminuant les revenus imposables au moment de la succession: une évasion fiscale qui empiétait sur la fraude.

Primauté de la réserve donc, et de curieux contrastes : les pauvres communs, une masse amorphe et anonyme au départ, sont nommés, fichés, obligés d'avoir un signe de reconnaissance ; pour les honteux, par contre, le fait d'être connu est la condition préliminaire pour devenir anonymes. Les statuts de 1491 de la Confrérie ferraraise de Saint Martin, spécialisée en pauvres honteux, insistent : « les décisions de cette compagnie soient secrètes »; que les aumônes se fassent « le plus secrètement possible, ou le soir, de nuit, ou le matin avant la lumière ». La confrérie de Saint Antonin porte les secours la nuit aux patriciens déchus, dans la Venise du XVIe siècle (et collabore avec le conservatoire des Zitelle pour découvrir des cas de prostitution secrète). La nuit les Disciplinants pisans frappent à la porte des honteux, déposent une aumône et s'enfuient, imitant le don de saint Nicolas aux trois vierges, mythe fondateur de toutes ces actions. A Rome l'hôpital Saint Roc, fondé en l'an 1500, accueille dans le secret absolu les infirmes de condition civile ou noble. Quant à la Compagnie de Saint Grégoire à Faïence, en 1517 elle convoque, pour accomplir ses enquêtes « secrètes », les demandeurs dans certains « lieux lointains » ; et en 1633, non satisfaite, elle demande à ses confrères de jurer « de garder le secret et le silence des négoces qui se traitent ».

Mais encore. La charité secrète est le signe de distinction des confréries du Divin Amour, qui se répandent dans l'Italie du XVe siècle.[11] A Sienne, vers la fin du XVIe, la compagnie de la Vierge Marie distribue des bourses d'études aux jeunes nobles en difficulté. Ici on utilise des « informateurs secrets » capables d'enquêter « adroitement », et

---

11 Cf. D. SOLFAROLI CAMILLOCCI, *I devoti della carità. Le confraternite del Divino Amore nell'Italia del primo Cinquecento*, Napoli 2002, pp. 37–74, 181–187.

puis de référer « par le biais de demi-mots qui à leur discrète prudence semblent plus opportuns ». A l'époque, la compagnie de Saint Paul de Turin brûle chaque année les papiers compromettants, « afin qu'il n'apparaisse pas le vestige du prénom et du nom des pauvres ».

Le secret, on l'a vu, crée aussi des obstacles à l'accumulation des archives. En fait, la non – inscription des pauvres dans les registres d'assistance était une pratique courante – et constitue parfois un obstacle pour l'historien d'aujourd'hui. A Florence, tous n'avaient pas changé de route comme la compagnie d'Orsanmichele. La corporation de Calimala note ainsi certaines distributions de blé en 1335 : « à certains pauvres honteux dont on ne dit pas le nom ici pour ne pas leur faire honte ». Quant aux Buonomini di San Martino – sans doute la compagnie spécialisée la plus célèbre, fondée en 1442 sous l'impulsion de saint Antonin de Florence – ils rapportaient les noms, mais aujourd'hui encore ceux qui travaillent dans leurs archives doivent s'engager à ne pas les publier. La congrégation jésuite de Sainte Couronne aussi, fondée à Milan en 1601, « pourra taire le nom » des bénéficiaires sur son grand livre, « s'ils devaient être si honteux au point de ne pas vouloir être connus ».

Alors que l'Etat moderne et bureaucratique grandissait, accorder le secret avec la bonne administration devenait une tâche difficile, qui pouvait rencontrer des résistances exceptionnelles. Des sondages hors de l'Italie le confirment. « En secret » raconte Saint-Simon en 1669 – la comtesse de Pontchartrain « allait toujours à la chasse de pauvres honteux, gentilshommes et donzelles besogneux ».[12] Mais entre-temps Anne d'Autriche, épouse de Louis XIII, repoussait avec de mauvaises paroles ceux qui lui montraient les reçus signés par les honteux auxquels elle avait fait l'aumône. D'autres, en France, moins royalement, cherchaient des solutions plus réelles. A Aix-en-Provence, la Miséricorde rédigeait la liste des noms des assistés dans un registre secret qui était détruit périodiquement ; et à un moment difficile, à la moitié du XVIe siècle, elle refusa l'aide de la municipalité qui demandait en échange de voir le registre. Mais encore le 16 mai 1789 – les Etats Généraux étaient déjà réunis – une famille « honnête » remercia

---

12 SAINT-SIMON, *Mémoires*, par G. TRUC, I, Paris 1970, p. 653.

la Charité de Lyon pour l'avoir inscrite sous un « faux » nom, la sauvant d'une « humiliation ».

Entre-temps le thème du nom, vrai ou faux, nous impose une considération. Il y a plusieurs années, Carlo Ginzburg et Carlo Poni suggéraient d'utiliser la méthode nominative comme « fil d'Ariane » dans le « labyrinthe des archives »[13]. Cette approche vise à construire une histoire qui tienne compte de la complexité des rapports qui lient l'individu à la société. Sans doute se profile aussi la possibilité d'analyses prosopographiques étendues à des classes plus vastes et plus basses que celles généralement prises en considération. Aux acquisitions basées sur la méthode nominative le cas fuyant des pauvres honteux constitue un défi spécial.

Privilèges et escroqueries des pauvres honteux

Légion sont les témoignages relatifs aux escroqueries, aux duperies et aux méprises capables de se développer autour des pauvres honteux et de leur attitude particulière, la simulation : jusqu'où la simulation était-elle légitime ?

Juan Luis Vivès percevait qu'il fallait beaucoup de prudence, autour des honteux, pour ne pas engendrer de « soupçons ». Les nombreux privilèges dont jouissaient les honteux faisaient envie. Et l'ordre de leur monde silencieux provoquait des désordres cachés, contrairement à ce que pensait au XVIᵉ siècle le juriste Pierre Grégoire (« Celui qui est gêné de mendier n'exerce pas les tromperies des mendiants valides »). Mais ce vice était ancien. A l'hospice pour bourgeois ruinés de Lille, il arrivait souvent que des personnes aisées se faisaient entretenir, malgré les protestations des échevins. En 1472 le Duc Charles le Téméraire dut s'en occuper en personne : « sont entretenus et accueillis dans cet hospice des individus qui en vérité ne sont pas du tout indigents, mais qui étaient et qui sont riches et puissants ». Quelque chose de similaire arriva à Lyon. En 1519, on supprima la distribution annuelle de pain de la confrérie de la Sainte-Trinité, à partir du moment où se présentaient « beaucoup de personnes non besogneuses ni indigentes

---

13 Cf. C. Ginzburg, C. Poni, « Il nome e il come: scambio ineguale e mercato storiografico », dans : *Quaderni storici*, XIV, 1979, n. 40, pp. 181–190.

avec femmes, enfants, servants et servantes ». Par contre, personne ne blâmera les bourgeois de Genève qui, ruinés par la crise de subsistance de 1649, n'osaient mendier et envoyaient leurs domestiques le faire.

D'autres fois, on dupait en simulant une volonté de dissimulation. En 1456 les Etats Généraux du Languedoc se plaignaient de « certains vêtus en marchands ou en hommes honnêtes » qui vendaient à travers les villages de « faux lingots d'or ou d'argent, en feignant d'appartenir à de grandes familles et de ne pas vouloir être reconnus ». D'une manière analogue, en 1766 à Sienne le voyageur français Jérôme Richard remarquait des individus louches « mal habillés mais avec une épée sur le côté », qui offraient de faux chefs d'œuvres aux étrangers, feignant d'être des « chevaliers de grandes familles » contraints de se défaire de leurs biens. Il était inévitable que la littérature s'approprie de situations si imprégnées de théâtralité ; et tout aussi inévitable était la contiguïté avec le filon des textes de gueuserie. Au XVe siècle, la liste de tromperies de mendiants connue sous le nom de *Basler Ratsmandat* comprend aussi des nobles ou des marchands qui feignent d'être frappés par des revers de fortune (*Küsche Narunge*). En Allemagne, vers 1510, le *Liber vagatorum* fait la même chose (*le terme qui y est utilisé est Kandierer*), dont une préface successive de Luther assurera la notoriété européenne.[14]

Sur ces premières bases fleurirent dans toute l'Europe les comptes-rendus du monde des gueux. Ils se situaient à mi-chemin entre la dénonciation sociale et le divertissement – et laissent ouvert le problème du rapport avec la réalité. Même des lettrés cultivés, de Noël du Faïl à Michel-Ange Buonarroti le Jeune, de Molière à Francisco de Quevedo, décrivaient les duperies et les malentendus liés au monde de la pauvreté honteuse. Mais la lutte qui se déchaîna en France au XVe siècle contre les pauvres *glorieux* appartenait à la réalité tangible. Les *glorieux* étaient des hommes du peuple qui bénéficiaient d'aumônes prévues pour les pauvres secrets, mais de façon abusive, puisque pour eux le travail n'était pas une honte. Cette action fut conduite en première ligne par les jésuites Honoré Chaurand et André Guevarre,

---

14 Cf. F. KLUGE, *Rotwelsch, Quellen und Wortschatz der Gaunersprache und der verwandten Geheimsprachen*, Strasbourg 1901, pp. 11–12, 38, 49.

fondateurs en Bretagne, en Provence et au Languedoc d'une centaine d'Hôpitaux Généraux et Bureaux de Charité.

Kiel et Constantinople (via Venise)

Nombreuses sont les oppositions dans cette histoire de pauvres honteux. Riche/pauvre, naturellement ; puis passé/présent, secret/public, oisiveté/travail, honneur social/sexuel ; et enfin une opposition Nord/Sud qui comprend toutes les précédentes. Nous aurions déjà dû le soupçonner, en observant que presque tous les exemples fournis proviennent de l'espace catholique d'Italie, de France et d'Espagne. Mais maintenant une comparaison aussi nous est permise entre les deux mers intérieures d'Europe, la mer Baltique et la mer Méditerranée.

Kiel, 1591. Durant la crise de subsistance de cette année-là, dans les rues de Kiel, capitale du Duché de Holstein, on voyait des gentilshommes danois chercher ouvertement de l'argent en prêt. Un témoin, l'historien Anders Sœrensen Vedel, s'en plaignait accusant les taux d'intérêts usuraires et le poids des impôts.[15] Mais le phénomène était là, et il était dû à l'évolution de l'ancien système de privilèges vers un système de marché moderne. Indépendamment des données économiques, un spectacle de ce genre aurait pu difficilement se voir dans une ville à la fois catholique et méditerranéenne. Cela aurait été empêché par la culture prononcée de l'honneur, et donc par l'implication des classes dirigeantes dans les actions caritatives et législatives qui assainissaient, ou du moins cachaient, ces problèmes.

Constantinople-Venise 1794. L'ambassadeur de Venise auprès du Sultan signala plusieurs fois à son gouvernement que le gentilhomme Domenico Giuseppe Marin circulait « mendiant, en haillons et besogneux » dans les rues de Constantinople.[16] Le problème de la noblesse pauvre était chronique à Venise, mais jamais on n'était tombé

---

15 Cf. E. L. Petersen, « La crise de la noblesse danoise entre 1580 et 1650 », dans : *Annales ESC* XXIII, 1968, en part. p. 1243.
16 Cf. P. Preto, *Venezia e i turchi*, Firenze 1975, pp. 203–204.

si bas.[17] Dans leur patrie maternelle des malheureux comme Marin ne mendiaient pas, la république le leur empêchait de force ou avec une généreuse bienveillance, pour éviter de nuire à l'image de toute l'oligarchie. Ayant fini au Levant, le gentilhomme enfreignait la « dignité du caractère patricien » parmi les ennemis infidèles, les Turcs, plutôt que de faire appel à la charité de ses concitoyens et coreligionnaires. Ce que l'on voyait à Kiel, qui ne se voyait pas à Venise, pouvait se voir à nouveau au-delà de la frontière mentale, à Constantinople. Quoi qu'il en soit, on est proche de la fin. En 1796, Venise tomba entre les mains des Français, ce qui mit fin à un ancien régime de sauvegarde des pauvres honteux. Et dans les années suivantes, même à Venise on commença à parler de travail pour eux : travail secret, en suivant l'exemple lancé par le comte de Rumford à Munich.

Pauvres honteux/pauvres vicieux

En 1798 un prêtre catholique italien gagné par les idées démocratiques françaises, Luigi Morandi, avait réservé ces paroles aux institutions pour les honteux : « établissements aristocratiques ordonnés à maintenir la différence des rangs », qui « n'égalent pas le secours au besoin mais aux commodités et aux décences » et conduisent « à l'inertie de vivre sans rien faire » ; dignes pour cela de s'appeler « plutôt des vicieux que des honteux ». La force polémique venait de l'esprit jacobin et tapait certainement dans le mille quand elle condamnait les privilèges d'assistance. Mais aujourd'hui notre jugement est plus nuancé. Nous voyons des œuvres pieuses qui jouent le rôle d'amortisseurs sociaux, tendant à freiner, ralentir, pour un peu occulter aussi les chutes sociales désastreuses ; mais il est vrai qu' aucun individu ou famille n'est entretenu à l'infini. Tout choix comporte un mélange de solidarité collective et de responsabilité individuelle. La mesure de ces deux ingrédients, évaluée avec un mètre actuel, n'est certainement pas satisfaisante. Les institutions pour les besogneux avaient de toute façon mis en évidence les deux ingrédients et je dirai que même aujourd'hui les politiques sociales ne peuvent en faire abstraction.

---

17 Cf. G. Cozzi, *Giustizia « contaminata ». Vicende giudiziarie di nobili ed ebrei nella Venezia del Settecento*, Venezia 1996, pp. 51–71. Plus en général, M.L. Bush, *Rich Noble, Poor Noble*, Manchester-New York 1988.

Mais un aspect s'est totalement renversé, c'est le rôle de la honte. Désormais nous sommes plongés dans une société techniquement sans pudeur,[18] où on exhibe en public les plis les plus intimes de sa vie, de son âme, de son corps. Seul la honte du pauvre reste — ou parfois même s'accentue. Mais ce n'est plus un privilège réservé à quelques déchus, mais bien une obligation ou une condamnation qui incombe sur tous les pauvres, les nouveaux pauvres, les chômeurs expulsés du monde du travail. Ainsi la honte, loin de garantir assistance et faveurs, comme dans l'Ancien Régime, pousse celui qui en est frappé à accepter n'importe quel compromis, n'importe quelle condition, pourvu qu'il rentre dans le cycle. Nouvelle fonction sociale d'un sentiment, devenu un élément très important des profits : « La honte devrait être cotée en Bourse » conclut Viviane Forrester.[19]

En tout cas, au dessous et à l'intérieur des institutions et des processus sociaux se cachent des vies individuelles, comme nous l'a appris l'expert en matière de déclassés sorti du siècle bourgeois, François Béchard. C'est pourquoi la conclusion sur un phénomène à la fois social et mental lui revient : « Dans cet enfer se rencontrent toutes les contradictions, le luxe dans l'indigence, l'ennui dans le plaisir, la misère dans la vanité, l'impuissance dans les prétentions, le vice jusque dans la vertu ; contrée toujours trop peuplée et que peuplent tous les jours davantage les révolutions et les victimes des désastres particuliers qui les suivent, les passions et les naufragés des fortunes qu'elles engloutissent… empire si démesurément étendu. »[20]

---

18 Cf. L. WURMSER, *The Mask of Shame*, Northvale, N.J.-Londres 1994.
19 V. FORRESTER, *L'horreur économique*, Paris 1996.
20 F. BÉCHARD, *Les déclassés*, cit., p. 7.

Crossing the Poverty Line or Can Poverty Be Considered Hereditary?
———————— Torsten Fischer ————————

I. Introductory Notes

For many years, researchers from various scientific disciplines have been working on the image and the explanation of poverty as a social phenomenon. In 1987, the Polish historian and later foreign minister Bronislaw Geremek pointed out the important role of historical research in this respect: "Les processus de paupérisation et les conflits sociaux parallèles à la naissance et au développement du capitalisme obligent les idéologues et les politiciens à affronter la pauvreté comme un phénomène d'envergure sociale. Dans les polémiques qui se développent, c'est l'histoire qui est la principale source dans laquelle on puise des arguments et des exemples".[1] Thus, many historians have been publishing and discussing aspects of poverty during the last three decades, with a hiatus in the early nineties. It is surprising, however, that many results deriving from sociological research have not yet been taken into account. As early as 1977, Anne-Marie Rabier and Guy Picquet had already referred to possible reasons for the hereditary character of poverty in their sociological study "Soleil interdit". However, their study was hardly considered by historians. Rabier and Picquet tried to prove that a poor family could only, in very few cases, manage to reach a sufficient level of existence. In addition, the authors were able to cite some of the parameters determining the continuity of poverty among different generations within one family.[2]

Thomas Riis referred to the approach of Rabier/Picquet, when describing the destiny of two Scottish immigrant families in early modern Helsingør. He was able to retrace their declining financial

---

1 BRONISLAW GEREMEK, *La potence ou la pitié. L'Europe et les pauvres du Moyen Age à nos jours*, Paris 1987, p. 5.
2 ANNE-MARIE RABIER & GUY PICQUET, *Soleil interdit ou deux siècles de l'exclusion d'un peuple*, Pierrelaye 1977 [Igloos 96].

means throughout a century.[3] Riis also underlined the methodological difficulties of such an analysis: the properties of poor families could not be easily defined solely based on manuscript sources. Only the fortunes of wealthier families were systematically mentioned in the documents and could thus be translated into detailed figures.[4]

Despite the high methodological value of the two studies, they were based on a limited scope, namely, from the topographical and chronological perspective as well as concerning the main body of manuscript sources. The present article aims to transcend these limitations by maintaining at the same time the idea of analysing the transmission of means throughout several generations within poor families. This objective leads to the following two working hypotheses:

Poverty is hereditary in the early modern times. Once a family has fallen below the poverty line, it is not able to cross it again in a long-term perspective.

In a given early modern European community public relief is not sufficient in order to help poor families to cross the poverty line in the long run.

II. Methodological and Terminological Considerations, Manuscript Sources and Historical Background

At first glance, the claim that poor individuals are in danger of inheriting their status from the previous generation seems to be evident. Hence, the problem must be explained in more detail: in fact, an individual defined as a 'poor person' is not always a *nihil habens*. When referring to the early modern silk capital Lyons, for instance, the French historian Jean-Pierre Gutton calculated that approximately sixteen per cent of the urban community (around 150,000 inhabitants) were living below the poverty line.[5] The same applies to another

---

3 Thomas Riis, 'Les mouvements de longue durée: le déclin économique et les causes de la pauvreté,' in Jean-Claude Caillaux et al. (ed.), *Démocratie et pauvreté. Du quatrième ordre au quart monde*, Paris 1991, pp. 433–438.

4 *Ibid.*, p. 434.

5 Jean-Pierre Gutton, *La société et les pauvres. L'exemple de la généralité de Lyon 1534–1789*, Paris 1971, pp. 50–51.

early modern European agglomeration: in the modest town of A-berdeen in Scotland, between fifteen and twentyfive per cent of the population had to apply for public poor relief in the late seventeenth and early eighteenth centuries.[6] In both cases, it would be mathematically astonishing if not at least a few of the poor families' descendants could succeed in their fight against poverty, thus offering a perspective for a better life to the following generation. Furthermore, it would be logical in this sense to analyse, how these potential achievements coincided with the reform of public poor relief in the early modern period. In fact, both ecclesiastical and secular authorities had left the traditional medieval perception of poverty and begun to create a new poor relief system in the early sixteenth century. The intellectual basis had been provided by the publications of Juan Luis Vives and Ignatius de Loyola.[7] It is of interest to examine the effectiveness of the reformed social policy within early modern Europe by tracking the property development of poor urban families.

The early modern silk capital Lyons is a suitable example for such a study. The reason for this is not only the rich archives, but Lyons was also well known for the rapid implementation of a new municipal relief system, similar to the one established in Ypres and thus influenced by the ideas of Juan Luis Vives. The municipality took the decision to undertake this step after a serious food riot in 1529 (the '*Grande Rebeyne*'). It created a centralised body that organised the poor relief *intra-muros*, the so-called *Aumône générale*. This body built the *Hôpital Notre Dame de la Charité* in 1622 in order to isolate the poor from society and to put the able-bodied to work. The *Corps des*

---

6 GORDON RUSSELL DESBRISAY/ELISABE EWAN/H. LESLEY DIACK, "Life in the Two Towns," in E. PATRICIA DENNISON/ DAVID DITCHBURN/MICHAEL LYNCH (eds.), *Aberdeen before 1800: A New History*, East Linton 2002, pp. 44–70, here: p. 63.

7 ROBERT JÜTTE, *Poverty and Deviance in Early Modern Europe*, Cambridge 1999 [New Approaches to European History 4], pp. 100–101. Vives argued in favour of a new poor relief system based on two principles: every poor person living *intra muros* should put their name down on lists for the distribution of public alms, and the 'able-bodied' poor should be made to partake in forced labour (JUAN LUIS VIVES, *De subventione pauperum*, Bruges 1526). The first town that implemented these ideas for the reform of the public relief system was Flemish Ypres. Many urban communities in Western Europe followed this example.

Vieillards became important a little later in 1716 and 1742, when more than a half of the interns living in the *Charité* (about 600 people) were counted as elderly poor.[8]

The Scottish town of Aberdeen on the North Sea appears to be appropriate as a counter-example. It provides a completely different political and socio-economic environment for the same study,[9] having implemented a well-documented public poor relief system on the basis of the Scottish '*Act anent the Poor*'. The perception of the poor in Aberdeen, as in other Scottish towns in early modern times, was largely influenced by the two 'Books of Discipline',[10] and the

---

8 GUTTON 1971, pp. 249ff. A study of the property situation of the elderly interned in the *Corps des Vieillards* proves that this kind of relief was well accepted by the poor themselves. They undertook considerable efforts to join the corps. It was very often thanks to reference letters written by wealthier members of Lyons society, or thanks to testaments bequeathing the last properties to the *Aumône générale*, that they were received in the house. So this kind of relief can still be considered as rather a 'selective' one (see TORSTEN FISCHER, *Y-a-t-il une fatalité d'hérédité dans la pauvreté? Dans l'Europe moderne: les cas d'Aberdeen et de Lyon*, Stuttgart 2006 [Beihefte VSWG 187], pp. 58ff.

9 In 1640, Aberdeen had around 9,000 inhabitants, a population that declined after the Civil Wars to 7,140. Until 1755, the number of inhabitants had increased very slowly to 10,785 (see ROBERT E. TYSON, 'People in the Two Towns', in DENNISON/ DITCHBURN/ LYNCH (eds.), (as note 7), pp. 111–128, here: p. 112 and p. 50. Unlike the Lyons economy, based on the trade in luxury products, the merchants of Aberdeen were very active in the wool trade with the Scottish Lowlands and the Baltic countries. The economic situation was very unstable due to bad harvests in the late seventeenth century, 1740–41 and 1782–83 (for more details, see IAN BLANCHARD/ ELIZABETH GEMMILL/ NICHOLAS MAYEW/ IAN D. WHYTE, 'The Economy: Town and Country', in DENNISON/ DITCHBURN/ LYNCH (eds.), (as note 7), pp. 129–158, here: p. 158.

10 JAMES K. CAMERON (ed.), *The First Book of Discipline*, Edinburgh 1972 and JAMES KING (ed.), *The Second Book of Discipline*, Edinburgh 1980.

relief system was thus mainly organised by the Presbyterian Kirk.[11] Similar to other Scottish urban communities, Aberdonian residents had the priority to public assistance. The members of the 'Seven Incorporated' trades and guilds – as well as their relatives – were allowed to receive special forms of relief: they were eligible for indoor relief by the Trades' hospital and could also benefit from special collections.[12] The non-incorporated Aberdonian poor, on the other hand, had to ask for public assistance from the Kirk and the Town Council.[13]

In times of economic regression, as, for instance, during the Great Famine (1695–1699), the Town Council could give a so-called 'token' to the deserving poor. This was then a symbol for the Aberdonians that these poor had public permission to ask for personal alms. It is noteworthy that a number of money recipients waived their monetary relief in order to ask for this 'beggar's badge'. Apparently, the income from this – then 'positive' – stigma for the poor was at a higher value than the yearly average of monetary relief from special

---

11 Concerning the '*Act anent the Poor*', see Parliaments of Scotland, *Acts of the Parliaments of Scotland* (APS), vol. III, London 1814–1875, here III, 88, 14; quoted in ROSALIND MITCHISON, *The Old Poor Law in Scotland: The Experience of Poverty, 1574–1845*, Edinburgh 2000, here: p. 7. In a formal perspective, the Scottish act was a copy of the Poor Law established in England. The 'able-bodied poor' were to be set to work, the towns and parishes were asked to levy taxes for the financing of the relief system. However, the practical implementation of the rules did not turn out as in England, because the Scottish parishes were not obliged to create the framework for this system. Moreover, the English law was followed by a number of legal amendments established by the central authorities. In Scotland, the biggest part of the territories depended upon the intentions and the power of the landed aristocracy. This is why during the whole seventeenth century, the poor relief in Scottish rural areas was based on the dependence of the poor on the lairds and barons. Hence, the Scottish relief system can be considered as being quite arbitrary, or, expressed more positively, in a much more 'flexible' way than in countries with strong centralised power (see, in this respect, THOMAS M. DEVINE, *The Scottish Nation 1700–2000*, Edinburgh 1999, p. 102). In the years after the Union, there was no further amendment made to the Poor Law. The different Scottish counties and the Kirk sessions continued to organise their own relief (see MITCHISON 2000, p.109; and MITCHISON, 'The Making of the Old Scottish Poor Law', *Past and Present*, 63/ 1974, pp. 58–93, here: pp. 88ff.).

12 FISCHER, *Hérédité de la pauvreté*, 2006, pp. 144ff.

13 In the second half of the eighteenth century, the income of the Town Council for poor relief was transferred to a United Fund containing, among other things, information about the means for the Aberdeen 'Poor's Hospital'; see *ibid.*, pp. 121ff.

collections.[14] The average amount of the yearly monetary relief paid by the Town Council could be calculated at about £ 2–10 Scots at the end of the seventeenth century; later it was increased to the sum of between £ 8 and £ 8–10 Scots.[15] The Aberdeen Kirk Session paid out a yearly average of £ 14 Scots at the end of the seventeenth century.[16] This was, of course, not enough for a minimum subsistence level. Hence, the historiography considered the relief system in Aberdeen to be non-efficient.[17] However, an electronic filtration of the names of those assisted by these institutions yielded the conclusion that many of them were receiving money from both charitable institutions! Some of them even obtained relief from the Aberdeen Incorporated Trades, so that – thanks to this complementary relief system – many Aberdonian poor received more than £ 30 Scots a year.[18]

Manuscript sources for genealogical poverty research in Aberdeen and Lyons

With regard to the sources for genealogical studies, the archival situation in the two chosen cities is equally promising. Both offer a well-registered body of serial sources for genealogical research,

---

14 *Ibid.*, pp. 142–144. The average value of the yearly monetary relief given to those requiring (instead of the monetary relief) the 'beggar's badge' in Aberdeen was £ 5 Scots (for 1779–1783, see *ibid.*, p. 142).

15 *Ibid.*, pp. 128–129.

16 *Ibid.*, pp. 129–131.

17 See the recent and interesting summary of the Aberdonian poor relief system in GORDON RUSSELL DESBRISAY/ ELISABETH EWAN/H. LESLEY DIACK, "Life in the Two Towns," in DENNISON/ DITCHBURN/ LYNCH (eds.), (as note 7) , pp. 44–70. The negative, but premature conclusion about the 'almons paid out to Aberdonians' is made on pp. 63–64.

18 See examples of poor having received 'complementary alms' in FISCHER, *Hérédité de la pauvreté*, 2006, pp. 132–133.

such as parish registers.[19] However, it is not always easy to retrace the families' whereabouts for the different generations, since the poor individuals' level of mobility was high.

Concerning the Lyons case study, the wedding contracts are a very important source for the identification of poor individuals and their properties. Lyons was actually one of the few early modern towns in which this type of document was required from every couple, even from the poor.[20] In addition, many serial sources and also personal documents related to poor individuals can be found in the archives of the Lyons hospitals, especially in the archives of the hospital *Charité Lyon* (maintained by the *Aumône générale*).[21] Other sources like tax lists are less beneficial for a study about poorer individuals and their families, because often the poor were exempt from taxes and thus do not appear on the nominal tax lists.[22] Another kind of problem concerns the interrogation protocols of the *Maréchaussée*, a special police created in Lyons for the arrest of beggars and the punishment of criminal

---

19 For Lyons, see Archives Municipales de Lyon (AML), 1 GG 001–1GG 0780, Parish Registers Lyon (microfilm 2 Mi 09 0001–2 Mi 09 0323), 1566–1792. Concerning Aberdeen, the parish registers can be consulted in the General Register Office of Scotland at Edinburgh (the GRO is part of the Scottish Record Office, since 1999 the National Archives of Scotland). Furthermore, the Mormon Corporation has created an open access database for genealogical research, see Aberdeen City Library, Section Local Studies (ACLLS), Corporation of the Church of Jesus Christ of Latter Day Saints, Old Parish Registers, 0036–0071 (microfilm), Index of Parish Registers, Christening 1531 to 1855 classified by surnames, Scotland-Aberdeenshire (including parish of St. Nicholas), available on the web at www.familysearch.org).

20 See MAURICE GARDEN, *Lyon et les Lyonnais au XVIIIᵉ siècle*, Paris 1970, p. XI. Most of the wedding contracts are well preserved and can be consulted in the Archives Départementales Rhône (ADR), sous-série 3E (classified following the notaries' surnames).

21 See, first of all, the nominal lists of entries of the '*Corps des Vieillards*' (Charité Lyon, F 12–F 25: Titres et papiers provenant des vieux hommes admis et décédés à la Charité, 1540–1790; Charité Lyon, F 26–F 39: Titres et papiers provenant des vieilles femmes admises et décédées à la Charité, 1545–1790). For this study, the personal documents of nearly 600 poor individuals have been registered in a database. In addition, the nominal lists of poor individuals receiving bread alms can be found at Charité Lyon, E 1469–E 1477: Distribution de consommation de pain, 1710–1774.

22 Concerning the problem of tax lists in poverty research, see GUIDO PAMPALONI, 'La povertà a Prato nella seconda metà del Quattrocento', in THOMAS RIIS (ed.), *Aspects of Poverty in Early Modern Europe* II, Odense 1986, pp. 105–119, here: p. 105; see also *ibid.*, pp. 217–218.

offences committed by them. In the documents of the *Maréchaussée*, it can be noticed that poor individuals were often lying about their living circumstances in order to avoid arrest. Furthermore, the minute taker described the examined person in such a subjective manner, that this kind of report could not be used for our study.[23]

In Aberdeen, a similar method as in Lyons can be applied for retracing poor individuals' families. Although the notarial archives do not offer the same opportunities as in Lyons, the poor individuals can be found in the 'Mortification Accounts' ('under the Charge of the Provost, Magistrates and Town Council of Aberdeen', MPMTCA). These accounts provide names of the assisted poor individuals and detailed information about the given relief.[24] A similar list was held by the Kirk in its session accounts, where nominative lists of poor individuals receiving relief are still accessible.[25] The most interesting information on the Aberdonian poor, however, is (surprisingly) accessible at the library at Robert Gordon's College in Aberdeen: it is the Minutes and Register of Interns of Aberdeen's Poors' Hospital or Poor House. In these records, ample information about living conditions, reasons for the entry of poor individuals, their whereabouts, etc., can be found. The relatively unexpected location is perhaps the reason why historical research about poverty in Aberdeen has not taken these sources into account until now.[26] Other evidence can complete the picture of the poor relief system in Aberdeen, derived

---

23 The interrogation protocols of the Maréchaussée are accessible at the ADR, sous-série 7B, Maréchaussée, 1631–1790.

24 Aberdeen City Archives (ACA) 10/5 I–XII: Mortification Accounts, Aberdeen City Council, vol. I–XII, 1615–1812.

25 ACA CH2/448/70, Kirk Session Minutes, parish of St. Nicholas, General Accounts, 1768–1803. Important other lists for this study can be found in the earlier ACA, Kirk Session Accounts 10/14, parish of St. Nicholas, 1602–1704, here: 1690–1692, as well as in the Account Bundles of the Presbyterian Council: ACA, Kirk and Bridge Work Accounts (KBA), vol. II–III, 1670–1725.

26 Robert Gordon's College Aberdeen (RGC), Aberdeen Poor's Hospital, Register of Interns, 1779–1814. See also RGC, Aberdeen Poor's Hospital. First Book of Minutes of the Directors of the Poor's Hospital, 1739–1744. The latest analysis of the lives of the Aberdonian poor has unfortunately not referred to these sources (see DESBRISAY/ EWAN/ DIACK (as note 7) , pp. 44–70).

mostly from the accounts of the Seven Incorporated Trades[27] and the records of the Aberdeen Royal Infirmary,[28] where many of the poor had been treated free of charge.[29]

Terminological considerations

The sources referring to the lower social categories of early modern urban communities represent a remarkable variety when it comes to the description of poor individuals.[30] The definition of the concept poor is already controversial. In the present study, a poor individual will be seen as someone who does not have any or has only a part of the consumables he or she would need to obtain sufficient living standards. These comprise, according to Montesquieu, "une existence assurée, la nourriture, les habits suffisants ainsi qu'une qualité de vie qui ne met pas en danger la santé de la personne concernée".[31] If one adds the missing physical and intellectual capacities, no specialised professional education, the lack of liberty and personal dignity, the image of the poor seems to be complete. However, for an empirical study of the property situation, this definition might be too vague. Hence, the definition of a statistical poverty line is important in order

---

27 The records of the trades are accessible at Trinity Hall, Aberdeen. For the present study, the following documents have been consulted: Seven Incorporated Trades of Aberdeen, Convener Court Book, vol. I, 1626–1699; Master of Trades Hospital, Warrant Book, 1807–1839; Hammermen Trade Aberdeen, Hospital Book, 1807–1839; Hammermen Trade Aberdeen, Court Book, 1762–1793.

28 Scottish Northern Health Services Archives (NHSA), Minutes relating to the Institution of the Aberdeen Infirmary & Lunatic Asylum, 1739–1742; NHSA, The Minutes of the Sederunt Book of the Infirmary at Aberdeen; NHSA, GRHP 1/3, Admission and Discharge Registers of the Aberdeen Royal Infirmary, 1753– 1880; NHSA, GRHP 1/4 1–40, Clinical Records of the Aberdeen Royal Infirmary, 1743–1807.

29 Every person mentioned in these various name lists was entered into an Excel database (by the author) containing personal information about more than 10,000 Aberdonian inhabitants considered as being poor. Finally, this was the basis for the genealogical research and the estimation of the property situation.

30 A very useful summary of the terminology of poverty in the *Généralité de Lyon* is given by JEAN-PIERRE GUTTON 1971, pp. 7–13. See also the good overview in JEAN LOUIS ROCH, *Les mots aussi sont de l'histoire: vocabulaire de la pauvreté et de la marginalisation, 1450–1550*, Lille 1986.

31 CHARLES LOUIS DE SECONDAT, BARON DE MONTESQUIEU, *De l'esprit des lois*, livre XXIII chapitre XXIX, edition LAURENT VERSINI, Paris 1995, p. 143.

to estimate whether a member of a family can be considered as poor or not. For the present study, the poverty line suggested by Richard Gascon will be applied: he has defined this line as a threshold beneath which 50% of the resources of a household (containing four people) with only one salary were taken up by the expenditure for cereals.[32] In this study, we will go further and suppose – in case a calculation is not possible because of insufficient documentation – that the people living in a household receiving poor relief can be considered as being poor.

The distinction between the so-called 'ordinary poor' (or the '*pauvres ordinaires*') and the 'shamefaced poor' (or the '*pauvres honteux*') is crucial for understanding the contents of the sources. The first group consists of people who lived below the poverty line despite their salaries and the assistance given by the public relief system. The social status of the shamefaced poor would make it possible to classify them into the wealthier categories of an early modern society, but, from an economic point of view, they have to be considered indigent or poor (mostly due to bankruptcy). The shamefaced poor were often assisted by special donations organised outside the usual public relief system. It was a more efficient relief in terms of quantity and quality than the alms given to the ordinary poor.[33] In the present study, the shamefaced poor are excluded.

---

32 RICHARD GASCON, *Grand commerce et vie urbaine au XVIe siècle. Lyon et ses marchands*, 2 vol., Paris-Den Haag 1971, here: vol. I, p. 402; as well as ANDRÉ LATREILLE (ÉD.) & RICHARD GASCON et al., *Histoire de Lyon et du Lyonnais*, Toulouse 1975, p. 165. For further details concerning the discussion on the poverty line, see THOMAS RIIS, 'Poverty and Urban Development in Early Modern Europe: A General View', in RIIS (ed.), *Aspects of Poverty in Early Modern Europe* I, Stuttgart 1981, pp. 1–28, here: p. 9. Later also BRONISLAW GEREMEK, (as note 2), p. 142.

33 For an in-depth analysis of the shamefaced poor, see AMLETO SPICCIANI, 'The "Poveri Vergognosi" in 15th Century Florence', in RIIS (ed.), *Aspects of Poverty I* (as note 32), pp. 119–183, here: p. 119. The shamefaced poor in Lyon have been studied by GUTTON 1971, pp. 23ff. and FISCHER, *Hérédité de la pauvreté*, 2006, pp. 71–78 and pp. 103–115. See also STUART WOOLF, *The Poor in Western Europe in the Eighteenth and Nineteenth Centuries*, London-New York 1986, here: pp. 27–28; as well as GIOVANNI RICCI, *Povertà, vergogna, superbia: i declassati fra Medioevo e Età moderna*, Bologna 1996.

Methodological reflections concerning the comparison of currency value in Early Modern Times

The problem of inflation of early modern currencies needs to be solved before comparing the monetary value of properties owned by different generations of a poor family. In fact, the correction of the highly fluctuant *Livre tournois* of the French Ancien Régime is possible, because a detailed calculation of the monetary value of the *Livre tournois* had already been published in 1857 and can still be used.[34] In Britain, the value of the pound Sterling remained relatively stable in early modern times, with the value of the pound Scots worth one twelfth of it between 1600 and 1707.[35]

As a matter of comparison, it is useful to know that the average price of 100kg of wheat in local currency (at the value for the year 1602) was 6 *Livres tournois* (L.t.) 16 sols (s) 10 *deniers* (d) in Lyons and 64 pounds (£) 7 shillings (s) 0 pence (d) Scots in Scotland.[36]

III. Transmission of Poverty in Early Modern Lyons : A Case Study

The family history of the master carpenter Claude Antoine called 'le jeune' is a typical but eloquent example of the transmission of ordinary poverty throughout different generations in early mod-

---

34 NATALIS DE WAILLY, *Mémoire sur les variations de la livre tournois depuis le règne de Saint-Louis jusqu'à l'établissement de la monnaie décimale* [Mémoires de l'Institut impérial de France, vol. XXI, part 2], Paris 1857; in particular 'Tableau comparatif du pied des principales espèces d'or et du pied des principales espèces d'argent', WAILLY 1857, pp. 397–406. In the following case studies, the nominative monetary sum will be given first, the reader will find the corrected value in brackets. Only the latter can be used for the comparison of properties throughout the generations. See a detailed description of the correction of monetary value of the Livre tournois in FISCHER, *Hérédité de la pauvreté*, 2006, pp. 19–20.

35 The value of the pound Sterling rose slowly before the creation of the Union in 1707, when 100 pounds Sterling were sold for 1,300 pounds Scots; see JOHN M. HENDERSON, Scottish Reckonings of Time, Money, Weights and Measures, *Historical Association of Scotland Pamphlets*, no. 4 (1926), pp. 8–16, here: pp. 8–10.

36 See for wheat prices in France WILHELM ABEL, *Crises agraires en Europe (XIIIᵉ–XXᵉ siècles)*, Paris 1973 [in German: *Agrarkrisen und Massenarmut*, Hamburg-Berlin 1966], p. 433; concerning the price development in Scotland and more precisely in Aberdeen, see T. CHRISTOPHER SMOUT & A. J. S. GIBSON, *Prices, Food and Wages in Scotland, 1500–1800*, Cambridge 1995.

ern Lyons.[37] His biography, illustrated in the documents he delivered when entering the *Corps des Vieillards* in 1733,[38] is marked by considerable fluctuations in his financial situation.

In fact, he did not seem to be a poor person in the year of his second wedding with the shoemaker widow Anne Fayat in 1715 (no. 23, see diagram 1, part 1).[39] According to the sums quoted in the wedding contract, Claude Antoine (19) offered the sum of 1,500 Livres tournois (inflation-adjusted referring to the value of the Livre tournois in 1602: 918 L.t. 9s 10d) as a marriage portion.[40] In the following months, Claude Antoine suffered from the general economic recession: the Livre tournois actually lost twenty per cent of its value in December 1715. The couple decided to set up a testament, in which their common properties were quoted as 'the sum of 150 Livres' (inflation-adjusted to 64 L.t. 4s 2d).[41] Taking into account this rapid loss of assets, it is not surprising that the master carpenter had to apply for public assistance in the *Corps des Vieillards*. The rectors of the *Charité* decided quickly to receive him as an intern in the hospital, where he died two years later without leaving any children. His properties passed into possession of the *Charité*.[42]

---

37 See also and in more detail FISCHER, *Hérédité de la pauvreté*, 2006, pp. 95–102.

38 Charité Lyon F 12, dossier Claude Antoine, 1733.

39 The genealogical tree shows one generation in a horizontal line. For a better identification of the individual persons there is numbering in chronological order from the top to the bottom; wedding dates are given if they are named in the documents: the double frame of a family member's name designates the person who was identified in the sources as poor and who was thus serving as the starting point of the genealogical research: the grey colour of the frame designates the family member having been identified as being poor, whereas the colours grey and white are used for dependents who, after calculation of their properties, could not be identified without any doubts as to them being poor; the white frame symbolises people either being identified as not being poor or whose means could not be calculated at all due to a lack of sources.

40 Charité Lyon F 12 No. 18, dossier Claude Antoine, here: wedding contract Claude Antoine and Marie Fayat (notary Benoît Laurent), 27 October 1715 = Archives départementales Rhône (ADR), sous-série 3 E, 6059.

41 Charité Lyon F 12 no. 12, dossier Claude Antoine, here: testament Claude Antoine and Marie Fayat (notary Benoît Laurent), 1 February 1716 = ADR 3 E 6059.

42 Charité Lyon F 12, dossier Claude Antoine; see also Archives Municipales de Lyon (AML), 2 Mi 09 0321, register of deaths of the Charité, 1666–1737, here: 1735.

A look at the other branches of the Antoine family shows why the relatives could not assist him. In fact, the destiny of Claude the younger was not unique in the Antoine family. Claude's father Jean Antoine (10), a master carpenter (also a skilled craftsman), died poor long before the above-mentioned second wedding of his son.[43] The development of his economic situation was similar: on the occasion of his wedding, he received a dowry of 985 Livres tournois (inflation-adjusted to 607 L.t. 3s 10d) from his wife's family.[44] After the death of his first wife, Jean decided to marry again. In the wedding contract, the notary recorded a dowry of 530 Livres tournois (inflation-adjusted to 337 L.t. 12s) offered by the bride Benoite Malasaigne (39).[45] However, all they bequeathed to their son Benoît Antoine (16) after their death was the sum of 30 Livres tournois, "including a ring worth six Livres tournois", according to the quotation in the receipt signed by Benoît Antoine.[46] The reason for this poor inheritance was the "little value of the properties of the quoted Jean Antoine, who bequeathed only his furniture and the products of his work as a carpenter".[47] It is not surprising to see that Benoît (16) also had to fight against poverty in this period of macro-economic depression. The two other brothers of Claude the younger (19), Etienne (17) and Claude the elder (18), were not mentioned at all in the testaments.

---

43 AML 2 Mi 09 10 0143 no. 661, parish register 'Lyon de la Platière', burial of Jean Antoine, 24 June 1696.

44 Charité Lyon F 12 no. 16 and no. 17, dossier Claude Antoine, here: wedding contract of Jean Antoine and Magdelaine Aujart (notary Arthaud, copied by notary Delatant), 25 August 1662; confirmation of dowry by Jean Antoine in favour of Magdelaine Aujart, his wife (notary Delatant), 4 March 1672. The parents of Jean Antoine (10), Claude Antoine (03) and Claudine Gatton (04) did not add any marriage portion. The peasant Claude Antoine (03) had already died in 1657 (see AML 2 Mi 10 01, name list of the parish register 'Lyon de la Platière', 1649–1665).

45 ADR 3 E 3639 (notary André Clerc), wedding contract of Jean Antoine and Benoite Malasaigne, 16 November 1686. It is interesting to see that both the bridegroom Jean (10) as well as his brother and witness Claude Antoine (08) signed the contract, whereas they had declared themselves unable to do so on the occasion of Jean's first wedding.

46 Translation of Charité Lyon F 12 no. 20, dossier Claude Antoine, here: quittance of Benoît Antoine on behalf of Claude Antoine, his brother (notary Benoît Laurent), 16 October 1722.

47 Charité Lyon F 12 no. 17, dossier Claude Antoine, here: quittance of Benoît Antoine on behalf of Claude Antoine, his brother (notary Romieu), 25 June 1714.

The fluctuations in the economic situation within three generations were considerable, as can be seen in the following diagram:

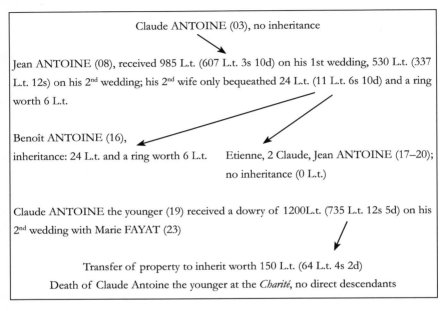

Claude ANTOINE (03), no inheritance

Jean ANTOINE (08), received 985 L.t. (607 L.t. 3s 10d) on his 1st wedding, 530 L.t. (337 L.t. 12s) on his 2nd wedding; his 2nd wife only bequeathed 24 L.t. (11 L.t. 6s 10d) and a ring worth 6 L.t.

Benoît ANTOINE (16),
inheritance: 24 L.t. and a ring worth 6 L.t.   Etienne, 2 Claude, Jean ANTOINE (17–20); no inheritance (0 L.t.)

Claude ANTOINE the younger (19) received a dowry of 1200L.t. (735 L.t. 12s 5d) on his 2nd wedding with Marie FAYAT (23)

Transfer of property to inherit worth 150 L.t. (64 L.t. 4s 2d)
Death of Claude Antoine the younger at the *Charité*, no direct descendants

It is noteworthy that every male descendant of Claude Antoine (03) received a large sum of money as a dowry. But despite good professional skills, none of them were able to maintain the level of financial property (inflation-adjusted) in times of macro-economic recession. On the contrary, they could not bequeath any inheritance of financial value which could have served as an important starting point for the lives of the following generation above the poverty line. Apparently, the income earned by the work as a skilled craftsman was also too low to secure a permanent life at a higher standard than the subsistence level. Nevertheless, the destiny of the following generations illustrates that low income and missing inheritance were only two parameters causing poverty within the Antoine family.

Claude Antoine the elder (18) was also a skilled craftsman, working as a master armourer. In 1685, he married the craftsman's daughter Jeanne Boléda (22) with whom he had six children.[48] One can easily imagine that the family fell below the poverty line in 1708 at the latest, when Claude the elder died at the age of 43.[49] Even if the other family members tried to assist the widow with her children – in other words, the family network was still existing – their help was certainly not enough for providing more than the minimum of subsistence.[50]

The reason for the weak efficiency of the family network can also be found in the destiny of the other family members: Jean-Baptiste Antoine (32) founded a family without any noteworthy property. The wedding contract he signed together with his in-laws did not contain any financial means nor any other valuables.[51] At the wedding of Claude Antoine (30), another brother of Jean-Baptiste (32), the directors of the *Charité* were present as witnesses and signed the wedding contract: the bride Louise Fontanel (36) was an adopted daughter of the *Aumône générale*, so it can be concluded that it was a couple of orphans who obviously had to fight against poverty,[52] although Claude (30) had a modest income as a master shoemaker. In 1722, their daugh-

---

48 AML 2 Mi 09 0141 no. 1490, parish register 'Lyon de la Platière', wedding of Claude Antoine and Jeanne Boléda, 13 February 1685 (transferred to parish register 'Lyon Saint Nizier'); AML 2 Mi 09 0142 and 0143, parish register 'Lyon de la Platière', baptisms, 1691–1701.

49 AML 2 Mi 09 0143, no. 212, burial of Claude Antoine, 31 May 1708.

50 For instance, Jeanne Bouche (21, wife of Etienne Antoine (17)) was godmother to Claude (30), see AML 2 Mi 09 0138 no. 309, here: baptism of Claude Antoine, 2 August 1695.

51 AML 2 Mi 09 0186 no. 17, parish register of 'Lyon Sainte-Croix', weddings, here: Jean-Baptiste Antoine and Etiennette Prost, 29 January 1733. The contract had been signed one week before the wedding in church; see ADR 3 E 4741 (notary Pierre Faure), wedding contract of Jean-Baptiste Antoine and Etiennette Prost, 22 January 1733; the wedding contract can also be found in the control registers of the royal central administration (ADR, Sous-série 10 C: Contrôle des actes, notaires et sous seing privé, insinuations et droits joints (1693–1791), here: ADR 10 C 896, 29 January 1733).

52 AML 2 Mi 09 0067 no. 892, wedding of Claude Antoine and Louise Fontanel, 21 September 1721. The orphans living in Charité were often married to unmarried craftsmen of the community; see, in this respect, JEAN-PIERRE GUTTON, 'L'insertion sociale des enfants recueillis par la Charité de Lyon au XVIIIe siècle. Un bilan provisoire', in J. P. BARDET (ed.) et al., *Lorsque l'enfant grandit. Entre dépendance et autonomie*, Paris 2003, pp. 929–939, here: p. 937.

Diagram 1. The Ordinary Poor in Lyons: Genealogical Tree of Claude Antoine's Family (I)

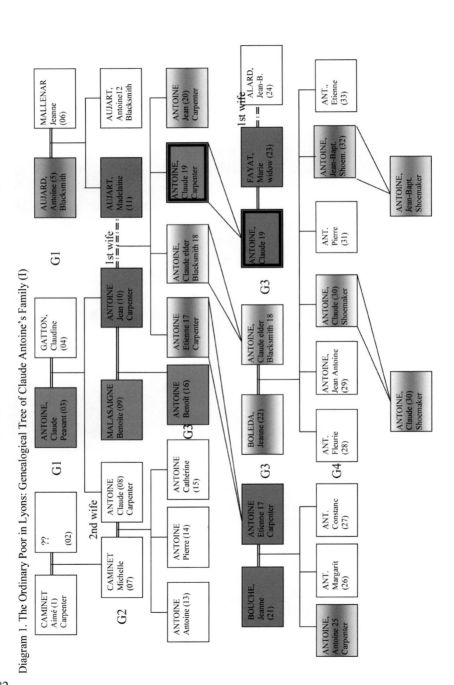

Diagram 1. The Ordinary Poor in Lyons: Genealogical Tree of Claude Antoine's Family (II)

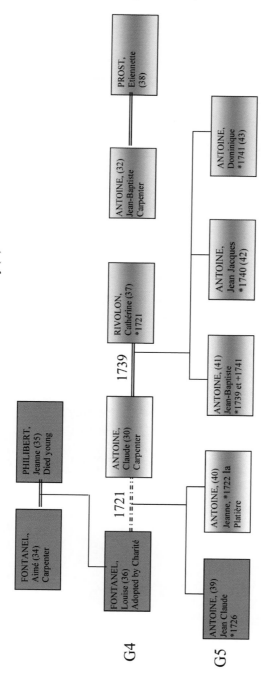

ter Jeanne (40) was born without any disorder, but the young mother died at the birth of the second child Jean Claude (39) in 1726.[53] It is easily imaginable that the family's quality of life was considerably reduced at this moment. Only thirteen years later the shoemaker decided to marry again, this time seventeen year old Catherine Rivolon (37). Apparently, Claude Antoine was able to start again a normal family life, because shortly after the wedding, the young woman gave birth to three children.[54] But the situation once again turned into a disaster, when in 1741 Jean-Baptiste (41) died, and only a year later the mother, too, at the age of thirty.[55] The master shoemaker had to try again to organise the family life without wife and mother. The family network appeared to be still existing, because Jean-Baptiste Antoine (32) was godfather to his nephew (41), but once again the network was not sufficient to help out in the long run. As illustrated by the wedding contract of Jean-Baptiste (32), neither himself nor his wife were in the financial position to assist with much more than their moral support.

The Antoine family could not be followed any more in the documents relating to the sixth generation. Nevertheless, already the destiny of the five generations could tell a lot about the setbacks suffered by poorer families in their fight for a better quality of life. For the Antoine family, it can be summarised that most of the 43 members that could be followed in the documents had to live below the poverty line. Poverty was transferred from one generation to the other. The high level of infant mortality and the deaths of the young mothers were certainly no exception. They were due to the characteristic features of the poor families' living conditions: bad nutrition, the unhygienic state of the rooms in which they were living (especially serious for women in childbed), illnesses and insufficient medical care. In the case of the Antoine family it is also remarkable that every generation

---

53 AML 2 Mi 09 0143 no. 1310 and no. 1315, parish register 'Lyon de la Platière', baptisms and burials, here: burial of Jean Claude Antoine, burial of Louise Fontanel, 7 January 1726.

54 AML 2 Mi 09 0143, no. 1751, no. 173 and no. 748, parish register 'Lyon de la Platière', here: baptisms of Jean-Baptiste Antoine (41) 9 February 1739, Jean Jacques Antoine (42) 22 April 1740, Dominique Antoine (43) 8 April 1741.

55 AML 2 Mi 09 0143, parish register 'Lyon de la Platière', here: burial of Catherine Rivolon, 29 November 1742.

had to live below the poverty line, despite the fact that every male member was a skilled craftsman. This shows how the living conditions influenced the life of families belonging to the lower categories of urban communities, such as the less skilled workers, day labourers and other marginalised groups (e.g., the so-called 'sans aveu', dishonest and itinerant people, the unemployed, the shirkers or even the beggars).[56]

It is striking that the Lyons *Aumône générale*, as the responsible administration for public poor relief, only appeared twice in the Antoine family's history (as the responsible body of the *Corps des Vieillards*, where Claude the younger (19) finished his life, and as the tutor of the orphan Louise Fontanel (36) until she married). These two cases cannot serve as proof of sufficient coverage of the poor families by the urban public poor relief system. Furthermore, the example of the Antoine family shows that inadequate public assistance was only one of the reasons for the transmission of poverty in early modern times. The different parameters will again be analysed in a separate section of this study. Before looking at the summary of the reasons for urban poverty, the case of a poor family living in a completely different urban environment, namely in Aberdeen, Scotland, will be presented as a counter-example.

IV. Poor Families in Early Modern Aberdeen: The Family of the Tailor George Hill

The name of the tailor George Hill (no. 01, see diagram 2) can be found on the Town Council's list of alms recipients. In 1695, at the beginning of the Great Famine in Aberdeen, the Council assisted him with the sum of £ 1 Scots.[57] Apparently, his situation did not improve over the following years, as he asked to be put on different recipient lists by the Town Council. In 1698, he received the overall sum of £2 8s Scots.[58] This was of course not enough to survive. Apparently the municipal authorities in Aberdeen were aware of

---

56 For a more detailed description of the 'sans aveu' in Lyons, see GUTTON, pp. 12ff.
57 ACA 10/5 II, MPMTCA, 1673/74–1699/1700, here: 1695, alms for George Hill, 'older' tailor.
58 ACA 10/5 II, MPMTCA, 1673/74–1699/1700, here: 1695–1699, alms for George Hill, 'older' tailor.

this fact, because they also put George Hill's wife Isabell White (02) on the Town Council's recipient list. In 1698, she was able to benefit from an additional yearly sum of £1 8s Scots. Altogether, the couple received four pounds Scots per year, so it is easily imaginable that they had problems acquiring the necessary income for paying their own food. Presumably, their four children could not help out,[59] because all of them were living below the poverty line.

The only son of the couple, the later tailor Thomas Hill (06), can also be considered as poor.[60] At the beginning of the Great Famine in 1695, he was married to Elspet Steven (07). The couple lived in the Footdee area throughout their whole life. Thanks to their sedentariness, the family structure can be easily retraced: they had two sons and two daughters. But seemingly, Thomas (06) could not rid himself of the poverty transferred from his father's generation: in 1725, he could not pay his taxes to the Town Council,[61] and, in 1746, he had to ask that the inflammation of a badly healed cut on his thigh be cured at the municipal hospital. On his admission to the hospital, he declared himself to be a resident of the Aberdeen Poor's Hospital.[62]

The poverty of George and Thomas Hill was also transferred onto the third generation. Actually, at least three out of the four children of Thomas Hill can be found in the documents as poor individuals: Katherine Hill (15) is only mentioned once when baptised in the church of St. Nicholas of New Aberdeen.[63] The destiny of the two sons Alexander (10) and George (13) can be retraced in the documents: both of them learned the same profession as their father and grandfather. Still, they also lived below the poverty line, this is at least

---

59 IGI C111684 7916, parish of St. Nicholas, baptism of Marjory Hill, 16 June 1661; IGI C111684 8355, parish of St. Nicholas, baptism of Elisabeth Hill, 9 July 1663; IGI C111684 10440, parish of St. Nicholas, baptism of Margaret Hill, 16 April 1672.

60 His baptism is recorded in the parish register of St. Nicholas, on 14 February 1667; see IGI, C111684 9169.

61 ACA, Tax Debts Outstanding, 1725.

62 NHSA, GRHP 1/4 1, Daily Journal, 1743–1747, here: November 1746; see also NHSA, GRHP 1/1 2, Minutes of the Sederunt Book for the Directors of Aberdeen Royal Infirmary, 1742–1751, here: admission of Thomas Hill, November 1746.

63 IGI C111685 5639, parish of St. Nicholas, baptism of Katherine Hill, 19 June 1698.

what can be proven at one point in their life. Alexander did not pay his tax in 1725 and died young in 1736. His widow had to ask for public relief and received it between 1737 and 1740. She benefited from a yearly sum of £ 4 Scots.[64]

In 1717, George Hill (13),[65] second son of Thomas Hill (06), married the servant Margaret Tosh (14). The family network was apparently existing, since both fathers were witnesses of their minor children at the ceremony. This is at least what can be understood from the notice left in the parochial register of St. Nicholas: 'George Hill taylor and Margaret Toash a servant young woman in Aberdeen having contracted and cautioned for the man Thomas Hill taylor and for the woman John Craig baxter, payed two pound Scots'.[66] Unfortunately, it is not possible to retrace the destiny of this young couple in the documents. They did not enrol on any of the recipient lists of the municipal relief. Still, it seems unlikely that they were able to support George's parents.

The fourth generation of the family of George Hill (01) proves the methodological difficulty when it comes to the reconstruction of poor families' genealogical trees: the sources do not allow for the possibility to retrace the destiny of the children belonging to the couple George Hill (13) and Margaret Tosh (14). Three of them were baptised in St. Nicholas Church of (New) Aberdeen: Janet (18) in 1718, Patrick (19) in 1722 and finally George Hill (17) in 1724.[67] Only George the younger (17) reappears in the documents after his wedding:[68] he put his name down on the list of Aberdonian men preparing for the defence of the city against an expected attack of

---

64 ACA, Tax Debts Outstanding, 1725; and ACA, PR 10/5/VI, MPMTCA 1737/1738–1749/1750; here: public alms paid out to the widow of Alexander Hill, 1737–1740.

65 IGI C111685 4584, parish of Saint Nicholas, baptism of George Hill, 5 February 1693.

66 ACLLS, FR 4117, wedding of George Hill to Margaret To(a)sh, 21 February 1717.

67 IGI C111686 2544, parish of St. Nicholas, baptism of Janet Hill, 30 September 1718; IGI C111686 3191, parish of St. Nicholas, baptism of Patrick Hill, 6 May 1722; IGI C111686 3572, parish of St. Nicholas, baptism of George Hill, 28 June 1724.

68 IGI M119064, parish of Old Machar [Old Aberdeen, T. F.], wedding of George Hill and Christian Marshall, 23 July 1753.

Diagram 2. The Ordinary Poor in Aberdeen: Genealogical Tree of George Hill's Family

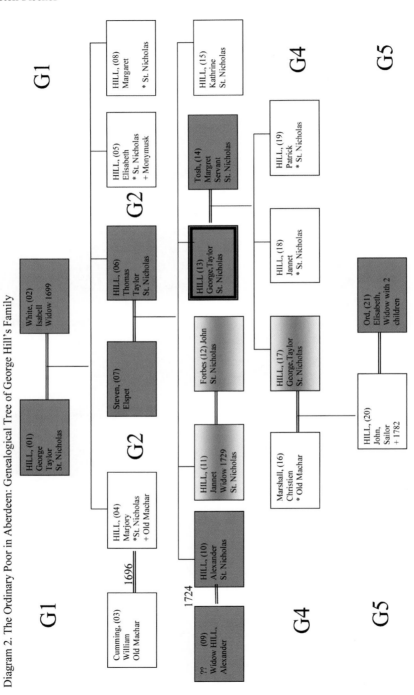

French troops in 1759.[69] He was mentioned in the list of men living in Footdee, so it might have been possible that he had taken over his father's tailor shop in this Aberdeen district. However, it is not possible to find any clues as to his property situation. On the one hand, it is possible that his fight against poverty was successful, because there is no mention of him in the recipient lists. On the other hand, there are also other conceivable reasons for his name not appearing, such as premature death. In any case, he had one son John Hill (20) whose short life left a few trails in the sources.

John Hill (20) was baptised on 17 May 1754 in New Aberdeen, in the same church as four generations of his ancestors.[70] It is interesting to note that he was the first sailor in the Hill family. Apparently, this profession did not give him enough income to maintain his own family. His wife Elisabeth Ord (21) can be found on the recipient lists of the 'United Funds', a collection organised by the municipality for poor relief and paid out by the directors of the Poor's Hospital. She received the sum of six shillings Sterling and one 'peck of meal' per month, for herself and her 'two infant childs'.[71] Given the fact that the committee of directors referred to her as a 'relict', it can be supposed that John Hill had perished at sea just before his wife asked to be enrolled on the 'Poor's Table' of the Poor's Hospital. After this event, any traces of the Hill family are lost: the widow of John (20) did not receive poor relief in Aberdeen any more.

In total, 21 members of the family of George Hill (a tailor in Aberdeen) can be found in the sources. It can be summarised that, apart from the poor relief the municipal authorities accorded to the family throughout five generations, there was a high level of sedentariness and a continuity in the profession learned by the male members. This could not ameliorate the family's economic situation.

---

69 This remarkable list was created by the Aberdeen Town Council in late August 1759. It is highly valuable for the population research of Aberdeen in the 18th century, since it contains the name, age and profession of every male Aberdonian resident older than sixteen (in total, 2,258 people), who were able for military service at that time; see ACA, Press 18/59 1–24, 28–30, List of Men aged sixteen and above in Aberdeen, 1759.
70 IGI C111686 6738, parish of St. Nicholas, baptism of John Hill, 17 May 1754.
71 Quotations from RGC, Aberdeen Poor's Hospital, Register of Interns I, here: alms paid out to Elisabeth Ord, relict of John Hill, 3 September 1782.

Although the sources could not give detailed information about every descendent, it can be seen that the family was not able to cross the poverty line in the long run. In other words, the status of poverty was transferred from one generation to another at least between 1696 and 1782. Instead of calculating the property of the households, we could base our observations on the possible value of the public relief given to the different generations of the Hill family. Four of them received alms in the form of money or medical treatment free of charge. On the other hand, none of them benefited from the public relief organised by the Presbyterian Kirk. Eight family members were regularly enrolled on the recipient list for public alms, but the sums paid out were probably not large enough for a successful fight against the family's poverty. In other words, and unlike the French case of the Antoine family, the public relief administration contributed frequently and actively to the family income, in particular in the years of social and economic pressure. This was especially the case during the Great Famine at the end of the seventeenth century.

It seems appropriate in the following section to analyse in more detail the parameters that caused poverty in the two case studies.

V. Parameters of the Hereditary Character of Poverty in Early Modern Europe: The 'Vicious Circle of Poverty'

The comparison of the case studies illustrated for early modern Lyons and Aberdeen show certain similarities: the ordinary poor cannot cross the poverty line, even if they make considerable efforts to do so. In a few cases, one generation is able to cross the poverty line. However, it can be seen that the family once again finds itself in a miserable situation as soon as there is an accidental cause, like the death of the breadwinner, or a cyclical cause, like (macro-)economic depression.

The degree of poverty then depends upon various parameters that have come to the fore in the two genealogical case studies of the families of Claude Antoine and George Hill. In Lyons, the people responsible for the centralised relief system were obviously acting with a certain selection of the deserving poor. The poor who did not have any network could easily be excluded from the charity.[72]

In Aberdeen, the relief system seems to be more flexible indeed than the one established in early modern Lyons. The different resources for relief – clerical and secular ones – can be called 'complementary': the poor who were on different recipient lists at the same time could avoid at least the physical poverty for a certain period in their life. But the poverty status could not be avoided in the long run, as shown in the case of George Hill's family.[73]

The most important reasons for the poverty seem to be inherent in the individual poor person. If these are to be described in an abstract manner, one has to place this poor individual in the centre of the analysis; the factors behind the status and those influencing the degree of its poverty would then have to be put in relation both to the individual person and to each other (see diagram 3, The Vicious Circle of Poverty).

In the three circles that surround the ordinary poor in the diagram, the personal constitution of the poor individual is the only parameters he or she can influence directly. These are the 'property situation', the 'willingness to survive', the 'social reputation' and the 'self-confidence'. These four parameters influence each other in the sense that if the quality of one parameter is declining, the other three decline as well and so on. These seem to be the most relevant factors of a vicious circle of poverty, because it is through its personal constitution that the poor individual makes contact with the society in which he or she lives.

The four mentioned parameters of the inner circle are influenced by the parameters shown in an intermediate circle, containing all the other causes of poverty that have appeared in our comparative approach. Again, these parameters exert mutual influence on each other, classified as they are in four different clusters (in diagram 3 these can be distinguished by the different fonts): these four clusters are the 'qual-

---

72 These observations can also be proved by the cases of four other families of the ordinary poor in early modern Lyons; see FISCHER, *Hérédité de la pauvreté*, 2006, pp. 78–95.
73 Two further case studies of Aberdonian ordinary poor are described in *ibid.*, pp. 153–162.

ity of life of the poor individual', the 'attitude of the society towards the poor' (the objective of the poor relief system is strongly related to this cluster), the 'conditions for contribution of poor relief, set by the charitable institutions' and finally the 'poor family'. Once the quality of one cluster has declined, it would have negative consequences for the inner circle and vice-versa. The same applies to positive fluctuations in the quality of one of the parameters. In this sense, there is a strong interdependence between the inner circle and the intermediate circle.

The schematic illustration of the first two parts of the vicious circle of poverty shows that the poor individuals did not have the choice of different strategies to fight against poverty.[74] On the contrary, they depended on their environment and the society. The example of the family of Claude Antoine (30) can serve to illustrate this: the shoemaker 'inherited' the status of being poor from his ancestor generation. At the time of his wedding, so to say, the time when he founded his own family, he did not have any high value property of his own. At the time, his esteem in the Lyons urban society was relatively low. This lack of social reputation certainly influenced his self-confidence and the estimation of his own possibilities to succeed in the fight against poverty. In other words, it was a bad start to family life. His professional career was apparently more successful, at least at the beginning when he acquired the master craftsman's diploma. However, we know that the income of a master craftsman in early modern Lyons was subject to considerable fluctuations: in particular in times of cyclical crises, it was not enough to avoid poverty for a household with four children.[75] In this situation, a decrease in the quality of one of the described parameters within the inner circle or the intermediate circle could cause the setting in motion of the whole 'automatism' of the vicious circle of poverty.

---

74 This is the supposition of the analysis written by MARCO VAN LEEUWEN, 'Histories of Risk and Welfare in Europe during the 18th and 19th Centuries', in OLE PETER GRELL/ ANDREW CUNNINGHAM/ ROBERT JÜTTE (eds.), *Health Care and Poor Relief in 18th and 19th Century Northern Europe*, Aldershot 2002, pp. 32–66, here: p. 34.
75 Concerning the high fluctuations in income for craftsmen in early modern Lyons, see GASCON, *Grand commerce* , vol. I, pp. 403ff.

Diagram 3. The Vicious Circle of Ordinary Poverty in Early Modern Europe

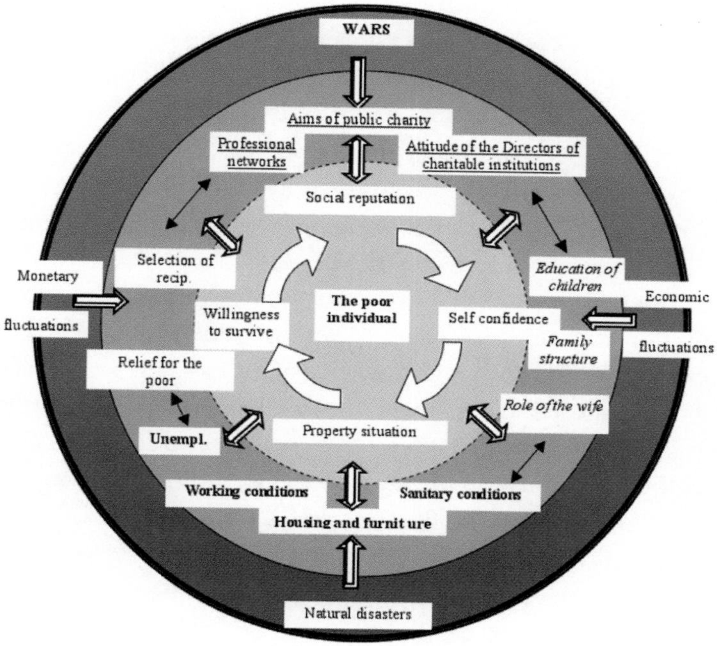

The different fields of parameters in the intermediate circle are represented by the following colours:
- **Cluster 1. The poor individual**
- Cluster 2. The attitude of the society towards the poor and public assistance
- Cluster 3. The conditions for contribution of relief set by the charitable institutions
- *The poor family*

Supposing, for instance, that the income of the master crafts-man had decreased significantly and thus influenced negatively his property circumstances, in the worst case, he would have run up debts in order to avoid the physical poverty of his family. This could have again had negative consequences for his self-confidence and his repu-tation in society. The effects on the parameters of the intermediate circle are obvious: the quality of nutrition declined, illnesses could not be adequately cured and probable higher costs for maintaining the dwelling in winter times (e.g., for the acquisition of firewood) could not be compensated. In other words, the living conditions declined in general. For the family of Claude Antoine, this situation was fatal, since – obviously due to bad sanitary conditions – his wife died im-mediately after the birth of his son Jean-Claude (39). The structure of the whole family was broken by this incident, with a considerable weakening of the family's living situation as a result. According to the terminology of the diagram illustrating the vicious circle of poverty, the quality of all the other parameters within the different clusters declined, and this again influenced the parameters of the inner circle. The consequences of the deaths of his second wife Catherine Rivo-lon (37) and further children are easily imaginable: the parameter of the two circles was again negatively influenced: the economic and so-cial situation deteriorated again, and there was no way to break the vicious circle of poverty.

The remedies of the public relief system and the possibilities of the family network were insufficient to help Claude Antoine in his fight against poverty. He actually transferred this status to the families of his descendants in the same way he had inherited it from his own father. It is in this respect noteworthy that the vicious circle could not be broken, although various other parameters did not appear in the family history: the sources do not mention any direct influence of political or (macro-)economic fluctuations. We do not learn anything about wars or natural disasters that could have influenced family life. With reference to the diagram of the vicious circle of early modern poverty, this is why one should place these parameters in an external circle. They have only got indirect consequences for the poor indi-vidual's life, but they can influence every parameter represented in the intermediate circle and the inner circle. Hence, the parameter of the external circle in the diagram has an impact in only one direction, and the poor individual cannot have any direct influence on it. He or she will not be able to cross the poverty line, even if they make every effort to improve their situation, reaching the parameters in the inner circle and the intermediate circle. As long as these macro-parameters can influence positively the destiny of the poor, there is no way to avoid poverty in the long run. On the contrary, compared to wealthier social categories of the urban society, the ordinary poor did not have any access to more functional networks, like those we can find in the environment of the shamefaced poor.[76] This is why in the early modern period the ordinary poor transferred their social and economic status to the next generation. Their opportunity for social mobility was extremely restricted, and so the status of being poor has to be considered hereditary.

VI. Conclusion and Outlook

The case studies of the families of the Lyons and the Aberdeen craftsmen Claude Antoine and George Hill can give many indications why and in which circumstances poverty can be considered hereditary in early modern Europe. Both families were more or less assisted by the public poor relief system, but they could not fight their poverty in the long run. Thus, it seems that the public poor relief system was not efficient enough to fight ordinary poverty. The hypotheses in the studies of Anne Marie Rabier and Thomas Riis can be extended by adding the model of the vicious circle of poverty. Only in the event of the poor individual having efficient and solid networks, he or she could break this circle. However, the ordinary poor living in an early modern urban community did not have this kind of network.

---

76 An analysis of four genealogical trees of shamefaced poor in Aberdeen and in Lyons has been able to prove that they were actually able to cross the poverty line in the long run thanks to their very efficient 'professional' and 'personal networks'. In Lyons, the sources mention a special form of alms for the shamefaced poor, the so-called 'Aumône secrète', see, in particular, Charité Lyon E 1232: Dépenses. Aumône secrete, January 1696–April 1781). Hence, this kind of poverty cannot be considered 'hereditary'; see, in this respect, FISCHER, *Hérédité de la pauvreté*, 2006, pp. 114–115 and pp. 173–174.

Of course, some of the poor had links with the wealthier social categories, for instance, in the case of a poor servant.[77] But these links were obviously too weak to help out in the fight against poverty in the long run. The findings for the professional group of craftsmen in an early modern society can be found in other marginalised groups of an urban society, even if they cannot be retraced in the sources over several generations.

On the basis of these results, it is interesting to ask how historiography could enhance and thus validate the approach applied in Lyons and Aberdeen. To what extent could the vicious circle of poverty be recognised as the constitutive element of poverty in other urban societies within early modern Europe? Can the mechanisms described in this study be applied to other socio-political, economic and cultural environments?

The application of the model in rural societies seems to be worthwhile, as in this environment the possibility of public relief was even more restricted than in urban communities. Furthermore, an analysis of the hereditary character of poverty in earlier periods would be desirable, as the contents of manuscript sources diverge considerably from those used for the present study. The model of the vicious circle of poverty could also apply to later periods of Modern Times, at least the sources are supposed to be more abundant.

Last but not least, it should be asked whether an interdisciplinary approach could add some parameters from neighbouring disciplines, such as Sociology, Political Science or Economics. At first glance, the methodo-logical and terminological obstacles seem to be too sophisticated for such an effort. However, the historian could help to overcome at least some of these.[78] The present model of the vicious circle of poverty and the parameters classified in the diagram are only a small contribution to future research in order to find inter-

---

77 The networks of servants are described, for instance, in Jean-Pierre Gutton, *Domestiques et serviteurs dans la France de l'Ancien Régime*, Paris 1981.

78 The Treves Collaborative Research Center on 'Fremdheit und Armut. Wandel von Inklusions- und Exklusionsformen von der Antike bis zur Gegenwart' has been working since 2002 on problems of poverty throughout history.

disciplinary solutions to the social problem of poverty; a problem that is becoming more and more urgent nowadays.

Bibliography
Manuscript sources

A. Archives des Hospices Civils de Lyon
Charité de Lyon
Série E: Administration de l'Etablissement, délibérations, nominations, budget, économat.
E 71: Délibérations du bureau de l'Aumône générale. Le corps des vieux et celui des vieilles, 1712–1737.
E 97: Délibérations du bureau de l'Aumône Générale à l'usage du recteur ayant la direction du Corps des Vieux, 1531–1774.
E 1232: Dépenses. Aumône secrète, January 1696–April 1781.
E 1469–E 1477: Distribution de consommation de pain, 1710–1774.
Série F: Registres d'entrées et de sortie de personnes admises dans l'Etablissement – Demande d'emploi et d'admission.
F 12: Titres et papiers provenant des vieux hommes admis et décédés à la Charité (ADR-BLA), 1616–1790.

B. Archives Départementales Rhône (ADR)
Série B: Cour et Juridiction.
Sous-série 7B: Maréchaussée.
7 B 5–7 B 92: Procédures, 1631–1790.
Série C: Administration provinciale: Intendance et généralité du Lyonnais.
Sous-série 10 C: Contrôle des actes notaires et sous seing privé, insinuations et droits joints (1693–1791).
10C 1–2319: 32 inspection points; documents used for this text are quoted in detail in the footnotes.
Sous-série 3E (Notaries)
Classified in alphabetical order of notaries' surnames; documents used for this text are quoted in detail in the footnotes.

C. Archives Municipales de Lyon (AML)

1 GG 0011–1 GG 780, Parish Registers Lyons (Microfilm 2 Mi 09 0001–2 Mi 09 0323), 1566–1792.

Used for this text:

1 GG 001–1 GG 220: Parish Register Saint-Nizier (= Microfilm 2 Mi 09 0001–2 Mi 09 0095), 1547–1792.

1 GG 159 I a: Fragments of Parish Register Saint-Nizier (damaged by fire on 26 December 1825, again published on microfilm in 1990; = 2 Mi 24).

1 GG 287–1 GG 340: Parish Register La Platière (= Microfilm 2 Mi 09 0126–2 Mi 09 0151), 1593–1792.

1 GG 700–1 GG 712: Parish Register Charité (= Microfilm 2 Mi 09 0319–2 Mi 09 323), 1666–1792.

D. City Archives, Aberdeen Town House, Charter Room (ACA)

ACA, Kirk and Bridge Work Accounts (KBA), vol. II–III, 1670–1725.

ACA CH2/448/70, Kirk Session Minutes, parish of St. Nicholas, General Accounts, 1768–1803.

ACA, Kirk Session Accounts 10/14, parish of St. Nicholas, 1602–1705.

ACA (not classified), Stent Roll Bundles (outstanding tax debts, borough of Aberdeen), 1718–1725.

ACA, 10/5 I–XII: Mortification Accounts, Aberdeen City Council, vol. I–XII, 1615–1812.

ACA, Press 18/59 1–24, 28–30, List of Men aged sixteen and above in Aberdeen, 1759.

E. Central Library Aberdeen, Section local studies (ACLLS)

Corporation of the Church of Jesus Christ of Latter Day Saints, Old parish registers, 0036–0071 (microfilm), Index of Parish Registers, 1531–1855 classified by surnames, Scotland – Aberdeenshire (including parish of St. Nicholas), available on the web at www.familysearch.org, accessed 15 October 2004.

F. Scottish Northern Health Services Archives (NHSA)

NHSA, Minutes relating to the Institution of the Aberdeen Infirmary

& Lunatic Asylum, 1739–1742. Copied from the original Register of the Infirmary.

NHSA, GRHP 1/1 1–4, The Minutes of the Sederunt Book of the Infirmary at Aberdeen,1742–1767.

NHSA, GRHP 1/1 5, Royal Infirmary. Index of the Sederunt Books from 1739–1834.

NHSA, GRHP 1/3, Admission and Discharge Registers of the Aberdeen Royal Infirmary, 1753–1880.

NHSA, GRHP 1/4 1–40, Clinical Records of the Aberdeen Royal Infirmary, 1743–1807.

G. Archives of Robert Gordon's College, Aberdeen (RGC)

RGC, Aberdeen Poor's Hospital. First Book of Minutes of the Directors of the Poor's Hospital, 1739–1744.

RGC, Aberdeen Poor's Hospital, Register of Interns, vol. I–V, 1779–1814.

H. Trinity Hall, Aberdeen

Seven Incorporated Trades of Aberdeen, Convener Court Book, vol. I, 1626–1699.

Master of Trades Hospital, Warrant Book, 1807–1839.

Hammermen Trade Aberdeen, Hospital Book, 1807–1839.

Hammermen Trade Aberdeen, Court Book, 1762–1793.

Secondary works

ABEL, WILHELM, *Crises agraires en Europe (XIIIe–XXe siècles)*, Paris 1973 [German: *Agrarkrisen und Massenarmut*, Hamburg-Berlin 1966].

BLANCHARD, IAN/ GEMMILL, ELIZABETH/ MAYEW, NICHOLAS/ WHYTE, IAN D., 'The Economy: Town and Country', in DENNISON/ DITCHBURN/ LYNCH (eds.), *Aberdeen before 1800: A New history*, East Linton 2002, pp. 129–158.

CAILLAUX, JEAN-CLAUDE et al. (eds.), *Démocratie et pauvreté. Du quatrième ordre au quart monde*, Paris 1991.

CAMERON, JAMES K. (ed.), *The First Book of Discipline*, Edinburgh 1972.

DENNISON, E. PATRICIA/ DITCHBURN, DAVID/ LYNCH, MICHAEL (eds.), *Aberdeen before 1800: A New History*, East Linton 2002.

DESBRISAY, GORDON RUSSELL/ EWAN, ELISABETH/ DIACK, H. LESLEY, 'Life in the Two Towns', in DENNISON/ DITCHBURN/ LYNCH (eds.), *Aberdeen before 1800: A New History*, East Linton 2002, pp. 44–70.

DEVINE, THOMAS M., *The Scottish Nation 1700–2000*, Edinburgh 1999.

FISCHER, TORSTEN, *Y-a-t-il une fatalité d'hérédité dans la pauvreté? Dans l'Europe moderne: les cas d'Aberdeen et de Lyon*, Stuttgart 2006 [Beihefte VSWG, Nr. 187].

FISCHER, TORSTEN, 'Die Erblichkeit der Armut im Europa der Frühen Neuzeit', in GERHARD FOUQUET et al. (eds.), *Von Menschen, Ländern, Meeren. Festschrift für Thomas Riis zum 65. Geburtstag*, Tönning 2006, pp. 373–393.

FOUQUET, GERHARD et al. (eds.), *Von Menschen, Ländern, Meeren. Festschrift für Thomas Riis zum 65. Geburtstag*, Tönning 2006.

GARDEN, MAURICE, *Lyon et les Lyonnais au XVIIIe siècle*, Paris 1970.

GASCON, RICHARD, *Grand commerce et vie urbaine au XVIe siècle. Lyon et ses marchands*, volume I, Paris-The Hague 1971.

GEREMEK, BRONISLAW, *La Potence ou la pitié: l'Europe et les pauvres du Moyen Age à nos jours*, Paris 1987 (German translation: *Geschichte der Armut. Elend und Barmherzigkeit in Europa*, Munich 1991).

GRELL, OLE PETER/ CUNNINGHAM, ANDREW/ JÜTTE, ROBERT (eds.), *Health Care and Poor Relief in 18th and 19th Century Northern Europe*, Aldershot 2002.

GUTTON, JEAN-PIERRE, 'L'insertion sociale des enfants recueillis par la Charité de Lyon au XVIIIe siècle. Un bilan provisoire', in J. P. BARDET (ed.) et al., *Lorsque l'enfant grandit. Entre dépendance et autonomie*, Paris 2003, pp. 929–939.

GUTTON, JEAN-PIERRE, *Domestiques et serviteurs dans la France de l'Ancien Régime*, Paris 1981.

GUTTON, JEAN-PIERRE, *La société et les pauvres. L'exemple de la généralité de Lyon 1534–1789*, Paris 1971.

HENDERSON, JOHN M., 'Scottish Reckonings of Time, Money, Weights and Measures', *Historical Association of Scotland Pamphlets*, no. 4 (1926), pp. 8–16.

JÜTTE, ROBERT, *Poverty and Deviance in Early Modern Europe*,
Cambridge 1999 [New Approaches to European History 4].

KING, JAMES (ed.), *The Second Book of Discipline*, Edinburgh 1980.

LATREILLE, ANDRÉ & GASCON, RICHARD et al. (eds.), *Histoire de Lyon et du Lyonnais*, Toulouse 1975.

LEEUWEN, MARCO VAN, 'Histories of Risk and Welfare in Europe during the 18th and 19th Centuries', in OLE PETER GRELL/ ANDREW CUNNINGHAM/ ROBERT JÜTTE (eds.), *Health Care and Poor Relief in 18th and 19th Century Northern Europe*, Aldershot 2002, pp. 32–66.

MITCHISON, ROSALIND, *The Old Poor Law in Scotland: The Experience of Poverty, 1574–1845*, Edinburgh 2000.

MITCHISON, ROSALIND, 'The Making of the Old Scottish Poor Law', *Past and Present*, 63/1974, pp. 58–93.

MOLLAT, MICHEL, 'Assistance et assistés', in: *Actes du 97e congrès national des sociétés savantes de Nantes 1972*, volume II, 1979, pp. 8–27.

MONTESQUIEU, BARON CHARLES LOUIS SECONDAT DE, *De l'esprit des lois*, livre XXIII, LAURENT VERSINI (ed.), Paris 1995.

PAMPALONI, GUIDO, 'La povertà a Prato nella seconda metà del Quattrocento', in RIIS, (ed.), *Aspects of Poverty in Early Modern Europe II. La réaction des pauvres à la pauvreté*, Odense 1986, pp. 105–119.

RABIER, ANNE-MARIE & PICQUET, GUY, *Soleil interdit ou deux siècles de l'exclusion d'un peuple*, Pierrelaye 1977 [Igloos 96].

RICCI, GIOVANNI, *Povertà, vergogna, superbia: i declassati fra Medioevo e Età moderna*, Bologna 1996.

RIIS, THOMAS, 'Freedom from Fear and Want (ou « vivre à l'abri de la peur et du besoin »)', in *La liberté dans tous ses états. Liber amicorum en l'honneur de Jacques Georgel*, Rennes 1998, pp. 367–374.

RIIS, THOMAS, 'Les mouvements de longue durée: le déclin économique et les causes de la pauvreté', in CAILLAUX et al. (eds.), *Démocratie et pauvreté. Du quatrième ordre au quart monde*, Paris 1991, pp. 433–438.

RIIS, THOMAS (ed.), *Aspects of Poverty in Early Modern Europe III. La pauvreté dans les pays nordiques 1500–1800*, Odense 1990.

RIIS, THOMAS (ed.), *Aspects of Poverty in Early Modern Europe II. La réaction des pauvres à la pauvreté*, Odense 1986.

RIIS, THOMAS (ed.), *Aspects of Poverty in Early Modern Europe I*, Stuttgart 1981.

RIIS, THOMAS, Poverty and Urban Development in Early Modern Europe (15th–18th/19th Centuries): A General View, in Riis (ed.), *Aspects of Poverty in Early Modern Europe I*, pp. 1–28.

ROCH, JEAN-LOUIS, *Les mots aussi sont de l'histoire: vocabulaire de la pauvreté et de la marginalisation*, 1450–1550, Lille 1986.

SMOUT, T. CHRISTOPHER & GIBSON, A. J. S., *Prices, Food and Wages in Scotland, 1500–1800*, Cambridge 1995.

SPICCIANI, AMLETO, 'The "Poveri Vergognosi" in 15th Century Florence', in RIIS (ed.), *Aspects of Poverty in Early Modern Europe I*, Stuttgart 1981, pp. 119–183.

TYSON, ROBERT E., 'People in the Two Towns', in DENNISON/ DITCHBURN/ LYNCH (eds.), *Aberdeen before 1800: A New History*, East Linton 2002, pp. 111–128.

WAILLY, NATALIS DE, *Mémoire sur les variations de la livre tournois depuis le règne de Saint-Louis jusqu'à l'établissement de la monnaie décimale*, Paris 1857 [Mémoires de l'Institut impérial de France, vol. XXI].

WOOLF, STUART, *The Poor in Western Europe in the Eighteenth and Nineteenth Century*, London-New York 1986.

Constructing Unemployment: Britain and France in Historical Perspective
Noel Whiteside

Introduction

Over the last twenty years, the question of unemployment as a primary cause of poverty has become central to many European states. On the one hand, industrial restructuring has forced the decline of heavy industry in Western Europe and the disappearance of many unskilled jobs. On the other, rising levels of social dependency are increasingly translated into financial burdens for the welfare state. Policy responses have reformed social protection and reoriented European social politics away from the provision of benefits and towards the promotion of employability and lifelong learning. The meaning of employment itself is moving away from the lifelong career with a single employer and towards more chequered patterns requiring constant personal adaptation to new technical and economic imperatives. Jobs are no longer an automatic by-product of economic growth. We can now recognise traditional employment relationships as the product of a post-war socio-political compromise, founded on Keynesian principles that are now undermined by international pressures reflecting the consequences of growing global competition. In many respects, we are currently returning to employment patterns reminiscent of a much earlier age. The cost of labour market risk has shifted over the last fifty years from employers in the post-war period, to the state in the 1980s and now rests increasingly on the shoulders of individuals themselves. With this comes a concomitant risk of poverty.

Reduced state benefits generate multiple outcomes: a growth in early retirement, in incapacity benefit claims and, not least, in the 'black' economy that fails to conform to legal norms about the nature of employment and obligations between employer and the employed. Employment (and hence unemployment) is structured by law and custom as well by levels of economic activity. The categorisation of the unemployed embraces moral criteria when distinguishing deserving from undeserving cases, enforcing moral orders that have long been applied to the mass of the poor themselves. The form these have taken and their application have varied considerably by time and place. A historical assessment of past and current understandings of unemployment demonstrates dramatic shifts in meaning: in terms of changing regulation governing classification of social dependency – reflecting changing expectations about the proper structure of a working life and who should be expected to undertake it. Such a perspective belies a purely economic view of unemployment as a problem reflecting the results of economic downturn on a labour market whose boundaries are fixed and where the experience of work is uniform. Hence, for example, fifty years ago the 'good mother' was expected to stay in the house to care for her children as an unwaged domestic worker, in return for a share of hearth and home. Today, as divorce rates rise and hearth and home divide, all mothers are expected to undertake waged work – and most EU governments actively encourage them to do so. Equally, older workers, discharged during industrial restructuring in the late twentieth century, were classified as sick or in early retirement – and not as unemployed.[1] The economic activity rates of adult males aged 55–65 (i.e. below retirement age) have dipped alarmingly since the 1950s and remain well below 50% in many major EU countries. These labour market rejects are rarely understood as 'unemployed'.

Hence unemployment – or, indeed, any social classification – is not established fact, but a socio-political product that responds to prevailing circumstances. Many critical appraisals of official unemployment statistics implicitly accept the normative view that there is somewhere a 'real' rate of unemployment that can be calculated with greater precision following careful reappraisal. This paper argues that this is fallacious. Using a historical perspective, it examines how the idea was conceived, developed and implemented in the early twentieth century and concludes with a brief appraisal of its pertinence to current debates. The period of relative economic growth following the Second World War gave the concept a greater degree of stability than it had previously (or has subsequently) enjoyed; this has helped cre-

---

1 A.-M. GUILLEMARD, *L'âge de l'emploi*, Paris 2003.

ate an unmerited aura of permanence. The object is to demonstrate how political debate and social expectation combined to delineate the dimensions of a problem assumed to be a principle cause of poverty – and the ways in which it should be addressed. Evidence is largely drawn from two co-edited works: one examining the roots of the issue and the other, the creation of the post-war settlements in Britain and France.[2] I acknowledge the research of contributors to this paper; the opinions expressed here are essentially my own.

Discovering unemployment:

The terms 'unemployment' and 'chômage' entered common parlance in the late nineteenth century. Both emerged during an era of chronic economic fluctuation: the 1880s and 1890s witnessed growing poverty accompanied by social disruption during periods of downturn in both economies. This attracted official attention to the labour market and its organisation as central to the 'social question'. However, the problem was not interpreted in the same way: debates were set in very different contexts and generated very different results. This reflected in part the contrasting economic profiles of the countries concerned. As is widely recognised, British patterns of industrialisation and urbanisation fostered a higher degree of reliance on waged employment than that found in France at that time. In the latter, patterns of land ownership and artisan traditions of production allowed traditional forms of work to co-exist alongside more modern patterns found in heavy industry. Geographically, French industrial production was confined to the north-east and the Parisian basin of a country whose economic profile reflected the strength of artisan skill in the creation of luxury and technologically advanced products of international repute. Lower levels of urbanisation and continued links of even Le Creusot workers with the land meant that any shrinkage in the demand for labour tended to hit the British urban worker harder

---

2 M. MANSFIELD, R. SALAIS and N. WHITESIDE (dirs.) *Aux sources du chômage, 1880–1914: une comparaison interdisciplinaire entre la France et la Grande-Bretagne*, Paris 1992; NOEL WHITESIDE and ROBERT SALAIS (eds.) *Governance, Industry and Labour Markets in Britain and France: the modernising state in the mid-twentieth century*, London 1998.

than it did his French counterpart, exacerbating for him the link between loss of waged work and poverty.

However, different constructions of unemployment also sprang from the role the state and law played in guaranteeing social protection and citizenship rights. In France, in contrast to Britain, republican ideals embodied political principles that required the state to define and protect civil liberties – including mutual obligations between employers and employed. Following the collapse of the Second Empire and the establishment of the Third Republic in 1872, constitutional instabilities encouraged republican politicians to foster working class support for their new-born regime, which faced extensive monarchist and Bonapartist opposition. The creation of a republic required a decentralisation of power (particularly over social questions) to democratically elected local authorities that challenged a Catholic Church closely associated both with the relief of poverty and with monarchist politics. Republicans needed to convince the populace that the state, not the church, offered help for the destitute and secured social justice. Founding the republic also involved recognition of a (hitherto largely illegal) trade union movement, a democratisation of the mutuelles (mutual aid societies) and a reform of the Civil Code to establish a contract of employment that stipulated obligations between employers and employed. Here the state was charged with guaranteeing social order in accordance with collectively agreed principles. In Britain, by contrast, constitutional stability was not in question and both sides of industry viewed state interventions in economic or commercial matters (including the labour market) as an infringement of liberty. Work contracts remained essentially private and state help for the indigent was punitive. In Britain, public relief under the poor laws entailed a loss of personal freedom, civil rights and the acceptance of the status of pauper that was, socially speaking, second in opprobrium only to that of the convicted criminal. Here, we observe two states with opposing traditions: the former understanding official provision of civil rights as essential to national well-being: the latter understanding well-being as primarily a matter of individual responsibility. Yet, almost paradoxically, it is the latter that makes the first breach, generates the first national identity of the unemployed and, with this, the earliest national statistical series claiming regular measurement of the problem's incidence.

The recessions of the 1880s witnessed rising social distress in both countries and fostered public discussion of its causes and potential systems of relief, allowing 'unemployment' to emerge in its own right as a focal point for concern. The identification of the 'unemployed' was no simple matter: it required the identification of 'real' cases, who merited help, from those whose lack of waged work was due to laziness, incompetence or incapacity due to old age. In both countries, those poor from want of waged work had long been held personally responsible for their plight, which was assumed to reflect poor character: a failure to conform with social expectation to save against hard times or insufficient effort to find work. Such moral codes did not disappear overnight: on the contrary, major controversy emerged about how to distinguish those whose joblessness was not the consequence of personal failing from the rest. Thanks to industrialisation, waged work was increasingly the labourer's major source of sustenance; if unable to earn a living, he and his family were liable to fall into destitution and become a burden on the local community. In this way, prevention (or alternative systems of support) became a social issue rather than simply an individual obligation. For we must recall that unemployment is adult and male: a masculinity reflecting legal and moral assumptions about the duties of fathers and husbands to sustain families. Finally, while unemployment is accepted as a cause of destitution, the reasons for its rising political significance can be found in a wider set of social and economic issues. In other words, not all the unemployed are poor.

In the pre-1914 era, defining unemployment and classifying its victims proved complex and ultimately inconclusive. In France, debate took place on multiple levels; no single definition dominated, no single statistical series was generated and in consequence, no single history has been written. The earliest attempts to quantify a national incidence of the problem are in the 1896 census, which created 'unemployed' as a separate category. The object was to identify those situations attributable to the unexpected rupture of a permanent employment contract: evidence of dependence on a single employer.

Here, paradoxically, the subordination to a single employer was to be the foundation of the worker's liberty[3] as this endowed him with social rights guaranteed in law. Those with a permanent contract of employment, subordinate to a single employer or establishment, were capable – if that contract were broken – of becoming unemployed. Central authority wanted to distinguish unemployment that was predictable (due to regular slack seasons, to be accommodated by means of personal savings or collective prévoyance) from the unforeseeable job loss that provoked domestic crisis. This legal definition, which lasted until the 1930s, meant that those working for an employer by sub-contract (i.e. whose legal obligations were defined by the task to be completed, not by subordination to management) would not 'count' as unemployed when that contract terminated. It was also adapted to distinguish the isolée dependent on a single employer from the out-worker who had several masters. Implementing the census definition, however, revealed multiple problems: in no small part due to the predominantly artisanal and agricultural nature of the French economy and to the consequently ambivalent distinctions between 'employed', 'self-employed' and 'petit patron'.[4] The isolées (in domestic services, textiles or the clothing industry) were particularly problematic. The clothing industry, for example, supplied 41.5% of all isolées, but only 10.5% of employees (factory workers). Here, an isolée might be desperately poor, taking in any work she could get, or a professional skilled milliner, who could choose her work and whose elevated rate of pay did not force her to work regularly. Neither would 'count' as 'unemployed' when idle. Female workers proved a major source of difficulty: domestic industries generated 17.5% of female 'unemployed' and 39% of women whose situation was 'unknown' – probably signifying women working for different employers on an irregular or part-time basis, whose status simply did not conform to census regulations. While female workers raised most of these difficulties, male workers in construction industries posed similar pro-

---

3 SALAIS in: *Aux sources…*(as note 2), p. 17.
4 Most of what follows is taken from B. REYNAUD "La genèse de la catégorie "chômeur" and C. DIDRY "Le chômage entre conciliation et contrat de travail", both in *Aux sources* (as note 2). See also CHRISTIAN TOPOLOV, *Naissance du chômeur, 1880–1910*, Paris 1994.

blems for the enumerators – not least because of the presumption that personal prévoyance should see workers through the winter months when outdoor work was scarce.

The pure juridical definition was thus extremely narrow. While it offered possible redress in law against summary dismissal, thereby reinforcing professional protection, it did not, at this time, offer any state help. While national debate was creating a definition, local experience – and perception – of the problem was far more varied. Such help as was available remained limited until 1914, being largely confined to local charity (*bureaux de bienfaisance*) which a few municipalities were prepared to subsidise. Here, careful distinction between 'good' and 'bad' cases revolved around the acceptance of an offer of work from a benevolent employer or on municipal public works, thereby dividing the sheep from the goats, allowing the latter to be directed to the *depôts de mendicité*. Here the 'real' unemployed are not distinguished by the cause of their situation, but by more traditional means: their willingness to take work – any work. A third construction of the problem can be observed in the operation of the *bourses du travail*: urban agencies run by local trade unions, which essentially acted as placement agencies for the unemployed. Political initiatives to convert revolutionary syndicalism into republican virtue fostered the spread of the urban bourses, to enable trade unions to organise local labour markets: to place suitable men in suitable jobs in accordance with union terms. Here, unemployment is cast within the locality and the trade: the status of the skilled man is respected. In official eyes, keeping local men in local jobs discouraged drift into major urban centres where those desperate for work might undercut native labour and provoke unrest. In this instance, the link with poverty is at its weakest: political motives dominate the interpretation of unemployment.

Voluntary unemployment insurance was officially well regarded in France (receiving both municipal and national subsidies from 1905), but was hardly widespread.[5] French trade unionists retained their revolutionary tradition inherited from the Paris Commune and

---

[5] Dijon and Moulins being two exceptional cases – P. HESSE in: WHITESIDE and SALAIS, *Governance, Industry and Labour Markets* (as note 2), p. 202.

remained unconvinced that it was the job of workers to pool their savings to prop up capitalism. Outside the printing industries, trade union benefit funds hardly existed.[6] Opposition to contributory insurance as a mechanism for protecting workers against risk was not confined to trade unions. The strong association of this type of social protection with authoritarian regimes, witnessed in the policies of Napoleon III as well as those of Bismarck and reinforced by their association with a German enemy, encouraged republicans to seek alternative remedies. As Didier Renard has demonstrated,[7] the general preference was for local assistance to be given in cases of need; from 1905, those whose destitution was due to old age, invalidity or insufficient means to feed a large family had recourse to municipal assistance schemes, which judged cases on their merits. Here in particular we witness how the municipality was to take over the role traditionally performed by the Church. Municipal funds for the unemployed, with national subsidies, were set up from 1914 and subsequently extended in the interwar years. During the Slump of the 1930s, adding up the numbers relieved locally, town by town, became the main method for creating a national total estimate of the numbers of unemployed (see next section). In this way, national statistics were eventually calibrated through a series of local assessments, not through the central imposition of a single definition.

In Britain, the early twentieth century witnessed the opposite trend. Official concern was not centred on an equitable distribution of legal rights but on the twin problems of poverty and pauperism. Following official and unofficial investigation, the former was understood as a source of industrial inefficiency: a source of physical degeneration, of economic – and imperial – decline. The latter meant a drain on local resources where poor law claimants lived- which, by the early twentieth century, were being propped up by loans from the

---

6 DREYFUS, KOTT, PIGENET and WHITESIDE, "Les bases multiples des syndicalismes au XIX⁰ siècle" in J-L. ROBERT, F. BOLL and A. PROST (dirs), *L'invention des syndicalismes,* Paris 1997.

7 In MIRE (LA MISSION DE RECHERCHE ET EXPERIMENTATION), *Rencontres et Recherches: comparer les systèmes de protection sociale en Europe* vol.I, Rencontres d'Oxford, (SICOM, Paris, 1995).

Exchequer. Pauperised communities fostered criminality and immorality, provoking multiple causes for official concern, that could, in practical terms, be mapped onto Britain's major cities.[8] Such perceptions stimulated professional debate; their role in promoting social reform has been extensively documented.[9] The situation appeared almost perverse. Statistical appraisal demonstrated how industrial wage rates were rising in the closing decades of the century. Yet these years witnessed growing social unrest in major conurbations during economic recession – with rioters and looting indicating the inability of the poor to save against hard times or otherwise to protect themselves against the exigencies of a working life.[10] Moral imperative allied with fears concerning Britain's commercial future in social scientific debate. Workers at risk of destitution must be taught how to manage their lives – to invest in learning a skill and to save against the risk of redundancy, illness and the inevitable decline in earning power in old age. This agenda and the political strategies it promoted stimulated the identification of the 'unemployed' within the pauper host. The objective was less the relief of poverty per se than the identification (and support) of regular workers thrown out of work by trade fluctuations beyond their control. Although appearing similar to the French agenda, the dimensions of the problem were apprehended in very different ways.

Unemployment protection was already practiced by some skilled trade unions in construction, engineering, shipbuilding and so on (where cyclical and seasonal changes in labour demand were endemic). Unemployment here had less to do with poverty than with systems of trade regulation: union benefits were designed to prevent unemployed members being forced, through desperation, to take work on non-union terms. Rights to benefit were subject to nation-

---

8 Topolov, *Naissance du chômeur* (as note 4) uses the maps of East London, developed by Charles Booth's investigations in the late nineteenth century, to demonstrate correlations between casual work, slum housing, criminality, poor school attendance and multiple general social evils. See especially ch. 10.

9 E.g. J. Harris, *Unemployment and politics*, Oxford 1972.

10 H. Barkai, "Travail, emploi, salaires dans l'économie néo-classique" in *Aux sources* ...(as note 2).

ally agreed rules; branches acted as placement agencies for members and guaranteed the skills of the men concerned. Such systems operated unevenly as not all branches exercised the total control over local labour markets necessary for their enforcement. In principle, high contributions from relatively well-paid workers funded a range of 'friendly' benefits (help for the sick, injured, aged or unemployed); rights varied by sector, by length of membership and by level of skill. Members were supported for refusing work offered on non-union terms: where the union rate was not paid, for example, or in firms employing too many apprentices. Equally, members were fined for accepting such work or for working alongside non-members when there were union men 'on the books'.[11] Fines held the same status as contribution arrears: union support was denied until they were paid. Hence union benefit schemes regulated work practices in skilled trades, where mass strike action was consequently rare. They also sustained membership: seniority frequently translated into higher benefit rates or extended rights. Although unemployment benefits were not universal, numbers covered expanded steadily in the decades preceding the First World War, reaching 1.84 million by 1908. Trade union provision of friendly benefits was officially well regarded.[12] Their close association with trade dispute was not. The policy debate about unemployment, therefore, was partly shaped by state aims to re-calibrate trade union systems of classsification, to distinguish the unemployed, the retired and the sick from strikers – provoking dissent within the union movement and opposition to state intervention as a result.[13]

Most official attention, however, focused on the other end of the labour market, where enquiry revealed the close relationship between chronic poverty, physical incapacity and irregular (or casual) employment – closely associated with the rising levels of pauperism

---

11 N. WHITESIDE, "Définir le chômage; traditions syndicales et politique nationale" in *Aux sources…*(as note 2) n.b. the language here is not sexist: there were few female trade union members in trades offering such support.

12 See, for example, Royal Commission on Labour, *Final Report*, C.1421, 1894 (HMSO) p. 24 and p. 28. Union unemployment statistics taken from N.WHITESIDE , *loc. cit.*, p.386.

13 N. WHITESIDE, "Welfare legislation and the unions during the First World War", *Historical Journal*, 23, 1980, pp. 857–874.

caused by the crisis in poor law finance in many major cities. Here, the national space was reconstructed along social scientific lines: impartial enquiry would reveal the source of the problem and professional impartiality would administer the cure. A logic of rationalisation, based on a uniform definition of the length and form of the working life, underpinned policy development (with the working life largely delineated by criteria of productive efficiency). This replaced the earlier (and more varied) systems of unemployment relief that had, since the mid-1880s, concentrated on the provision of municipal works and charitable help for the unemployed, in ways similar to their French counterparts.

To avoid the punitive poor law, those desperate for work crowded the casual labour markets found in the UK's major ports, urban building sites and gasworks, where the heavy nature of the work, the competition for jobs and daily fluctuations in the demand for labour meant that secure employment was nearly impossible.[14] Here, good character, skill and regular work habits counted for nothing in the daily round of hiring and firing. Casual labour was widely recognised as a major source of inefficiency (large numbers of casuals were incapable of regular work), of social and moral degeneration (poverty bred criminality, sickness and incapacity) and this posed a major threat to Britain's industrial (and imperial) pre-eminence.

"those who ... come to be casual labourers are almost inevitably demoralised by their circumstances. Irregular work and earnings make for irregular habits; conditions of employment in which a man stands to gain or lose so little by his good or bad behaviour make for irresponsibility, laziness, insubordination. ...The line between independence and dependence, between the efficient and the unemployable, must be made clearer. Every place in 'free' industry, carrying with it the rights of citizenship – civil liberty, fatherhood, conduct of one's own life and government of a family – should be a 'whole' place involving full employment and earnings up to a definite minimum."[15]

---

14 See G. PHILLIPS and N. WHITESIDE, *Casual Labour*, Oxford 1986, chs 2–4.

15 W. H. BEVERIDGE, "The Problem of the Unemployed," *Sociological Papers*, 1907, pp. 326–327.

Hence, under-employment bred unemployability: if treated like a pauper, the unemployed regular man would eventually behave like one, ending up as another casual labourer incapable of holding down a permanent job.[16] The only way to break this cycle, reformers argued, was to protect the regular man and distinguish his treatment from that of the pauper, the habitual casual, the vagrant, the drunkard and the petty criminal: the sources of 'the social problem'. The solution lay not in the provision of municipal public works that were widely used in both British and European major conurbations to relieve the unemployed. This merely added the chance of another short-term job, exacerbating the problems of casualism and irregularity. Instead, inter-linked labour exchanges should rationalise the labour market: to eliminate the inefficient, the idle, the vagrant and habitually irregular workers and to concentrate work in the hands of the most efficient, thereby improving industrial and commercial performance. In short, far from seeking to remove or relieve the problem of unemployment, policy was designed to create it.[17]

This strategy underpinned the reforms introduced by Liberal governments in Britain: the Labour Exchanges Act (1908), the National Insurance Act (1911) and the introduction of old age pensions (1908). Unlike either the municipal *bureaux de bienfaisance* or the *bourses du travail*, designed to keep unemployed workers in their local communities, the British labour exchanges offered a national network, to promote total labour mobility between as well as within trades and towns. New information technologies (the telephone) enabled the immediate exchange of information about vacancies and applicants, allowing state officials to send the most efficient to fill vacancies. Networks of official surveillance could identify applicants of good character, skill and sound working habits, in whose capable hands all available work should be concentrated, thereby eliminating the inefficient and promoting industrial prosperity to the advantage of employers seeking workers. Contributory national insurance reinforced this strategy. It was in the employer's interest to avoid hiring day labourers, as each

---

16 W. H. BEVERIDGE, *Unemployment: a problem of industry*, London 1909.
17 M. MANSFIELD, "Naissance d'une définition institutionelle du chômage en Grande Bretagne" in *Aux sources...*(as note 2).

required a weekly contribution for health insurance purposes – a payment that was doubled if the worker was also a member of the unemployment scheme.[18] Regulations covering access to benefit, based on actuarial calculation, would separate the regular contributor from the rest (the 'morality of mathematics' according to the young Winston Churchill). An established contributory record and the limitation of benefit to 15 weeks p.a. meant that support was only available to short-term claimants with a record of regular employment. Long term unemployment therefore did not exist: once benefit rights were exhausted, the claimant re-entered the pauper class. Rules disqualified claimants whose unemployment was due to dismissal for misconduct or to industrial dispute. The previous employer (not the trade union) was to certify the reasons for dismissal (this allowed coal owners in South Wales in the 1920s to punish workers who refused pay cuts by claiming their unemployment was due to a trade dispute). From the legislative detail the British unemployed emerge: a select group of regularly employed men whose services were temporarily surplus to immediate requirements, in a scheme initially confined to trades known to suffer from seasonal fluctuations in demand.

While both countries sought to identify (and help) those out of work through no fault of their own, little conceptual equivalence is visible. The international conference in Paris in 1910 on the subject of unemployment was a non-event; it failed to discover any common ground: the nature of the labour market, the geographical construction of the problem and possible avenues for state intervention were so disparate that discussion was impossible. British proposals to promote mobility on a national scale were incomprehensible in France, where policy sought to incorporate trade unions into the governing process, not transfer labour market management to state officials. French jurisprudence offered the possibility of compensation to workers whose permanent employment contract had been unexpectedly broken; seasonal fluctuations remained the provenance of personal responsibil-

---

18 Part II of the 1911 National Insurance Act offered unemployment insurance that covered a restricted number of trades – largely those with skilled unions offering unemployment benefits, i.e. shipbuilding, engineering, construction and metal working. The Act was extended to all manual workers earning less than £ 250 p.a. in 1920.

ity. In Britain, by contrast, the 1911 unemployment scheme was confined to trades (such as shipbuilding) where men moved from yard to yard, working for several masters. Here, actuarial calculations were based on trade fluctuations and were designed to help those subject to such variation to save against slack times, as the industry required a 'reserve' to be sustained in an efficient state. While the vision of how a labour market should operate is broadly similar, the points of state intervention – and their focal objectives – are different in each case. So is the location of a solution: in Britain, the policy framework shifts from the local to the national in the pre-war decades while the French trajectory is in the opposite direction.

In the pre-war era, the twin issues of unemployment and poverty thus became embedded in national politics in very different ways. In both the countries studied here, poverty was considered to be a problem: in each case it posed a different type of threat and the contribution of unemployment to that menace was only one factor among many for state intervention in labour markets. In the UK, the problem of poverty was located in the context of industrial and national efficiency (and its consequences for British commercial and imperial pre-eminence) on the one hand – and in the collapse of local poor law finance on the other. The threat posed by the poor was not political, but economic. The solution lay in rationalising the distribution of work, to remove the dross and to protect workers needed to meet fluctuations in trade, who were identified 'unemployed'. As for the rest of the rejected poor, policy remained hazy about their fate: punitive poor law treatment was tightened up in 1911, in the wake of the passage of new legislation. In France, the identification of the unemployed developed within twin agendas, both focused on the future security of the republic. In the first place, juridical reform permitted the creation of an employment contract as a compact between state and worker that enforced legal responsibilities on employers. In the second, to reinforce the local foundations and popular support for the new regime, republicans offered state protection against hazards liable to provoke destitution, thereby undermining the appeal of a monarchist Catholic Church while also offering trade unionists control over local labour markets. Here, the agenda is highly politicised. Poverty is perceived as a source of potential radicalism; its relief can secure the future of the Third Republic by guaranteeing democracy and preventing the return to authoritarian rule – the fate of France's earlier republican regimes.

Constructions of unemployment may have differed radically, but local circumstance and varied employment meant that policy was never fully translated into effective practice. In the UK, the vision of a professional, centralised and expert system of labour market management never materialised: the decasualisation project was strongly opposed by employers and workers alike. Although the attempt was made during the First World War, union opposition ensured its demise. Unemployment rose in the 1920s, attempts at labour market rationalisation were abandoned and policy switched to fostering work sharing and short-time working[19] as the official gaze shifted from casual labour markets and towards the 'depressed areas', the locus of long-term unemployment. In France, the transfer of Alsace-Lorraine into French territory in 1918 forced debate on the extension of social insurance to all workers, as these new French citizens refused to abandon privileges acquired under German rule. Although this eventually generated social insurance to cover family allowances, old age pensions and sickness benefits (1928–1930), the unemployed were not an object for central reform. Instead, as the Slump bit and numbers out of work rose, municipal assistance funds and voluntary municipal insurance – extensively subsidised by national government – were extended to bridge the gap. While circumstances changed how the unemployed were identified in both countries, it did not create a more uniform definition.

The Slump and unemployment in the 1930s

The Slump years pushed unemployment back into the limelight of policy discussion. The length and depth of the crisis changed managerial practices; employers concentrated work in fewer hands – abandoning common strategies of spreading work over a number of men in slack periods, in order to retain their services when conditions

---

19 "Deconstructing unemployment: developments in Britain in the interwar years", *Economic History Review*, XLIV, Nov. 1991, pp. 665–682.

improved. Small business could no longer afford to share available work to sustain the marginal and unproductive. Equally, in mining, engineering and metal working, employers cast off elderly, physically impaired or otherwise unproductive workers in an attempt to cut costs. Growing destitution forced governments to introduce reforms. The British scheme of unemployment insurance, which had struggled in deficit throughout the 1920s, was reappraised and a national scheme of means-tested assistance was created. In France, local assistance spread like wildfire to meet growing destitution. Following mass strike action in 1936, the Popular Front government initiated a more extensive programme of state intervention in industrial affairs. Perhaps the most important political legacy for both countries lay in the way that new strategies, coupled with public reaction to the crisis, generated a standardised working week: one foundation of the post-war Keynesian systems of economic management (albeit that Keynes' thesis was read in different ways in each country). Hence the Slump created the conditions for new national post-war settlements that were to solve the vexed problem of what 'employment' meant and who should be responsible in the event of its termination. After 1945, waged work assumed 'modern' dimensions and characteristics; in consequence, the meaning of unemployment became better defined.

During the 1930s, the profile of French unemployment changed. In comparison with the UK, Germany and the USA, the Slump years affected France both later and less severely; still, the situation was grave enough to provoke changes in the understanding of unemployment and the treatment of its victims. First, numbers claiming assistance as unemployed in major conurbations rose. Municipal funds to help the unemployed and desperate were largely to be found in towns of over 10,000 (but embracing c. 39% of the population).[20] While regulations governing access to state funds were supposed to be uniform, it is clear that the nature of the local economy, accessibility and the provision of alternative employment shaped registration at the local labour bureaux. Second, following the wave of strikes that hit the Paris region in 1936, the Popular Front government passed le-

---

20   R. Salais, N. Bavarez and B. Reynaud, *L'invention du chômage*, Paris 1986, pp. 117–118.

gislation to introduce a forty-hour week and two weeks paid holiday for all permanently employed: cutting hours of work was designed to create more jobs. Compulsory arbitration was revived and government was empowered to extend collective agreements over specified industrial sectors, thereby standardising levels of professional qualification, apprenticeship ratios as well as rates of pay and working practices. This led to a uniform codification of work relations in private companies. For example, a collective work agreement signed in September 1936 between the master printers and the CGT *Fédération du Livre* was extended in May 1937 to the whole of France. It stipulated weekly work schedules, overtime rates, indexed salaries and apprenticeship regulation: all reinforced as virtually statutory law.[21] Work agreements pioneered in the Parisian metal industries were adapted, under negotiated arbitration, in other metal-working districts, to reflect different production systems; this was subsequently reinforced and extended after the war.[22] Such developments fostered more standardised work practices, more uniform systems of remuneration and more legitimate assessments. It eventually produced closer co-ordination between the census measurement of unemployment and its registration: albeit that the fragile economic situation meant that the significance of these developments proved greater in the long rather than the short term.

In the 1930s, the position remained far less precise. In the south, urban authorities were not sympathetic to the claims for help made by immigrants from North Africa or other Mediterranean countries – who were encouraged to migrate back from whence they came. Equally, municipal relief was not granted to women who lost work due to the recession. Here, conventions of family responsibility affected the assessment of individual rights to support. Wives of men in work were very occasionally helped if destitution threatened the household, but generally were not. Unmarried juveniles living in the parental home were not considered proper recipients either. And, all over the country, the plight of the 'isolées' remained unexamined and untouched; the amount of work on offer fell, but we know nothing

---

21 Zancarini FOURNEL, in WHITESIDE & SALAIS, *Governance, Industry and Labour Markets* (as note 2), p. 186.
22 DIDRY in: WHITESIDE & SALAIS, *Governance, Industry and Labour Markets* (as note 2).

about how this affected home-based workers whose situation did not accommodate classification as either 'employed' or 'unemployed'. In agricultural districts the picture remains equally unclear. On the one hand, many industrial workers retained an interest in the land. The numbers of urban workers who declared themselves 'sick' during the later summer months in wine growing regions even after the Second World War remained very high and evidently reflected a need to return home to help with the harvest. We might expect, therefore, urban workers faced with redundancy would tend to return to the family smallholding rather than join a queue for a place on menial public works or a minimal level of assistance. Neither census nor relief policy took much notice of agricultural work – or of those who did it. Here, above all, the status of workers (frequently both employed and self employed in accordance with the season of the year) was beyond classification.

The consequences of such developments are reflected in French statistical compilations for the Slump years. There is no statistical correlation between the growth of unemployment and the diminution of waged jobs in the years 1931–36 at the level of the département, except in those where heavy industry was dominant.[23] For the country as a whole, the 1931 census enumerated 452,000 out of work – a number that almost doubled in five years, when the census counted 864,000 unemployed. These were mostly men aged between 25 and 59 years of age who worked in industry of some type. Over the same period and according to the same sources, the numbers classed as 'economically active' fell by 1,760,000 (including the number of workers that fell by 1,423,000).[24] From this we can only conclude that the process of counting those out of work was largely disconnected from changing levels of occupation. It was only the political creation of employment norms and their more universal enforcement in postwar France that enabled a more linked set of figures. The concepts that permitted a better correlation were tied to the recognition of a

---

23 R. SALAIS, N. BAVAREZ and B. REYNAUD, *L' invention du chômage* (as note 20), p. 121. For departments dominated by heavy industry, the linear correlation is 0.64 for men, as opposed to 0.21 departmental average for the country as a whole.

24 *Ibid.*, p. 77.

specific construction and length of working life under a Keynesian settlement.

In Britain, the identification of the unemployed remained tied to regulations governing access to state benefits under the unemployment scheme. These had originally stipulated a six-day waiting period (to disqualify casual workers), a contributory record of at least six-months' standing and a maximum duration of 15 weeks' benefit in any one year. From the first extension of the unemployment scheme in 1920 to all blue collar workers,[25] regulations were revised to accommodate political pressure resulting from high unemployment in Britain's old industrial heartlands: in the coal mines, metal foundries, engineering and shipbuilding plants, on the docks and in textile mills. Temporary extensions in unemployment benefit were initially supposed to be repaid when trade revived. Once offered, however, it proved impossible to rescind or abolish such measures and the British statute book is littered with modifications to the basic scheme throughout the 1920s and well into the 1930s. The net effects were twofold. First, the better-organised irregularly employed (both casuals and short-time workers) managed to supplement their incomes with unemployment benefit, as employers and unions saw the Unemployment Fund (financed by their contributions) as a means to supplement wages.[26] Second, those claiming extended benefits became increasingly subject to additional requirements concerning work-seeking and their household arrangements.[27] Finally, while extending cover to organised male workers, the British government ruthlessly removed such rights as female workers possessed. Domestic work was not covered by the scheme and the exchanges were instructed to offer female claimants a domestic position. These women were thus trapped. If they accepted the position, they left the unemployment scheme and if they refused

---

25 In 1920, a ceiling of £220 p.a. income was set, below which membership of the state scheme was compulsory. Agriculture, domestic service and bank employees were not covered.

26 Regulations required registration at the exchanges continuously for 3 days out of 6 – with two periods of such registration within a period of 6 weeks 'counting' for one week's benefit as unemployed.

27 Those living with a person in work were commonly disqualified.

it, their claim was disqualified.[28] Uniform regulations were thus re-shaped to political circumstance, industrial practice and expectations of family responsibility: the construction of unemployment reflected immediate priorities.

As the Slump bit and unemployment rose, so work-sharing strategies (as in France) diminished and long-term unemployment moved centre-stage in political debate. Following Britain's financial crisis of 1931, the whole scheme was recalibrated in a renewed attempt to accommodate different aspects of unemployment, to allow the temporarily unemployed (who retained benefit rights) to be distinguished from long-term cases. In 1934, reform separated unemployment insurance from unemployment assistance and reinforced the distinction. Throughout the 1930s, the imposition of means-tests (associated with the disgrace of pauperism) on skilled men in the depressed areas provoked hostility. At the same time, then as now, numbers of older workers with little hope of re-employment transferred across to claim sickness or invalidity benefits.[29] The ensuing quarrels with the Ministry of Health about whether (or not) a claimant was 'physically capable of work' when (s)he suffered from bronchitis, varicose veins, flat feet and a host of other middle-range infirmities – led to pointless but prolonged bouts of claimant shuffling and re-categorisation. Unemployment, notably long-term unemployment, caused poverty and poverty exacerbated illnesses – as much then as it has done recently. Sickness and disability rates collapsed as a consequence of labour shortages following the onset of the war.[30] In the course of the interwar years, the cause for concern in the British construction of the unemployment problem shifted – away from the casual worker who had been central to policy discussion before 1914 and towards the long-term claimant in a depressed area with no hope of finding

---

28 For refusing a job they were capable of doing.

29 For evidence of this see WHITESIDE, "Counting the cost: sickness and disability among working people in an era of industrial recession," *Economic History Review*, XL, 1987, pp. 228–246. Unfortunately, too little work has been done on the French sickness insurance scheme in the 1930s, to see if high unemployment translated into higher sickness rates there as well.

30 WHITESIDE, "Counting the cost ..." (as note 29).

work. Again, the experience of the 1930s shaped the politics of the 1940s: in this case, the adoption by UK governments of Keynesian strategies to sustain an agenda of jobs for all.

By 1939, there are signs of convergence in the meaning of unemployment, but less about the relationship between state and labour market. In France, 'classic' unemployment was related to industrial modernisation: a modernisation that invoked state powers to extend collectively negotiated and standardised work practices to all in the specified trade or sector. This builds on earlier foundations: the state, through negotiation and arbitration, is a source of social justice and the means of co-ordinating relations between employer and employed. In the context of post-1945 reconstruction, this agenda develops new dimensions. Modernisation and planning are adopted across the whole remit of industrial production, to strengthen the French economy by adapting technologically advanced production systems that require contracted employment of skilled workers under a standardised working week for a specified working lifetime. The object of post-war French social security is to reinforce this trend, to attract the rising generation away from traditional work in rural and small town communities, to city jobs in modern industry, by offering protection against predefined risks and a retirement pension at the end of a working life.[31] This is central to the French Keynesian settlement. The experience of the Slump years is noted less for high unemployment than the failure (again) of France to secure its borders and the need for France to contain its German neighbour. Full employment is the object of policy: here, stress is on the second word, the object is to extend formal subordination and employment contracts to a higher proportion of the working population. In Britain, in contrast, post-war reconstruction focused on jobs for all – full employment would guarantee that the Slump years and mass unemployment would never return. Far from planning a modern industrial future, post-war reconstruction focuses on a renewal of social protection, but leaves industrial modernisation and work practices to the province of free collective bargaining. External to these pro-

---

31 NOEL WHITESIDE and ROBERT SALAIS, "Comparing welfare states: social protection and industrial politics in France and Britain, 1930–60," *Journal of European Social Policy*, 8, 2, 1998, pp. 139–155.

cesses, state policy remains confined to rescuing casualties. Keynesian strategies have less to do with planning than with deficit budgeting, regulating domestic demand to accord with macro-economic policy.

Conclusions

This paper has traced what Robert Salais would term the convention of unemployment: its birth in the late nineteenth century and its emergence in the mid-twentieth century as a uniform construct, building on a specific socio-political settlement. In each of the countries examined here, this convention took different forms as the political contexts within which it was realised were far from identical. Moreover, while the concept becomes more uniform, working practices do not: transformations in the post-war decades are slow and uneven. In France, we witness how, during the 1950s and 1960s, the protection offered for contracted employees slowly convinces hitherto independent workers of the advantages to be gained from subordination to a standard working life. In the UK, where short-time working or casual employment had been endemic in industries like coal mining and port transport for as long as anyone could remember, the post-war productivity drive and new standardised work patterns exert enormous pressure on the workforce, resulting in absenteeism and strikes. In other words, the emergence of standard employment does not entail its automatic translation into the world of work. This took decades. The decasualisation of dock work, a project dear to the hearts of British reformers before 1914, is finally agreed (amid much industrial unrest) in the early 1970s. The final stage is implemented two years before the election of Mrs Thatcher who, unsurprisingly, promptly destroys the scheme in the name of labour market deregulation.

Such trajectories demonstrate the transitory nature of the Keynesian settlement that does, however, last long enough to be considered 'normal' – and to leave behind classificatory vocabularies still widely used by statisticians concerning 'standard' and 'non-standard' or 'a-typical' employment. We should note that such terminology is highly gender specific. The Keynesian settlement assumes a structure of domestic dependency of what we now regard as a traditional type, with wage-earning and caring tasks carefully delimited by sex and social protection dedicated to wage replacement in the case of predefined risks. Wage-earning wives in the UK in particular are generally excluded from registered unemployment, thanks to their proclivity for part-time work and their payment of social insurance contributions at a lower rate. In consequence, post-war statistics continue to tell us comparatively little about female unemployment. Here we see how concepts of family responsibility, labour market activity and the risk of poverty combine to create a construction of unemployment that is neither a simple measure of joblessness – nor, necessarily, an indicator of poverty. Precisely what distribution of work creates 'unemployment'? Is the worker who is out of work three days out of six more (or less) likely to suffer from poverty than the worker who is jobless for three months out of six? Why should the latter 'count' as unemployed when the former does not? What expectations about the ability to budget, to accommodate reduced circumstances, underpin our expectations? Why do they change? What moral orders remain embedded in our understanding of unemployment and in our identification of its 'real' victims?

This paper has illustrated how politics and political expectations has shaped the answers to these questions, but in only two of Europe's major economies. We know that, in other countries faced by labour market crisis, the convention of unemployment was interpreted in different ways.[32] Comparative historical trajectories therefore throw into question the utility of using measurement of unemployment as an indicator of national economic well-being – or of personal poverty. Although not properly the subject here, more recent literature on current labour market developments is replete with references to the 'working poor': a term used commonly in reference to 'a-typical' or 'precarious' employment where statutory protection is limited and personal risk is high. As the Keynesian convention collapses, so the

---

32 B. ZIMMERMAN, "Deux modes de construction statistique du chômage au tournant du siècle" in B. ZIMMERMAN, C. DIDRY and P. WAGNER (dirs), *Le travail et la nation*, Paris 1999.

remit of such employment is extending, below if not above board.[33] Here, potential sources of poverty are at their richest. In the UK, in partial recognition of this, we are witnessing a revival of old poor law treatments for the partially and under employed: the tax credit system that subsidises those unable to make ends meet, under the new guise of 'making work pay'. As this paper has indicated, the statistical apprehension of waged work and its distribution has long reflected a moral agenda concerning the proper distribution of responsibilities and desirable labour market behaviour. During periods of decline, these are called into question, modified and misapplied, generating conflict and political debate. We are living through such a period of uncertainty today – although whether this presages a return to earlier uniformities appears extremely uncertain. Instead, in the UK in particular, the labour market appears to revert to its late nineteenth century form, when poverty became more apparent in the midst of rising prosperity and when official intervention proved a necessary precursor to the effective classification of its causes in order to secure their cure.

---

33 Noel Whiteside, "From full employment to flexibility: Britain and France , 1960–2000" in Bo Ström (ed), *After Full Employment: European discourses on work and flexibility*, Brussels 2000, pp. 107–135.

Popular Unrest, Bread Riot, Legitimism. Power and Poverty in Ferrara under the Este Rule
—————— Matteo Provasi ——————

In Spring of 1574 the cityscape of Ferrara was transformed by a blizzard of anonymous posters placed in the most noticeable locations. Roughly, their content read thus: "Cristoforo Sfregiato step aside / you know that you have ruined The Poverty / but if this time it has gone badly, next time it won't fail / because God will grant it."[1] We shall have time later to linger over the syntactic and semantic aspects of these lines of protest. But in the early stages, they offer an important contribution: they introduce more or less two of the central characters of this story. On one side Cristoforo da Fiume, better known with the derogatory nickname "Sfregiato" (Scarface): that is one of many examples of intermediate economic and fiscal power, within an Italian dominion of the modern age. On the other side Poverty: a word deliberately written by the anonymous satirist, and subsequently used in all contemporary chronicles, with an initial capital letter. In this sense Poverty is not used as an indication of state or material condition of life; but as a social class and, without over-emphasizing the purposes of public opinion at that time, as a political interlocutor.

It is only a minor episode, which is politically and historically marginal if compared with the European scope of the Workshop. Nonetheless through its ordinary uniqueness I hope to offer a concrete evidence of factual and symbolic elements able to interact with the general theme and useful for the reconstruction of a bigger universe.[2]

---

1 M.A. GUARINI, *Diario di tutte le cose accadute nella nobilissima città di Ferrara dal 1570 al 1598*, Biblioteca Estense di Modena (from here onward BEMo), ms. It. 285 (alpha H.2.16), foll. 91–92: "in diversi luochi della città si ritrovò affissi alcuni billittini che dicevano Cristofaro Sfrisà fatti da là / tu sai c'hai rovinato la Povertà / ma s'adess l'è andà falà / un'altra volta sa non falirà / perché Dio lo permeterà."
2 For these notations of historic methodology C. GINZBURG – C. PONI, "Il nome e il come: scambio ineguale e mercato storiografico", *Quaderni storici*, n. 40, 1979, pp. 181–190; C. GINZBURG, *Miti emblemi spie. Morfologia e storia*, Torino 1986; J. REVEL (ed.), *Giochi di scala. La microstoria alla prova dell'esperienza*, Roma 2006.

My analysis will be substantially divided into three parts. The first one will encompass an economic evaluation: a quantitative and qualitative picture of the spread of misery in Ferrara, on one side by taking account of the trends of the period (thus the entire sixteenth century), and on the other side by paying attention to their variations (but it would be more honest to define them as accelerations), recorded during the years 1565–1575. It's during this time span that the most important episodes in the life of our story's main character, Cristoforo da Fiume, take place. From the simple role of a contractor of local taxes, through a skilful evolution of his political career, Da Fiume manages to become the main fiscal authority of Ferrara (and its territory). From this privileged position he will manage to benefit himself, and will contribute to a great extent to the deterioration of the living conditions of the subjects of Alfonso II d'Este. In essence, with his anti-popular policies, he can justifiably be considered a creator of poverty.

The second perspective of analysis concentrates on the actual behaviour determined by the events. The economic aspect introduces a classic combination of the social and political history of the modern age: that of poverty and revolt. Suffering, poverty and a lack of basic victuals lead to protests, turmoil and revolt. In this sense, Ferrara is no exception. It remains to understand at what level of awareness, which practical objectives and by what means these protests took place.

Lastly, here is the third point of view: the cultural consequences. Several decades ago Edward Thompson had already criticized a reading levelled at the economic aspects of popular unrests (he spoke expressly about "economic reductionism").[3] In the case of Ferrara, the apparent simple reading of the conflict leaves the field open to an interpretative complication. In the first place for the interlocutors called to the cause: in fact, on the social scene we find at various levels the legitimate authority of the Este dominion, the intermediate powers and actual executors of the dominion's policies (of whom Cristoforo da Fiume is the most meaningful example), and the people

---

3 E.P. THOMPSON, "The Moral Economy of the English Crown in the Eighteenth Century", *Past and Present*, n. 50, 1971, pp. 76–79.

(or Poverty) whom they ruled, but they were often able to influence through different forms of pressure. The nature of the popular disturbances is also significant, and in this case appears to have a clear legitimist background. The intersection of these components yields its most tangible expression during the final phase of our story (the public funeral of Da Fiume) and leads us to concentrate on abstract concepts such as power and poverty, and over the continuous, unstable balance between mediation, repression and protest that inevitably marks the interrelations between them.

Poverty and the fiscal system

Groups of paupers who wander around the town crying for mercy and begging for a slice of bread. Children who die of hunger in the arms of their mothers at the doors of churches, where they are asking for charity. Enterprising men who try to avoid the bans on buying or trading bread outside the dukedom. Finally, desperate heads of families who kill their children, tired of seeing them suffer from hardship and lack of food; or worse, in order to eat the flesh in a kind of survival cannibalism.[4] These are all scenes of everyday poverty taken from the Ferrara chronicle by Giovanni Maria Zerbinati, a ducal official, from a family of notaries, who without any doubt was strongly linked to the lordly power of the Estes. The year in question, and the date at which we must begin, is 1505.[5]

I deliberately recovered a rather dated testimony in respect to the decade in which Cristoforo da Fiume worked. To demonstrate how much the severe fiscal policies of the administrator acted simply as accelerators in a context which was already dramatically marked by urban poverty. A few more references in loose order bring us closer to the years we are most interested in. In 1533, with obvious fatherly behaviour and in conjunction with several religious brotherhoods, the Este Court instituted the *Monte delle Farine*. This was a charitable orga-

---

4 On the human regression to bestial status during periodic food shortages and episodes of desperate anthropophagy, see P. CAMPORESI, *Il pane selvaggio*, Bologna 1983 [first ed. 1980], pp. 39–61.

5 G.M. ZERBINATI, *Croniche di Ferrara. Quali comenzano del anno 1500 sino al 1527*, edited by M.G. MUZZARELLI, Ferrara 1988, pp. 56–58.

nisation to help the many poor present in the city, who could depend on an adequate supply of grain in times of famine, and which allowed bread to be sold at a price far lower than the internal market laws.[6] In 1539, during a severe famine, there was the need to carry out a census of the poor in Ferrara: the rough estimates suggested at least ten thousand genuine cases in the urban area or about one fifth of the total population.[7]

A long lasting trend singled out the 1500s as a decisive moment, a watershed century, in the history of poverty at a European level:[8] the mechanism and the dimensions of the production of poverty change, but still more important is the cultural and political approach towards it, which undergoes a transformation. The explosion of the population and the rise of prices represent wide ranging factors. Alongside these, or possibly in dialectic relation to these, unfavourable circumstances are taken into account, such as a particularly cold winter, a poor harvest or an outbreak of the plague. Usually, it is a mixture of general trends and specific problems that causes poverty and destitution, and this is in a way what happened in Ferrara in the *annus horribilis* of 1505, or in a more dramatic manner during the decade that best concerns our study, when the direct presence of Cristoforo da Fiume leaves its mark in the economy of the town.

On the peculiar nature of the ever increasing power of the "Sfregiato", as his contemporaries used to call him, a consideration is required. After more than two centuries of ruling by the Este family, the process of transformation of the old magistracies of communal tradition into something adjusted to the lordship system had been al-

---

6 F. CAZZOLA, *La città, il principe, i contadini. Ricerche sull'economia ferrarese nel Rinascimento 1450–1630*, Ferrara 2003, pp. 261–293.

7 The news is extracted from the cronicles of M. EQUICOLA DI ALVETO, *Annali della città di Ferrara*, Biblioteca Ariostea di Ferrara (from here onward BAFe), ms. classe I, 355, fol. 105r; A. ISNARDI, *Ricordi diversi della città di Ferrara*, BEMo, ms. It. 530 (alpha R.4.2), fol. 107.

8 Essential on this theme, J.P. GUTTON, *La société et les pauvres en Europe (XVIᵉ–XVIIIᵉ siècles)*, Paris 1974; B. GEREMEK, *Poverty. A history*, Oxford 1997.

most completed.[9] But in our case we are not facing a direct instrument of the duke's: Da Fiume is not embedded in the mechanism of the court but acts more like a private speculator, with such a wide field of manoeuvre to deeply influence public policies. He can do so by taking advantage of the lack of interest by the main authority, Duke Alfonso II, who at that time, had just inaugurated a strategy of total discharge of commitment on the economic front. As part of the strategy the collection of taxes was entirely entrusted to external contractors with the primary objective to obtain a secure and readily usable source of cash for the exhausted ducal coffers, with no particular attention to the methods used by those who collected it. Another important consequence of the new fiscal strategy is that the duke can transfer any complaints from the tax-burdened population to the contractors.[10]

Cristoforo da Fiume takes advantage of the new policy and exploits all possible discretionary spaces left to him, often venturing far beyond them. He officially entered the Este economic system in 1564, obtaining together with other speculators the duty of the *beccaria* (of the butchers). However, some references predate the first meeting between the administrator and the population of Ferrara: by 1562, he was already present in Comacchio, an area near the mouth of the River Po, economically very important for the trade in fish and salt. Before that, under the rule of Ercole II d'Este, predecessor of Alfonso II ruling until 1559, he had managed to become entrusted with the temporary collection of the wine tax.[11] By all means the enrolment of Cristoforo da Fiume in the heart of the Este economic mecha-

---

9 On the evolution of the ruling system, see T. DEAN, "Commune and Despot: The Commune of Ferrara under Este Rule, 1300–1450", in T. DEAN – C. WICKHAM (eds.), *City and countryside in late Medieval and Renaissance Italy*, London and Ronceverte 1990, pp. 183–197; L. TURCHI, "Istituzioni cittadine e governo signorile a Ferrara (fine sec. XIV – prima metà sec. XVI)", in A. PROSPERI (ed.), *Storia di Ferrara*, vol. VI, Ferrara 2000, pp. 130–158.

10 For a general picture on fiscal policies and tax administration of the Italian states during the XVI century, see G. MUTO, "Modelli di organizzazione finanziaria nell'esperienza degli stati italiani della prima età moderna", in G. CHITTOLINI, A. MOLHO, P. SCHIERA (eds.), *Origini dello Stato. Processi di formazione statale in Italia fra medioevo ed età moderna*, Bologna 1994, pp. 287–302.

11 Respectively F. RODI, *Annali di Ferrara*, BAFe, ms. classe I 645, fol. 646r; C. RONDONI, *Dei successi di Ferrara e il suo dominio sino ad Alfonso II*, BEMo, ms. It. 485 (alpha J.4.17), foll. 313r–314v.

nism occurs in successive steps, and each of them encompasses a progressive enlargement of the field of action. This went on up to the crucial year 1569, in which Scarface obtained the entire contract for the city levies. The news gets a lot of attention in the contemporary chronicles, which often contain little supplemental notes with negative judgements or worried comments from the population of the town.[12]

From this moment the unpopular project of Scarface takes shape following two parallel schemes. The first one is coherent with the typology of contracting: for the investment to be fruitful the collection of taxes and its control system must be made more rigorous.[13] The second refers to the enormous level of discretionary measures that this type of activity allowed: not satisfied with the increase of old taxes, Da Fiume introduces new ones. The new fiscal policy affects invariably all sectors of commerce but with particularly negative consequences for the basic commodities. In this order: a duty on the fishing trade, on cheese, on oil, on loans (in an economic system where an updated form of bartering still survived), and finally on wood for burning.[14]

Particular attention deserves the control on bread. We are talking here about the food which represented the principal, and for the poor the only possible source of nourishment in sixteenth-century Ferrara; the mainstay of the diet.[15] In this area Scarface built a true monopoly, which included production and trading. He became a pro-

---

12 Some examples: A. DE MONTE, *Storia di Ferrara. Tomo II. Delle cose al tempo dei duchi*, BEMo, ms. It. 217 (alpha W.6.18), foll. 407v–408r; C. RONDONI, *Dei successi*, cit., foll. 341v–342r, who retrospectively observes (his writings date back to the beginning of the seventeenth century) that the decision to fully entrust the tax collection to Da Fiume would ruin many families of artisans, peasants and citizens.

13 This mechanism is perfectly explained by G. SARDI, *Libro delle historie ferraresi [...] Aggiuntivi di più quattro Libri del Sig. Dottore Faustini sino alla Devoluzione del Ducato di Ferrara*, Ferrara 1646 [anast. ed. Bologna 1967], p. 52 of Faustini: "egli, per non rimetterci nell'affitto, faceva molte estorsioni, attirando le querele di tutto il popolo".

14 For a full list, see L. CHIAPPINI, *Gli Estensi. Mille anni di storia*, Ferrara 2001, pp. 327–328.

15 F. CAZZOLA, "La città e il pane: produzione agricola e consumi alimentari a Ferrara tra Medioevo ed Età moderna", in J. BENTINI, A. CHIAPPINI, G.B. PANATTA, A. VISSER TRAVAGLI (eds.), *A tavola con il Principe. Materiali per una mostra su alimentazione e cultura nella Ferrara degli Estensi*, Ferrara 1988, pp. 21–37.

ducer himself, then issued very few licences for private production, and if at all, only after payment of a heavy tax, and he also strictly controlled the prices.[16] To assure himself almost total power, in 1571 he tried to close the *Monte delle Farine*, the alternative centre for bread sales at limited prices. But in this case the measure was short lived because of the direct intervention of the Holy See.[17]

In short, a dramatic outlook for the people of Ferrara, soon made worse by other factors mainly of a climatic nature. During the years from 1567 onwards a series of very poor harvests were recorded, which in turn had a negative influence on all other economic activities. To worsen an already difficult situation we can add particularly cold winters in the same period, so rigid that in 1572 a witness reports "on the beginning of November in few days the Po river froze completely [...] and the ice lasted until the eighth of January 1573; the ice was so thick that it was possible to go from one bank of the river to the other with a horse."[18] Lastly an unpredictable event, a natural disaster: the most serious earthquake ever recorded in Ferrara struck the town in 1570 (with a series of aftershocks into 1571), devastating an urban environment unused to dealing with this kind of emergency.[19] The cataclysm created chaos, death, material damage and a general alteration of all social dynamics that the anti-fiscal policy of Scarface magnified.

During the same years Alfonso II committed himself directly in a campaign for raising funds from the already vexed population of the town. On the other hand the onerous costs of representation of

---

16 See F. RODI, *Annali*, cit., foll. 646r-v.

17 See C. RONDONI, *Dei successi*, cit., foll. 346v-347r.

18 G.G. and P. MONFERRATO, *Giornale d'alcune cose della città di Ferrara e d'alcune altre domestiche (1557–1573)*, Biblioteca Apostolica Vaticana (from here onward BAV), Vat. Lat. 12592, fol. 27r.

19 For further evidence, see G.G. and P. MONFERRATO, *Giornale d'alcune cose*, cit., fol. 18v-19v; I. ROBERTI, *Cronichetta che comincia il 3 ottobre 1559 e termina il 10 maggio 1592*, BAFe, ms. coll. Antonelli, 294b, foll. 4r-5v. For a historic reconstruction, A. SOLERTI, *Ferrara e la corte estense nella seconda metà del secolo Decimosesto. I discorsi di Annibale Romei*, Citta di Castello 1900, pp. CLXI–CLXXIII; E. GUIDOBONI, "Riti di calamità: Terremoti a Ferrara nel 1570–74," *Quaderni storici*, n. 55, 1984, pp. 107–135.

the court had drained the ducal coffers.[20] Only in the initial years of his rule at least five important and very expensive public ceremonies can be recorded: in the fall 1559 the succession of the new lord and the sumptuous and elaborate funeral of the former Duke Ercole II.[21] Just few months later the solemn entrance of Lucrezia de Medici in the court and between 1565 and 1566 the luxurious rite for the admission of the duke's second wife Barbara d'Austria (paid by a specific loan requested by the court from the most affluent citizens of the town). And lastly the campaign of Hungary, firmly imposed by Alfonso and in reality nothing more than a parade of military ornaments (the Este army counted at least four thousand men richly clothed). To remedy the constant lack of money, this same duke was committed to constructing a particularly unprincipled fiscal machine,[22] in respect of which the system of contracting represented only one of the solutions.

Protest and riot

With its heavy consequences for the local community, this situation leads to open demonstration of intolerance. We can observe the protest expressing itself through actions at different levels of materiality: beginning with voices of dissatisfaction and ending with concrete attempts at revolt or threats to the personal security of Scarface. At a European level we can notice an obvious increase in episodes of urban unrest during the course of the 1500s, at the same time as the rise in poverty. An example, macroscopic but significant: in France George Huppert counted at least four hundred and fifty uprisings

---

20 On the importance of the policy of representation among Italian lordships, see B. Mitchell, *Italian civic pageantry in the high Renaissance. A descriptive bibliography of Triumphal entries and selected other festivals for state occasion*, Firenze 1979 (pp. 28–34 for the performances in Ferrara).

21 For detailed informations on these events, see G. Ricci, *Il principe e la morte. Corpo, cuore, effigie nel Rinascimento*, Bologna 1998, in part. pp. 25–60.

22 The chronicler C. Rondoni, *Dei successi*, cit., foll. 332r-334r, does not hesitate to define these measures as "brutal abuses" ("angarie"). Other comments can also be found in A. Isnardi, *Ricordi diversi*, cit., fol. 144; AA.VV., *Croniche giornali scritte da vari autori* [...], BAV, Vat. Lat. 12587, fol. 84; F. Rodi, *Annali*, cit., fol. 647v.

with economic causes during the sixteenth century.[23] These numbers should be interpreted loosely, because it is often true that the spark that lights the fuse of popular revolt is an economic crisis. Alongside this, ideas of a political nature take shape.

I have deliberately used the term "ideas" instead of the more connotative "objectives" as the latter would imply some sort of consciousness and an organization of the protest which are totally absent from the events here described. As a matter of fact the majority of historiographical studies on Early Modern popular revolts tend to concentrate on this dichotomy of interpretation. On one side the natural, spontaneous tension generated by food shortages; on the other a more complex organization with precise objectives how to change the system power.[24] In our case of study it is evident that the first type of situation tends to prevail. The aim of the revolt is the diffusion of the sense of dissatisfaction toward the power and its administration. The concrete action, be it verbal of physical, creates a code of communication universally shared and through which the protest is expressed and spread.

So let us now turn to the events. The first evidence of open conflict against the fiscal system created by Cristoforo da Fiume emerged from the guild of craftsmen bakers. We find ourselves facing the first anomaly: usually in urban revolts with economic objectives, at least for most of the eighteenth century, millers and bakers, producers and sellers of the basic commodity of survival, are on the opposing side. They represent the lowest step of middle power against which the population hurls its impatience, exasperated by hunger. The *Grande Rebeine* of Lyons in 1529 had the bakers' shops as one of the principal targets of popular violence, as well as the public granaries and

---

23 See G. HUPPERT, *After the Black Death. A Social History of Early Modern Europe*, Bloomington and Indianapolis 1986.

24 This debate, on which a vast bibliography is available, takes shape around conflicting opinions of Boris Poršnev and Roland Mousnier. I will just quote J.H. ELLIOTT, "Revolution and Continuity in Early Modern Europe", *Past and Present*, n. 42, 1969, pp. 35–56, particularly useful for our perspective. For a more complete coverage of the issue you will find a precious aid in F. BENIGNO, *Specchi della rivoluzione. Conflitto e identità politica nell'Europa moderna*, Roma 1999, pp. 7–103.

the houses of the rich.[25] Limiting the field of research to the Italian context during the seventeenth century we have plenty of material: the assault on the bakeries in Milan during the plague of 1630 has been made famous by Alessandro Manzoni's novel *I Promessi Sposi*; but Bologna too, some years later, would be the stage of similar episodes invariably targeted to get bread.[26]

But that is not enough. Ferrara bakers of the 1500s assume the roles of actors rather than targets of the protest. Moreover in my view, their opposition does not hide a form of pressure on political power: they do not present themselves as a lobby looking for favourable legislation to profit from the famine. Theirs is a simple protest of subsistence: if they cannot produce and sell bread freely, they will find it difficult to survive. In July 1570, immediately after the severe impositions of Scarface, bakers take advantage of institutional channels. A delegation makes its way in front of the public authorities: the Judge of the *Savi* Antonio Rondinelli (the most important of the municipal magistracies of communal tradition) and, among other representatives of the lord, the secretary Gian Battista Pigna. They asked for "justice" in general, which could be translated as a more open market. The meeting substantially ended with a reconfirmation of the previous dispositions, undertaken by Da Fiume and sustained by the duke, with the resolve of having them respected through the publication of specific provisions against the offenders.[27] It is a sort of dialogue between two parties without any power: the bakers had none, subject to heavy external interventions in their market;[28] and the Judge of the *Savi* had been substantially deprived of his authority. In fact, at the end of the same year, Antonio Rondinelli renounced his office, and had great

---

25 See B. GEREMEK, *Poverty*, cit. (note 8), for the town of Lyons; G. RUDÉ, *The Crowd in History 1730–1848*, London 1981, for examples from the eighteenth century.

26 For this last episode see L. FERRANTE, "Tumulto di più persone per causa del calo del pane…". Saccheggi e repressione a Bologna (1671, 1677)", *Rivista Storica Italiana*, 1978, pp. 770–807.

27 M. EQUICOLA DI ALVETO, *Annali*, cit., foll. 136v-137r; A. ISNARDI, *Ricordi diversi*, cit., fol. 153.

28 For an example of the actual organization of the bread market outside the town of Ferrara consult A. GUENZI, "Un mercato regolato: pane e fornai a Bologna nell'età moderna", *Quaderni storici*, n. 37, 1978, pp. 370–397.

difficulty in finding a successor: most eminent citizens refuse the job: "for not being subject to the will of Scarface."[29]

The real need to find bread forced the urban population to threatening forms of looting. In May 1570, the ducal authorities confiscated a wagon filled with bread, probably ready to be exported to Chioggia under the supervision of Scarface. Here, we touch upon another typical element of economic revolt: the hate on the exporters, guilty of taking goods from a population already in a state of destitution. The load was weighed and found to be irregular: we are probably talking about mixed bread ("pane ignobile"), made from ingredients other than wheat. Sometimes mixing broad bean, rye, bran, barley, rice, acorn, chestnuts and even vegetal roots was necessary to increase the selling weight or just for growing the production when plain flour lacked.[30] Whether nutritious or vile, the load never actually arrived at the court, because it was attacked and looted by "twelve poor men and two bakers;"[31] and with the first intention of destroying rather than stealing.

A number of years passed, during which the bad harvests, the human costs of the earthquake and further taxes imposed by Scarface increased the poverty problem, and the protest gained the fullest and most violent aspects of a riot, using the double register of verbal and physical violence. Some chroniclers registered the attempted murder of Cristoforo da Fiume: a shot from an harquebus from which the iniquitous administrator escaped miraculously. The concrete threat to his unscathed physique was not linked to a planned attack but it is more precise to suppose a momentary expression of revolt. What is important to underline is the relationship of the involved parties: the

---

29 A. DE MONTE, *Storia di Ferrara*, cit., foll. 415v-416r. Some interesting information on the commitment of Rondinelli against the abuses of Scarface can be found in A. MARESTI, *Cronologia et istoria de Capi e Giudici de Savii della Città di Ferrara*, Ferrara 1683, p. 76.

30 For a brief overview of the different recipes of bread produced for the poor see T. GARZONI, *La piazza universale di tutte le professioni del mondo*, edited by P. CHERCHI and B. COLLINA, Torino 1996 [or. ed. Ferrara 1586], vol. II, pp. 1352–1355; G.B. SEGNI, *Discorso sopra la carestia, e fame*, Ferrara 1591, pp. 40–44.

31 C. RONDONI, *Dei successi*, cit., foll. 343v-345r; G. TESTI, *Libro di alcuni raccordi della città di Ferrara, et altri luochi (fino al 1602)*, BEMo, ms. It. 1689 (alpha K.1.35), foll. 125–126; AA.VV., *Croniche giornali*, cit., foll. 192v-193r.

people formed a shield around the sole attacker, thus protecting his anonymity. Once he found out the identity of the culprit, the duke of Ferrara opted for a fundamentally soft punishment considering the gravity of the crime. It is probable that the increasing dissatisfaction and the concrete risk of prompting a general insubordination had suggested to Alfonso II to opt for a low profile, far removed from exemplary rigidity.[32]

The lines which I used to open my lecture refer specifically to the episode of this attempted murder. Let us see them again: "but if today has gone badly / another time it will not fail"; it is clear that this refers to the harquebus shot that did not reach its target and the hope that a second attempt might be more successful. It is the language of infamy, that is almost as aggressive and dangerous as the physical actions that strike Scarface. In a society where the anthropologic category honour-shame is a central element, anonymous letters, leaflets, satiric parodies are the expressive tools commonly used to target the respectability of the intermediate powers.[33] A language that is universally shared and that enriches even its macabre framework: next to the leaflets in the public square and literally in front of the stall from which Da Fiume sold bread, lay a blood-soaked loaf of bread.

The topography of symbols is not decided at random and the same holds true for their semantic meaning. The leaflets were affixed in the areas of highest human density of the urban context, precisely to highlight the need to publicise the rebellion. The positioning of the blood-soaked loaf of bread thus assumes even greater symbolic value: by night, in an anonymous and therefore untraceable way, the macabre object was placed in front of the physical place where the iniquity of Scarface was expressed (thus where poverty was produced). The stylistic interpretation of the lampoon is even more interesting:

---

32 See for example M.A. GUARINI, *Diario*, cit., foll. 91–92; C. RONDONI, *Dei successi*, cit., foll. 348v-349r; A. DE MONTE, *Storia di Ferrara*, cit., foll. 418v-419r.
33 On this subject see P. BURKE, *The Historical Anthropology of Early Modern Italy. Essays on Perception and Communication*, Cambridge 1987, pp. 95–109; G. RICCI, *Povertà, vergogna, superbia. I declassati tra Medioevo e Età moderna*, Bologna 1996, pp. 89–108; O. NICCOLI, *Rinascimento anticlericale. Infamia, propaganda e satira in Italia tra Quattro e Cinquecento*, Roma-Bari 2005, pp. 29–48.

few verses, simple words and the use of rhyme made it a fundamental instrument for an effective infamy. Through this a large part of the semi-illiterate population could memorise the content of the leaflet, thus transforming the mix of words into a refrain to repeat (a task given mainly to the children) around the city to spread the message.[34] In some ways the use of the macabre object had the same function: the union of image and footnote made the spreading of the message easier. Furthermore, it reminds us of the late medieval practice of infamy paintings, often used by the legitimate powers in order to judge by default those guilty.[35]

Finally the persistence of this particular language of infamy over the course of the centuries is surprising. It can even be found in atmospheric, social and chronological contexts that are entirely different, but which are always linked to popular revolts with an economic matrix. In Nottingham in 1812, in other words at the dawn of capitalist society, a group of women demonstrated in the city with a loaf upon a pole, streaked with red and tied with black crepe, emblematic of "bleeding famine decked in Sackecloth". Some time later in Plymouth, we find another public demonstration of a loaf of bread soaked in blood beside a heart.[36] Therefore the emotional force of the instruments used did not diminish, even two and a half centuries after the events in Ferrara. And the intrinsic significance did not change: the corrupt administrator with his unpopular policies enforced destitution and created poverty to such an extent that he removed bread as well as blood, the vital sap from the people.[37]

However let us return to Ferrara in 1574, to the practical results caused by infamous booklets and macabre images. The historian from Ferrara Filippo Rodi described the reaction of the population the morning following the billposting of the leaflet in this way: "when

---

34 On the stylistic instruments see C. EVANGELISTI, "Libelli famosi": processi per scritte infamanti nella Bologna di fine '500', *Annali della Fondazione Luigi Einaudi*, vol. XXVI, 1992, pp. 181–239.

35 G. ORTALLI, *"Pingatur in Palatio". La pittura infamante nei secoli XIII–XVI*, Roma 1979.

36 E.P. THOMPSON, "The Moral Economy", cit. (note 3), pp. 131–136.

37 On the multiform meaning of blood see P. CAMPORESI, *Il sugo della vita. Simbolismo e magia del sangue*, Milano 1997.

it was seen by the people each person expressed his own opinion, and they all began to be pleased that there was someone who took care of damaging his reputation [obviously referring to Scarface], in order that his life might be damaged."[38] According to this reading, the verbal infamy and the attack on the honour of the administrator could have acted as a prelude to a physical attack; it could have been the source of courage that led the community to concrete action against the enemy of the people. To confirm this theory we have got the summary of two contemporary chroniclers, Claudio Rondoni and Alessandro De Monte: as a matter of fact, both reversed the chronological order of the events.[39] The lampoon and the threatening object would have been prior to the attempted murder of Scarface, resulting no longer in a consequence of the latter but rather as its cause. Thus responding to the definition present in many modern legal texts of the crime of "shouts of rebellion" ("*grida seditiose*").[40] In addition it is interesting to notice that all those forms of protest take place in an interval of time (between February and April 1574) when the authority of the lord was not directly present over the town: Alfonso II was in fact travelling outside Italy creating a sort of temporary suspension of power that made it relatively easier to advance social claims.[41]

The legitimist perspective

Let us move now to the last stage. In 1575 fate substituted the noisy and ineffective aggressiveness that the people of Ferrara had against him. Scarface died of "*mal di preda*" (presumably liver stones) after some months of atrocious suffering; and the news created obvious signs of joy among the citizens. Taking inspiration from the

---

38 F. RODI, *Annali*, cit., foll. 685v-686r: "la matina quando fu vista dalla gente ogn'uno disse la sua et cominciarono le persone a ralegrarsi che ci fosse qualcheduno che si pigliasse cura di cominciarlo a intacar nella riputazione per poterlo altra volta intacarlo nella vita."

39 For these references to the text see note 32.

40 See M. SBRICCOLI, *Crimen laesae maiestatis. Il problema del reato politico alle soglie della scienza penalistica moderna*, Milano 1974, pp. 267–294. For an example of the modern penal theory G.B. DE LUCA, *Il dottor volgare. Overo il compendio di tutta la legge Civile, Canonica, Feudale e Municipale nelle cose più ricevute in pratica*, Roma 1678, pp. 250–262.

41 On this subject a useful reference is G. AGAMBEN, *Stato di eccezione*, Torino 2003.

circumstances of the death, the pungent eye of the artisan Giovanni Maria di Massa, for example, attributes it to the efficiency of divine justice: not only it had finally saved the community from its enemy, but it also had made him suffer from a long illness. In the end, the people of Ferrara, who had greatly suffered the abuses of Scarface, had its moral compensation.[42] However, it was especially the funeral service that offered other significant elements. We know about the signs of popular jubilation that accompanied the coffin with red drapes and festive shouting. The scene appears like a grotesque performance, with a continuous intertwining of joy and mourning symbolism.

The behaviour of the Este seigniory was more ambiguous as it was taken up with the opposing aims of repression and excitement. Cristoforo da Fiume therefore received luxurious funeral rites ("magnificent" as witnesses say):[43] as a public expression of intermediate powers, after all he represented the lordship in matters of taxation. To exalt the death of the functionary meant more or less re-establishing the image of authority.[44] On the other hand though, Duke Alfonso II realized the necessity of a net estrangement from the politics and the methods of the unjust administrator. That is to say, honour to the office and additional shame to the person. As before the attempt to impress the public imagination was entrusted to a major public performance. The court, contemporarily to the rich funeral procession, actually made a spectacular show of confiscating the goods of Scarface: pillaging his house, taking huge quantities of property and carrying them to the public weigh house, in order to try and show that

---

42 G.M. di Massa, *Memorie di Ferrara (1582–1585)*, edited by M. Provasi, Ferrara 2004, p. 113: "d'ongni gravo pechatto che lui aveva chomesso chontra il popullo di Ferrara elli fu remunerato dal signor Idio, ché il stete mesi quatro che gridò chome una anima danata dì e note di mal di preda, et alla fine se ne morsse". Similar comments can be found in AA.VV., *Croniche giornali*, cit., fol. 106v.

43 The antropologic and historiographic analysis on passage rituals has greatly taken advantage from the studies of A. Van Gennep e R. Hertz; I just mention the more recent text of R. Huntington – P. Metcalf, *Celebration of Death. The Anthropology of Mortuary Ritual*, Cambridge 1979; D.J. Davies, *Death Ritual and Belief: the rhetoric of funerary rites*, London 1996.

44 On the defence of intermediate powers as expression of power see the Venetian cases explained in G. Ruggiero, *Violence in Early Renaissance Venice*, New Brunswick 1980.

the House of Este had been cheated by Da Fiume as much as the citizens had been. In reality, this theatrical act also absolved a necessary practice: that of avoiding violent pillage and theft of money by the people, who, in these circumstances, traditionally crowded in front of the iniquitous administrator's office to destroy the accounting books and to take possession of the remaining goods.[45]

Once the possibility had disappeared of concentrating the violence in the destruction of the objects of oppression, the crowd's sense of intolerance poured out directly on to Cristoforo Da Fiume's body. The people tried literally to take the corpse from the procession and to punish him with the extra disgrace of a post-mortem lynching. The loss of the body integrity and of any human resemblance after the mutilation of the corpse; the negation of the purifying power of the burial: we are in front of the most cruel episodes among the ones infamy can produce, a sort of convergence of primaeval anthropologic tensions and identified political symbols (following the dynamics of capital executions).[46] This reminded Filippo Rodi of the tragic end of Tommaso da Tortona, *Podestà* of Ferrara in 1385, brutally murdered by the rioters in revolt, then quartered, cut to bits and burnt in the public square along with his accounting books:[47] "had it not been for the love of the lordship, where for his respect no brutality was used against his corpse, he would have received a bigger torture than the one suffered by Tommaso da Tortona in the same

---

45 On the subject of ritual plundering see C. GINZBURG, "Saccheggi rituali. Premesse a una ricerca in corso", *Quaderni storici*, n. 65, 1987, pp. 615–636; for a perspective of it from the town of Ferrara G. RICCI, "Solenni entrate e violenze rituali negli Stati estensi fra Quattro e Cinquecento", in G. VENTURI (ed.), *L'età di Alfonso I e la pittura di Dosso*, Modena 2004, pp. 93–102.

46 For some examples set in the context of the Italian Renaissance S. BERTELLI, *Il corpo del re. Sacralità del potere nell'Europa medievale e moderna*, Firenze 1990, pp. 209–231; A. ZORZI , "Rituali di violenza giovanile nelle società urbane del tardo Medioevo", in O. NICCOLI (ed.), *Infanzie. Funzioni di un gruppo liminale dal mondo classico all'Età moderna*, Firenze 1993, pp. 185–209; O. NICCOLI, *Il seme della violenza. Putti, fanciulli e mammoli nell'Italia tra Cinque e Seicento*, Roma-Bari 1995, pp. 24–39; G. RICCI, *Il principe*, cit. (note 21), pp. 109–118; L. MARTINES, *April Blood. Florence and the Plot against the Medici*, London 2003, pp. 138–149.

47 See J.E. LAW, "Popular unrest in Ferrara in 1385", in J. SALMONS – W. MORETTI (eds.), *The Renaissance in Ferrara and its European horizons – Il Rinascimento a Ferrara e i suoi orizzonti europei*, Cardiff-Ravenna 1984, pp. 41–60.

town."[48] In this case the anger felt by the people of Ferrara, who were impoverished by Cristoforo da Fiume, and the wish to physically destroy the enemy of the community, are evident. This probably did not take place only because of a general sense of respect for the authority. But Guarini's evidence gives us an account of facts that is more pragmatic: actually the lynching was avoided thanks to the decisive action of some garrisons of ducal guards standing around the coffin with raised lances, thus forming a protective barrier.[49]

In conclusion let us try to evaluate this local episode in a wider perspective. The strong component linked to subsistence in popular revolts is clearly evident; but it would be perhaps an unfair reduction to consider them only as a "rebellion of the belly". Then how should we consider them? Probably in a sort of free zone that surpasses the dimension of the material needs, but without attaining the awareness of political revenge. There is a lot of a legitimist perspective in the rise and fall of Scarface. According to the valid definition given by Eric J. Hobsbawn, there are two main supporting concepts of popular legitimism: the safeguarding of the established order and the idea of justice embodied by his lordship.[50] In practice they are expressed in a short range protest, in which the episodes of rebellion do not regard the authority (in this case the duke of Este), but especially hit the intermediate powers, the material executors.

Cristoforo da Fiume embodies all the elements of cultural oppositions to the intermediate powers. He is first of all an outsider; and this is a characteristic that in the small closed world of cities in the sixteenth century marked him as a dangerous person not to be trusted.[51] It is not a case as frequent in Ferrara as in other places, where one

---

48 F. RODI, *Annali*, cit., foll. 688v-689v: "se non era il principe così amabile, come era, onde per suo rispetto non fu ch'usasse severità contra al cadavero di quello al sicuro tutte le genti correvano a dilaniarlo, et ci faria maggior straccio assai di quello che nella medesima città fu fatto della persona di Tommaso da Tortona."

49 M.A. GUARINI, *Diario*, cit., foll. 96–97.

50 For a definition of popular legitimism see E.J. HOBSBAWM, *Primitive Rebels. Studies in Archaic Forms of Social Movement in the 19th and 20th Centuries*, Manchester 1959, pp. 108–125. But the analysis in this case starts from the middle of the eighteenth century.

51 M. BERENGO, *L'Europa delle città. Il volto della società urbana europea tra Medioevo e Età moderna*, Torino 1999, pp. 521–586.

of the first defence measures of the community was the expulsion of foreigners, when the material conditions became more difficult in moments of crisis. If the topographical reference in his surname does not deceive you, Cristoforo originally came from a small town, which was on Venetian soil in the sixteenth century, and today situated in the province of Pordenone in the Friuli. Before settling in Ferrara, Da Fiume had already made a name for himself: there are several sources which highlight his infamy. His illegal dealings, including that of operating a prostitution racket, are also documented, as well as his eagerness to secure money through unfair speculation. Some chroniclers positively affirm that he fled to Ferrara primarily because Venice had banished him from its lands. And our administrator carried in his face a tangible sign of the popular hostility generated by his dealings: a scar, the result of a cut from a knife (hence the nickname).[52] Coming from another place meant not being able to share the habitual values, the unwritten rules of the society of Ferrara.

Strictly connected to this protective vision is the perception that Scarface, with his continuous imposition of new taxes, interferes with the rules of the community. In a logic of moral economy, the novelty is a synonym of social threat. Contemporary chroniclers comment the introduction of any new levy with the resented affirmation "tax that never existed before."[53] Along this line a devastating action for the subsistence economy of the town such as the shutdown of the *Monte delle Farine*, is compared in importance with the elimination of the Monday market in San Giorgio, a mechanism consolidated over the centuries. To conclude this point, I may add that the social collocation of the rebels is not to be searched among the marginal fringes of the beggars: we are speaking of integrated poverty, of the weakest categories of an impoverished community. An element that exalts the defensive and traditionalist soul of the protest even more.[54]

---

52 For this information, M. SAVONAROLA, *Memorie di Ferrara*, BAFe, ms. coll. Antonelli, 226, fol. 42; G. MERENDA, *Annali di Ferrara*, BAFe, ms. classe I, 107, foll. 81–82; *Cronaca della città di Ferrara dall'origine del mondo sino al 1574*, BAFe, ms. coll. Antonelli, 862, *ad annum*.

53 The concept is perfectly expressed by E.P. THOMPSON, "The Moral Economy", cit. (note 3).

54 G. HUPPERT, *After the Black Death*, cit. (note 23).

And what was Alfonso II of Este's role? Where does he fit in this reasoning? The evidences of time do not express equal judgements on the duke's actions, and can not be otherwise. However they all substantially agree on one aspect: the protest against Scarface expressed the wish of individual attacks. There is never the impression that the aggressiveness against the corrupt governor actually hides a criticism to the lordship rule through a third party. The contemporaries, with their attitude, appear to be seeking some sort of justification for the duke, trying to save at least the ideal image of the prince as a good father of his subjects.[55] A few examples let us understand this aspect better: Alessandro de Monte knows that many new taxes have been expressly decided by Alfonso d'Este, but he alleviates the lord's responsibility pointing his finger against the bad advisors.[56] In 1570, during the confusion produced by the earthquake, the chronicler Antonio Isnardi expressly compares the reaction of Scarface with the one of Alfonso II: while the first one starts his project of monopolising the bread business, the second one, together with many gentlemen, joins in the setting up of the bank of alms for the poor.[57] Even more adventurous is Marc'Antonio Guarini's version: nearly like a wizard, with his own "astuteness" he had made the duke go mad, he had "bewitched" him.[58]

We can probably conclude that the rioting people of Ferrara in the years 1565–1575, could be labelled with the slogan so dear to the French farmers in the late sixteenth century *"Vive le Roi et sans la gabelle!"*.[59] But as a matter of fact the unconditional entrusting of the fiscal policy to dishonest speculators will outlive at least by a decade the death of Scarface.

---

55 Useful references on the subject can be found in Y.M. BERCÉ, *Le roi caché. Sauveurs et imposteur. Mythes politiques dans l'Europe moderne*, Paris 1990.

56 A. DE MONTE, *Storia di Ferrara*, cit., foll. 391v-393r.

57 A. ISNARDI, *Ricordi diversi*, cit., fol. 152.

58 M.A. GUARINI, *Diario*, cit., foll. 69–70

59 In the Italian meaning of "viva il re, mora il malgoverno". See A. MUSI, "La fedeltà al re nella prima età moderna. (A proposito di un libro di Rosario Villari)", *Scienza e politica*, n. 12, 1995, pp. 3–17.

Communication II : Les causes de la pauvreté : maladies et conjonctures
—————————— Thomas Riis ——————————

Nous savons tous que partout, l'orphelin est considéré avoir droit à l'assistance, la disparition d'un parent, surtout du père, est donc une cause reconnue de la pauvreté.

Non seulement la mort, mais aussi la maladie est souvent à l'origine de la pauvreté, surtout si elle touche les parents de famille. Parmi les 39 familles assistées par les Buonomini di San Martino de Florence dont on connaît la raison de l'aide, 16 en avaient besoin parce que le chef de famille était malade.[1] D'abord, les revenus manquaient pendant la maladie, qui souvent entraînait des dépenses supplémentaires pour des soins médicaux ; si la maladie était mortelle, ce fut souvent le coût des funérailles qui rendait le bilan déficitaire, comme nous montrent les exemples d'Elseneur au XVIIe siècle :

Le coût des funérailles à Elseneur 1626–1663 (en daler à 64 skilling)

		Funérailles	Surplus/déficit
1626	David Lyall II	64	- 638
1643	James Greenwood	90	+ 120
1651	Epouse de Hans Jack	28	- 11
1652	Epouse de Hans Hansen	9	- 2
1652	Veuve de James Black	44	- 68
1654	Alexander Glen	22	- 168
1656	Hans Adamsen et épouse	73	- 88
1659	James Kerse	39	- 89
1659	Epouse d'Albert Skrædder	28	+ 4
1663	William Jack	172	- 275

Source : THOMAS RIIS, « Les mouvements de longue durée : le déclin économique et les causes de la pauvreté » dans : *Démocratie et pauvreté. Du quatrième ordre au quart monde*, Paris 1991, p. 436.

———————————

1   AMLETO SPICCIANI, « The « Poveri Vergognosi » in Fifteenth-Century Florence. The first 30 years' activity of the Buonomini di S. Martino », dans : THOMAS RIIS éd., *Aspects of Poverty in Early Modern Europe*, Stuttgart 1981, pp. 152–153.

Cependant, il y a souvent des coûts indirects causés par la maladie (ou la disparition) de la ménagère : c'est difficile de cuisiner de façon économique faute de temps, et pour la même raison on ne peut guère profiter des offres avantageuses. En tout cas, nous constatons que dans deux tiers des familles assistées, le chef de famille était incapable de travailler.

Les causes de l'assistance aux familles, Florence 1466–1470

Chef de famille malade	16
Epoux quitté la maison	8
Epoux en prison	2
Personnes âgées à nourrir	3
Epouse enceinte	3
Enfants en bas âge	3
Enfants adultes incapables de travailler	1
Filles adultes à nourrir	1
Sans foyer	1
Chef de famille veuf	1

Source : AMLETO SPICCIANI, « The « Poveri Vergognosi » », p. 152.

Ces chiffres montrent clairement que la famille allait glisser vers la pauvreté, sitôt le chef de famille (en général le mari) était incapable de travailler. Mais aussi le rôle de la mère dans l'économie familiale était signifiant, ce que démontrent le cas du veuf et ceux dans lesquels la grossesse de la mère l'empêchait de travailler. Même si elle ne s'occupait pas en dehors de la maison, la famille dépendait d'elle pour cuisiner, pour réparer les vêtements, bref pour gouverner le ménage de façon économique. Les personnes à nourrir – vieilles ou jeunes – seraient des charges supplémentaires pour la famille (huit cas), surtout si elles ne pouvaient pas contribuer aux revenus de cette dernière.

Aussi aujourd'hui, la combinaison de chômage et de maladie constitue une raison importante de la pauvreté, car elle prolonge l'état de chômage de quatre mois. Ceci vaut pour un cinquième des chômeurs. En 1926 cas, le besoin d'assistance pouvait être attribuée à une situation sociale particulière :

Les causes du besoin d'assistance à Kiel (Allemagne) 1997

Divorce	1004	52,1 %
Naissance d'un enfant	342	17,8 %
Manque de foyer	300	15,6 %
Dépendance des drogues, d'alcool	120	6,2 %
Mort d'un membre de famille	91	4,7 %
Autres causes	69	3,6 %

Source : *Bericht über die Entwicklung der Armut in Kiel*, pp. 30–31, diagramme 26.

Ainsi, la fragmentation de la famille est comme cause de la pauvreté aussi importante à Kiel aux années 1990 qu'à Florence au XVe siècle.

Comparées aux hommes, plus de femmes recevaient une aide sociale, surtout comme des mères célibataires (18–34 ans) ou comme des retraitées (au-dessus de 65 et surtout de 80 ans).[2] Probablement, le dernier groupe était composé de celles qui avaient été élevées selon les trois idéaux traditionnels « *Kirche, Kinder, Küche* » (Eglise, Enfants, Cuisine). Rarement, elles avaient appris un métier, et si elles travaillaient, leur occupation exigeait rarement de grandes qualifications. Par cette raison, elle ne réussissaient guère à faire des économies, et peut-être plus que la moitié se trouvaient chefs de famille à cause de la deuxième guerre mondiale. Cinquante ans après la fin des combats les veuves de guerre auraient soixante-dix à quatre-vingts ans. De nouveau, on voit les effets de longue durée de la fragmentation des familles.

Les fluctuations monétaires

Vers 1560, on constate, dans le *Reich*, une pénurie grandissante d'argent, qui entraîna une augmentation du prix de l'argent ; avec le temps, la bonne monnaie disparaissait de la circulation (loi de Gresham). La valeur du *Reichstaler* augmentait : de 68 *Kreuzer* par *Taler* en

---

2 *Bericht über die Entwicklung der Armut in Kiel*, Kiel 1998, pp. 26–28.

1570 à 90 *Kreuzer* en 1611. Cette évolution se trouve aussi au Dane-mark, pays étroitement lié à l'économie du *Reich*, comme démontre la tabelle.

L'équivalent d'un Reichstaler en Skilling danois et en Schilling de Lübeck

	Skilling danois	Schilling de Lübeck
Milieu XVIᵉ siècle	48	31
1572	32	31
1602	66	33
1609	68	34
1616	80	-
1618	84	-
1619, confirmé 1625	96	-

Source : *Corpus Constitutionum Daniæ*, éd. V. A. SECHER I, Copenhague 1887–1888, nos. 190, 205, 609, III, Copenhague 1891–1894, nos. 173, 295, 433, 495, IV, Copenhague 1897, no. 158.

Ainsi, il y avait des facteurs de longue durée défavorables.[3] A ces derniers s'ajoutaient les facteurs à court terme, avant tout le début de la guerre en 1618. En automne 1620 un *Reichstaler* valait deux gulden (florins), au printemps 1621 six et une année plus tard dix. On avait assez de petite monnaie, mais à cause de l'inflation forte, les prix augmentaient. La bonne monnaie disparaissait, la cause en était une pénurie de marchandises. En 1622–1623, la population refusa d'accepter la petite monnaie comme paiement et le commerce eut lieu comme du troc. Malgré le fait qu'en Tirol la récolte de 1622 fut bonne (ce qui ne fut pas le cas en Europe du Nord), les paysans ne voulaient pas vendre leur surplus par peur d'être payés en mauvaise monnaie.

---

3 Les taux d'échange au Danemark montrent que dès 1602 la valeur du Reichstaler était déjà hors contrôle.

En 1623, enfin, le système monétaire du *Reich* fut réformé. La petite (et mauvaise) monnaie devait être échangée contre une nouvelle ; on procéda à la régularisation des prix et des salaires en introduisant des maxima.[4]

Un intermezzo lombard

Aussi à Milan, les années 1619–1622 étaient une période difficile, car plusieurs signes laissent conclure à une crise économique. A cause de la guerre de succession de Mantoue 1613–1617 les dépenses publiques avaient augmenté ; les entreprises élargissaient leurs activités dans l'espoir de pouvoir récupérer une partie des sommes payées comme salaire aux mercenaires. Aussi, l'évolution conjoncturelle en Europe était favorable aux métiers d'exportation milanais ; à cause de l'augmentation de 50 % des prix des tissus de laine l'industrie de la laine florissait, finalement, entre 1611 et 1618 on frappait cinq fois plus de monnaie que pendant la première décennie du siècle.

Au printemps de 1619, cette évolution s'arrêta, et ceci pour plusieurs raisons : début de la guerre en 1618, le chaos monétaire dans le *Reich* (dont Milan faisait toujours partie), la diminution des importations d'argent américain, ce qui causa une contraction du commerce. Quand le gouvernement milanais essayait à freiner l'inflation en fixant des taux d'échange des pièces d'or et d'argent en relation de la lira locale, les articles milanais d'exportation devenaient trop chers, et en même temps, la demande internationale fléchissait.[5]

---

4 HANS-JÜRGEN GERHARD, « Ursachen und Folgen der Wandlungen im Währungssystem des Deutschen Reiches 1500–1625 », dans : *Geld und Währung vom 16. Jahrhundert bis zur Gegenwart*, ed. ECKART SCHREMMER, Stuttgart 1993, pp. 69–84 ; PAUL W. ROTH, « Die Kipper- und Wipperzeit in den Habsburgischen Ländern, 1620 bis 1623, », dans : *ibid.*, pp. 85–104.
5 G. VIGO, « Manovre Monetarie e Crisi Economica nello Stato di Milano (1619–1622) », *Studi Storici* XVII, 1976, pp. 101–126.

L'Allemagne au lendemain de la première guerre mondiale

Apparemment, l'inflation du lendemain de la guerre était moins causée par les réparations à payer par l'Allemagne vaincue que par d'autres circonstances. En partie, la guerre avait été financée par des emprunts de guerre, qui maintenant devaient être remboursés, mais le résultat de la guerre les avait fait perdre beaucoup de leur valeur ; ainsi, beaucoup d'Allemands perdirent leurs économies. A cause de la production de marchandises insuffisante pendant la guerre, le pouvoir d'achat s'était accumulé, en outre, il fallait payer des subventions aux veuves de guerre, aux invalides, des pensions aux soldats professionnels. Tout demandait de l'argent, que l'état n'avait pas, c'est pourquoi on imprimait plus de billets de banque et les mettait en circulation, ce qui accélérait l'inflation. Par cette raison, aussi les subventions et les pensions perdaient de valeur.

Au printemps 1919, on avait levé les restrictions sur les prix des vivres, mais il fallait attendre 1921 pour voir les effets de l'inflation. Entre juin et novembre les prix des vivres augmentaient de 150 à 300 % ; à partir d'août 1922 le mark s'effritait pour finir dans le débâcle de 1923 sous impression de l'occupation de la région du Ruhr. Seulement en 1923, une reconstruction monétaire mit une fin à l'inflation.

Les emprunts de guerre avaient perdu leur valeur, il en était de même pour les pensions à cause de l'inflation ; à ces circonstances il faut ajouter la situation intérieure peu stable (les coups manqués de Kapp et de Lüttwitz en 1920 ainsi que de Hitler en 1923). Il est vrai que beaucoup de dettes furent payées avec l'aide de l'inflation, mais en revanche, nombreux étaient ceux qui avaient perdu leurs économies, toute la classe moyenne fut paupérisée et son existence était menacée. Tout ceci préparait un sol fertile pour des mouvements autoritaires et antidémocrates.

Dans le cas allemand d'après-guerre la causalité entre troubles monétaires et pauvreté est évidente, nous avons raison à croire que l'inflation dans le *Reich* pendant les deux premières décennies du XVIIe siècle avait des effets analogues, ainsi qu'à Milan, la politique de déflation a entraîné le fléchissement de la demande internationale, ce qui, à son tour, a dû faire augmenter le chômage.

Seismic Disasters and Poverty: Some Data and Reflections on Past and Current Trends
—— Emanuela Guidoboni & James Jackson ——

Abstract

Strong earthquakes and tsunamis, like other natural disasters (storms, hurricanes, floods) are destructive events that strongly affect the standard of living of the populations they hit. Their impact on human societies varies according to the frequency with which they occur, the quality of the buildings, the demographic density and the economy of the areas involved.

In areas with a precarious economic equilibrium, natural disasters have increased the speed of impoverishment in the short and medium term. The economic and social impact of seismic disasters over the medium and long term can be assessed by analysing the quality of reconstruction work and the time taken to carry it out. Historical and recent records show that when reconstruction is slow and funds are largely or totally lacking, there is a negative effect even on later generations, increasing the vulnerability of the buildings and therefore increasing the hazard from other later destructive events. At times when reconstruction work is being carried out, now as in the past, local economic crises, emigration, famine, plague may also occur, leading to further losses.

In so far as the increasing disparity in living standards across the world is affected by seismic disasters, the scenarios we find today tend to be new, since earthquakes and tsunamis of the same size can have effects of widely varying severity depending on the context. The poorest and most densely populated areas in the world (Near East, Asia, and along the coast of South America), are those most likely to suffer major disasters in the near future. This general trend does not exclude the possibility of economically strong regions being struck by natural disasters resulting in high death tolls and serious economic damage (see the case of New Orleans, in 2004). The technological systems on which urban life depends are in fact very vulnerable. But the difference lies in the resources available for recovery and the time required to effect it. We can therefore be sure, not only that very poor and highly populated areas will suffer the worst natural disasters, but also that the destructive effects of these disasters will tend to worsen pre-existing poverty levels.

The authors present some cases that highlight this historical and current trend in Iran, Pakistan and Italy. For Italy, they present a historical case study of Calabria over the last three centuries. A sequence of destructive earthquakes has played a crucial role in the economy and the culture of that region, which is today one of the poorest in Italy. Historical research has shown that this kind of poverty results from the loss, not only of houses and other buildings needed for production purposes, but also of knowledge, skills and trade exchanges.

Introduction: Earthquakes and Seismic Disasters

Earthquakes are natural frequent phenomena in the life of the Earth. They can be disastrous, triggering off economic and social crises, or over a period of time harm the areas that are affected by them frequently. However, the relationship between earthquakes and disasters is not always clear, as multiple and pre-existing economic, social and cultural factors can interact with the natural phenomenon itself to determine whether the earthquake becomes a 'disaster' or not. Here we try to shed light on some aspects of these inter-relationships where they affect relatively poor areas of the globe. We discuss two standpoints: I) the natural one, that is, the earthquake phenomenon itself and its distribution around the world; and II) the human one, observing some of the social and economic dynamics initiated by earthquakes, when the areas hit are already sociologically or economically fragile, sometimes as a result of demographic changes involving population growth or decline. In our opinion, the cases we present are of interest from historical, anthropological and economic perspectives, and may also be useful towards understanding ongoing trends.

On a macro-level we consider the entire country of Iran, an ancient country and society that long ago developed particular ways of living with the threat posed by earthquakes, remnants of which are preserved in some of its rural communities and the locations of its larger towns and cities. On a much smaller scale, we consider the case of a southern Italian region, Calabria, today one of the least developed areas of an economically developed country. This region of the Mediterranean region experiences strong and relatively frequent earthquakes, which represent an important local environmental characteristic, and one that has influenced many aspects of its history and development. Iran and Calabria, a great country and a small Mediterranean region, respectively, are completely different areas, and both geographically and culturally very far apart. Yet in both areas earthquakes have influenced their resident populations in ways that have marked their history and the development, though in different ways, consequently earthquakes, along with other elements, are an integral part of their long-term economic and social dynamics.

What are earthquakes?

Earthquakes are a natural part of the processes that deform rocks on our planet. They occur when rocks break or slide suddenly on knife-like cuts ('faults') in response to the accumulation of forces ('stresses') in the outer part of the Earth. The energy responsible for these earthquakes ultimately comes from interactions between the rigid spherical caps ('plates') that form a mosaic on the Earth's surface, whose movement is related to how the Earth loses its interior heat. Most earthquakes occur on the boundaries between adjacent plates where they move against each other, the rocks involved first bending, then breaking, rather like a plank of wood. The movement in a single earthquake depends on its size, but even in the biggest earthquakes, the amount of slip on the fault is only a few metres; for example, about 20m in the great Sumatra event of 2004, which was the second biggest of the last 100 years, and to which seismologists assigned a magnitude of 9.2. Smaller earthquakes involve less slip on shorter faults, but are still capable of causing great damage, such as the catastrophic earthquake of 2003 at Bam in Iran (magnitude 6.5, and about twothousand times less energetic than the Sumatra earthquake), in which the fault slipped only about 2m. Earthquakes repeat on the same faults, but typically at intervals of hundreds or thousands of years, which is why several generations of people can live near an earthquake-inducing fault without experiencing an earthquake themselves. Although the movement in a single earthquake is small, repeated earthquakes on the same faults over the millions of years that characterize geological time lead to large offsets, ultimately creating the mountains and basins that form the landscape in earthquake-prone regions. In such places, the landscape itself thus contains clues to the earthquake activity, and one of the goals of modern research is to learn to read the signals it contains. Those signals are not always obvious: some earthquake faults do not rupture the Earth's surface at all, but are entirely contained underground, causing the surface to warp into folds or ridges instead. Recognizing the geomorphological expression of such 'blind' faults is a relatively new capability, dating back only to the 1980s. Although some structures can be ripped apart if they straddle a fault that breaks the surface, most damage in an earthquake occurs from the sound waves or vibrations that are radiated from the fault when it slips: the reverberations or shudders when you push a brick along a table-top are a reasonable analogue of this process.

From the simplified description above, it can be seen why historical research into earthquakes is so important. Modern scientific methods can study earthquake processes in extreme detail, but observations are limited to a few decades; a time-scale that is simply too short to provide a reliable picture of the long-term earthquake activity in a particular region, because the repeat-time of earthquakes on faults is so much longer. There are two ways to improve this situation: one is to learn to read the clues to previous earthquakes that are preserved in the landscape, and the other is to make use of the documented historical record which, in favourable circumstances, can extend the earthquake record back several centuries at least.

This contribution is principally concerned with exploiting the historical record. Not only can that record provide important geological information about earthquakes that occurred in the past, but it also greatly extends our knowledge of how earthquakes affect populations, which is the focus of this paper. The damage suffered is often the cause of impoverishment, but history also shows man's capacity to adapt to the earthquake hazard and to develop survival strategies in situations characterised by major environmental challenges.

Living with earthquakes

Important civilisations have developed over the millennia of human history in strongly seismic areas. Numerous inhabited sites, towns and villages have, in the course of time, been destroyed by seismic disasters, which have caused countless deaths, ruin and substantial economic damage. The earthquakes are located in well-known areas of the Earth's surface. In fig. 1 (see page 349) we have mapped the earthquakes of the Mediterranean, the Middle East and Asia recorded in the past forty years or so, 1964–2002. As can be seen, the earthquakes follow, and are ultimately responsible for the growth of, the mountains that run from Italy to China, and are caused by the northward motion of Africa, Arabia and India into Eurasia. The ancient E-W trade routes (shown as black lines in quoted fig. 1), follow the earthquake belts along the edges of the mountains, avoiding the inhospitable deserts adjoining them. Habitations along these routes have evolved from small villages, into towns, and now cities of a million or more people. Thus earthquakes which, in the past, killed a few hundreds or thousands, will now kill many more, when they recur.

And yet in the seismic areas of the planet there has been nearly everywhere a sort of cohabitation with earthquakes. Not always can such persistence be attributed to cultural ties and territorial considerations. At times the presence of water and the use of materials available for building determine this indissoluble bond between earthquake and inhabitants. Some examples come to us from Iran (Jackson, 2008). A global general view in Guidoboni & Ebel (2009, pp. 356–358).

Table 1. Earthquakes in Iran that killed more than 10,000 people over the last thousand years

	Date		Dead	Lat.	Long.	Place	Source
1008	04	27	16,000	34.6	47.4	Dinevar	MR01
1042	11	04	40,000	38.1	46.3	Tabriz	MR01
1336	10	22	25,000	24.7	59.7	Khwaf	MR01
1405	11	31	30,000	36.5	59.0	Nishapur	MR01
1641	02	05	13,000	27.9	46.1	Tabriz	Utsu
1667	11	18	12,000	37.2	57.5	Shirvan	Utsu
1721	04	26	40,000	37.9	46.1	SE Tabriz	MR01
1780	01	08	50,000	38.2	57.5	Tabriz	MR01
1824	06	25	20,000	29.8	46.0	Shiraz	MR01
1893	11	17	15,000	37.0	52.4	Quchan	MR01
1962	09	01	12,000	35.6	58.4	Buyin Zara	MR01
1968	08	31	12,000	34.0	59.0	Dasht-e-Bayaz	MR01
1978	09	16	20,000	33.3	57.4	Tabas*	MR01
1990	06	20	40,000	37.0	49.2	Rudbar	MR01
2003	12	26	40,000	29.0	58.3	Bam	Jackson

* The figure for Tabas includes other villages in the oasis; 11,000 died in the town itself.

Note that 5 of these 15 earthquakes occurred in the last 50 years.

Sources are MUNICH RE (MR01), UTSU (2002), and JACKSON (2006). Fatality figures are uncertain, especially for older earthquakes, and the ones here are generally lower estimates; discussions of the older events are in AMBRASEYS & MELVILLE (1982). Even for the 2003 Bam earthquake, the official fatality figure was 24,000, though most people believe it was considerably more.

The desert oasis of Tabas (table 1), properly known as Tabas-e-Golshan (lit. 'Tabas the flower garden'), visited by Marco Polo in the 13th century, was destroyed in 1978 by earthquake movement on a series of blind faults, whose associated folds are clearly visible in satellite imagery (fig. 2, see page 350). The water supply for Tabas comes from the adjacent range front by man-made underground tunnels, locally called *qanats*, which penetrate the nearby fold. The fold is also cut by the ephemeral Sardar river, which has incised a deep gorge through the rising ridge. In the past, the river caused problems of its own, when flash summer thunderstorms in the mountains produced great volumes of water that were trapped within the Sardar gorge and then discharged when the river emerged through the fold, to flood

Tabas. The local response, attributed to Shah Abbas (17th century) was to build a dam or water-gate where the river leaves the mountains; but one in which there is a vaulted arch at the base to allow the bed-load of the river through, while limiting the head of water to a height that was manageable. This ingenious, maintenance-free solution has stood for 350 years, and is still effective today.

After the devastating 1968 earthquake at Dasht-e-Bayaz in eastern Iran (magnitude 7.1, c.12,000 killed) several *qanats* were cut and offset by horizontal movement on the causative fault, which slipped up to 4 m in places. These *qanats* were then either abandoned or re-paired by reconnecting the offset channels. There is clear evidence on the ground, and in air photos, for earlier generations of *qanats* that had been offset and abandoned in previous earthquakes. Even more remarkable, are subsidiary, minor, *qanat* tunnels that had been dug long ago so as to feed into the main channels, and which followed precisely the line of the 1968 fault rupture. These side-tunnels exploit a change in water-table level across the fault, caused by the imperme-able clay ('fault-gouge') that builds up as successive earthquakes grind the rocks to a flour, to tap and increase the water flow into the main tunnels. Thus the local tunnel-builders were aware, and had exploited, the fault-related hydrology for a considerable time before the modern earthquake (and before seismologists or geologists understood any of this).

The town of Ferdows, destroyed in 1968 (1,000 killed), lies towards a fault-bounded range front. The houses are built of adobe-brick walls, with roofs either of mud-brick domes or of poplar logs laid horizontally and sealed with mud. Most of the roofs have a dis-tinctive blueish hue, caused by the clay that is used to seal against the winter rains. The clay that is used comes from a quarry at the foot of the range front, and is in fact the fault-gouge itself, made from ground volcanic rocks. The material is suitable for this purpose, being fine and relatively impermeable. Such blueish mud roofs are a common sight at range-front villages in eastern Iran.

Villages, megacities and population growth

For centuries, desert populations in Iran had established a way of living with earthquakes. Earthquake faulting, and the topography it produces, is largely responsible for the water resources and for the locations of habitations and agriculture, as well as of some building materials. Occasionally, earthquakes moved the faults, and villages were destroyed, but the repeat times of earthquakes on individual faults are measured in thousands of years and they are most unlikely to recur on a timescale relevant for human memory. When earthquakes do occur, the destruction, and particularly the mortality, can be shocking, because of the vulnerable local building styles. Thus in the town of Tabas in 1978, more than 80 % of the population (11,000 out of 13,000) were killed outright; at Bam in 2003 the figure was nearer 30 % (Berberian, 2005). Most places are, nonetheless, rebuilt and resettled because their location is, in the end, determined by where water is available and agriculture is possible. In the past, when rural populations were relatively small and dispersed, the frequent strong earthquakes of magnitude 6–7 that occur in Iran would kill typically a few hundred or thousand people. A modern example is the recent earthquake in the mountains near Zarand, in February 2005 (magnitude 6.4), which destroyed two villages, killing 500 (Talebian et al., 2006).

But the population and its density have grown strongly since the mid-20th century, an effect that can transform relatively moderate-sized earthquakes into catastrophes. As the villages have grown rapidly, building quality has remained vulnerable, though it may have changed from weak adobe houses to poorly-built multi-story apartment blocks. As a result, mortality rates remain appallingly high. Thus the isolated village of Sefidabeh (where a moderate-sized earthquake killed 6 in 1984) can become the large rural town as Tabas, or the small cities of Bam (40,000 killed in 2003; fig. 3a, see page 351) or Rudbar (40,000 killed in 1990), or the megacity of Tehran, which now has a daytime population of 10–12 million (fig. 3b, see page 351).

The case of Tehran is particularly instructive. This city is situated at the base of the Alborz mountain range front (fig. 4, see page 352), which is elevated by movement on an active earthquake-generating fault. Several other active faults are also situated nearby. In former times, the site was occupied by relatively small towns on a major trade route. These predecessors of modern Tehran were damaged or destroyed completely in earthquakes of probable magnitude ~7 in the 4th century BC, 855, 958, 1177 and 1830 (Ambraseys & Melville, 1982; Berberian & Yeats, 1999), but the number of killed was probably quite small by modern standards, perhaps measured in hundreds or thousands. The modern Tehran is a megacity that grew rapidly on the same site in the later 20th century. While the Tehran site was occupied by relatively small towns, the city of Tabriz was always bigger, more prosperous and far more important as a trade-route crossroads. Tabriz, a city today of 1,200,000 inhabitants, was devastated by major earthquakes on its nearby faults in 1721 (more than 40,000 killed) and 1780 (more than 50,000 killed), at a time when the population was a small fraction of today's. The message is quite clear: there is no sign that the concentration of population into large towns and cities in Iran is accompanied by a decrease in the proportion of deaths due to earthquakes. Many major towns and cities are situated adjacent to range fronts and faults, in places that made sense when they were initiated as agricultural settlements, and they retain that vulnerability to earthquakes. The situation is similar throughout much of the Mediterranean-Middle East-central Asia earthquake belt.

Seismic destruction and number of deaths

The number of deaths, from the historical and social standpoints, can reasonably be considered to be a strong indicator of the impact of earthquakes on a population. Indeed a high number of deaths also indicates a high level of destruction. Above all, in countries with an economy based prevalently on primitive agricultural methods (as used to be the case in the pre-industrial economies), today called 'poor', earthquakes can bring about a further lowering in the standards of living in the short and medium term. This is because earthquakes do not only destroy buildings, but also the exchange and services networks that make social life possible (schools, trade, roadways, craftsmen's workshops, communications, etc.). Reconstruction requires substantial economic means, and within relatively short timescales; means that are hardly ever available today in many non-industrialised seismic areas of the world. Earthquake disasters can therefore trigger off processes of relentless impoverishment, if they hit areas that are already poor and marginal.

Thus we come to the 2005 Pakistan earthquake (magnitude 7.5) which destroyed the Himalayan town of Muzaffrabad, killing 86,000 people. The fault responsible for this earthquake is part of a fault system that has thrust Tibet over India and is ultimately responsible for building the Himalayan range itself. The part that moved in 2005 was a 100 km section of a much longer system of faults that stretches E-W for 3,000 km, from NW Pakistan to Assam (fig. 5, see page 353), all of which moves because India and Tibet converge at about 20 mm per year. This figure shows the locations of earlier earthquakes on this fault system, some of them much larger than the earthquake in 2005. Three such earthquakes happened in the last century, in 1905, 1934 and 1950. Each one killed a few thousand people, but since those times the population of the Ganges basin has increased dramatically, and it is now one of the most densely inhabited regions on Earth, with many cities of over a million people. The flat plain of the Ganges valley contains thick sediment sequences containing water-saturated sand and mud washed off the rising Himalaya and deposited by the river. When shaken in strong earthquakes, the sediments liquefy, releasing water which spouts to the surface as springs and sand 'volcanoes', as was observed in the earthquake of 1934. The effect is similar to walking on a sandy beach just washed by an incoming wave: water-saturated sand 'flows' easily through one's toes.

A large earthquake on the Himalayan front will cause such effects over a substantial part of the Ganges valley, liquefying an area perhaps 100–200 km long and several tens of km from the mountain front. The consequences of such liquefaction for multistory buildings is to make them sink, then collapse (as was observed widely in the 1964 Niigata earthquake in Japan). An important difference between the situations in 1934 and today is that the population throughout the Ganges valley is now not only much bigger, but is concentrated in large cities and living in poorly-constructed multi-storey apartment blocks. Of particular concern is the obvious 'gap' in earthquakes along the Himalayan front north of Delhi, where no major event has occurred since at least 1500 and where the concentration of major cities is particularly dense.

There is little doubt that earthquakes which once killed a few thousand would now kill many more, perhaps hundreds of thousands or more, when they recur in the future, as is inevitable. Thus the earthquake at Muzaffrabad in 2005, though by no means the biggest known earthquake along the Himalayan front and certainly not in the most densely populated part of it, killed many more people than any of the previous known earthquakes in fig. 5 (see page 353). The lesson of Muzaffrabad is that there is worse to come.

Case history. Earthquakes and poverty: the Calabria region (southern Italy) in the last three centuries

Calabria is the Italian region with the lowest economic level and the highest emigration rate. Its surface area, 15,000 km^2 (5 % of the national territory), is mostly mountainous. Calabria is situated between the Tyrrhenian and the Ionian Seas, separated from Sicily by the Strait of Messina, a channel that is about three kilometres wide (fig. 6, see page 354).

Table 2. Earthquakes in Calabria (southern Italy) from the mid-18th century to 20th

date			h	lat	long	I0	Imax	Me	Epicentral zone
1743	12	07	00:05	38 42	16 22	VIII	VIII–IX	5.7	Central Calabria (Serre)
1744	03	21	20:30	39 02	16 47	VIII	IX	5.7	Crotonese
1767	07	14	01:05	39 22	16 17	VIII–IX	VIII–IX	6.0	Cosentino
1783	02	05	12:00	38 18	15 58	XI	XI	7.0	Calabria
1783	02	06	00:20	38 13	15 38	VIII–IX	IX–X	6.2	Southern Calabria Messina
1783	02	07	13:10	38 35	16 12	X–XI	X–XI	6.6	Calabria
1783	03	01	01:40	38 46	16 18	IX	IX–X	5.9	Central Calabria
1783	03	28	18:55	38 47	16 28	XI	XI	7.0	Calabria
1791	10	13	01:20	38 38	16 16	IX	IX	6.0	Central Calabria
1832	03	08	18:30	39 05	16 55	X	X	6.5	Crotonese
1835	10	12	22:35	39 20	16 18	IX	X	5.9	Cosentino
1836	04	25	00:20	39 34	16 44	IX	X	6.3	Northern Calabria
1854	02	12	17:50	39 15	16 18	X	X	6.1	Cosentino
1870	10	04	16:55	39 13	16 20	IX–X	X	6.1	Cosentino
1887	12	03	03:45	39 34	16 13	VIII	IX	5.5	Northern Calabria
1894	11	16	17:52	38 17	15 52	IX	IX	6.2	Northern Calabria
1905	09	08	01:43	38 40	16 04	X	X–XI	6.8	Calabria
1907	10	23	20:28	38 08	16 00	VIII–IX	IX	6.0	Southern Calabria
1908	12	28	04:20	38 09	15 41	XI	XI	7.1	Southern Calabria Messina
1913	06	28	08:53	39 32	16 14	VIII	VIII–IX	5.7	Northern Calabria
1947	05	11	06:32	38 39	16 31	VIII	IX	5.7	Central Calabria
1975	01	16	00:09	38 07	15 39	VII-VIII	VII-VIII	5.3	Strait of Messina
1978	03	11	19:20	38 01	15 59	VIII	VIII	5.5	Southern Calabria

I0 = Epicentral intensity

Imax = Maximum intensity;

Me = Equivalent magnitude value

Source: *CFTI4 MED*, see Guidoboni et al. (2007-).

In spite of its attempts to develop as a tourist area, Calabria is still a poor region, even though it belongs to a developed country. There are many causes responsible for this situation: the nature of the landscape (rugged mountains, isolated villages, centuries-long lack of roads, etc.); the scarce population density; the region's role as a peripheral area, first in the Kingdom of Naples, then in the Kingdom of Italy (since 1860) and up until now; and a shortage of investment and market activity. Earthquakes must be added to these historical and economic factors. Indeed, this region's past has been dramatically shaped by extensive and frequent destruction (table 2). The analysis of the history of Calabria highlights the perhaps critical importance of the area's seismic activity (Guidoboni, 2008).

Calabria is part of an earthquake belt that stretches from North Africa, through Sicily, along the Apennines and into the Alps. The Calabria-Apennine mountain chain in particular produces frequent earthquakes in the magnitude 6–7 range, and in the last three centuries Calabria has had more strong earthquakes than all the rest of Italy. Such seismic destruction has contributed to increase poverty and underdevelopment. Even when, in the last few decades of the 18th century, ambitious projects for reconstruction were made by the central government of Naples, the strong local territorial powers of Calabria, of a feudal kind, obstructed and slowed down the development of this region.

The history of Calabria in the last three centuries shows that when the elapsed time between one destructive earthquake and the next is too short to allow for a real recovery of the local economy, poverty arises and becomes stable, triggering off population migration, which further impoverishes the economic and social situation. From this point of view, it can be said that each reconstruction in Calabria has been a 'poor' one, as there was not the chance to rebuild properly, something that could have saved human lives and resources from the subsequent earthquakes. Perhaps excluding the last reconstruction in 1908, most of the residents in Calabria have always rebuilt with a view to achieving immediate survival.

The data provided by historical seismology allow us to know about the seismicity of Calabria with a good level of detail and with quite a complete historical coverage starting from the 17th century (compared to the preceding period back to the ancient world, for which the data are more sporadic). But here we shall only take into consideration the last three centuries, from around the mid-18th century until the mid-20th century.[1] For this period the earthquakes that

---

1 The data relating to the earthquakes mentioned here are contained, unless otherwise stated, in the *Catalogue of Strong Earthquakes in Italy 461 B.C. – 1997*: see GUIDOBONI et al. (2007-).

have caused serious damage are 152. Figure 7 (see page 355) shows all the known epicentres in black and those of the earthquakes considered here in red.

The dramatic 18th century in Calabria

The year 1743 is sadly known in the chronicles of southern Italy as a year of plague and earthquakes. While the plague spread across Sicily and attempts were made to create a cordon sanitaire to prevent the spread in Calabria, on December 1743, an earthquake struck central Calabria and in particular the area of the Serre (in the low part of the Sila massif), just south of the isthmus of Marcellinara. The worst hit villages were Olivadi, Capistrano, Chiaravalle Centrale, San Vito sullo Ionio and Vallelonga; a further sixteen villages suffered substantial damage.

Just three months later, on 21st March 1744, another earthquake hit Calabria.[2] Although the effects were serious and the area of damage extensive, this earthquake had until now remained unknown to historical seismology, and had only been highlighted by recent studies. The most serious effects were detected at Roccabernarda, where two thirds of the houses collapsed and the others were seriously damaged. Collapses and serious damage in houses and ecclesiastical buildings occurred in a further six localities, including the city of Catanzaro, where some churches were also badly damaged. Less serious damage was detected in a further twelve locations.

On 14th July 1767 the valley of the Crati, north of Cosenza, was hit. In that year there had been a poor wheat harvest and the production of silk had been very low, elements that alone had caused a serious indigence in the population. The earthquake destroyed, in addition to the houses of at least six villages, also the food stocks and the livestock, lost under the debris of the stables and the barns.

---

2 This earthquake is analysed in detail, with the bibliography of the archival sources, in E. GUIDOBONI & D. MARIOTTI, 2005. *Revisione e integrazione di ricerca riguardante il massimo terremoto storico della Puglia: 20 febbraio 1743*, RPT SGA no. 272, October 2005, unpublished report, available from the central library of the Istituto Nazionale di Geofisica e Vulcanologia, Rome and from the Milan section.

Sixteen years later, between February and March 1783, a long and devastating earthquake sequence, comprising five strong shocks succeeding one another in the space of about fifty days, represented a major historical phase for the economic, social and cultural life of Calabria.[3] It was the greatest seismic event since the earthquake of Lisbon in 1755 and as that one did, caused disquiet in European cultural circles. On 5th February 1783 the first earthquake started; there then followed the earthquakes of 6th and 7th February, 1st March and 28th March. The overlapping effects of each earthquake, distributed along the Apennine chain in the north-easterly direction, produced a large area of destruction. The five main earthquakes were preceded and followed by several hundreds of minor shocks, which had a devastating cumulative effect over a territory of several thousand square km, lasting for several years.

The cumulative picture of the damage is huge and extraordinarily serious: the destructive effects, accompanied by extensive ground rupture in landslides and disruption of water systems, affected a vast area comprising all of southern Calabria, from the isthmus of Marcellinara to the Strait. Across the Strait, Sicily was hit as well in the area of Messina. (fig. 8, see page 356). In 182 villages of Calabria the destruction was almost complete; thirtythree of these had to be reconstructed in different sites. In the most damaged areas, out of a population of a little over about 400,000 inhabitants, the victims numbered over 35,000 (about 8 % of the whole resident population).

The seismic events of 1783 shook the existing social order at its foundations, an order that had already shown signs of crisis in the previous years. Elements of unrest in public order and the spreading of epidemics, accompanied by a general conviction that earthquakes

---

3 The five strong earthquakes of 1783 are documented by countless sources of various types: administrative acts, treatises, reports of scholars, literati and scientists of the day: see GUIDOBONI et al. (2007-). This vast production of writings is due to the very strong impact of earthquakes across the whole of southern society and in European culture. The historical events in 18th century Calabria before this seismic disaster have also been studied by Italian historiography: fundamental are the studies of Augusto Placanica, who, besides investigating the cultural reactions to the earthquake, also published a substantial amount of contemporary documentation. For the bibliography and the analysis of the sources, see GUIDOBONI et al. (2007-).

represented a point-of-no-return, represented some of the elements characterising the social imprint left by the earthquakes on the society of the day. These amounted to conditioning that acted not only in the immediate aftermath, but also in the long term, interweaving with the decisive political events at the turn of the 18th century.[4]

The effects on the natural environment were so important and spectacular that they became the subject of specific surveys by the scientists and naturalists of the day: landslides, cleavages, slips, collapses, detachments and lake formation, as well as the effects of liquefaction, for the first time became the subject of drawings and surveys (fig. 9, see page 357). Entire hills, falling into the valleys, had in some cases dragged houses with them and obstructed the water ways, thereby creating hundreds of new dykes. On the Tyrrhenian coast, near Scilla, in the night between 5th and 6th February, an enormous landslide occurred off the mount Campallà, and gave rise to a substantial tsunami: the water invaded the coast violently, penetrating the hinterland for over 160 metres, causing new destructions and 1,300 deaths.

The enormous scope of the destruction also affected important urban centres for the political and economic and military life of the Kingdom of Naples, such as Reggio Calabria and Catanzaro. For the Bourbon government of Naples this seismic disaster represented a chance to attempt the redistribution of resources, above all the landholdings. A complex process of generalised expropriation of goods was enacted regarding Church properties in Calabria, planned by the Bourbon government in June 1784, through the setting up of the *Cassa Sacra*. From the administration and the sale of the ecclesiastic assets the aim was to collect the resources for the reconstruction and at the same time to initiate, through the land redistribution, a phase of development for the areas that had for centuries been situated on the margins of the social and economic life of the kingdom. The aim of reabsorbing the upheaval and the laceration of the social fabric did not, however, achieve the hoped-for effects, although the causes of the backwardness and the penury of Calabria had been well identified

---

4 See, in particular, PLACANICA (1985).

by the intellectuals and the reformers of the day, who indicated: I) the permanence of feudal structures (83 % of the Calabria territory was subjected to baronage); II) absenteeism of the great landlords; III) decay of the territory's agricultural, woodland and grazing facilities; IV) the expense of the central fiscal system, and, last but not least, V) the weakness of the State *vis-à-vis* the baronial power. These factors were not greatly affected during the lengthy reconstruction phase.

To these elements were added the exodus of the population from the countryside towards the more important inhabited areas: in subsequent years these migratory shifts accentuated the already serious problems of lack of manpower in the rural sector in the marginal areas.

The mortality and the disastrous effects on the economic and social life, consequent to the seismic events in 1783, first of all accentuated then contributed to repressing the demographic development of Calabria compared with the other regions of the Kingdom of Naples, at least until the mid-19th century. Not even the economic and social life of the Calabrian cities returned to the pace and the characteristics that preceded these seismic events. In some centres, the direct and indirect consequences of the earthquakes caused a strong productive crisis: at Palmi the wool and silk industries were seriously damaged and after the earthquake there was an epidemic fever. At Pizzo, a few people died in the ruins of their homes, but subsequently a serious epidemic caused many deaths. Some villages, such as Seminara, Oppido Mamertina and Briatico were ravaged by another epidemic fever that spread in the summer of 1783, which alone caused nearly 19,000 deaths.

In the initial dispositions of the central government, the reconstruction should have constituted a significant improvement for the affected area, both as regards the urban lay-out of the houses, and the characteristics and the quality of the materials of the buildings. Indeed, as had never previously occurred in the past, academics and engineers on surveillance missions in the destroyed areas, related the damage effects to the existing building types. They noted that two characteristics, apparently antithetical, in the local way of building, constituted just as many factors of weakness: on the one hand, there was an excessive height in the buildings, a heaviness in the load-bearing structures with decorative elements, an excessive weight in the rafters of the roofs, and insufficient foundations; on the other hand, as in a tragic *pendant*, the building materials were poor (clay, mud, straw, unseasoned timber) and the construction techniques were judged to be very poor. These elements were combined with other characteristics common to the various inhabited areas, such as the excessive narrowness of the roads, the strong gradients on which the village buildings were erected, and the absence of open spaces inside the inhabited areas: all elements that had worsened the effects of those earthquakes.

Thanks to the reports provided by technicians and scientists of the day, the central government decided to adopt building regulations to be followed in the reconstruction phase. The aim was to impose the compliance with the specific building techniques, inspired by earthquake-resistant criteria. The plans of entire villages were redrawn, where the size of the new inhabited area was supposed to be proportionate to the number of inhabitants. Furthermore, the plan of the village was supposed to develop in an orthogonal reticulum in order to safeguard the regular pattern of the urban design. For the buildings the adoption of a particular construction technique was demanded of a "*baraccato*" kind: this consisted in a load-bearing wooden framework, containing the brickwork structure. In addition, the supra-elevation of the buildings was forbidden, limited to just one inhabitable floor.

However, such innovative dispositions immediately clashed with the actual availability and the local reality, and many of these measures remained only on paper. The lack of wood in many damaged areas required construction systems that were not based on timber. Owing to the chronic shortage of materials and their very high prices, rubble was used, recovering timber, iron, stones or even pillaging them from falling buildings. In the subsequent years, the protracted reconstruction times and the social conflict that accompanied it, contributed to depressing the social and economic scenario. As the years passed the constraints initially set by the government eased, and solutions inspired by a rationale of compromise were adopted, and the rules were completely ignored. The effects of such neglect and carelessness later became dramatically apparent when in the subsequent decades other earthquakes occurred.

Indeed, a few years later, on 13th October 1791, a strong shock hit mountain towns and villages, already devastated in 1783. Central and southern Calabria was hit, in particular the internal Apennine villages: there were collapses and ruins in around thirty locations; cracks to the walls and lighter damage occurred in a further thirtyfive villages.

The long-suffering Calabria economy, based on subsistence agriculture, was unable to deal with this chronic emergency. Most of the population lived in precarious hygienic conditions in wooden sheds (however, this element probably managed to limit the number of victims in 1791). The government intervention for this reconstruction was limited to the mere distribution of wooden planks to the homeless, for the repairs to the damaged houses or for the construction of new sheds. In the same period a flood wreaked fresh havoc.

19th century: seven earthquakes in a period of economic crisis and political change

Even the following century for Calabria was a period afflicted by strong earthquakes. In the 1830s the Bourbon kingdom was hit by a serious political and economic crisis, which made it ever less capable of intervening actively after a seismic disaster.

<u>1832 earthquake:</u> A new earthquake struck Calabria on 8th March 1832, in the north-eastern area of the presentday province of Catanzaro, causing very serious destruction to a dozen or so villages, three of which (Cutro, Mesoraca and Rocca di Netro) had to be reconstructed on sites other than the pre-existing ones. In a further forty localities many buildings either collapsed or became uninhabitable. In Catanzaro the shock caused the collapse of many houses and damaged nearly all the others, which mostly became unfit for human habitation. In the city, badly performed repair work following the damage by the 1783 earthquakes enhanced the damage. According to the documents of the Calabria authorities (the 'Intendenza'), most of the new damage was due to the inadequate repair work carried out on the buildings damaged in 1783.

The effects of the tsunami were also substantial: the water invaded a stretch almost 30 km long of the coast running between Steccato and Marina di Catanzaro, then a semi-marshland area. Furthermore, the earthquake triggered off landslides and slips. Rain and strong wind further aggravated the static conditions of the damaged buildings and the discomfort for the populace forced to live outdoors.

1835 earthquake: Just three years later, on 12th October 1835 the upper valley of the Crati north-east of Cosenza was hit. The damage was particularly serious in the locations that rose up on the alluvial grounds: Castiglione Cosentino was completely destroyed; in another three villages most of the houses collapsed and the remainder were uninhabitable. In a dozen or so other localities there were collapses or serious cracks to the buildings. Although few buildings fell to pieces in Cosenza, nearly all of them were substantially cracked; many remained in danger of collapse in the numerous aftershocks that followed. The villages affected in the Valle Cosentino had between 1,000 and 2,000 inhabitants, and were characterised by a traditional, fragile rural economy, so that the disruption from the earthquake contributed to making the poor living standards even worse. The city of Cosenza, thanks to its urban lay-out and its greater economic potential, recovered more quickly than the outlying villages.

1836 earthquake: The earthquake that hit the Cosentino, and in particular the area around Rossano, followed just a few months later, on 25th April 1836. The village of Crosia was almost completely destroyed; at Calopezzati most of the houses collapsed. The building stock of Rossano was heavily hit: out of a total of 1,538 buildings, 370 (24 %) were destroyed; 392 (26 %) were damaged beyond repair and the other 776 (50 %) suffered repairable damage. In another 15 localities on the Ionian side of the province of Cosenza there were landslides and cracks to buildings. In the city of Cosenza and in some villages on the Tyrrhenian coast, already hit by the earthquake on 12th October 1835, there was slight damage, but to buildings that were already dangerously unstable (fig. 10, see page 358).

The area most hit by this earthquake was a fertile agricultural zone: the widespread destruction of the infrastructure (warehouses, oil-mills, depots and stables) caused the near-complete loss of the produce already prepared the previous year and of a large number of livestock. This event produced an economic crisis, which public intervention did not do enough to redress. The only public measures drew upon charity funds and were limited to the most urgent interventions of the earliest emergency. No fiscal measures were planned, nor were other forms of financial support: this increased the number of indigent people and significantly increased poverty levels, already widespread in Calabria in those years. The economic burden of the reconstruction had strong repercussions on the local economies for over twenty years.

1854 earthquake: Again the Cosentino area, together with the whole city of Cosenza, were violently hit by the earthquake on 2nd December 1854 as well. In Cosenza, that then had about 14,000 inhabitants (today it is a small city with a population of 73,000 inhabitants), there was extensive destruction. Over fifty or so towns and villages of its provinces had their houses so damaged or cracked as to make their stability for living purposes an abstract concept for a whole generation. The demographic size of the municipalities hit was between 1,000 and 4,000 people.

In the whole area in which the earthquake caused the most serious effects there opened large and deep cracks in the ground and there were slips and landslides. The frequency of news relating to phenomena of crumbling or detachment makes us suppose that the violence of the shock triggered and accelerated extensive slope instabilities, due to the intense deforestation of the previous decades. The intense and continuous rainfall of the two months previous to the earthquake had probably made the phenomenon worse.

In those days Calabria had very few roadways and those of the interior were practically just mule tracks; the rivers had no bridges and were crossed on horseback: the difficult transport conditions also made organising aid very difficult.

1870 earthquake: It was again the province of Cosenza that was overwhelmed by another very strong earthquake on 4th October 1870: many villages situated between the valleys of the Crati and the Savuto, such as Mangone and Cellara, were almost completely destroyed. Total or partial collapses and large cracks left the inhabitants of about twenty other villages homeless, including the centres of the Sila and the Ionian and the Tyrrhenian coasts. Overall in the whole province of Cosenza, 1,600 houses either collapsed or became uninhabitable. Many of these buildings had been seriously damaged by the earthquake of 1854 and had been repaired inadequately (for example, the cracks had been summarily filled in with layers of quicklime).

The area hit was characterised by a very modest industrial activity, by an agriculture linked to backward systems and by an insufficient or non-existent road network. It is also necessary to remember that the unification of the Kingdom of Italy, to which Calabria was annexed along with the whole of the Bourbon Kingdom in 1860, had not had a positive impact on the economy of the area, causing a serious crisis in the weak industrial and agricultural apparatus, incapable of standing up to the competition of the northern Italian and European industries and the specialised agricultural activities. This context of widespread economic backwardness had repercussions also on the quality of the local building stock and on its maintenance, thereby increasing the vulnerability of the buildings.

1887 earthquake: In the valley of the river Crati there was a strong earthquake on 3rd December 1887: the most serious damage occurred in some centres of the mid-valley of the Crati; the most damaged village was Bisignano. The damage effects were diverse: an important role was played by the presence of different types of houses, due to a significant social stratification also within the poor villages themselves. At Roggiano Gravina, for example, the poorer farm labourers lived in huts, one beside the other, whose walls were made of wicker or interwoven wood, and the roofs were made of a layer of clayey earth mixed with straw. These houses had little damage and above all few victims. The most serious damage instead occurred in the small buildings made of brickwork belonging to the medium-lower classes of the villages: they were old and badly built houses, with heavy roofs, and with inadequate or lacking foundations.

The reconstruction did not channel economic resources: the government decreed some tax breaks and made available to the local administrations only modest subsidies and about twenty lots of land for the most damaged families of Bisignano. As there was a strong disproportion between available resources and needs, the lots were put to the draw, an element that caused much discontent and strong social unrest.

<u>1894 earthquake:</u> After years of earthquakes in the central area, it was southern Calabria that was violently hit on 16th November 1894. The most destructive effects extended over an area of 80 km² to the north-western slopes of the Aspromonte. The dead numbered about a hundred with a thousand injured, but the number of victims could have been higher if the shocks prior to the strongest one had not alarmed the population. The buildings were greatly hit: according to the official government data, in 124 municipalities of southern Calabria, out of a total of about 105,000 houses, 35,639 (equal to 33.9 %) were damaged; in particular, 916 houses (0.9 %) collapsed completely, 3,527 (3.3 %) suffered partial collapses, 10,488 (10 %) were seriously cracked and 20,708 (19.7 %) were slightly cracked. In Reggio Calabria nearly all of the buildings suffered extensive cracks to the walls.

Besides the material damage, this earthquake paralysed every sort of productive activity, in the crafts and in agriculture. In spite of the detailed reports of the scientific world on the analysis of the damage and on how to rebuild (the first of contemporary Italy), there were no legislative and administrative measures to foster the social and economic life that had been so deeply disrupted (fig. 11 and 12, see pages 359–360).

Two strong earthquakes before the seismic disaster in 1908

It is fair to say, however, that the worst was yet to come. The new century, the 20th century, began for Calabria with a series of earthquakes, which culminated in the 1908 disaster of the Strait of Messina, and continued further with the earthquake of 1913. It can be said that in the first two decades of the 20th century nearly all of the Calabrese building stock was undermined, making it unstable and dangerous to live in an enormous number of villages and even in the chief towns, like Reggio Calabria. In a very brief summary, here are the dramatic phases.

<u>1905 earthquake:</u> The earthquake on 8th September 1905 fell upon the current province of Vibo Valenza and partly upon that of Catanzaro, seriously damaging 326 villages, inhabited by 1,189,300 people altogether, and causing in a few seconds 560 deaths and making 300,000 people homeless. More than 8,000 houses were so damaged as to have to be completely knocked down as they were beyond repair; the ones that needed to be propped up were nearly 7,500. Only the good constructions had withstood the earthquake impact. The houses of the so-called "Americans", that is, the better off emigrants, built with suitable materials and in compliance with more adequate building rules, were definitely more resistant than the others, even in the zones closer to the epicentral area.

This earthquake occurred in a period of strong economic depression: the unfavourable rural situation in the last decades of the 19th century and the subsequent protectionist tariffs (1887) had not allowed for a productive development, so the Calabrese agriculture had remained within a traditional framework. In this economic context, the earthquake had devastating effects for the population: one year after the disaster thousands of families were reduced to starvation and were desperate owing to their homeless state. The great landholders either had had their homes repaired by the civil and military engineers or had abandoned them. The small landowners did not have the means to repair the damaged houses and lived with families of up to 8 or 10 people in very few precariously patched up rooms. In those years many very poor farmhands from Calabria abandoned their villages. Those who remained tried to repair the damaged houses by reusing the same materials as before, extracted from the rubbles and by using the same building systems, generally the least expensive. From one earthquake to the next the weakness and the vulnerability of the Calabrese building stock had been a chronic problem.

<u>1907 earthquake:</u> Only two years later, on 23rd October 1907, an earthquake violently shook the villages of the southern Ionian coast of Calabria: at Ferruzzano, Sant'Ilario dello Ionio, Palizzi, Pietrapennata and Casalnuovo, the damage overall concerned between 30 and 50 % of the building stock. But also the northern Tyrrhenian slopes of the Aspromonte, in particular in the municipalities of Sinopoli

and Oppido Mamertina, and in the immediate hinterland of Reggio Calabria, there were collapses and cracks to the walls. In the province of Reggio Calabria alone, according to official data, the houses that had collapsed or needed to be rebuilt were 1,505, the ones that had become uninhabitable 7,147 and a further 10,994 were damaged less seriously. In the province of Catanzaro, the earthquake caused damage in localities already hit two years before, where many buildings had not yet been repaired (fig. 13, see page 361).

1908: the large earthquake of the Strait of Messina

Just little more than a year from this latest event, on 28th December 1908, a seismic event occurred that left an indelible mark not only on the overall situation of the destroyed areas – southern Calabria and the Messina area – but also in the conscience and the historical memory of Italy. This earthquake, considered to be one of the events with the highest magnitude in the Italian seismic history (7.1), from the standpoint of the most serious effects affected an area of 6,000 km². The shock was recorded by 103 Italian and foreign seismic stations and was felt by people over a huge area. In many Calabria localities the destruction was the dramatic and inevitable result of the overlapping of the effects of the earthquakes that had occurred in the previous years. In Calabria, the 1908 earthquake had destructive effects across an area comprising all the slopes of the Aspromonte massif, in particular in 25 villages. The area within which the effects of the shock were terrible was very large. Reggio Calabria was almost completely destroyed, but its reconstruction was only started some ten years afterwards, in the midst of indescribable difficulties and a near-total precariousness in living conditions.

In Messina (Sicily) about 42 % of the population fell victim to the earthquake; in Reggio Calabria about 27 % (12,000): overall, across the affected territory, both Calabrese and Sicilian, the victims numbered over 65,000. A tsunami of a huge size for the Italian shores struck eastern Sicily, from Messina to Catania, and the Calabrese coastline. Waves between 6 and 12 metres in height swept away even the rubble of the buildings that had previously collapsed, alone causing over 2,000 deaths (fig. 14, see page 361).

As regards the economic damage, several parties compared this earthquake to a lost war, to a great national emergency. The earthquake devastated urbanised regions, characterised by modern dynamics of economic and commercial growth, as well as areas marginalised from the commercial and industrial flows, and the specialised agricultural activities. It was in the latter poorer context, in particular, that the earthquake reduced the already scarce opportunities of coming out of the isolation and the economic backwardness. In the more productive circumstances, the economic recovery was more rapid. For example, in the industrial areas of Villa San Giovanni, Cannitello and Santa Caterina, where there were silk-working factories, which had been seriously damaged by the earthquake, as early as 1910, 62 % of the productive potential had been re-established. Instead, for the agricultural sector, and for the classes dependent upon it, the earthquake meant a sort of obligated reconversion to other activities.

Waves of emigration followed this seismic destruction. There were phenomena of internal migration, as well as migration towards other countries, above all Canada and the United States. The destroyed villages became repopulated, even if very slowly, because they offered job opportunities for the impoverished populations from the inner villages. A widespread loss of cultural identity characterised these populations for decades. The stability of daily life, made of human ties and habits, was broken for dozens of years, and for many Calabrese, forever.

The Italian government passed a series of laws that outlined the normative framework within which the institutional response to the emergency was then organised. There was no lack of resources to deal with the consequences of the earthquake, also in consideration of the fact that Italian society was going through a laboured transition phase towards the modern industrial economy. The period 1896–1908 was indeed characterised by an annual growth in industrial production of 6.7 %, the highest in the period 1881–1913. Fiscal incentives and special funds were created for the reconstruction, but the speculation that accompanied this enormous flow of public funds, in some cases, even aggravated the population's hardships.

After 1908 until today

Northern Calabria had only been brushed by the great event in 1908, but on 28th June 1913 an earthquake struck the northen part of the province of Cosenza, substantially damaging the building stock of other 30 villages. There were no deaths, but the building stock was profoundly undermined. The most hit location was Roggiano Gravina, where there were numerous total collapses, serious lesions in nearly all the houses, roofs fell in; collapses of houses and damage also hit some other villages. Indeed, the government did not adopt measures addressed to funding the repair work, but limited itself to delivering a very modest subsidy, which was reserved only to people completely deprived of their means of economic sustenance.

As only outlying (from the economic and political standpoints) areas were concerned, and no important urban centres were involved, the State's attention and that of the national press very soon shifted away from the problem of this reconstruction. Just a few months after the earthquake, even the official deeds failed to record the most significant decisions. Thus, the repairs to the damage for many years weighed upon a very poor rural economy, also because of the lack of public measures and the pre-existing economic precariousness of the local administration.

The widespread damage to the houses, even if not such as to require demolitions, created a general situation of uprooting and disruption in the population's everyday life. The reconstruction often came to a halt before the lack of building materials suited to reinforcing the cracked and unstable buildings (rafters, tiles, bricks).

After a truce lasting a few decades (but in the meantime there had been the two world wars: 1914–18 and 1943–45), on 11th May 1947 a strong earthquake struck the Ionian side of central Calabria, at the level of the Squillace Gulf, seriously damaging over 20 locations in the province of Catanzaro. The worst hit village was Isca sullo Ionio, where about two-thirds of the dwellings were declared unsafe. Hundreds of families ended up homeless.

The impact on the social and economic conditions of the damaged villages was accentuated by the precarious economic situation in the post-Second World War period. The reconstruction works, funded by the State were conceived of as an instrument of intervention upon the labour market, as the whole of the affected area already had a very high unemployment rate: the building reconstruction work thus set itself structural economic goals, which were resolved only to a small extent.

After these earthquakes, two more events have struck Calabria, although to a much lesser extent than the previous ones: on 16th January 1975 and 11th March 1978. There were cracks and signs of instability above all in the buildings built after the 1908 earthquake. After these more recent events no important seismic activity has been recorded in Calabria, in other words capable of causing substantial damage.

Public assistance, low productivity, devastating seismic destruction today add up to a worrying legacy for Calabria, which slows down the economic development and depresses the whole regional area. The role of the seismic disasters appears to be historically strong. In the graph in fig. 15 (see page 362) the known earthquakes in this region are shown starting from the year 1600 (table 2): in this case too, owing to the region's rather particular position from the geophysical standpoint, which we mentioned at the beginning of the paper, we can suppose that, unfortunately, the future will not be very different from the recent past.

Earthquake vulnerability in the modern world

The exposure of villages and towns to the damage of seismic disasters is strong even in relatively developed countries, as has been seen in the historical case of Calabria, but it is even more dramatic in the poorer and more populous parts of the planet. The link between how and where people live and earthquakes is particularly dramatic in Iran, Pakistan, India, but for many other parts of the great earthquake and mountain belts that run from Italy to China, the situation is similar.

Throughout this region the topography is largely created by fault movement in earthquakes, ultimately the result of the ongoing collision between the Eurasian plate and the African, Arabian and Indian plates to the south. Large tracts of this area are either low, barren, inhospitable deserts, or high, inaccessible and also inhospitable plateau, such as Tibet. Habitations concentrate around the edges of these regions, at the range fronts, because their locations are on trade routes, are of strategic importance controlling access, or are near water supplies. Many habitations have been destroyed in past earthquakes when their populations were relatively small, but have now grown into very large, and very vulnerable, cities.

The relentless rise in global population and in the growth of megacities in the developing world is discussed in a number of papers by Bilham (1996, 1998, 2004). As he points out, the existence of earthquake building codes has had little effect in many of the countries concerned, and the mortality remains shockingly high: for example, 20–35 % of the population (between 240,000 and 500,000) died in the 1976 Tangshan earthquake in China. Half the world's megacities of more than 10 million inhabitants are in locations vulnerable to earthquakes (fig. 16a, see page 363), and the reason we have not yet had an extreme catastrophe in one of them is probably because they have only been exposed for a short time (about 50 years) compared with typical recurrence times of earthquakes (hundreds or thousands of years).

Figure 16b (see page 363) shows the most damaging earthquakes, in terms of lives lost, of the last 1000 years. Accurate fatality figures for historical earthquakes, and even for modern extreme events like the 1976 Tangshan and 2004 Sumatra earthquakes, are notoriously difficult to obtain. Figure 16b (see page 363) is an updated and amended version of an earlier figure from Bilham (1996), with most of the fatality data from Munich Re (1991), and updated for recent events. The map simply distinguishes earthquakes that killed more than 10,000 people from those that killed more than 100,000. At that level of discrimination it is probably accurate, in spite of the uncertainty in the precise figures. These two maps are alarming because they highlight the vulnerability of cities in the Mediterranean-Middle East-central Asia earthquake belt, as well as the coastal regions of south and central America and Indonesia, for which tsunamis pose an additional risk, as demonstrated by the event in Sumatra in 2004 (283,000 deaths). Many of the red dots indicate earthquakes that killed more than 10,000 people at times when the cities involved had populations far lower than they have today. Of the 113 earthquakes included in figure 16b over the last 1,000 years, 34 occurred in the last 100 years alone.

Another way of viewing the situation is with the histogram in fig. 17 (see page 364), which shows the number of earthquakes killing more than 10,000 (grey) and 50,000 (black) per century for the last 1000 years. These data suffer from the scarcity of information for the more distant centuries, due to the lack of historical sources or the lack of research. Furthermore, it is necessary to bear in mind, as has already been observed above, that the demographic scale in the past was much smaller than the present one; in other words it was much harder to kill 10,000 people in the relatively small cities of the past than it is now. Hence, the graph does not make the data on the deaths over the long-term wholly comparable. In spite of these limitations, the histogram shows the relentless increase in fatalities with the expanding global population after 1600, and it is quite clear where the trend is heading (see also Bilham, 2004). This century is only nine years old, but already we have had the catastrophes of the earthquakes in Gujurat (Bhuj) (2001: 19,000 victims), Bam (2003: 40,000 dead), Sumatra (2004: 283,000 victims, though many of these perished in the tsunami), and Pakistan (2005: 86,000 dead).

What can we expect for the future?

An article of this sort should not end without at least some comment on what can or should be done about the earthquake vulnerability of large megacities in the developing world. The problem is immense and urgent, and most of it is both beyond the scope of this article and the competence of their authors. It is a problem that is being addressed by committed individuals, agencies and professional organisations of many kinds (Tucker, 2004).

The great success of the developed nations in reducing the earthquake hazard of their urban populations is limited to moderate-sized earthquakes. In California, and increasingly in Japan, earthquakes of magnitude 6–7, which can routinely kill tens of thousands of people in rural areas of the Middle East and Asia, now principally cause economic loss. The earthquakes at Loma Prieta in northern California

(1989, magnitude 7.1, 64 killed) and Northridge in southern California (1994, magnitude 6.8, 50 killed) occurred in regions that would be considered urban or suburban compared with the cases discussed at Bam or Tabas in Iran. Expressed as proportions of the population, the number of deaths of the Californian earthquakes are insignificant compared to those of Bam and Tabas (which lost roughly 30 % and 85 % of their populations). But also for Italy these comparisons are relevant: in November 1980 a magnitude 6.7 earthquake that struck the regions of Irpinia and Basilicata (two mountainous and poor zones in central-southern Italy) caused over 2,000 deaths; in the same period an earthquake of similar magnitude in California injured just a few people. This comparison is not to lessen the importance of economic loss, since that can be devastating for developing countries, as can also be seen in the case of Calabria.

As Tucker (2004) points out, the costs of the 1989 and 1994 Californian earthquakes were 0.2 % and 1 %, respectively, of the regional (not national) gross domestic product (GDP), while the cost of the 1972 Nicaragua and 1986 El Salvador earthquakes were 40 % and 30 %, respectively, of those countries' entire GDP. The experiences of California and Japan are testaments to good building design codes, sensibly enforced, though whether those same designs will prove effective in earthquakes much bigger than magnitude 7, in which shaking durations and ground displacements are much larger, is uncertain (Heaton et al., 1995).

Living with an earthquake hazard should not necessarily imply getting ready for the suffering endured by the past generations and by those of the present. But this will only become true through preparation, that is by building new houses well and adequately reinforcing the existing ones, and organising a conscious and responsible social behaviour. It will also be helped by education and better international awareness: when the people of Iran realize, based on their awareness of the Californian experience, that thousands of deaths in moderate earthquakes of magnitude ~6 are not inevitable, and demand progress towards that alternative state, an important step forward will have been taken. A new culture trained in safety should enable the resident populations to adopt adequate solutions, which today are available in the scientific and the technical fields, in order to mitigate and overcome earthquake damage.

But reducing the effects of earthquakes does not just involve steps that need to be taken to prepare for the inevitable extreme catastrophe, so as at least to attempt to cope with its consequences. As Tucker (2004) points out, it also needs a sustained determined effort at hazard mitigation and reduction before such a catastrophe occurs, and one that must embrace a large number of cities. The problem which accompanied the rapid growth of these megacities, viz. what to do about populations that are already housed in poorly-constructed apartment blocks, is particularly difficult. One thing at least is clear: we can expect 2 billion people to be added to the cities of developing countries over the next 20 years (Bilham, 2004; Tucker, 2004). This will be the biggest construction boom in history, and for those people at least, we should try to ensure that this construction conforms to good building practise and good land-use planning.

References

AMBRASEYS, N. N. & MELVILLE, C. P., 1982. *A History of Persian Earthquakes*, Cambridge: Cambridge University Press.

BERBERIAN, M., 2005. "The 2003 Bam urban earthquake: a predictable seismotectonic pattern along the western margin of the rigid lut block, south east Iran," *Earthquake Spectra, EERI,* 21, no. S1, pp. S35–S99.

BERBERIAN, M. & YEATS, R.S., 1999. "Patterns of Historical Earthquakes Rupture in the Iranian Plateau," *Bulletin of the Seismological Society of America*, 89, pp. 120–139.

BILHAM, R., 2004. "Urban Earthquake Fatalities: A Safer World, or Worse to Come?," *Seismological Research Letters*, 75, pp. 706–712.

BILHAM, R., 1998. "Earthquakes and Urban Development," *Nature*, 336, pp. 625–626.

BILHAM, R., 1996. "Global Fatalities from Earthquakes in the Past 2000 Years: Prognosis for the Next 30," in *Reduction and Predictability of Natural Disasters*, edited by J. B. RUNDLE, D.

L. TURCOTTE & W. KLEIN, Santa Fe Institute Studies in the Sciences of Complexity, XXV, Reading, Mass.: Addison Wesley, pp. 19–31.

GUIDOBONI, E. & EBEL, J. E., 2009. *Earthquakes and Tsunamis in the Past: A Guide to Techniques in Historical Seismology*, Cambridge: Cambridge University Press.

GUIDOBONI, E., 2008. "I terremoti e i maremoti della Calabria: una riflessione sui loro effetti nel lungo periodo," in *La Calabria e i terremoti*, edited by L. MELIGRANA, Centro Studi di Parghelia.

GUIDOBONI, E., FERRARI, G., MARIOTTI, D., COMASTRI, A., TARABUSI, G. & VALENSIS G., 2007-. *CFTI4 MED. Catalogue of Strong Earthquakes in Italy 461 B.C. – 1997 and Mediterranean Area 760 B.C. – 1500. An Advanced Laboratory of Historical Seismology*, available at: http://storing.ingv.it/cfti4med/.

HEATON, T. H., HALL, J. F., WALD, D. J. & HALLING, M. W., 1995. "Response of High-rise and Base-isolated Buildings to a Hypothetical Mw 7.0 Blind Thrust Earthquake," *Science*, 267, pp. 206–211.

JACKSON, J., 2008. "Surviving Natural Disasters," in: *Survival, 2006 Darwin Lectures*, edited by E. SHUCKBURGH, Cambridge: Cambridge University Press, pp. 123–145.

JACKSON, J., 2006. "Fatal Attraction: Living With Earthquakes, The Growth of Villages into Megacities, and Earthquake Vulnerability in the Modern World," *Philosophical Transactions of the Royal Society of London*, 364A, pp. 1911–1925.

MUNICH RE, 1991, *World Map of Natural Hazards*, DIN A4, Ordner 17272-V-e, München: Münchener Rückversicherung-Gesellschaft, 36 pp.

PLACANICA, A., 1985. *Il filosofo e la catastrofe. Un terremoto del Settecento*, Turin: Einaudi.

TALEBIAN, M., BIGGS, J., BOLOURCHI, M., COPLEY, A., GHASSEMI, A., GHORASHI, M., HOLLINGSWORTH, J., JACKSON, J., NISSEN, E., OVEISI, B., PARSONS, B., PRIESTLEY, K. & SAIIDI, A., 2006. "The Dahuiyeh (Zarand) Earthquake of 2005 February 22 in Central Iran:

Reactivation of an Intra-mountain Thrust," *Geophysical Journal International*, 164, pp. 137–148.

TUCKER, B., 2004. "Trends in Global Urban Earthquake Risk: A Call to the International Earth Science and Earthquake Engineering Communities," *Seismological Research Letters*, 75, pp. 695–700.

UTSU, T., 2002. "A list of Deadly Earthquakes in the World: 1500–2000," in: *IASPEI Handbook of Earthquake Engineering and Seismology*, Part A, edited by W. H. LEE, H. KANAMORI, P.JENNINGS, & C. KISSLINGER, Amsterdam; London: Academic Press, pp. 691–717.

Guerre et pauvreté
René Leboutte

La guerre : à la fois source de profits et de misère

Les relations entre la guerre et l'appauvrissement des populations sont ambivalentes. Que la pauvreté fasse partie des misères de la guerre, personne n'en doute. Il suffit d'évoquer les dessins de Jacques Callot (1592–1635) ou les innombrables photographies et reportages qui accompagnent l'avancée des troupes alliées en Europe en 1944–1945. Que la guerre constitue aussi une source de revenus, un métier, une occasion d'enrichissement rapide pour certains est tout aussi vrai : accapareurs, trafiquants, profiteurs du marché noir font partie du « climat de guerre ». Que dire alors des mercenaires: jadis la guerre était une source normale de revenus pour les jeunes gens pauvres ; hier comme aujourd'hui, entrer dans l'armée est un moyen de sortir de la précarité, d'échapper au chômage, d'être reconnu socialement. L'Italie de la Renaissance regorgeait de condottieri, de soudards qui se vendaient au plus offrant. Le métier de mercenaire a sorti de la misère des jeunes hommes désœuvrés, des paysans qui combinaient la culture des champs et le métier des armes.

Les relations entre guerre et crise économique sont tout aussi complexes. Comme nous le verrons, les guerres anciennes, la guerre de Trente Ans comme les campagnes napoléoniennes, se sont soldées par un appauvrissement structurel de certaines régions. Toutefois, la guerre a aussi servi de « sortie de crise économique » en éliminant le chômage endémique et en stimulant la production industrielle. La Première Guerre mondiale a en grande partie apuré la pauvreté et le chômage en Grande-Bretagne. La grande dépression des années 1930 a été stoppée par les programmes de réarmement, puis par l'économie de guerre. Alors qu'en 1945, l'Europe était exsangue, moins de trois ans plus tard, elle s'engageait dans une phase de croissance économique sans précédent : les « Trente Glorieuses », c'est-à-dire une période de croissance économique exceptionnelle par sa puissance et par sa durée (1946–1975). Il est vrai que cet essor aurait été impossible sans le coup d'accélérateur du *European Recovery Program* (Plan Marshall), c'est-à-dire la preuve même d'une Amérique prospère.

La guerre en tant que remède à la pauvreté, au chômage, à la stagnation économique est en fait une vision cynique et à courte vue. L'économie tant en Europe qu'aux États-Unis après la Première Guerre mondiale s'est vite révélée fort instable. Dès 1921, pour la première fois dans l'histoire contemporaine, les pays industrialisés sont confrontés au phénomène de chômage structurel – fléau qui, depuis le milieu des années 1970, est le problème majeur de nombreux pays occidentaux. Comme l'a démontré Paul Bairoch, cette forme nouvelle de chômage de masse s'observe dans tous les pays européens (exception faite de la Suisse et de la Belgique) entre 1922 et 1929.[1] Par ailleurs, le passage de l'économie de guerre à l'économie de paix a été tellement difficile dans les années 1920 que c'est précisément pourquoi, durant la Seconde Guerre mondiale, le retour à la paix a été soigneusement préparé.

Si la guerre profite à certains, elle reste la première cause d'appauvrissement, avant les catastrophes naturelles, les crises agricoles, les épidémies.[2] En effet, la guerre exerce un effet cumulatif. Outre les soldats tués (provoquant le phénomène de classes creuses dans la pyramide des âges) et les victimes civiles, elle détruit les réserves alimentaires et de combustibles, les moyens de production et surtout de transport, et entraîne donc des privations équivalentes à une disette. L'insuffisance alimentaire est un terrain tout préparé non seulement pour les épidémies, mais encore pour un affaiblissement physique à long terme qui hypothèque la capacité à gagner sa vie. Enfin, la guerre provoque des migrations forcées, des déplacements de population qui favorisent la diffusion des épidémies.

La Première Guerre mondiale a engendré une pauvreté nouvelle sur le Continent européen (la Grande-Bretagne a en revanche été épargnée) : celle de la petite bourgeoisie frappée par la brusque augmentation du coût de la vie. Le déclenchement de la guerre a en

---

1 Paul Bairoch, *Victoires et déboires histoire économique et sociale du monde du XVIe siècle à nos jours*, t. III, Paris 1997, pp. 46–49.

2 Source: http://www.gdrc.org/icm/poverty-causes.htm (05/11/05).

effet stoppé la marche quotidienne des affaires, du commerce, des services et tout particulier des organismes de crédit. La mobilisation en masse a privé le monde du travail de samain-d'œuvre, ce qui a, il est vrai, donné l'occasion aux femmes de prendre pied dans des secteurs jadis réservés aux hommes.

Les gouvernements ont dû affronter des problèmes économiques complexes. Il a fallu recourir au cours forcé de la monnaie, à la mise en circulation de moyens d'échange de substitution, d'introduire les bons de rationnement, etc.. Ces mesures n'ont pas suffi à enrayer l'appauvrissement des populations civiles, en particulier dans les grandes villes. En France, le manque de combustible a été un problème majeur et une source de pauvreté. En matière alimentaire, les paysans français (mais c'est évidemment vrai dans les autres pays) se sont engagés dans un malthusianisme économique qui a aggravé la pénurie. C'est ainsi que sont réapparues les denrées plus ou moins comestibles qui rappellent la misère de la Guerre de Trente Ans : rutabaga, orties, fanes de carottes, pommes de terre de piètre qualité, etc.[3]

Guerres et pauvreté aux Temps Modernes
Les Cavaliers de l'Apocalypse

Comme l'a bien montré Nicole Haesenne-Peremans, la guerre exerce une triple action de paupérisation : endettement des communautés villageoises et des villes ; ruine des familles paysannes dont les récoltes sont ravagées ou réquisitionnées et, à partir du régime napoléonien, enrôlement par la conscription des jeunes hommes des classes les plus défavorisées.[4]

La guerre ne vient jamais seule. Elle est accompagnée d'incendies, de pillages, de disettes et d'épidémies comme le note le curé du village d'Emael, près de Visé en 1636 : « cette année, nous avons été éprouvés d'une façon étonnante par les maladies, la guerre, la famine et le feu. D'abord, une peste violente s'abattit sur le village pendant

---

3 GABRIEL PERREUX « *La vie quotidienne des civils en France pendant la guerre* » Paris 1966 ; MARC FERRO, *The Great War 1914–1918*, Londres 1973.

4 NICOLE HAESENNE-PEREMANS, *La pauvreté dans la région liégeoise à l'aube de la révolution industrielle*, Paris 1981, pp. 147–156 ; H. VAN HOUTTE, *Les occupations étrangères en Belgique sous l'Ancien Régime*, 2 vol. Gand-Paris 1930.

les mois de juin et de juillet et y fit 17 victimes. Immédiatement après vint la guerre. L'armée tout entière du roi d'Espagne [...] construisit d'abord un fort à Navagne, près de la Meuse. Ensuite, faisant semblant de vouloir assiéger la ville de Maestricht, ils vinrent camper [à Emael]. Ces gens-là étaient pires que des barbares ; ils détruisaient tout ; ils abattaient les arbres, démolissaient un grand nombre de maisons de fond en comble et foulaient aux pieds les grains qu'ils ne pouvaient pas enlever, ne laissant même pas aux pauvres cultivateurs de quoi apaiser leur faim ».[5]

La guerre : ruine des communautés rurales

Le passage des troupes en campagne était donc l'un des pires fléaux que tout le monde redoutait. Aux XVIIe – XVIIIe siècles, la manière de conduire la guerre a certes évolué dans le sens d'une plus grande discipline des troupes, d'une professionnalisation. Les troupes privées de soudards ont peu à peu été remplacées par des armées « nationales ». Cette discipline nouvelle n'a eu cependant que peu d'effets positifs sur l'appauvrissement dû à la guerre.[6] En effet, la règle suivant laquelle les soldats devaient vivre des ressources du pays (ami ou ennemi d'ailleurs) est demeurée d'application au moins jusqu'à la fin des guerres napoléoniennes. Le premier effet de l'annonce de l'arrivée de soldats, armées « amies » ou ennemies peu importe, était de semer la terreur parce que, hier pas moins qu'aujourd'hui, c'étaient les populations civiles qui avaient le plus à perdre : leur vie d'abord, leurs biens ensuite. La seule traversée d'un village par un millier de soldats avec chevaux, matériels, gens à demi vagabonds qui fermaient la marche signifiait à coup sûr une crise de l'économie locale : piétinement des futures moissons, pillage des granges, vol des bestiaux... Ainsi la belle récolte de l'été 1652 qui aurait permis aux villageois de la région parisienne de sortir de plusieurs années de privation fut totalement détruite

5 Carl Havelange, Etienne Hélin, René Leboutte, *Vivre et survivre. Témoignages sur la condition populaire au pays de Liège XIIe – XXe siècles*, Liège 1994, p. 28.
6 Nombreux exemples d'appauvrissement par la guerre en France aux XVIe–XVIIe siècles dans André Corvisier, Jean Jacquart (sous la direction de), *Les Malheurs de la guerre*. Vol. 1 : De la guerre à l'ancienne à la guerre réglée, (119e congrès national des sociétés historiques et scientifiques, Amiens, 1994), Editions du CTHS, 1996.

par les passages de troupes et les opérations militaires des Frondeurs, des Royalistes et des Lorrains. L'année suivante, pas de semences en suffisance : le cycle vicieux de la disette a repris. En effet, comme le note à juste titre, Jean Jacquart, le drame de la guerre ancienne réside en sa répétition, année après année lors du « siècle de malheur », le XVIIe siècle. Ce furent en effet en Europe les mêmes territoires, les mêmes vallées qui ont fait les frais de la guerre. « Parfois, désespéré, [le paysan] quitte le village et vient grossir la foule des errants sans feu ni lieu. On comprend alors que la baisse de la production globale du sol cesse d'être un accident pour devenir un phénomène général et durable. Dix ans après les campagnes de 1649 et de 1652, on voyait en Ile-de-France des vignes abandonnées et en friche ».[7]

Pour discerner l'impact de la guerre sur l'appauvrissement des populations, il faut distinguer l'espace urbain du monde rural. La ville a été la principale cible des guerres qui, aux Temps Modernes, étaient d'abord des guerres de siège. La population urbaine est réduite à supporter de longs sièges durant parfois plus d'une année. La ville est aussi la cible des troupes de passage parce qu'elle offre, contrainte et forcée, le logement chez l'habitant et des ressources en vivres, moyens de transport, combustible. Les populations urbaines sont donc victimes de contributions de guerre et de la présence de la soldatesque (accompagnée d'une foule de gens qui suivaient les armées : domestiques, femmes, enfants). Dans les campagnes, la guerre prenait une autre tournure. Il s'agissait surtout de passages répétés de troupes qui pillaient, détruisaient et rançonnaient les paysans. Semer la peur et répandre la misère faisaient partie de la stratégie des officiers. Alors que les populations urbaines restaient généralement à l'intérieur des enceintes, les villageois désertaient plutôt leur hameau à l'annonce de l'arrivée des soldats. L'errance devenait alors une forme de pauvreté, de misère même, car les gens sans aveu étaient vite assimilés à des vagabonds.

---

7 JEAN JACQUART, « Les inerties terriennes », dans PIERRE DEYON, JEAN JACQUART, *Les hésitations de la croissance (1580–1740)*, (PIERRE LÉON, Histoire économique et sociale du monde, t. 2), Paris 1978, pp. 380–381.

Fuir ou rester ?

Violences, viols, massacres n'étaient pas les seuls dangers d'un passage de soldats. La « peste », c'est-à-dire l'épidémie sous ses formes multiples, suivait les armées et le monde bigarré des vagabonds, des « domestiques » femmes et hommes qui accompagnaient les soldats. Sous l'emprise de la panique, la fuite dans les forêts voisines ou à la ville la plus proche était la première réaction. En Picardie, durant la guerre de Trente Ans, des villageois se cachèrent dans des souterrains ; ailleurs, en Ardennes, ils cherchèrent refuge dans des grottes au fond des forêts. Des villes comme Lyon ou Bergamo ont été régulièrement envahies par des hordes de paysans affamés et terrorisés aux XVIᵉ–XVIIIᵉ siècles : les institutions charitables étaient dans l'impossibilité de subvenir à ces pauvres.[8]

Quitter le village à l'annonce de troupes était souvent le seul moyen d'échapper aux violences, à la mort, mais pas à la misère. Les rumeurs des atrocités commises par les soudards engendraient une telle peur anticipée que les paysans n'hésitaient pas à tout laisser pour sauver leur peau. Durant la guerre de Hollande (1671–1679), le village des Avins près de Liège a été abandonné pendant trois ans. Les sources sont muettes sur le sort des villageois : ont-ils erré à travers le pays ou ont-ils cherché refuge en ville ? A leur retour, le village n'était plus que ruine : fermes pillées, champs retournés en friche, vergers détruits. Tout était à reconstruire à une époque où la disette était endémique. En 1697, c'est le tour d'Hannêche d'être vidé du jour au lendemain de ses habitants terrorisés par l'arrivée de soudards. Les champs ont été laissés en friche pendant plus d'une année.[9] Jetés sur les routes, les paysans devenaient des gens sans aveu et, dès lors, privés de ressources et d'aides, soupçonnés de vagabondage. Les villes n'étaient qu'un refuge hypothétique. Les institutions urbaines qui avaient déjà leur lot de pauvres n'étaient pas en mesure d'affronter l'afflux des villageois des faubourgs et environs, encore moins des étrangers. La guerre a donc poussé à l'errance. Cependant, l'état de « gens sans aveu », de vagabonds, était aussi dangereux que le fait d'affronter le passage des

---

8 STUART WOOLF, *Porca miseria. Poveri e assistenza nell'età moderna*, Rome-Bari 1988, p. 11.

9 NICOLE HAESENNE-PEREMANS, *La pauvreté dans la région liégeoise* (comme note 4), pp. 147–156.

troupes. En effet, quitter son pays natal signifiait immanquablement plonger dans la misère, c'est-à-dire un état pire que la pauvreté puisqu'il est assimilé à la criminalité. Comme on vient de le voir, la fuite et l'errance signifiaient également la rupture du calendrier des « travaux et des jours » du monde paysan : moissons ou vendanges perdues, retour en friche des champs, labours retardés, semailles empêchées, dispersion du bétail. Sans compter l'état dans lequel on retrouvait les fermes au retour : le terme « arse », brûlé, revient régulièrement dans les archives des communautés rurales au XVIIe siècle.[10] Aussi, dans certains villages au XVIIe siècle, les paysans ont fait le choix de défendre tant bien que mal leurs biens, leurs récoltes, leur bétail. Myron Gutmann a démontré que ce choix, fait par les villageois de la Basse-Meuse entre Liège et Maastricht au XVIIe siècle, a finalement été le bon. Certes, les populations rurales ont durement subi la violence des pillages, des rançons, des destructions, mais ils ont aussi très rapidement pu reprendre leurs activités et ainsi échapper à la misère engendrée par l'errance.[11]

Rançons et contributions de guerre

Cette volonté de résister se payait généralement fort cher. Les rançons et contributions de guerre ont été une source majeure d'appauvrissement durable. Au XVIIe siècle, l'intendance reste rudimentaire et ne fonctionne qu'au bénéfice des garnisons des principales places fortes. Les troupes qui prennent leurs quartiers d'hiver dans les villages n'ont d'autres ressources que de razzier le bétail, piller les provisions et les ustensiles de fer, tuer les paysans pour les dépouiller de leurs vêtements. Quant aux officiers, ils exigent des rançons, sommes d'autant plus difficiles à réunir que l'économie villageoise reposait sur les échanges de produits en nature et de services, et donc que la mon-

---

10 Comme note 7.

11 MYRON GUTMANN, « Why they stayed. The problem of wartime population loss », dans *Tijdschrift voor Geschiedenis*, 91, 1978, pp. 407–428; *Idem*, « War, the tithe, and agricultural production : the Meuse basin North of Liege, 1660–1740 », dans H. VAN DER WEE, E. VAN CAUWENBERGHE, *Productivity of land and agricultural innovation in the Low Countries (1250–1800)*, Leuven University Press, 1978, pp. 65–76; H.VAN DER WEE, « Putting crises in perspective. The impact of war on civilian population in the 17th century », dans *Annales de démographie historique*, 1977, pp. 101–128 ; *Idem, War and rural life in the Early Modern Low Countries*, Princeton 1980.

naie était rare. Les villageois étaient condamnés à recourir à l'emprunt à des taux prohibitifs et en engageant les biens communaux. Le moindre retard dans le paiement entraîne l'incendie des fermes, la saisie des biens communaux.

L'incendie du village de Sart (Wallonie) en 1651 illustre bien la tactique des militaires : refus de tout compromis, exécution immédiate en cas de non-paiement de la rançon. L'officier « commanda à trois cents dragons de mettre pied à terre et mettre (pendant trois quarts d'heure de temps) tout le bourg du Sart en feu, et en flamme, tuer ou faire de prise tous ceux qu'ils pouvaient attraper ».

Les guerres de Louis XIV mettent en campagne des armées de plus en plus nombreuses. On passe de quelques dizaines de milliers d'hommes à plusieurs centaines de milliers. Pour conserver la cohésion de telles masses, pour empêcher la désertion, les généraux améliorent l'intendance ; ils préfèrent le casernement au logement chez l'habitant, ils ont recours à des munitionnaires qui leur procurent la multitude des rations dont ils ne peuvent plus se passer. Cela signifie que mener la guerre coûte de plus en plus cher et donc que pour faire rentrer les contributions de guerre, il faut pressurer les paysans plutôt que d'incendier leurs fermes. Bon gré mal gré, les villageois entrent dans la logique de l'oppression par et pour l'argent : vendre ou hypothéquer les biens communaux, s'endetter, alourdir la fiscalité locale, produire davantage, obliger femmes, enfants, vieillards à travailler pour rien dans les ateliers familiaux. La survie est à ce prix.[12]

Les quartiers d'hiver pèsent particulièrement lourd sur l'économie villageoise : des milliers de soldats, accompagnés de domestiques, femmes et enfants campaient dans les champs, exigeant le ravitaillement et le combustible, et ce pendant des mois. En pays ennemi, l'exploitation systématique des ressources, « la mise en coupe réglée », faisait évidemment partie de l'arsenal de la guerre : ruiner, appauvrir afin de pousser l'adversaire à la défaite.

Plus à l'Est de l'Europe, ainsi que dans le pourtour de la Méditerranée, la guerre a longtemps pris la forme de razzias : arrivée sou-

---

12 CARL HAVELANGE, ETIENNE HÉLIN, RENÉ LEBOUTTE, *Vivre et survivre* (comme note 5), pp. 28–31.

daine de bandes tartares et de Cosaques dans le Sud-Est et en Pologne de 1605 à 1633 ; opérations de pirates turcs et maures. Ces troupes – mais peut-on encore parler de guerre ? – détruisaient les villages, emportant le bétail et déportant les hommes, vendus ensuite comme esclaves.[13]

Destruction des récoltes et des ressources forestières

A la campagne, les passages de troupes à travers champs anéantissaient les récoltes tandis que la destruction des denrées engrangées compromettait les approvisionnements d'hiver et les semences pour les futures récoltes. Les forêts aussi sont pillées comme le montre Jérôme Buridant à propos du Laonnois au XVIIe siècle.[14]

Les petits paysans, les « journaliers », les ouvriers de la protoindustrie survivaient grâce aux ressources fournies par les biens communaux qui permettaient d'entretenir une vache, un cochon et d'obtenir du bois de charpente et de chauffage. Les rançons et autres contributions de guerre ont nécessité le recours à des emprunts à n'importe quel taux et donc l'hypothèque de ces biens communaux. Ce mécanisme a constitué une source majeure d'appauvrissement comme suite à la guerre. Ainsi, la communauté de Hamoir a perdu la presque totalité de ses biens communaux dans le remboursement des dettes contractées lors des guerres du XVIIe siècle. En 1753, la communauté de Jalhay est contrainte de débourser 22.000 écus au titre de contribution de guerre, c'est-à-dire l'équivalent de 150.000 journées de manœuvre… Une telle somme frappant un village d'un millier d'habitants signifie un appauvrissement généralisé. Ces passages de troupes, ces contributions de guerre se multiplient. Pour le seul XVIIIe siècle, le comté de Logne a subi une douzaine d'invasions, tandis que la charge cumulée des quartiers d'hiver dans la principauté de Stavelot-Malmédy atteint la somme considérable d'un million de florins.[15]

---

13 Comme note 7.

14 Jérôme Buridant, « Guerres et paysages forestiers : l'exemple laonnois au XVIIe siècle », dans André Corvisier, Jean Jacquart (sous la direction de), *Les Malheurs de la guerre*. Vol. 1 : (comme note 6), pp. 193–200.

15 N. Haesenne-Peremans, *La pauvreté dans la région liégeoise* (comme note 4), pp. 147–156 ; H. van Houtte, *Les occupations étrangères en Belgique sous l'Ancien Régime*, 2 vol. Gand, Paris, 1930.

Déserteurs et brigands

A l'occupation militaire, il faut aussi ajouter les exactions des nombreux déserteurs. Durant les guerres de Louis XIV, la région de Huy est infestée de soudards qui se mêlent aux vagabonds pour piller les villages. Le brigandage est endémique et rend tout déplacement extrêmement hasardeux.[16]

Guerre, industrie et pauvreté

La guerre ne profite pas nécessairement à l'industrie, car les moulins et usines étaient la proie des militaires. De plus, l'insécurité des transports réduisait le commerce et frappait donc la production. Ainsi dans la région de Huy, les guerres des XVIIe–XVIIIe siècles ont entraîné la disparition de l'industrie sidérurgique.[17] Dans le bassin charbonnier liégeois à l'époque de la guerre de Sept Ans, la réquisition de tous les chevaux utilisés pour actionner les treuils des fosses à charbon a provoqué un chômage forcé de plusieurs mois pour des centaines d'ouvriers mineurs. A Herstal, la misère était telle que les ouvriers et leurs familles ne fréquentaient plus la messe dominicale faute de vêtements… Deux ans plus tard, nouveau passage de troupes et nouvelles réquisitions des chevaux et des charrettes, cette fois la misère due au chômage, à la fermeture des mines, est si grande à Herstal et dans les villages voisins que le curé adressa une longue requête au Prince-Evêque pour demander une aide d'urgence.

Les charbonnages étaient particulièrement vulnérables : il suffisait en effet d'arrêter ou d'endommager le système de pompage pour provoquer le noyage des galeries. Il fallait plusieurs mois, après la guerre, pour remettre la mine en état et ce, à grands frais. La destruction des charbonnages a connu une ampleur sans précédent durant la Première Guerre mondiale dans le bassin du Nord/Pas-de-Calais. Comme l'exploitation charbonnière est une industrie de main-d'œuvre, la fermeture forcée des mines par fait de guerre signifiait donc un appauvrissement des familles de mineurs. Lors de la guerre de succession d'Autriche, les soldats réquisitionnèrent le fourrage nécessaire

---

16 Jean-Pierre Rorive, *Les misères de la guerre sous le Roi Soleil*, Liège 2000.
17 Comme note 9.

aux chevaux des charbonnages de Herstal, près de Liège, les outils et le matériel des houillères, contraignant des centaines d'ouvriers au chômage forcé. Une des sociétés charbonnières qui a échappé de justesse à la faillite n'a d'autre recours que de faire creuser un nouveau puits, les autres ayant été irrémédiablement noyés et détruits. En juin 1758, le prince-évêque de Liège autorisa le séjour à Herstal d'un régiment de cavalerie (donc des troupes « amies ») qui y est resté jusqu'en mai 1759 : la réquisition des chevaux de houillère, du fourrage, de denrées alimentaires, a réduit la communauté dans son ensemble dans la misère. Tous les charbonnages ou presque ont chômé pendant plus d'un an. Dix ans après cette occupation, les familles de mineurs étaient toujours dans une misère telle qu'elles en appelèrent aux Etats de la principauté pour obtenir une aide d'urgence.[18]

L'appauvrissement des populations urbaines

Comme l'a bien montré Jean-Pierre Rorive, les villes ne sont pas seulement victimes de sièges, de pillages et de destructions, elles sont la cible privilégiée des contributions de guerre et des logements de soldats. Huy, par exemple, a subi un pressurage constant de 1674 à 1718 : troupes impériales (1674–1675), occupations françaises et hollandaises. La ville a dû recourir aux emprunts s'endettant gravement. Malgré ces contributions de guerre, elle n'a pas échappé aux pillages, au saccage des maisons. Vergers, jardins, vignobles ont été mis en coupe réglée. La destruction des ponts et l'insécurité des voies de communication aggravent la pénurie en combustible et denrées alimentaires.[19]

Comme l'explique un habitant de Verviers en 1701, la ville est exsangue après des années de guerre. « Les passages, les campements, les logements, quartiers d'hiver, contributions et cent pareille semences de misère ont achevé la ruine du public et du particulier de cette ville ».[20] Pourtant, cette ville devra encore subir de nouveaux

---

18 René Leboutte, *Reconversions de la main-d'œuvre industrielle et transition démographique. Les bassins industriels en aval de Liège, XVIIe–XXe siècles*, (Bibliothèque de la Faculté de Philosophie et Lettres de l'Université de Liège, fascicule CCLI), Liège-Paris 1988, p. 101.

19 Comme note 16.

20 Laurent Deschêne, *Industrie drapière de la Vesdre avant 1800*, Paris 1926, p. 247.

passages de troupes en 1715–1719, 1735–1736, 1746–1748… Les bourgeois sont forcés de loger non seulement les soldats, mais encore une foule de domestiques et de gens qui suivent les troupes. Au logement forcé s'ajoute l'obligation de ravitailler en pain, viande et bière toute cette foule bigarrée. Les bourgeois doivent aussi fournir les rations de fourrage pour les chevaux. A titre d'exemple, le quartier d'hiver de 1678–1679 a coûté plus de 470.000 florins aux habitants de Verviers, une somme considérable pour l'époque. En fait, du milieu du XVIIe siècle qu'à la fin du siècle suivant (au moment où débute la Révolution industrielle), la ville se débat dans les dettes et la pauvreté est générale. Pour apurer les dettes dues aux contributions de guerre, la ville est obligée d'introduire en 1748 une taxe personnelle spéciale « tant sur les bourgeois, habitants, possessionnés, commerçants que sur les ouvriers et les ouvrières de la dite ville ». Ce nouvel impôt qui s'ajoute aux contributions courantes frappe inégalement : ce sont les ouvriers qui en supportent le plus durement le poids. En effet, comme le souligne Nicole Haesenne-Peremans, c'est une fiscalité indirecte, permanente et non progressive, qui appauvrit les plus défavorisés. En 1746–1747, Liège est forcée de fournir pour près de 150.000 florins en grains, alors que la disette sévit. La ville doit s'endetter pour longtemps.[21]

Les guerres de la Révolution et de l'Empire : pas d'amélioration…

Elles présentent une différence par rapport aux guerres antérieures sous deux aspects : d'abord l'ampleur et la masse des soldats mis en mouvement; ensuite l'introduction de la conscription.

L'occupation révolutionnaire : Les villes forcées de supporter l'action révolutionnaire

Les troupes révolutionnaires se considéraient chez elles dans les territoires rattachés à la République et envahis. Ainsi, entre 1789 et 1806, la ville de Huy a dû abriter à grands frais et de manière régulière des troupes de passage. Ainsi de novembre 1805 à mai 1806, les

---

21 Comme note 9.

bourgeois ont dû assurer le logement et l'entretien de 25.000 hommes et de 21.300 chevaux. La population urbaine, tant à Huy qu'à Liège, a éprouvé un appauvrissement généralisé dû aux contributions de guerre, aux réquisitions, aux logements de troupes. En septembre 1814, le Conseil municipal de Huy en a été réduit à supplier une réduction de l'occupation compte tenu de « l'état de détresse où les logements militaires ont réduit cette malheureuse ville ».

Alors que s'était amorcée une protoindustrialisation prometteuse dans les années 1770–1790 et que les premiers signes de la Révolution industrielle apparaissaient dans le textile verviétois, les guerres de la Révolution ont cassé net cet élan plongeant en 1794–1795 la population des territoires annexés dans la plus grave crise économique depuis la fin du XVIIe siècle. C'est tout le secteur industriel qui a été touché : charbonnages fermés, chômage dans les ateliers de cuirs, la clouterie, la draperie. En l'an III, la guerre est considérée comme la cause immédiate de la stagnation de l'industrie et du commerce, la disette dont souffre la population liégeoise et la ruine « d'une infinité de familles honnêtes, de laborieux artisans, d'actifs petits commerçants, de nombre même de gens qui vivaient ci-devant économiquement du produit de quelques modiques rentes » (3 messidor an III). Ce texte, cité par Nicole Haesenne-Peremans, est révélateur : l'appauvrissement ne frappe plus seulement les paysans ou les ouvriers, c'est la petite bourgeoisie et les artisans qui font aussi les frais de la guerre.

Comme d'habitude, les villes n'ont d'autre possibilité que de recourir à l'emprunt pour satisfaire les exigences militaires : contribution de guerre, livraison des chevaux, des charrettes, du fourrage, des rations de pain, etc.. La ville de Huy a été à ce point endetté pendant les guerres napoléoniennes qu'en 1862 encore le Conseil municipal a dû contracter un emprunt pour apurer les dettes dues aux occupations militaires…

L'insécurité dans les campagnes

Dans les campagnes, la situation était tout aussi grave. D'abord, l'insécurité qui régnait en 1794–1795 en raison de la multitude de vagabonds et de bandits (les « chauffeurs ») empêchait tout commerce. Les fermes étaient attaquées et pillées pendant la nuit. Ensuite, les villages n'étaient pas épargnés de l'obligation d'entretenir les troupes. Ainsi, en 1814, Cras-Avernas, un village de 306 habitants a dû loger et nourrir près de 1000 cavaliers, fournir de l'avoine et du foin pour les chevaux et mettre à la disposition des armées tous les chevaux et toutes les charrettes.

Comme le souligne Nicole Haesenne-Peremans, les passages de troupes ont eu pour conséquence de ruiner la couche sociale des petits exploitants agricoles, c'est-à-dire les plus nombreux. En conséquence, ces paysans appauvris étaient hors d'état d'employer des ouvriers agricoles, des journaliers. L'appauvrissement s'est ainsi étendu en un mouvement de cascade. Et les institutions ? Dans les villes comme à la campagne, le nouveau régime avait bien instauré des comités du Bureau de bienfaisance, mais les caisses étaient vides. Ainsi, les membres du Bureau de bienfaisance de Villers-l'Evêque en sont réduits à constater, en 1806, que *tous* les habitants du village devraient figurer sur la liste des pauvres à la suite des campagnes militaires de 1794… « Les troupes républicaines commandées par les généraux Championnet et Morlot étant arrivées à Villers-l'Evêque, le 27 juillet 1794, au nombre de 30.000, y sont restées campées pendant 7 à 8 semaines, séjour qui a occasionné le fourragement [22] général de toute la campagne, par là, les habitants se sont trouvés sans grain, fourrage, légumes et ont été réduits à une profonde misère de sorte qu'ils n'ont pu rien payer au registre des pauvres pour 1794 et leurs champs ayant resté presque sans culture, faute de semence et de chevaux pour les labourer, ils n'ont encore rien fait en 1795 qu'une demi-récolte et voilà ce qui a occasionné la perte de 1200 francs au moins dans les revenus des pauvres parce que l'étant tous devenus, ils étaient dans l'impuissance de payer ».[23] Même situation en Ardennes, à La Reid. Pendant deux mois les soldats ont « ravagé » les campagnes, pris tous « les fourrages et presque généralement tous les légumes et pommes de terre », réduisant à la misère une paysannerie « dépouillée de toute sa moisson » (an III). Alors que la disette menace depuis 1789, les Républicains exigent la livraison d'énormes quantités de grains, sans

---

22 Vieux mot wallon qui signifie que les chevaux des soldats ont détruit les récoltes et dévoré le fourrage.

23 Archives de l'Etat à Liège, *Fonds français, Préfecture*, 1603, Villers-l'Evêque, 1806.

se soucier des risques de famine. Celle-ci va finir par éclater en 1794. On comptera plusieurs cas de décès par la faim, notamment à Verviers. Ainsi, à cause de la guerre, des passages des troupes révolutionnaires, la région liégeoise (elle n'est pas la seule) redécouvre la famine… Certes, les révolutionnaires promettaient dédommagement, mais en assignats. Ainsi, c'est toute la classe des petits agriculteurs, de la petite bourgeoisie urbaine qui ont rejoint l'immense masse des pauvres.

En 1814, une nouvelle arrivée de troupes achève d'appauvrir les petits exploitants agricoles qui étaient parvenus à survivre tant bien que mal. A la suite du logement des soldats prussiens, de nombreuses familles du canton de Stavelot « jouissant d'une honnête aisance » ont été ruinées et les plus pauvres « anéantis ».[24]

La conscription

Elle a frappé les plus pauvres : ouvriers, journaliers, petits agriculteurs, bref tous ceux qui étaient hors d'état de payer un remplaçant. La conscription a arraché aux familles pauvres les hommes valides, ceux dont dépendait le pain quotidien. Faut-il s'étonner dès lors que la conscription a été une source majeure d'appauvrissement ? Selon Nicole Haesenne-Peremans, 22 % des demandes de secours entre 1800 et 1809 proviennent de familles victimes de la conscription. Ce sont pour la plupart des veuves de conscrits surchargées d'enfants en bas âge et d'épouses de soldats. La conscription a donc accentué la pauvreté féminine, touchant ainsi les enfants également. Pour échapper à la conscription, nombre d'individus se sont mariés alors qu'ils étaient « sans autre ressource que le prix de leur travail pour vivre et sont venus avec leurs familles, grossir les rangs des indigents » (juillet 1818). D'autres rejoignaient la horde des vagabonds et gens sans aveu.[25]

C'est d'ailleurs en raison de la multiplication des vagabonds, des errants, des gens sans aveu, c'est-à-dire des pauvres, que les autorités républicaines ont instauré le « registre de population », instrument destiné à la police. Ces registres permettaient de contrôler les déplacements — un passeport était nécessaire pour sortir du département

---

24 Comme note 9.
25 *Loc. cit.*

— et de comptabiliser les pauvres. L'exploitation de cette source est éloquente pour la période 1795–1830 : dans la région liégeoise, les pauvres représentaient la moitié de la population.[26]

Il nous faut insister sur la pauvreté féminine provoquée par la guerre et la conscription. En effet, comme le rappelle un ouvrier armurier dans sa chronique écrite dans la seconde moitié du XIXe siècle, la pauvreté engendrée par les guerres de la République et de l'Empire a privé les femmes de la possibilité d'accéder à l'instruction. « Ma bonne mère n'avait aucune instruction. La misère alors répandue sur le pays par les guerres et invasions de la première République française et de l'Empire ne le permettait pas aux ouvriers même un peu aisés. Ma pauvre mère durant toute sa jeunesse avait dû travailler ferme aux plus durs travaux pour se procurer sa subsistance. [...] Ma mère se maria : elle fut encore dans la misère » (1877).[27]

Conclusions

La guerre offre un double visage sur le plan socio-économique : d'un côté, source de gagne-pain pour beaucoup de mercenaires et de soldats engagés dans les armées ; occasion de faire du butin ; chance d'enrichissement rapide pour tous les munitionnaires, accapareurs et profiteurs ; d'un autre côté, pour les victimes, c'est-à-dire les civils, la guerre était le comble de la misère parce qu'elle aggravait souvent durablement une situation économique déjà précaire et parce qu'elle favorisait la diffusion des épidémies.

Pour les historiens qui se sont penchés sur ce sujet, il ressort que l'appauvrissement dû aux guerres tient à l'endettement des communautés soumises à l'occupation et la désorganisation de l'économie locale durablement : désindustrialisation, abandon des champs et des vignobles.

Une différence s'observe entre villes et campagne : les premières étaient surtout victimes des contributions de guerre et des lo-

---

26 RENÉ LEBOUTTE, « Reconstitution des familles et dynamique des ménages : l'apport des registres de population belges », dans *Archives et Bibliothèques de Belgique, n° spécial 24 : Sources et méthodes de la démographie historique avant 1850*, Bruxelles 1984, pp. 89-112.
27 RENÉ LEBOUTTE , *L'archiviste des rumeurs. Chronique de Gaspard Marnette, armurier, Vottem 1857–1903*, (Collection d'études publiée par le Musée de la Vie Wallonne, n° 6), Liège 1991.

gements militaires qui ont fini par épuiser les ressources financières urbaines et donc ont empêché les institutions urbaines de venir en aide à leurs pauvres ; les communautés rurales généralement insolvables étaient tout simplement condamnées à l'incendie, aux pillages, aux réquisitions des réserves.

Campagnards et urbains n'avaient habituellement d'autre échappatoire que l'exil, l'errance, mais cette solution était parfois pire que de subir l'occupation militaire. Aussi, certains préféraient rester chez eux, défendre leurs biens, au risque de leur vie.

New Technologies as a Cause of Poverty
Thomas Riis

Today we are convinced that the technological development brings us mostly advantages, and we are glad that since the Middle Ages water or wind has ground our corn, otherwise we would have had to do it ourselves by rubbing it between two stones as they did it in the Stone Age. Already in the Middle Ages and the Early Modern period mechanical installations driven by wind or water made several processes easier, e.g. the blacksmith could leave the monotonous beating with a hammer to the machine. A beautiful example has survived in Annaberg-Buchholz in Saxony. Such machines must have made labour redundant, but movements of protest have not been mentioned in the surviving sources. These belonged rather to the Industrial Revolution.

Mechanization of the production of thread

Traditionally, the production of thread was a classical way to create work for the poor. Even most Handicapped could use their hands for spinning and were thus able to furnish thread e.g. for the production of textiles. In this way they could earn something and were not fully dependent on poor relief. A problem connected with the thread thus produced was its changing quality.

In the 1760s British engineers – Richard Arkwright (1732–1792) and James Hargreaves (1740–1778) – invented spinning machines; one of Arkwright's models was driven by water.[1]

For several reasons the mechanization meant a more profitable production. Skilled labour could be replaced by unskilled workers, even children, and work in the factory was more economic than work at home. But in this way factory work became the only possible in-

---

[1] As to the technical question, see H. CATLING, "The Evolution of Spinning" in J. GERAINT JENKINS, *The Wool Textile Industry in Great Britain*, London-Boston 1972, pp. 101–116.

come for the man, who could no longer engage himself as a journey-
man during harvest and that for reasons of transport. Also his wife
lost her work, because earlier she had been able to earn something by
spinning at home. Already Hargreaves's first machine made the work
of four women. No wonder then, that in the Blackburn region spinning machines were destroyed as early as 1768 by workers who feared
for their jobs. That this was not necessarily the case was shown by the
development after 1788, when because of the mechanical production
thread became so abundant that a shortage of weavers resulted.

Other parts of textile production were mechanized as well,
e.g. the finish of woollens at the beginning of the nineteenth century, which menaced the existence of skilled textile workers. In many
places in Yorkshire the machines were destroyed as a consequence.

Similar means were used by the so-called Luddites in order to
arrive at their aims. Also they worked in the textile industry, especially
knitting stockings. Frequently they had rented a sort of knitting machine driven by hand. Both the knitters and the workers of woollens
felt cornered by capitalist entrepreneurs; as a protest against the exploitation of workers the Luddites destroyed the machines, the workers in woollens did it in order to keep their job. The Luddite troubles
took place in 1811–1813, especially in Yorkshire and Nottinghamshire.
Similar excesses are known from France, when the sewing machine
was introduced. In 1841 a firm of Paris owned perhaps 81 sewing
machines, which were all destroyed by the crowd.[2]

The Scottish Example

The invention of the textile machines had taken place in England; in Scotland the new technology was introduced during the latter
half of the eighteenth century.

Because of the mechanization the production of thread in
England had become cheap and quick compared with the past. The

---

2 Cf. W. CUNNINGHAM, *The Growth of English Industry and Commerce in Modern Times II:
Laissez Faire*, Cambridge 1917, pp. 609–668; DAVID S. LANDES, *The Unbound Prometheus.
Technological Change and Industrial Development in Western Europe from 1750 to the Present*,
Cambridge 1969; MAXINE BERG, *The Machinery Question and the Making of Political Economy
1815–1848*, Cambridge 1982 (paperback), pp. 226–252.

product could be sold to Scotland, where because of lacking thread the skilled textile workers had been underemployed since the 1770s. Because of the penury of thread the Scots changed to cotton; as a result the cotton industry flourished in Clydeside (Glasgow and Paisley).

Rather soon the Scots introduced water driven machines for the spinning of cotton thread. During the first quarter of the nineteenth century the Scottish cotton industry was competitive, although the mechanization of weaving came rather late. Still in 1820 one reckoned about 2,000 weaving machines against 50,000 looms worked by hand. This had two reasons: cheap labour was available and the Scottish textile industry concentrated on fine textiles which could not be produced by the machines. Towards the end of the eighteenth century the Scottish weavers' conditions of life had been good, and the workers who had protested had done so less out of fear for losing their jobs than out of concern for the improvement of labour conditions. Because of the wars at the beginning of the nineteenth century real wages appeared to fall; consequently, the weavers claimed the fixation of a minimum of wages. Besides inflation caused by the wars, the massive influx into the craft had increased the offer of labour, as a result wages remained low. A movements of strikes appeared in 1812, but was broken by legal action against its leaders in the following year.

The next two decades saw both the declining prosperity in the traditional weavers' trade and in the 1820s the break-through of the mechanic loom. As a consequence wages fell as it can be seen from the table:

Average Weekly Wages of Clydeside Weavers 1810–1830

	Paisley Shawl Weavers	Glasgow Gingham and Pullicate Weavers
1810–1816	25 sh 0 d	20 sh 9
1816–1820 (sic)	21 sh 9 d	11 sh 9
1821–1825	18 sh 6 d	10 sh 9
1826–1830	11 sh 7 d	7 sh 6

Source: T. C. SMOUT, *A History of the Scottish People 1560–1830*, London 1969, pp. 427–428; paperback edition Glasgow 1979, p. 400.

Why did this unfortunate development take place? The cause was only to a limited extent the new technology, as this did not become significant before 1825. Much more important was it that labour had become abundant. The number of hand looms still increased, only after 1840 it began to decline. Moreover, the rules of the weavers' crafts did not formulate efficient claims to the education of new weavers. Weaving could be learnt rather easily; a family could use several looms at home and needed thus not to work in a factory. That labour had become abundant, is connected with the migration from the countryside into the towns, but this is a phenomenon which we know from other countries as well during their industrialization.[3]

Needlemakers and nailmakers

Despite the fact that the products of these crafts are very appropriate for industrial production – high quantities are needed and they ought to be cheap and fairly identical – the production of nails remained for a long period, actually the whole proto-industrial phase in England from 1760 to 1830, the activity of craftsmen. The coal and iron mines in the English Midlands furnished the raw materials, which were worked in the region round Birmingham. Considerable parts of this production were made as home work, e.g. the making of nails. This took place in a special room of the cottage where the father worked, assisted by other members of the family when necessary.

---

3 T.C. SMOUT, *A History of the Scottish People 1560–1830*, London 1969, pp. 253–255, 403–407, and 422–428; paperback edition Glasgow 1979, pp. 235–237, 377–381, and 395–401.

This professional structure remained dominant in the Midlands until well into the second half of the nineteenth century.[4]

In a related craft, the production of needles, machines were introduced at rather an early stage. In 1777 in the Westphalian town of Iserlohn the journeymen of the craft found the machines a threat to their source of income and consequently destroyed those belonging to the factory of the orphanage.[5] Probably this institution had been able to produce more cheaply, because the orphans were given lower wages, if any at all. Similar destructive action was taken in 1841 in Paris, when the seamstresses saw themselves menaced by the introduction of sewing-machines.[6]

Modern Times

Most of us remember Charlie Chaplin's wonderful film "Modern Times" in which he describes the struggle of "the man on the floor" against the machine. In various fields the machines have taken over parts of our work load, leaving us time for other things. But does this lead to an increased productivity like the one of the Protestant countries when the Reformation abolished many Catholic holidays? Perhaps not, because today the working week is as short as it was on the eve of the Reformation.[7] More probably, the opportunity is seized to dismiss employees and thus to save their wages.

The evolution in the secretariat is illustrative. Until the end of the nineteenth century documents (also administrative records) were handwritten. If more copies of a document were needed, they had to be written by hand, which explains why they are often slightly different from each other. Mechanical copies came in use about the middle of the nineteenth century, but with the typewriter and carbon paper, it became much more easy to take copies. Consequently, the need for se-

---

4   W.H.B. COURT, *A Concise Economic History of Britain from 1750 to Recent Times*, Cambridge 1967, pp. 49–57.
5   MARTIN RHEINHEIMER, *Arme, Bettler und Vaganten. Überleben in der Not 1450–1850*, Frankfurt am Main 2000, p. 47.
6   As note 2.
7   THOMAS RIIS, "An Analysis of Working Hours," *Diogenes* 149, Fiesole 1989, pp. 81–83.

cretarial work was reduced, and less labour was needed. The invention and subsequent diffusion of the computer meant a further facilitation in and reduction of secretarial work. The writing of identical copies is no problem any longer, corrections are easy to make and are not to be seen in the final text. Through this mechanization one person can make the work which formerly was done by several people. Does productivity increase ? rather not, as secretaries are dismissed in order to economize on their wages. At the same time ever more tasks are given to the 'scribes': administrative tasks proper, accounting etc.

It would be possible to go another way, if the saved potential were used to improve the administration, but so doing it would be impossible to economize on wages. In short: the mechanization allows the management to reduce the number of employees, mainly in the groups with modest salaries. These are from an economic point of view the most vulnerable individuals, e.g. single mothers or divorced persons at the end of their professional life. For these people a job as secretary could help them to make both ends meet without recourse to social assistance.

On top of this, although information technology – e.g. internet and emails – is useful, it claims preconditions which only half the adult German population is able to fulfil. The consequences are 1) the reduction of jobs because of mechanization, to what extent it is difficult to say as statistics are hardly available and 2) lesser possibilities to find an occupation for unskilled persons because of the higher qualifications needed. (Also physical, unskilled jobs have become less frequent because of mechanization). This evolution has been going on for several years, and at the same time the figures for receivers of social assistance at Kiel almost trebled between 1980 and 1996. In 1980 exactly half the receivers of social assistance had learnt a trade, 16 years later this group made up only 41 %.[8]

This image can be completed by the report on poverty in Schleswig-Holstein. In 1997 29.6 % of those receiving social assistance never completed an education (examination from school, ap-

---

8 Landeshauptstadt Kiel, Der Oberbürgermeister, Sozialdezernat: *Bericht über die Entwicklung der Armut in Kiel*, Kiel 1998, pp. 7 and 12–13.

prenticeship etc.). The figures are not quite certain, as in 41.8 % of cases an eventual education was not mentioned. The report underlines that "those entering the labour market without a formal education risk unemployment because of rationalization and increased international competition. The labour market's requirements to education are growing, and low qualification jobs are disappearing. Consequently, the less qualified have got only a modest chance of finding a sufficiently paid employment. In view of these tendencies an early maternity may (again) present itself as the better alternative to young, unqualified women who can hope neither for further education nor for a satisfactory job".[9]

A few older figures may be of interest. In 1981–1982 an investigation undertaken by the European Community estimated illiteracy in the total population of the then nine member states at 4 to 6 % or ten to fifteen million people, moreover their level of understanding did not exceed that of a thirteen year old school-child. In France in the middle of the 1980s one reckoned with a share of illiterates of 7.14 % in a class of conscripts. Still in France, a sample taken in 1976 in the Département Essonne (to the South East of Paris) showed that among the receivers of social aid 47 % of the men and 51 % of the women could neither read nor write at all, or only with great difficulty.[10]

Although this sample is already thirty years old, it fits almost too well with a German investigation published in 2000.[11] According to the latter, approximately half the persons asked were insufficiently

---

9 My translation from the original text „Wer heute ohne Berufsausbildung den Arbeitsmarkt betritt, ist durch Rationalisierungsmaßnahmen und verstärkte internationale Konkurrenz von Arbeitslosigkeit bedroht. Die Bildungsanforderungen auf dem Arbeitsmarkt werden höher. Arbeitsplätze mit geringen Qualifikationsanforderungen werden abgebaut. Unqualifizierte haben so nur geringe Chancen, ein ausreichendes Erwerbseinkommen zu erzielen. Angesichts dieser Tendenzen stellt sich für junge unqualifizierte Frauen, die weder Aussicht auf Aus- und Weiterbildung noch auf befriedigende Erwerbstätigkeit haben, eine frühe Mutterschaft (wieder) als die bessere Alternative dar". *Landesarmutsbericht Schleswig-Holstein*. Drucksache 14/2276, Kiel 1999, pp. 91–92 and 95 (Quotation from p. 95).
10 JOSEPH WRESINSKI, *Grande Pauvreté et Précarité économique et sociale. Rapport présenté au nom du Conseil économique et social* (Journal Officiel de la République Française 1987 no. 6, 28 Février 1987), p. 46.
11 Cf. the newspaper *Die Welt* September 20th, 2000.

qualified for the use of the new technology. The Wresinski report submitted in 1987 to the French Conseil économique et social said it clearly: "The right to a job is becoming ever more difficult for the less qualified".[12] According to this report, everybody should be given the possibility of an education which could secure for them permanent employment. Realising that this aim could not be arrived at within a short period, the report wanted nevertheless to keep it in mind, if "we want to avoid a polarised society…in which the less qualified workers are being marginalized" (my translation).[13]

With this knowledge we can look at the over-optimistic, silly-dogmatic declarations by politicians and managers according to whom we live in the best of worlds, when everybody has got access to the internet and communicates with others by email. Only about the turn of the century the European Commission realized the inherent danger of marginalization in the technological evolution. Thus "at Lisbon (March, 23rd–24th, 2000, Th.R.) the European Council realized that the new information society hides both a potential for the diminution of social marginalization through the creation of preconditions for greater wealth on the basis of increased economic growth and employment and through new possibilities for participation in society

---

12 WRESINSKI, *Grande Pauvreté* (as note 10), p. 101 (« Le droit à un travail est rendu difficile pour les travailleurs les moins qualifiés », my translation).

13 *Ibid.*, p. 101. My translation from the original text « si nous ne voulons pas que s'installe une société duale … dans laquelle les travailleurs les moins qualifiés sont mis à l'écart ». Already MONTESQUIEU had claimed as a human right the right to an occupation not threatening the health of the person (*De l'Esprit des Lois* XXIII chapitre XXIX), cf. THOMAS RIIS, « Freedom from Fear and Want (ou « vivre à l'abri de la peur et du besoin ») » dans: *La liberté dans tous ses états. Liber amicorum en l' honneur de Jacques Georgel*, Rennes 1998, p. 372.

and the danger of an increasingly broadening abyss, which separates those with access to the new knowledge from those who are excluded from it..." [14]

Conclusions

Mechanization leads to a lesser demand for labour, if the level of production remains stable. This is not necessarily bad in itself, but a crisis ensues, if at the same time the labour supply increases. This is what happened in the Scottish textile industry in the former half of the nineteenth century.

What today appears dangerous is the circumstance that mechanization has reached most areas of society. Tasks which formerly were performed by unskilled labour are becoming ever less numerous, and where can these persons find employment today? If anything happens at all, the streets are cleared of snow by machines and in order to work in an office you must know more than how to use a typewriter. The computer claims more qualifications, consequently, we must consider the new technology as one of the causes of poverty, but not as the only cause. Other circumstances play a role as well, as e.g. insufficient education in Kiel, in Schleswig-Holstein and in France.

---

14 My translation. In the words of the original "Der Europäische Rat hat in Lissabon ...festgestellt, daß die neue Wissensgesellschaft sowohl Potential für einen Abbau der sozialen Ausgrenzung durch Schaffung der wirtschaftlichen Voraussetzungen für größeren Wohlstand auf der Grundlage von mehr Wachstum und Beschäftigung und durch neue Möglichkeiten der Teilhabe an der Gesellschaft als auch die Gefahr eines immer breiter werdenden Grabens – zwischen denjenigen, die Zugang zum neuen Wissen haben und denjenigen, die davon ausgeschlossen sind – birgt..." European Commission 2000/0157(COD) of June 16th, 2000 „Vorschlag für einen Beschluss des Europäischen Parlaments und des Rates zur Auflage eines Aktionsprogramms der Gemeinschaft zur Förderung der Zusammenarbeit zwischen Mitgliedstaaten bei der Bekämpfung der sozialen Ausgrenzung", S. 9 (Preamble § 6).

To sum up:

1) the introduction of new technologies reduces the need for (mainly) unskilled labour and thus becomes a cause of poverty,
2) mechanization reduces the offer of unskilled jobs and thus prevents unskilled labour from finding a job;
3) new technologies may require such intellectual preconditions that great parts of the population do not possess, thus they become a cause of poverty;
4) mechanization makes production so efficient that too abundant a supply results. As a reaction enterprises tend to large scale dismissals, and also in this way mechanization becomes a cause of poverty.

Thus the concern about economic growth becomes a palliative to over-production with the ensuing necessity to create demands, e.g. through advertising. It could be worth while to consider the introduction of industrial production quotes as we know them from fishing as well as the use of labour less in industrial production than in the trades of repair.

These observations form another background to the over-optimistic statements of politicians and businessmen or – women. Again, I am not against the web or email – I use both regularly – but as a citizen I feel concerned, because mechanization has reached most areas of society. Tasks which formerly were performed by unskilled labour are becoming ever less numerous, and where can these persons find employment now? If anything happens at all, the streets are cleared of snow by machines and in order to work in an office you must today know more than how to use a typewriter. The computer claims more qualifications; consequently, we must consider the new technology as one of the causes of poverty, but not as the only cause. Other circumstances play a role as well, as e.g. insufficient education in Kiel, in Schleswig-Holstein and in France. The introduction of information technology is an advantage, but it has got a price that must be paid...not so much in cash, but in human capital.

Communication III : Les niveaux de vie et la « société de consommation »
Thomas Riis

La pauvreté comprend, nous le savons tous, la notion de la privation.[1] Même si la santé de la personne n'est pas menacée, cette dernière peut expérimenter la privation en comparaison avec des collègues, qui ont reçu la même formation, mais ont obtenu des postes mieux rémunérés. Il en est de même pour les familles distinguées aux ressources modestes, situation classique des pauvres honteux, pas seulement à l'époque contemporaine.[2] Cependant, une circonstance fait aggraver la situation, à savoir l'augmentation du niveau de vie et en même temps des exigences pour avoir une vie décente.[3]

Les exigences accrues

Au lendemain de la Deuxième Guerre Mondiale les autos privées étaient plutôt rares. Evidemment, il y avait des familles qui en avaient achetées déjà avant 1939 ; en dehors de ce groupe, on en trouvait surtout chez les médecins (chez qui la voiture était indispensable), chez les avocats ou chez les hommes d'affaires.

Aujourd'hui, cinquante ou soixante ans plus tard, il est normal que chaque famille ait au moins une voiture – par exemple une (grande) pour le père, une autre (plus petite) pour la mère, et une d'occasion pour le fils ou la fille à l'université. Parfois, les deux parents ont, tous les deux, besoin d'une auto à cause de leur travail, parfois, c'est seulement une question de commodité. Mais il faut aussi considérer le nombre de familles qui ne peuvent pas se permettre une petite voiture d'occasion.

---

1 WILFRED BECKERMAN, « The Measurement of Poverty » dans : *Aspects of Poverty in Early Modern Europe* [I], ed. THOMAS RIIS, Stuttgart 1981, p. 49.

2 Voir la description des aristocrates pauvres, qui pendant toute l'année font des économies afin de pouvoir recevoir une fois l'an comme il faut, par GIOVANNI VERGA, *Mastro Don Gesualdo*, 1888–1889. Selon la tradition, ce roman a lieu au XIXᵉ siècle à Vizzini (Sicile).

3 Constaté déjà en 1979 par WILFRED BECKERMAN, « The Measurement of Poverty » (comme note 1ère), p. 53.

Les vacances sont nécessaires pour la régénération du corps et de l'esprit après une année de travail ; pour cette raison dans certains pays, les employés sont obligés de placer une partie de leurs vacances en été. Il y a toujours été des endroits d'estivage plus chics que les autres : la Costa Smeralda en Sardaigne, la Versilia au nord de Pise, en France la Côte d'Azur, Biarritz ou Deauville, et pourquoi est-ce que, parmi les îles allemandes dans la Mer du Nord, Sylt attire une clientèle huppée contrairement aux îles voisines d'Amrum et de Föhr ? – et pourtant aux années 1840 le roi du Danemark passait ses vacances d'été à Föhr afin de profiter des bains de mer.

Pour ceux qui ne peuvent pas se permettre ni des vacances en un endroit chic, ni une maison de campagne, le tourisme de masse représente, à partir des années 1950, une solution. La semaine passée à Antalya (Turquie) ou à Majorque place la famille parmi celles qui peuvent se permettre des vacances « comme il faut ». Restent les excentriques qui préfèrent s'organiser autrement et tous ceux qui pour des raisons économiques doivent se contenter d'une excursion à la forêt ou à la plage.

Que le séjour en un endroit chic devient un fardeau, on le voit à travers le nombre diminuant de nuits passées à Sylt, à Timmendorfer Strand et à Travemünde ; en 2000 le nombre de nuits passées par touriste était à peu près la moitié du nombre noté pour 1970, tandis que le fléchissement était moins prononcé pour les stations balnéaires moins chics.

Tourisme balnéaire Scharbeutz, Timmendorfer Strand, Travemünde 1931–2000*

	Nuitées	Lits	Emploi des lits (Nuitées)	Hôtes	Nuitées par hôte
1931	111.585	-	-	-	-
1938	547.903	-	-	-	-
1950	334.875	-	-	-	-
1959	1.106.115	-	-	-	-
1970	2.260.238	22.892	98.7	227.484	9.9
1980	1.891.452	30.483	62.1	233.024	8.1
1990	1.237.759	13.572	91.2	228.093	5.4
2000	1.163.884	14.187	82.0	234.380	5.0

* 1931 seulement Travemünde, 1970 avec Haffkrug.

Source : *Beiträge zur historischen Statistik Schleswig-Holsteins*, Kiel 1967, pp. 154–155 tables 6 c–d ; *Statistisches Jahrbuch Schleswig-Holstein* 1971, pp. 125–126 table 11 ; *do.* 1981, pp. 130–131 table 11 ; *do.* 1991, pp. 104–105 table 10 ; *do.* 2001, pp. 148–149 table 11.

Tourisme balnéaire Sylt 1938–2000 *

	Nuitées	Lits	Emploi des lits (Nuitées)	Hôtes	Nuitées par hôte
1938	660.380	-	-	40.107	13.6
1950	453.536	-	-	28.310	13.6
1959	1.126.954	-	-	70.419	13.2
1970	3.057.758	36.727	83.3	193.973	15.8
1980	3.160.792	38.749	81.6	230.283	11.3
1990	1.906.307	19.169	99.5	184.955	10.3
2000	1.982.591	21.880	90.6	237.340	8.4

* 1938–1959 seulement Kampen, Wenningstedt et Westerland ; 1970–2000 aussi Hörnum, List, Rantum et Sylt Ost.

Source : *Beiträge zur historischen Statistik Schleswig-Holsteins*, Kiel 1967, pp. 154–155 tables 6 c–d ; *Statistisches Jahrbuch Schleswig-Holstein* 1971, pp. 125–126 table 11 ; *do.* 1981, pp. 130–131 table 11 ; *do.* 1991, pp. 104–105 table 10 ; *do.* 2001, pp. 148–149 table 11.

Aussi dans les programmes scolaires les voyages jouent un plus grand rôle qu'autrefois : visiter un pays dont on apprend la langue est devenu tout à fait normal, même si pour des raisons économiques certains élèves ne peuvent pas y participer.

Notre famille aimerait de temps à autre manger dans un bon restaurant, mais hésite devant le prix pour un couple avec deux enfants. Même si le restaurant n'est pas inabordable, on risque de payer autant que les dépenses ménagères pendant une semaine entière.

L'exercice est bon pour la santé, tout le monde en convient, mais aussi, il y a les sports chics et les autres. Au milieu du XIXe siècle, les « public schools » britanniques s'adonnaient au football, mais en face de la popularité grandissante de ce sport dans les classes populaires et de la possibilité de défaites à des équipes ouvrières, les institutions d'enseignement, elles, perdaient leur intérêt au football, préférant le rugby. De façon générale, les disciplines caractérisées par la force comme la boxe ou la lutte sont considérées moins distinguées que celles marquées par la vitesse comme l'aviron, le ski ou le tennis.[4]

Par notre propre expérience, nous avons pu constater la considération changeante de certains sports en Europe du Nord. Si, aux années 1970, le badminton était un sport préféré de maint étudiant, leurs parents économiquement consolidés étaient des partisans du tennis. Lentement, ce dernier devenait plus populaire. C'est pourquoi les couches aisées le délaissaient en faveur du squash et, surtout, du golf.[5] Comme l'équipement du « golfer » est bien plus coûteux que celui du joueur au tennis, nous constatons une polarisation sociale parmi les sportifs.

Avant la deuxième guerre mondiale, le phénomène des vêtements signés n'était pas très répandu en Europe du Nord pour se diffuser rapidement pendant le dernier tiers du XXe siècle. Même les écoliers « doivent » arborer certaines marques afin d'être acceptés socialement ; aussi ici, on constate la polarisation sociale et économiques de la population.

La promotion du niveau de vie chic (« lifestyle »)

L'accroissement des exigences, dont nous venons de voir des exemples, ne pourrait pas être si rapide ou si prononcé, s'il n'avait pas

---

4 HANS BONDE, « Den hurtige Mand. Mandsidealer i den tidlige danske sportsbevægelse », *Historisk Tidsskrift* 88, Copenhague 1988, pp. 34–43.

5 Ici, il faut se rappeler que le golf est un sport qu'on peut exercer même en un âge avancé.

été renforcé par les médias. Selon eux, il faut être jeune, beau/belle et riche, image diffusée par les magazines et par la publicité.[6] La question reste, si du point de vue économie politique, cette attitude ne révèle pas un manque de responsabilité sociale et économique ? Si l'on compare par exemple le temps de fonction d'une voiture sans réparation majeure avec le nombre d'autos produites, la conclusion est évidente : il y a une surproduction énorme dans l'industrie des automobiles et rares sont les entreprises qui fabriquent autres produits et de cette façon assurent du travail aux employés, si le marché des voitures allait fléchir. La seule action possible reste ainsi l'augmentation artificielle de la demande à l'aide de la publicité.

Les coûts du niveau de vie chic

La vie chic a son prix, d'abord parce qu'un revenu ne suffit que rarement. Par cette raison, les deux époux doivent travailler, ce qui nécessite souvent l'achat d'une deuxième voiture ; si le couple a des enfants, il faut leur trouver (et payer) une place dans une crèche ou dans un jardin d'enfants. C'était le problème d'un jeune collègue entré en fonction à Kiel en 2000 ; auparavant, la famille avait habité le Mecklembourg et la Saxe-Anhalt. Dans ces deux Bundesländer (non pas au Schleswig-Holstein), les jardins d'enfants et les crèches étaient gratuits et chaque enfant y avait droit à une place comme au temps de la RDA. C'est pourquoi l'initiative de la ministre fédérale de la famille, Madame von der Leyen (Démocratie chrétienne) pour augmenter le nombre des places de crèche, a été fortement critiqué, surtout au sein du parti de la ministre, comme voulant introduire des conditions comme dans la RDA.[7] Le résultat des places insuffisantes est plus de stress pour la famille et moins de temps pour les enfants et pour le conjoint, par contre, la création des crèches et des jardins d'enfants gratuits comme les écoles permettraient, si nécessaire, aux deux parents de travailler.

---

6 Voir pour la critique des images créées GÖRAN PALM, *Indoktrineringen i Sverige*, Stockholm 1968 , et de façon plus artistique, SIMONE DE BEAUVOIR, *Les belles images*, Paris 1972.

7 *Kieler Nachrichten* le 14 février 2007, p. 13 (rapport par CAROLA JESCHKE des conférences données par Madame von der Leyen à Kiel en février 2007).

Voici les coûts au niveau de la famille individuelle, mais aussi pour la société en général, le « lifestyle » a son prix. Il déclenche une polarisation de la société : d'un côté les jeunes, les beaux/belles et les riches,[8] de l'autre ceux qui n'arriveront jamais à ce niveau de vie. Dans ce dernier groupe le sens de la privation sans remède augmente jusqu'au moment, où la situation explose. On y arriva vers la fin de 2005 dans la banlieue parisienne,[9] mais il ne s'agit pas d'un phénomène exclusivement français. Partout, où le décalage entre la vie chic et la réalité quotidienne est devenu trop grand, on trouve un potentiel révolutionnaire, surtout si des problèmes de marginalisation ethnique s'y ajoutent, ce qui est souvent le cas, en France, comme en Allemagne, en Grande Bretagne, au Danemark ou au Pays Bas.

Que faire ?

C'est évident que les gouvernements doivent, enfin, prendre au sérieux les problèmes sociaux des ghettos, dans les banlieues comme ailleurs, en créant du travail pour les habitants et en les faisant intégrer dans la société. L'expérience du Mouvement ATD (Aide à toute détresse) Quart-Monde montre que les chances de succès s'améliorent si les pauvres et marginalisés contribuent au travail. La participation leur montre que la solution proposée n'est pas imposée par une autorité extérieure mais que les bénéficiaires de l'aide sont des partenaires dans l'exécution du projet.

Pour des raisons de prudence sociale, il faut faire diminuer l'aggressivité de la publicité pour le « lifestyle ». Sous cet aspect, les vêtements et les accessoires signés sont en eux-mêmes des exemples de publicité, car il s'agit, bien entendu, de faire reconnaître la carrosse de Hermès, le crocodile de Lacoste ou le dessin à carreaux de Burberry, etc. etc.

Une taxe de luxe sur les vêtements et les accessoires signés, sur la publicité pour le « lifestyle » ainsi que pour les voitures paraîtrait à beaucoup de personnes exagérée et injuste ; à vrai dire, il ne l'est pas plus que celle du tabac. On justifie cette dernière avec le souci de la

---

8 Une variante en est les soi-disants « Dinkies » = D(ouble) I(ncome) N(o) K(ids) = revenu double sans enfants.
9 Voir *Le Monde Diplomatique* Décembre 2005, pp. 1, 20–23 et 36.

santé de la personne, mais la taxe de luxe proposée profiterait à la santé de la société en évitant des explosions révolutionnaires et en diminuant les tensions sociales.

Les institutions charitables de l'Europe moderne et la question de leur efficacité
—————— Jean-Pierre Gutton ——————

Le Moyen Age laisse aux Temps modernes un réseau très dense d'institutions charitables. Ces institutions, hôpitaux et maladières, sont la plupart du temps de taille modeste et, pour les premiers, sont loin de toujours hospitaliser ceux qu'ils assistent. Elles sont, à la fin du Moyen Age, l'objet de critiques diverses. Certaines sont dues à des abus dans la gestion, mais beaucoup s'expliquent par une nouvelle vision de la pauvreté. L'identification des pauvres aux membres souffrants de Jésus-Christ demeure sans doute bien vivante. Cependant la détérioration des cadres traditionnels, puis les crises économiques ont multiplié les pauvres et les ont poussés vers les villes.[1] Les grandes pestes du milieu du XIVe s., entraînant vagabondage et pénurie de main d'œuvre, sont sans doute décisives pour comprendre le reflux de l'idée que la pauvreté est un signe d'élection. C'est le temps où plusieurs pays européens prennent des mesures contre la mendicité : la Castille en 1351, l'Angleterre en 1349 et 1351, la France en 1350. On voit s'instituer une distinction entre les « bons » et les « mauvais » pauvres et se multiplier les critiques contre les « aumônes » qui sont distribuées sans contrôle. Des essais de réformes voient le jour. Ainsi, dans le cadre du diocèse de Genève, on constate que dès 1446 l'évêque auxiliaire, Barthélemy Vitelleschi, est chargé de visiter et de réformer les institutions charitables. Un règlement de l'hôpital de Genève, en 1459, pose que la maladie ou l'infirmité sont les critères essentiels pour recevoir les pauvres dans l'établissement.[2]

---

1 G. Duby, « Les pauvres des campagnes dans l'Occident médiéval jusqu'au XIIIe siècle », *R. H. E. F.*, 1966, pp. 25–32. M. Mollat, *Les pauvres au Moyen Age. Etude sociale*, Paris 1978.

2 C. Hermann, *Assistance et charité dans le diocèse de Genève. Hôpitaux et maladières (milieu XIIIe – début XVIe siècle)*, Thèse Chambéry, 2005, 3 vol. Cf. T. 1 p. 160 sqq. et T. 2 p. 227.

Ce n'est cependant qu'au début du XVIe s. que les décisions essentielles sont prises. Une grande méfiance à l'égard des pauvres se développe alors. Le contexte des guerres civiles ou étrangères fait de l'errant un espion ou un colporteur de l'hérésie. Les désordres populaires font peur et si Lyon se dote en 1531 d'une Aumône générale c'est que le souvenir de la Grande Rebeyne de 1529 est très vif. Les pauvres sont aussi accusés d'être des agents de la peste : on a remarqué depuis longtemps qu'ils fournissent les victimes les plus nombreuses des épidémies et, en 1546, le médecin padouan Frascator expose une théorie de la transmission de la contagion. Et c'est aussi l'attitude à l'égard de la pauvreté qui a fini de se modifier en prenant de la distance vis à vis de l'idéalisation franciscaine de la pauvreté et de la mendicité. Les auteurs humanistes affirment volontiers que la pauvreté est un handicap à l'épanouissement humain, tandis que la littérature de la gueuserie dénonce les faux mendiants accentuant la distinction entre « bons » et « mauvais » pauvres. Cette transformation des idées sur la pauvreté passe par une critique de l'oisiveté et par une exaltation des vertus du travail. L'idée que travailler c'est prier, apparue dès le Moyen Age, finit de se répandre dans les pays catholiques comme dans les pays réformés. Cette évolution des idées suppose donc une réforme, voire une refondation, des systèmes d'assistance.

De fait, les différences confessionnelles ne semblent pas jouer de rôle décisif. Sans doute à Zurich le « Mandat » du 15 janvier 1525 qui organise l'assistance publique à l'égard des pauvres enregistrés, surveillés et interdits de mendicité doit autant à l'action de Zwingli qu'à celle de la municipalité. Cependant, les politiques d'assistance de Francfort, acquise à la Réforme, et de Cologne, restée fidèle au catholicisme, sont bien semblables. Et des réformes comparables sont réalisées à Nuremberg (1522), Strasbourg (1523), Mons et Ypres (1525), Lille (1527) et, plus généralement dans les Pays Bas grâce à un édit de Charles-Quint pris le 7 octobre 1531. Ainsi une organisation de l'assistance née dans des villes (Nuremberg, Strasbourg) catholiques mais pénétrées par les nouvelles doctrines religieuses inspirait la législation de Charles-Quint.[3] Et c'est à Bruges, le 17 mars 1526, que paraît le *De Subventione Pauperum,* promis à un grand retentissement et qui faisait, après coup, la théorie de ces réformes : rôle des magistrats des villes dans la gestion des fondations charitables ; renvoi, avec une passade, des pauvres étrangers ; emprisonnement des mendiants valides ; travail ou secours fournis aux pauvres. Centralisation des secours, réforme morale et nécessité de travailler étaient les idées force. Une telle politique se répand aussi en France. Ici, le rôle du pouvoir central pour interdire mendicité et vagabondage est affirmée par François Ier et Henri II dans une abondante législation qui laisse toutefois la responsabilité de l'application aux villes. Ces dernières agissent dans deux directions. D'une part, aidées là encore par des édits royaux, elles investissent les bureaux d'administration des hôpitaux, affirmant le caractère désormais public de l'assistance. D'autre part et surtout, « aumôsnes générales » ou « bureaux des pauvres » sont créés. Ici encore, c'est à partir des années 1525–1530 que des taxes pour les pauvres sont décidées à charge pour l'aumône générale de centraliser toutes les ressources de l'assistance, de recenser les pauvres et de les secourir et, bien sûr, d'empêcher la mendicité. L'Aumône générale de Lyon et le Grand Bureau de Pauvres de Paris ne sont que les plus connues de ces institutions. Les pauvres sont parfois contraints à porter une marque distinctive et ils reçoivent des secours dans des distributions régulières et ordonnées qui rompent avec les distributions à la porte des couvents génératrices de rixes. Les mendiants valides qui n'auront pas de travail sont contraints à travailler à la voirie, aux fortifications. Des « bedeaux » ou « chasse-coquins » veillent à faire respecter l'interdiction de la mendicité.

On retrouve dans beaucoup d'autres Etats européens des attitudes analogues. Venise lutte fermement contre la mendicité surtout à partir de 1540.[4] Dans les Etats pontificaux, Paul IV ou Sixte-Quint font de même. En Angleterre, le mouvement des enclosures a multi-

3 P. Bonenfant, « Les origines et le caractère de la réforme de la bienfaisance publique aux Pays-Bas sous le règne de Charles – Quint », *Revue belge de Philologie et d'Histoire*, 1926, pp. 887–904 et 1927, pp. 207–230.
4 B. Pullan, *Rich and Poor in Renaissance Venice. The Social Institutions of a Catholic State, to 1620*, Oxford, 1971.

plié les pauvres et les réformes religieuses d'Henri VIII ont fait table rase d'un système d'assistance ancien. Là encore les interdictions de mendier se multiplient. Le principe d'une taxe des pauvres s'impose tôt et devient obligatoire en 1562. Les ressources générées permettent de créer dans différentes villes – Londres, Norwich, Ipswich, Lincoln, Cambridge, … – des institutions spécialisées. En 1598 est prise une loi de circonstances qui deviendra, en 1601, la loi des Pauvres d'Elisabeth. Le système créé, applicable à l'Angleterre et au Pays de Galles, est nourri par la taxe hebdomadaire et obligatoire levée sur chaque paroisse qui finance trois types d'action : pauvres invalides et vieillards sont secourus ; les enfants pauvres sont mis en apprentissage ; les pauvres valides sont mis au travail. Cependant un pays demeure partiellement en marge de cette évolution. C'est l'Espagne où des « licences » de mendier sont délivrées par les curés à leurs paroissiens miséreux, par les recteurs aux étudiants pauvres. Cette nation, qui est la première puissance politique et militaire du monde chrétien, ne parvient pas à développer ses manufactures. Elle n'a pas le même culte du travail et elle ne suit que partiellement les idées de J. L. Vivès pourtant valencien. Certes, il y a, à partir de 1540, la création de bureaux des pauvres à Zamora, Salamanque, Valladolid. En mars 1545, paraissait à Salamanque l'ouvrage d'un bénédictin, Juan de Medina, proposant la suppression de la mendicité moyennant une taxe volontaire.[5] Les mendiants valides seraient contraints au travail forcé, des secours seraient donnés aux pauvres invalides et les enfants recevraient une éducation. Mais, en janvier de la même année Domingo de Soto avait pris la défense des mendiants dans sa *Deliberacion en la causa de los pobres* également parue à Salamanque. Il reconnaît aux pouvoirs publics le droit d'interdire la mendicité. Toutefois, si le nécessaire manque, mendier est légitime. Le jour du jugement, les pauvres ne risquent-ils pas de se dresser contre la cruauté des aisés ? Faut-il enlever aux riches l'occasion de faire leur salut ? C'est aussi le temps où les frères de la Charité de Jean de Dieu, établis à Grenade en 1540, ces « frères au cabas », collectent les aumônes le soir tombant, quand le chrétien

---

5 Sur les ouvrages espagnols relatifs à la pauvreté, commode choix de textes dans : *Le débat sur les pauvres et la pauvreté dans l'Espagne du siècle d'or (1520–1620)*. Les pièces du dossier p. p. R. Carrasco et M. Cavillac, Toulouse 1991.

est saisi par l'angoisse du salut. Plus tard, en 1564, le *De œconomia socia circo pauperum curam a Christo instituta* du moine espagnol Laurent de Villavicencio défend encore la mendicité en réponse à un nouveau plan d'assistance à Bruges. Il affirme aussi que le pouvoir civil n'a pas à réglementer ces matières.

Plus encore que les résistances ibériques, il convient de souligner le désenchantement qui suit, assez rapidement, la mise en place des nouvelles formes d'assistance en Europe. On a tôt fait de constater que les bureaux des pauvres ne font pas disparaître la mendicité et des revendications de mises à l'écart des pauvres sont désormais des pierres d'attente d'un enfermement que le XVIIe s. tentera de mettre en œuvre. C'est surtout l'Angleterre qui sera tentée par la déportation. Ailleurs c'est essentiellement l'enfermement dans des hôpitaux qui est mis en avant, notamment par une recommandation du concile de Bordeaux en 1583.[6] A Rome, Grégoire XIII et Sixte-Quint font interner des mendiants. A Amsterdam, le *Rasphuis* pour hommes et le *Spinhuis* pour femmes sont de vraies maisons de correction pour mendiants ; l'exemple hollandais sera, plus tard, souvent invoqué. Et l'Espagne même semble se rapprocher de ces solutions. Un manuscrit anonyme de 1560 condamne fermement l'aumône, recommande un impôt payé par tous sur les produits de première nécessité et permettant de regrouper les pauvres dans des hôpitaux généraux où ils seront éduqués et mis au travail.[7] Le *Tratato del remedio de pobres* (1579) de Miquel de Giginta, chanoine d'Elne, fournit une solution mixte mêlant charité publique et charité privée, enfermement et mendicité.[8] De 1574 à 1588, Giginta parcourt la péninsule ibérique de Perpignan à Lisbonne, par Barcelone, Madrid, Tolède, l'Andalousie pour convaincre les autorités. Il réussit à fonder des *Casas de Misericordia,* notamment à Tolède, à Madrid et à Barcelone, seule la dernière ayant une véritable longévité. Ces maisons comportent des ateliers qui servent surtout à réapprendre le

---

6 J. IMBERT, « Les prescriptions hospitalières du Concile de Trente et leur diffusion en France », *R. H. E. F.*, 1956, pp. 5–28.

7 J. SOUBEYROUX, « Sur un projet original de l'organisation de la bienfaisance en Espagne au XVIe siècle », *Bulletin hispanique*, 1972, pp. 118–4.

8 MIQUEL DE GIGINTA. *Chanoine d'Elne*, Perpignan 2003 (Actes du colloque des 5 et 6 juillet 2002).

travail. Mais elles demeurent ouvertes et on peut en sortir, notamment pour quêter au profit de l'institution. La mendicité est ici institution-nalisée. Quelque vingt ans plus tard, les neuf *Discursos del Amparo de los legítimos pobres, y reduccion de los fingidos y principio de los Albergues destos Reynos* (1598) du docteur Cristobàl Pérez de Herrera va plus loin. C'est un pro-jet de réforme économique et sociale qui se fonde sur le développement du secteur productif grâce à la mise au travail des pauvres mendiants. Certes les « pauvres légitimes » sont autorisés à mendier. Mais d'autres traits annoncent l'enfermement du XVIIᵉ s. : organisation conventuelle du temps, instruction religieuse obligatoire, rafle des vagabonds, travail obligatoire. La disparition de Philippe II réduisit le crédit de Herrera qui était médecin des galères et médecin du roi et peu de choses furent réalisées. On a pu noter que Herrera, fonctionnaire moyen, se sentait menacé par la hantise de la pureté de sang et qu'il voulait que la dignité soit désormais liée à l'utilité sociale et à une conception de l'honneur plus large et négligeant les clivages sociaux. C'était une condamnation de l'oisiveté que l'Espagne n'était pas encore prête à entendre.[9]

C'est le XVIIᵉ s. qui, un peu partout en Europe, allait créer de nouvelles institutions d'assistance. Ce sont assez largement des insti-tutions d'enfermement. Amsterdam et les Provinces-Unies en avaient donné l'exemple. Les Pays-Bas catholiques suivent et, en 1621, Bruxel-les se dote d'un *Tuchthuys* dans lequel les pauvres fabriquent du drap. En Angleterre, ce sont les *Bridewells*, maisons de correction, et les *Workhou-ses*, maisons de travail. L'Italie, notamment les Etats pontificaux et la Savoie, font de même. En France, les hôpitaux généraux se multiplient, soit par création, soit par transformation d'un ancien établissement. L'Aumône générale de Lyon, dont la fonction d'hôpital général est dé-cidée en 1614, sert de modèle. La monarchie, sans le financer, prescrit l'enfermement, particulièrement par un édit de juin 1662, un arrêt du conseil de juin 1673, une lettre aux évêques et aux intendants de juin 1676.

Il faut s'interroger sur les raisons de cette diffusion européenne de l'enfermement. Il est évident que les misères du temps y sont pour

---

9 M. CAVILLAC, « Noblesse et ambiguïté au temps de Cervantes : le cas du docteur Cristobal Pérez de Herrera (1556 ? – 1620) », *Mélanges de la Casa Velasquez*, XI, 1975, pp. 177–212.

beaucoup. Mais la volonté d'enfermer est surtout soutenue, un peu partout, par deux importants groupes de pression. Le premier est celui des mercantilistes. Enfermer les pauvres c'est imposer un système uniforme d'assistance et on retrouve ici le caractère unificateur, souvent relevé, du mercantilisme.[10] C'est aussi vouloir mettre tout le monde au travail. Les mercantilistes français – Laffémas, Montchrestien, La Gomberdière, Eon, Richelieu, … – y reviennent constamment. Le fait que les Provinces-Unies aient donné l'exemple de l'enfermement et que leur étonnante réussite économique intrigue et désole ne peut qu'aiguiser l'engagement des mercantilistes en faveur des hôpitaux généraux. Effectivement, des manufactures fonctionnent dans les hôpitaux généraux ou les *workhouses*. Elles ne sont pas toujours rentables mais on les conserve car elles sont aussi des écoles professionnelles et parce qu'elles exaltent les vertus du travail. Ce dernier dompte les passions ; il est donc entraînement à l'exercice du libre arbitre. Il a aussi une valeur éthique et religieuse. Pour ceux qui ne peuvent prier, il a valeur de prière. D'autant qu'à la même époque la création des filles séculières affirme qu'il n'y a pas de différence entre prière et travail. Au reste, le second groupe de pression est spirituel. En France, ce sont les dévots, les membres de la compagnie du Saint-Sacrement qui sont souvent à l'origine de la fondation d'un hôpital général, à commencer par celui de Paris, en 1656. Ce sont eux qui imposent, dans le monde clos de l'hôpital, une vie réglée, la périodicité des exercices du culte, le catéchisme plus encore. Tous ceux qui récusent un certain ordre religieux, moral, familial doivent être enfermés pour les contraindre à sauver leurs âmes. Il s'agit des mendiants et vagabonds, mais aussi des libertins, des enfants rebelles, des prostituées. L'âge classique considère que c'est le péché et le vice qui sont à l'origine de la pauvreté. Cette image pessimiste de la pauvreté soutenue par les représentations peintes ou gravées de rixes de mendiants et par la diffusion d'une littérature de la gueuserie conforte la volonté de séparer « bons » et « mauvais » pauvres. Au musée du Puy-en-Velay un tableau représente un bienfaiteur de l'hôpital général assis à sa table de travail. Une Bible y est ouverte au psaume 4 :

---

10 E. F. HECKSCHER, *Mercantilism*, Londres 1955.

fais du bien Yahvé, aux gens de bien,
qui ont au cœur la droiture
mais les tortueux, les dévoyés,
qu'il les repousse
Yahvé, avec les malfaisants.

Reste à dire cependant que les nouveautés du XVIIe s. ne se résument pas à la diffusion de l'enfermement. Les hôpitaux généraux bien loin d'enfermer de nombreux mendiants, accueillent surtout des vieillards qui demandent volontairement leur admission. Les formes anciennes de charité subsistent : aumônes, petits hôpitaux accueillant les passants demeurent actifs. Les vieux hôtels-Dieu entament une transformation dans le sens de la médicalisation : la visite quotidienne des médecins est souvent instaurée et surtout les filles séculières constituent désormais des soignantes au service des malades. Même en Angleterre la charité privée demeure plus importante que la charité institutionnelle.[11] De plus, au travers des hôpitaux généraux comme au travers d'écoles ouvertes dans les villes et dans les campagnes, le souci de scolariser les enfants pauvres est devenu très important. C'était certes la manifestation de l'idée que pour faire son salut, il faut un certain nombre de connaissances et, en France, la compagnie du Saint-Sacrement y insiste beaucoup. Mais, parce que l'enseignement professionnel n'était pas négligé, c'était aussi la reconnaissance de raisons matérielles et non plus seulement morales, dans le processsus de paupérisation. Le XVIIIe s. s'annonçait.

Ce siècle s'est beaucoup préoccupé d'institutions sociales et il le fit dans un esprit nouveau.[12] Dès la fin du XVIIe s., les « arithmé-ticiens politiques », anglais ou français, avaient notamment appris à compter les pauvres. De ce souci de dénombrement naît bientôt l'idée que économie et société peuvent être responsables du paupérisme. A partir des années 1610, les jésuites avec les « réductions », républiques communautaires chrétiennes, avaient d'ailleurs compris ce lien et don-né l'exemple d'une utopie réalisée. Les utopies du XVIIIe s. utilisent

---

11 W. K. Jordan, *Philanthropy in England, 1480–1660*, New York-Londres 1959.
12 Essai de synthèse dans J. P. Gutton, *La société et les pauvres en Europe (XVIe–XVIIIe siècles)*, Paris 1974.

alors le thème de la communauté des biens supprimant tout pauvre. Mais surtout, au-delà des constructions utopiques, se développent des réflexions sur le rôle du recrutement militaire, de la fiscalité, du prix des grains, du rapport entre paupérisme, population et subsistances, du marché de l'emploi. La formule de Montesquieu, dans *L'Esprit des lois* (1748), « Un homme n'est pas pauvre parce qu'il n'a rien, mais parce qu'il ne travaille pas » résume cette réflexion avec une acuité qui demeure, hélas, contemporaine. Au niveau des solutions, deux thèmes s'imposent bientôt. La charité ecclésiastique, tout comme les fondations, ont montré leur impuissance. C'est l'Etat qui doit prendre en charge l'assistance et, à ce titre, il a le droit de s'emparer des biens des fondations. Cela est particulièrement vrai dans les pays qui connaissent le despotisme éclairé.

A partir de ces principes, les Etats, au XVIIIᵉ s., tout en conservant les institutions charitables du passé, mettent en œuvre de nouveaux procédés. Mendicité et vagabondage, désormais sévèrement condamnés, y compris dans la péninsule ibérique, sont combattus par des maisons de correction ou de travail dans l'Espagne de Charles III, dans l'Empire de Joseph II par exemple. En France, des dépôts de mendicité (1768) assurent, pour la première fois, un véritable enfermement et permettent aux hôpitaux de mieux se consacrer aux malades. Partout aussi la création d'écoles, particulièrement d'écoles professionnelles, est à l'ordre du jour : en France, dans les Pays-Bas autrichiens, en Angleterre, en Espagne,… Cet accent mis sur l'école est gage d'une réhabilitation du travail. Celle-ci se manifeste par des ateliers de charité en France, des manufactures pour donner du travail à des journaliers sans emploi, des maisons de travail dans l'Empire et en Prusse. Dans ce dernier Etat s'ajoute la colonisation intérieure. Enfin la lutte contre la maladie fait désormais partie de la politique sociale.[13]

---

13 Voir par exemple pour la France les archives de la Société royale de médecine conservées à l'Académie de médecine (Paris). Pour l'Italie des Bourbons : S. RAFFAELE, *Della beneficenza all' assistenza. Momenti di politica assistenziale nella Sicilia moderna*, Catania 1990.

A ce tableau des nouveautés apportées au XVIIIe s. il convient, enfin, d'ajouter tout ce qui répond aux mutations du sentiment de sécurité. Un « transfert de ciel à terre » s'est opéré dans ce domaine.[14] On commence à vouloir construire la sécurité matérielle sans compter exclusivement sur la providence et les intercesseurs célestes. Ainsi le vieux problème du crédit est mieux maîtrisé. La diffusion des monts-de-piété, longtemps limitée aux Pays-Bas, à la péninsule italienne et à la France du Sud-Est, s'étend à l'Espagne, aux Provinces-Unies. La France les accueille bien modestement, mais Paris en est doté en 1777. Un autre type d'organisme charitable, assez proche, le mont frumentaire, se diffuse à partir des années 1700. Sans intérêt, ou avec un intérêt très modique, il prête des semences aux paysans d'Italie du Sud, de Provence, d'Espagne, de Suisse ou de Pologne. Plus encore, c'est le souci de prévoyance et d'épargne qui s'impose. Dès les années 1680, le système d'assurance, depuis longtemps appliqué au commerce, est appliqué aux risques maladie, vieillesse, décès. Defoe, dans son Essay in *Projects* de 1697 étendait même l'idée à l'assurance contre le chômage, pour faire en sorte que « toute créature si misérable et si pauvre qu'elle soit, puisse revendiquer sa subsistance comme un dû, au lieu de l'implorer comme une aumône ». Le comte de Boulainvilliers, Lavoisier proposent de tels systèmes. En Espagne, Campomanes favorise les *monte-pios* de métiers, caisses de secours mutuels qui, moyennant le versement d'une petite partie du salaire, assistent vieillards, veuves, invalides, orphelins.[15] Nous aurons à dire l'importance de l'aide apportée aux vieillards par de véritables pensions de retraite.

Une dernière remarque enfin. Présenter, comme nous avons tenté de le faire, les institutions charitables privilégiées par chaque sieclé de l'époque moderne demeure insuffisant si l'on n'insiste pas à nouveau sur le semis de très petits hôpitaux qui, y compris dans de très modestes communautés d'habitants, assurent des secours à domicile ou dans leurs murs. L'enquête conduite par le Comité des secours publics de l'Assemblée législative, en décembre 1791, fait état

---

14 L. FEBVRE, « Pour l'histoire d'un sentiment : le besoin de sécurité », *Annales. E. S. C.*, 1956, pp. 244–247.

15 L. DOMERGUE, *Jovellanos à la Société économique des Amis du Pays de Madrid (1778–1795)*, Toulouse 1971.

de 2326 établissements à cette date.[16] Encore faut-il ajouter que dans le cas français – et sans doute n'est-il pas isolé – des groupements associatifs jouent un grand rôle. C'est le cas des confréries. Les vieilles confréries de métier assistent leurs membres pauvres ou malades. La réforme catholique a vu l'éclosion de nouvelles confréries parfois très spécialisées (vouées au rachat des esclaves des Barbaresques par exemple), d'autres beaucoup plus « généralistes » sous le vocable de confréries de charité, filles de l'initiative de Vincent de Paul en 1617. Et, au XVIIIe s., de manière indépendante de l'Eglise de nombreux « bureaux de charité » verront le jour. Si ces thèmes sont bien connus depuis longtemps, on finit à peine en revanche de découvrir le rôle des confréries dans le crédit populaire. Pour l'Espagne, on a pu montrer combien, dans les Asturies, dans le Léon, les confréries constituent, au XVIIIe s., la majorité des prêteurs aux humbles.[17] Les confréries meusiennes jouent le même rôle.[18] Les sociétés de prêtres qui, sous des appellations diverses, sont si nombreuses sont en ce point comparables aux confréries. Dans le Val d'Aran, les fondateurs de messes ou d'obits sont liés aux paysans demandeurs de prêts par l'intermédiaire des sociétés de prêtres, l'Eglise apportant garanties et sécurité à cet échange qui nourrit un crédit populaire.[19] Les sociétés de prêtres de la région lyonnaise valident aussi ce modèle.[20]

Le second objet de ce rapport est d'évaluer l'efficacité de ces institutions dans la lutte contre la pauvreté. C'est une tâche singulièrement délicate, sans doute même en partie hors des prises de l'histo-

---

16 M. JEORGER, « La structure hospitalière de la France sous l'Ancien Régime », *Annales. E.S.C.*, 1977, pp. 1025–1051.

17 *L'endettement paysan et le crédit dans les campagnes de la France moderne*, Toulouse 1998, pp. 239–281: F. Brumont, « Le crédit rural en Espagne du Nord-Ouest à l'époque moderne ».

18 F. SCHWINDT, *La communauté et la foi. Confréries et société dans l'Ouest de l'espace lorrain (XIIIe–XXe siècles)*, Thèse univ. Nancy 2 (L. CHÂTELLIER dir.), 2004, 4 vol. Cf. chapitre 11.

19 *L'endettement paysan...*, pp. 217–237: S. BRUNET, « Fondations de messes, crédit rural et marché de la terre dans les Pyrénées centrales (XVe–XVIIIe siècles): les communautés de prêtres du Val d'Aran ».

20 Voir notamment L. REGARD, *Les communautés de prêtres dans le diocèse de Lyon. XVIIe–XVIIIe siècles. La Société de prêtres de Saint-Pierre à Saint-Chamond. Etude de cas*, Master I, (J. P. GUTTON dir.) univ. Lyon 2, 2005. Partie II : Les sociétaires et l'argent.

rien si l'on songe combien l'évaluation des politiques sociales actuelles donne lieu à des débats. Il faut ajouter que cette tâche suppose clarifiée la conception que les temps modernes ont de l'efficacité. Or, les buts recherchés sont, au XVIe s., le souci d'ordre, d'économies, mais surtout celui du salut des âmes. Le XVIIe s., en pays réformés comme en pays catholiques, renforce ces thèmes et y ajoute le thème du travail forme de prière. La volonté de mettre, ou de remettre, sur le marché du travail doit d'abord au mercantilisme. Et ici force est de constater que les manufactures qui fonctionnaient dans les hôpitaux généraux étaient rarement rentables, devaient souvent changer de production et avaient surtout la double justification du travail équivalent de la prière et de leur rôle, cette fois bien réel, dans la formation professionnelle. Inversement, lorsque, à partir des années 1680, on affirme que la pauvreté a ses racines dans un certain nombre de dysfonctionnements de la société, l'efficacité des institutions charitables commence à être mesurée dans un esprit proche du nôtre.

Tentons un bilan. Il convient d'abord de dire l'intérêt des travaux de Torsten Fischer sur l'hérédité de la pauvreté à l'époque moderne. A partir de deux échantillons archivistiques, ceux d'Aberdeen et de Lyon, Monsieur Fischer construit un modèle permettant l'évaluation de l'ensemble des paramètres influençant la pauvreté. Il étudie le destin des familles dont un membre a été repéré dans les archives des institutions charitables. A Lyon comme à Aberdeen, la conclusion de ces analyses est que le plus souvent l'assistance permet de subvenir aux besoins biologiques mais ne permet pas de briser le cercle de la pauvreté. Ce n'est que dans le cas des « pauvres honteux », c'est à dire de pauvres appartenant à des groupes sociaux qui sont normalement à l'abri du besoin et à qui le travail manuel est interdit, que la réinsertion s'avère possible. Pour les autres, la reproduction de la pauvreté tient à l'impossibilité à créer une marge de manœuvre suffisante pour surmonter, décès, maladie, accident, chômage, calamités. T. Fischer note toutefois que l'éducation offerte par le *Poor's Hospital* d'Aberdeen donne des chances de sortir de la misère.

De fait, c'est d'abord à propos des enfants qui ont pu profiter d'une éducation élémentaire qu'on saisit l'efficacité de l'assistance. Les petites écoles destinées aux pauvres, ouvertes avec l'aide des municipalités par des clercs ou des laïcs, celles aussi qui sont organisées à l'intérieur des hôtels-Dieu et des hôpitaux généraux pour des enfants recueillis ont d'abord l'immense mérite de diffuser la civilité. A partir du *De civitate morum puerilium* d'Erasme (1530), la *civilitas* fait partie des modèles de conduite des Européens. Dans les écoles élémentaires, des ouvrages servent à la fois de manuels de lecture et de manuel de civilité. Ce mot désigne la manière de s'habiller, de se comporter en maîtrisant son corps. On emploie assez souvent le mot de modestie. La civilité n'est plus un caractère distinctif de la société policée des gens du monde. C'est toute la société qui doit se policer. Cela permet d'exercer son libre arbitre en éliminant les passions mauvaises. C'est un apprentissage de l'ordre, de la discipline, du silence qui atténue quelque peu les différences de manières entre les groupes sociaux et tente de faire de chaque enfant un être socialisé. C'est là un atout pour échapper à la pauvreté, mais pas une assurance. S'y ajoute évidemment l'atout de l'enseignement élémentaire de lecture, écriture, jet.

L'étude de l'insertion sociale des enfants âgés de plus de sept ans qui sont recueillis par la Charité de Lyon au XVIIIᵉ s. fournit cependant des éléments encourageants.[21] Les enfants « adoptifs »,[22] orphelins de naissance légitime, reçoivent une éducation soignée et leur avenir est assuré. Les autres enfants sont, le plus souvent, placés à la campagne chez des parents « nourriciers ». Dans la seconde moitié du siècle, la physiocratie et la peur de la dépopulation aidant, ils demeurent parfois très longtemps à la campagne et il y a des cas d'adoption par les nourriciers, comme il y en a pour les enfants de moins de sept ans placés par l'hôtel-Dieu.[23] Si les enfants ne restent pas placés en

---

21 J. P. GUTTON, « L'insertion des enfants recueillis par la Charité de Lyon au XVIIIᵉ siècle. Un bilan provisoire », dans *Lorsque l'enfant grandit. Entre dépendance et autonomie* (J. P. BARDET, J. N. LUC, I. ROBIN-ROMERO, C. ROLLET dir.) Paris 2002, pp. 929–939. Comparer avec F. MEYER, « Les nourrices des Bauges au XVIIIᵉ siècle » dans *Les Bauges. Entre lacs et Isère*, Chambéry, Mémoires et documents de la S. S. H. A., CVII, 2004, pp. 167–188.
22 C'est à dire adoptés par l'établissement, les recteurs tenant le rôle de pères adoptifs.
23 J. ROUBERT, « L'adoption des enfants par des particuliers à Lyon sous l'ancien régime », *Bul. Sté. fr. d'hist. des hôpitaux*, 1978, n° 36 et 37, pp. 41–67.

campagne, ils reviennent à la Charité jusqu'à l'âge de quatorze ans et sont alors placés en apprentissage. Quatre enfants sur cinq sont placés dans les métiers de la soie. On ne peut dire que les recteurs de l'établissement se dupent sur les résultats. En effet, dans les *Règlements* de la Charité, on lit que « le métier qu'on leur fait apprendre ne leur donne souvent pas de quoi subsister et que, loin de soulager la Charité, ils en augmentent les dépenses par le pain qu'il faut leur donner, par les enfants qu'ils abandonnent quelquefois, et parce qu'ils viennent eux mêmes y finir leurs jours ». La Charité est pourvoyeuse de main d'œuvre et soupape de sûreté face aux « cessations de la Fabrique ». Cela étant dit, quelque 30 % des garçons placés en apprentissage deviendront compagnons. Ils bénéficient de protection de la part de la Charité : assurance d'être repris jusqu'à vingt-cinq ans en cas de chômage, visite des recteurs tous les trois mois chez le maître, retour une fois par mois à la Charité pour être interrogés sur les conditions de l'apprentissage. Mais ce pourcentage de 30 % signe bien un échec relatif. Le nombre des fugues, et des récidives de fugues, chez les garçons le fait aussi. Tout comme l'importance des engagements dans l'armée, « sans cause » écrivent les recteurs sur les registres. Il faut s'interroger enfin sur les cas les plus favorables, ceux d'enfants qui retrouvent ou qui fondent une famille. Les parents qui reprennent un enfant précédemment abandonné sont peu nombreux. Dans certains cas, des parents retirent « furtivement » ou « sans l'avis du bureau », ou encore enlèvent leur enfant. Cela signifie qu'ils connaissent fort bien l'identité de leur enfant en dépit de l'anonymat préservé des enfants exposés. L'étude du destin des enfants placés à la campagne et qui y sont restés devenus adultes est surtout possible pour ceux qui se marient, grâce aux registres paroissiaux et aux archives notariales. Les mariages entre enfants de la Charité sont nombreux. De plus un nombre important de filles épouse des veufs ou des hommes âgés, des garçons épousent des veuves ou des « filles anciennes ». Mais l'analyse des témoins de mariage ou de baptême montre une vraie intégration. A la seconde génération, le comportement des enfants de la Charité est semblable à celui des autochtones et il y a des réussites individuelles : accès à l'artisanat, à la fonction de marguillier.

Il semble pertinent de comparer ces résultats à ceux exposé par Isabelle Robin-Romero dans sa thèse.[24] Il s'agit ici d'orphelins et non pas d'enfants abandonnés. L'éducation générale et professionnelle que ces orphelins reçoivent n'a pas d'ambition de mobilité ascendante mais entend seulement les rendre à leur milieu d'origine. Presque tous sont placés sur le marché du travail. Il y a donc ici une réussite incontestable, mais une réussite qui rappelle celle des pauvres honteux de T. Fischer. L'assistance réussit quand il s'agit, « simplement » si l'on ose écrire, de réparer un accident de la vie. Mais la suite de leur vie peut les ramener vers l'assistance : Marie Barbe Ladet, pensionnaire de l'hôpital du Saint-Esprit à partir de 1787 sera journalière au faubourg Saint-Antoine ; à cinquante-huit ans, elle sera admise à La Salpétrière.

Le destin de Marie Barbe Ladet introduit à l'analyse des secours accordés à la vieillesse. Il y a ici de vrais résultats, au moins pour certains et à la fin de la période. Au XVIIe s., les hôpitaux généraux ont échoué à enfermer les mendiants. Mais des vieillards ont été recueillis, parfois après un long séjour de leurs noms sur une liste d'attente. C'est à ce moment que prend forme l'hospice de vieillards, pour quelques uns. C'est là, avec la diffusion dans la noblesse et la haute bourgeoisie du XVIIe s. de la retraite spirituelle, la raison d'une première reconnaissance de la spécificité de la vieillesse. Au siècle suivant, cette spécificité achève de s'affirmer avec l'image du « bon vieillard » et cela explique largement l'apparition de véritables pensions de retraite. Le mot de retraite pris dans cette acception date de 1737. Le « transfert de ciel à terre » du sentiment de sécurité invite au développement de systèmes protecteurs permettant de faire face aux aléas de l'âge mieux que par une retraite dans ou aux portes d'un couvent, ou encore mieux que par les clauses d'un contrat notarié. En Angleterre, une loi réserve les *workhouses* aux enfants, aux infirmes et aux vieillards. En Allemagne, les *Armenhäuser* sont ouvertes aux vieillards pauvres. Les Provinces-Unies, une fois de plus, sont novatrices en matière d'assistance puisqu'elles doublent les anciennes *hofjes*, maisons de retraite, par un système de pensions dont le revenu est constitué par une retenue sur

---

24 I. ROBIN-ROMERO, *Les établissements pour orphelins à Paris. XVIe–XVIIIe siècles*, thèse univ. Paris IV (J. P. BARDET dir.), 1997, 2 vol . Cf T. II, chapitre VI : « Sortir de l'hôpital ».

les revenus d'activité. En 1790, le duc de La Rochefoucauld-Liancourt en proposera le modèle à l'Assemblée Constituante. Il avait d'ailleurs déjà créé à Paris, puis à Orléans, une Maison philanthropique qui secourait à domicile les octogénaires indigents. Surtout, pour certaines professions, des pensions de retraite s'étaient mises en place dans la seconde moitié du siècle le plus souvent. L'Hôtel des Invalides, créé par Louis XIV, avait connu d'emblée un vif succès au point que certains anciens soldats bénéficiaient d'une réception avec la mention « logé dehors ». En 1764, Choiseul crée de vraies pensions d'invalidité qui deviendront, en 1776, des pensions de récompenses militaires. Les sous-ingénieurs des Ponts et Chaussées qui sont formés à l'Ecole du même nom bénéficient d'un statut qui prévoit notamment une retraite avec possibilité de réversion. D'autres administrations créent des pensions, notamment la Ferme Générale. Dans certains évêchés, des maisons de prêtres âgés apparaissent.[25] Dans différents pays, des pensions militaires sont également créées : en Angleterre pour les soldats de l'hospice de Chelsea ; dans l'Empire pour les soldats admis dans les établissements de Vienne, Buda, Prague,… ; en Prusse pour ceux de *l'Invalidenhaus* de Berlin. A Genève, un règlement de 1783 assure aux officiers et soldats de la République « des pensions de retraite pour le moment où l'épuisement de leurs forces, des infirmités graves ou des blessures reçues au service de l'Etat ne leur permettraient plus de continuer à le servir ».[26] Ainsi naissait un peu partout le type social du retraité, vieillard inactif qui a les moyens de vivre dans la dignité et qui est respecté.

Bien entendu, tout cela ne concerne qu'une petite minorité de vieillards. Il faut donc conclure sur la médiocre efficacité des institutions charitables, hors les cas de pauvres honteux, de vieillards et surtout d'enfants. Mais sans doute, faut-il dire aussi qu'un certain nombre d'aspects de la question nécessitent encore largement d'être étudiés. C'est sans doute vrai particulièrement des effets du crédit populaire,

---

25   *Notes historiques sur la Maison de Retraite des prêtres du diocèse de Lyon*, Lyon 1899.

26   Cité p. 98 de L. Mottu-Weber, « Etre vieux à Genève sous l'ancien régime », pp. 47–66 de G. Heller (éd.), *Le poids des ans. Une histoire de la vieillesse en Suisse romande*, Lausanne 1994.

crédit populaire dont nous avons suggéré la diversité. Or un travail[27] consacré à la consommation populaire en Avignon à partir des archives des Monts-de-Piété aboutit à d'intéressantes conclusions. Le recours au mont est, certes, signe de détresse. Mais il peut aussi être un moyen d'acheter à crédit, d'autant qu'il y a une circulation souterraine des billets émis lors de la « création du gage ». Ainsi le Mont contribue à une augmentation de la consommation populaire. Cette évolution concerne le mieux-être et, plus encore le mieux paraître. C'est à dire que le Mont favorise une forme de luxe et que ses clients découvrent que les objets sont mortels et que ces objets sont désirables. L'efficacité des œuvres d'assistance serait-elle parfois paradoxale dans ce monde pré-industriel ?

Les Institutions charitables de l'Europe moderne et la question de leur efficacité

A des stades divers et avec d'importantes différences nationales, l'époque moderne a connu trois grandes périodes de l'histoire de ses institutions charitables. Dans les années 1520-1530 surtout, la plupart des pays, mais avec une forte résistance de la péninsule ibérique, mettent en cause l'efficacité de l'aumône manuelle et des institutions traditionnelles au bénéfice d'aumônes générales ou d'autres organismes qui entendent centraliser et rationnaliser la charité. Parce que ces réformes donnent peu de résultats, dès les années 1580, se développent des tentatives d'enfermement des pauvres. Elles sont soucieuses de sauver des âmes et de mettre au travail les « oisifs ». Mais les enfermements du XVIIe s. créeront surtout l'hospice de vieillards et ce n'est qu'au XVIIIe s. que la mendicité et le vagabondage seront sévèrement réprimés. Si ces grands axes peuvent être aisément présentés, il demeure beaucoup d'incertitudes sur le rôle réel de multiples petites structures, souvent héritées du Moyen Age et qui, à l'échelon local, peuvent être efficaces. De même, dans le cas français, on est en train de finir de découvrir comment confréries et sociétés de prêtres peuvent avoir un rôle de prêteurs, mais aussi un rôle social dans les campagnes.

---

27 M. FERRIÈRES, *Le bien des pauvres. La consommation populaire en Avignon (1600–1800)*, Seyssel 2004.

La question de l'efficacité de ces différentes institutions est évidemment délicate car elle suppose clarifiée la conception que certains ont de l'efficacité. Or les buts recherchés sont au XVIIe s. le souci d'ordre, d'économies, mais surtout celui du salut des âmes. Et le XVIIe s. fera du travail une forme de prière. La volonté de mettre ou de remettre sur le marché du travail doit d'abord au mercantilisme qui entend mobiliser tous les bras. Lorsque, au XVIIIe s. se répand, notamment sous l'influence des « arithméticiens politiques », l'idée que la pauvreté a ses racines dans un certain nombre de dysfonctionnements de la société, l'efficacité des institutions sociales commence à être mesurée avec cette fois une mentalité proche de la nôtre. C'est sans doute à propos des enfants recueillis par les hôpitaux et des vieillards que l'on peut le moins difficilement se prononcer. L'enseignement qui est donné à ces enfants les fait participer aux progrès de la civilité qui intègrent à la vie sociale. Cela passe par une instruction générale et une instruction professionnelle qui permet d'accéder au compagnonnage. Au XVIIIe s. surtout, les placements d'enfants trouvés à la campagne permettent à l'historien d'étudier si et comment, l'âge du mariage venu, ils s'intègrent dans la nouvelle communauté. De fait, les mariages ont surtout lieu entre les enfants des hôpitaux et, s'il s'agit de mariage dont un des futurs n'est pas un enfant trouvé, c'est le plus souvent une « fille ancienne » qui épouse un enfant de l'hôpital. On doit aussi souligner la création des premières institutions protectrices de la vieillesse capables de lutter efficacement contre le déclassement par l'âge et d'éviter le recours à l'hôpital. En 1782, une loi réserve les *workhouses* aux enfants, aux infirmes et aux vieillards. Dans les Allemagnes, les *Armenhäuser*, multipliées après 1770, sont accessibles aux vieillards réduits à l'indigence. Les Provinces-Unies, toujours novatrices, doublent les *hofjes* par un système de pensions financées par un prélèvement sur les revenus du temps de l'activité. Le duc de La Rochefoucauld-Liancourt en proposera le modèle à l'Assemblée Constituante en 1790. Sa Maison philantropique s'était d'ailleurs notamment donné pour but de secourir à domicile les vieillards sans ressources à condition qu'ils soient … octogénaires. Surtout les pensions d'invalidité créées en 1764 deviennent de véritables pensions de retraite sous Louis XVI, alors que les ingénieurs sortis de l'Ecole des Ponts et Chaussées bénéficient d'un statut qui prévoit une retraite avec possibilité de réversion. Des pensions militaires apparaissent aussi en Angleterre et dans l'Empire. Le type social du retraité naissait, symbole d'une protection efficace.

Communication IV : Les réactions de la société à la pauvreté
Thomas Riis

Aujourd'hui, le terme d' « hôpital » s'applique surtout aux institutions dédiées au soin des malades, mais autrefois, ce mot avait plusieurs sens. Par exemple, les maisons du St Esprit médiévales n'étaient pas des hôpitaux au sens moderne, mais 1° des asiles pour les personnes âgées, dans lesquels on s'achetait une place en léguant ses possessions à l'institution, 2° des institutions pour les personnes dépendantes : pauvres, infirmes, malades et 3° des auberges pour les voyageurs.[1]

Aussi, il arrivait que l'objectif d'une institution changeait à travers les siècles, assumant ainsi une autre fonction dans l'assistance. Ceci fut le cas de l'Hospital Real de San Lazaro à Cordoue qui fut fondé comme léproserie et qui, à partir de 1346, travaillait à l'échelle nationale. Vers 1600, il commença à se consacrer à l'assistance aux pauvres, probablement à cause de la disparition de la lèpre en Europe occidentale pendant le bas Moyen-Age et les débuts des Temps Modernes.[2]

En France, nous trouvons trois types d'institutions : 1° l'hôpital offrant un grand nombre de formes d'assistance, 2° l'Hôtel-Dieu où les malades étaient soignés (« hôpital » au sens contemporain) et 3° l'Hôpital général qui était plutôt une maison de travail. En Europe du Nord, cette distinction des différents types d'institution paraît appartenir aux Temps Modernes, tandis que déjà au XIVe siècle, on commençait en Espagne à faire la différence entre les asiles pour les personnes âgées et les hôpitaux pour les malades. En 1676, le gouvernement français ordonna la création d'un Hôtel-Dieu et d'un hôpital général dans les grandes villes, et dans la même

---

1 SOLVEIGH HOLTMANN, *Hospitäler, Krankenhäuser und karitative Einrichtungen im Herzogtum Schleswig*, Dissertation Université de Kiel 1969, p. 8.
2 JESÚS BRAVO LOZANO, « La visita del Hospital Real de San Lazaro de Cordoba (1599–1603) », *Hispania* XXXIX, 1979, pp. 639–670.

année l'Hôtel des Invalides pour des anciens militaires fut fondé. Au XVIIIe siècle, ces types d'institutions se répandaient aux autres pays européens.[3]

Ainsi l'hôpital (au sens contemporain) paraît s'être développé au bas Moyen Age. En même temps, l'assistance médicale commençait à faire partie de l'assistance aux pauvres. Dans les villes hanséatiques de Brème, Hambourg et Lübeck les pauvres avaient droit à l'aide médicale gratuite et ceci depuis le XVIe siècle.[4] En 1578, à Edimbourg, les médicaments pour les pauvres furent payés par la ville, en 1627, la capitale écossaise nomma un médecin qui devait soigner les pauvres malades aux frais de la ville, ainsi en 1710 94 pauvres avaient droit au traitement médical gratuit. Il est très probable que l'exemple d'Edimbourg fut imité dans d'autres villes écossaises.[5]

Avec les veuves, les handicapés, les sinistrés et les personnes incapables de travailler, les orphelins appartenaient au groupe des pauvres classiques dignes d'être assistés. Assez tôt, on trouve des maisons pour les orphelins et les enfants trouvés, comme *l'Ospedale degli Innocenti* à Florence qui commença ses activités en 1445.

Ici, on recevait les enfants, on les éduquait et on se chargeait de l'éducation professionnelle des garçons, par exemple, on les inscrivait comme des apprentis chez un artisan. En général, les filles restaient dans l'institution jusqu'au mariage. Elles participaient aux travaux quotidiens, et l'institution leur donnait une aide pour leur trousseau.[6] En général, donc, une solution réussie de la part de la société d'un problème social. Cependant, il est légitime de demander pourquoi le

---

3 Muriel Jeorger, « La structure hospitalière de la France sous l'Ancien Régime », *Annales E.S.C.* XXXII, 1977, pp. 1025–1051.

4 Robert Jütte, « Health care provision and poor relief in early modern Hanseatic towns : Hamburg, Bremen and Lübeck », dans : *Health Care and Poor Relief in Protestant Europe 1500–1700* éd. Ole Peter Grell & Andrew Cunningham, Londres et New York 1997, pp. 115–119.

5 Rosalind Mitchison, « Poor relief and health care in Scotland, 1575–1710 », dans : *Health Care and Poor Relief* (comme note 4), pp. 227–228.

6 Philip Gavitt, « Economy, Charity, and Community in Florence, 1350–1450 », dans : *Aspects of Poverty in Early Modern Europe* [I], éd. Thomas Riis, Stuttgart 1981, pp. 103–104.

garçon devait apprendre un métier et pas se préparer à devenir négociant ou à faire des études, si son intelligence le permettait ?

Ainsi, l'orphelin était un pauvre accepté qu'il fallait aider – à cause de son avenir. Du mendiant, au contraire, il fallait se méfier, s'il n'appartenait pas aux catégories acceptées ; il était mal soigné et ne convenait pas à la société ordonnée ; il fallait donc s'en débarrasser, mais où l'envoyer ?

L'attitude plus rigide à l'égard des pauvres, on la constate en Italie vers 1400 ; on essayait de limiter, voire défendre la mendicité. Ainsi la place des pauvres serait à l'hôpital, non pas dans la rue.[7] Si l'histoire de l'Italie nous montre l'obligation de travailler[8] ainsi que le renfermement des pauvres, il faut attendre le milieu du XVIe siècle pour voir la combinaison de ces deux principes dans la maison de travail, dont le plus ancien exemple paraît le *Bridewell* de Londres.[9] Cette institution fut imitée en Angleterre et à l'étranger, surtout à Amsterdam dont le « *Tuchthuis* » fut fondé en 1595 et très vite acquit un rôle de modèle pour toute l'Europe du Nord.

La création faisait partie de la doctrine mercantiliste, car le chômage, n'était-il pas un gaspillage de ressources ? Cependant, il s'est avéré impossible de chercher des mendiants de la rue pour en faire, dans les plus brefs délais, des ouvriers de la soie qualifiés. Les manufactures de laine de Berlin à l'époque de Frédéric Guillaume Ier (1713–1740) étaient plus modestes, mais en même temps plus efficaces : on travaillait la laine du pays, la main-d'œuvre se trouvait déjà à Berlin, et les débouchés étaient assurés parce qu'on vendait les tissus à l'armée

---

7 Bronislaw Geremek, « Renfermement des pauvres en Italie (XIVe–XVIIe siècles). Remarques préliminaires », dans : *Mélanges en l'honneur de Fernand Braudel* I, Toulouse 1973, pp. 205–217.

8 On en trouve d'autres exemples au lendemain de la Peste Noire afin de remédier le manque de main-d'œuvre : Angleterre 1349, Suède-Finlande vers 1350, Castille 1351, Portugal 1375 ; au Danemark, une loi défendit en 1354 les exécutions et les mutilations à cause du manque de main-d'œuvre, voir Bronislaw Geremek, *La potence ou la pitié. L'Europe et les pauvres du Moyen Âge à nos jours*, Paris 1987, pp. 109–111; Eino Jutikkala, « Labour Policy and Urban Proletariat in Sweden-Finland » dans : Thomas Riis éd., *Aspects of Poverty in Early Modern Europe* II, Odense 1986, pp. 135–136. Loi danoise de 1354 : *Den danske Rigslovgivning indtil 1400* éd. Erik Kroman, Copenhague 1971, pp. 231–232 § 3.

9 Paul Slack, « Hospitals, workhouses and the relief of the poor in early modern London », dans : *Health Care and Poor Relief* (comme note 4), pp. 236–239.

pour en faire des uniformes. Les profits étaient élevés, vers les 30 % net, phénomène assez rare pour ce genre de manufacture.[10]

La maison de travail pouvait éloigner les mendiants de la rue, mais comme entreprise elle avait seulement du succès si ses activités restaient très simples ou si elle avait des débouchés assurés.

La chronique de Burchard Zinck nous informe qu'à Augsbourg un dépôt de blé fut fondé en 1451. En temps de cherté, il pouvait assurer l'approvisionnement des pauvres en blé.[11]

A la suite de la crise de 1437–1439 des magasins analogues furent fondés dans les grandes villes des Pays Bas, et on obligea les personnes aisées à créer des réserves de blé, ainsi à Groningue en 1425 et à Leyde en 1447. Afin de surmonter la crise de 1437–1439, plusieurs gouvernements urbains achetèrent du blé, ainsi Deventer en 1437, Gouda et Utrecht en 1438. Le blé venait de la région baltique, probablement de la Pologne.

Aussi dans les villes du duché de Schleswig-Holstein-Gottorf on créa des dépôts de blé en octobre 1709: la récolte de 1708 avait été mauvaise, l'hiver de 1708–1709 avait été très froid et les prix des céréales à Amsterdam étaient encore en 1709 très élevés.[12]

Le blé ne sert pas exclusivement à la production du pain, mais aussi à celle de la bière ou de l'eau-de-vie. Surtout cette dernière exige beaucoup de céréales, ce qui aggrava les effets des mauvaises récoltes de 1698–1699. Prévoyant une pénurie, le gouvernement royal de Schleswig-Holstein défendit en 1740 l'exportation de céréales ainsi

---

10   HELGA SCHULTZ, *Berlin 1650–1800. Sozialgeschichte einer Residenz*, Berlin 1987, pp. 107–116.

11   *Die Chroniken der deutschen Städte vom 14. bis in's 16. Jahrhundert* V, Leipzig 1866, p. 208.

12   R.VAN SCHAÏK, « Prijs- en levensmiddelenpolitiek in de Noordelijke Nederlanden van de 14de tot de 17e eeuw : bronnen en problemen », *Tijdschrift voor Geschiedenis* XCI, 1978, pp. 215–255, ici pp. 222–223 ; LARS N. HENNINGSEN, « Misvækst og kornspekulation i Sønderjylland 1698–1847. En studie i dyrtids- og hungerår og krisepolitik », *Sønderjyske Årbøger* 1981, pp. 11–13 ; ARNE BIALUSCHEWSKI, « Die Versorgungskrise von 1709 in Schleswig-Holstein. Getreidehandelspolitik und Landesherrschaft im Vergleich », dans : *Von Ländern, Menschen, Meeren* éd. GERHARD FOUQUET et alii, Tønning 2006, pp. 393–406.

que la distillation d'eau-de-vie. Aussi aux Pays Bas, la production de bière fut interdite quand les céréales se faisaient rares.[13]

En Angleterre, on fixait chaque année le poids des différents types de pain selon le prix des céréales. Ceci avait lieu au début de l'automne quand on pouvait estimer la récolte ainsi que la situation d'approvisionnement pour l'année à venir. Ainsi, les prix de pain restaient relativement stables, mais son poids changeait. Ce système était d'origine médiévale, il fut modifié en 1709 et définitivement aboli en 1822 pour Londres et quatorze ans plus tard pour le reste du pays.[14]

L'approvisionnement en céréales et le commerce de cette catégorie de vivres montrent un conflit prononcé entre les intérêts de la société et ceux des entreprises. C'est un problème qui aussi aujourd'hui a beaucoup d'actualité: est-ce que les intérêts de l'entreprise, sont-ils compatibles avec ceux de la société, et si non, qui doit céder, l'entreprise ou la société ?

En outre, l'approvisionnement pose des problèmes pratiques. C'est probable que vers 1700 la production céréalière de Schleswig-Holstein suffisait au moins à l'alimentation des habitants de la région. Cependant, son infrastructure était si peu développée que les Elbmarschen avaient plus d'intérêt à vendre leur surplus de céréales à Hambourg au lieu de le transporter vers les régions où le blé manquait.

Dans beaucoup de pays, nous trouvons des fondations responsables pour des distributions aux pauvres. Les vivres donnés par les Buonomini di S. Martino à Florence ne suffisaient pas à nourrir la famille, mais les femmes accouchées recevaient une aide et toute la famille le pain blanc, à Florence indispensable pour le maintien du statut social.[15] Aussi les distributions en argent du grand bureau des pauvres à Paris constituaient seulement une aide.[16]

---

13 SCHAÏK, « Prijs- en levensmiddelenpolitiek » (comme note 12), pp. 16–17.
14 ALAN S. C. ROSS, « The Assize of Bread », *The Economic History Review*, 2nd Series IX, 1956–1957, pp. 332–338.
15 AMLETO SPICCIANI, « The « Poveri Vergognosi » in Fifteenth-Century Florence. The first 30 years' activity of the Buonomini di S. Martino», dans : *Aspects of Poverty* (comme note 6), passim.
16 LÉON CAHEN, *Le grand bureau des pauvres de Paris au milieu du XVIIIᵉ siècle*, Paris 1904, pp. 17–19

Si les distributions citées visaient surtout les pauvres honteux, il en était autrement à Bruxelles depuis le bas Moyen Age. Ici, on distribuait régulièrement du pain (chaque jour, chaque semaine), et au début de l'hiver chaque personne assistée recevait une paire de chaussures et chaque deux ans quatre aunes de tissu de laine ainsi que six aunes de toile. A Noël et à Pâques les pauvres avaient droit à du porc salé, au début du Carême on leur distribuait des graisses et des petits pois secs, au Mi-Carême aussi des harengs.

Pendant le troisième quart du XVe siècle 350 à 400 pauvres furent assistés : à titre de comparaison, en 1496 316 ou 21 % des 1505 ménages appartenant à la paroisse Sainte Gudule furent considérés comme pauvres. Même si les distributions bruxelloises ne suffisaient pas aux besoins des pauvres, elles constituaient néanmoins une contribution importante.[17]

Pendant la crise économique italienne vers la fin du XVe siècle, la demande de crédits dépassait l'offre ; les emprunts devenaient ainsi plus chers. A l'initiative des Franciscains, un nouveau système de crédits fut inventé dans le but de fournir des crédits aux prix bas. La nouvelle institution – en général nommée Monte di Pietà – était considérée une œuvre de bienfaisance ; avec le temps, elle assumait d'autres fonctions bancaires comme la gestion des fortunes ou des dépôts.

En France, au XVIe siècle, les Monti di Pietà furent crées selon le modèle italien, mais en général, la caisse d'épargne fondée en 1778 par la « Patriotische Gesellschaft » (société patriotique) de Hambourg est considérée le plus ancien exemple de cette institution bancaire. C'était un trait nouveau que même de petites sommes étaient acceptées comme dépôts ; pour cette raison, plusieurs administrations d'assistance ont adopté l'idée de la caisse d'épargne.

---

17 G. DE GEEST, « Les distributions aux pauvres assurées par la paroisse Sainte-Gudule à Bruxelles au XVe siècle », *Annales de la Société Belge d'Histoire des Hôpitaux* VII, 1969, pp. 41–84 ; PAUL BONENFANT, « Achat de Draps pour les pauvres de Bruxelles aux Foires d'Anvers de 1393 à 1487. Contribution à l'histoire des petites draperies », dans: *Beiträge zur Wirtschafts- und Stadtgeschichte. Festschrift für H. Ammann*, éd. HERMANN AUBIN, Wiesbaden 1965, pp. 179–192.

L'exemple de Hambourg – plus tard imité à Kiel – est important, parce que nous y trouvons un système d'assistance global : aide aux incapables de travailler et aux sous-employés, création de travail pour les capables ; bref, on voulait plutôt empêcher la pauvreté au lieu d'y remédier. Les idées se sont avérées justes, car dix ans après la mise en marche du système on ne comptait que la moitié des pauvres adultes que dix ans auparavant.[18]

Les exemples des réactions des non-pauvres pour remédier à la pauvreté peuvent être multipliés à l'infini. Aujourd'hui, les caisses d'épargne sont devenues des banques ordinaires qui offrent des crédits aux conditions du marché. Certes, il ne serait aucune mauvaise idée si des instituts financiers étaient fondés afin de fournir aux pauvres en difficulté des crédits bon marché. Mais aussi en général, la politique sociale moderne aurait de l'intérêt à s'inspirer du système d'assistance, car aujourd'hui, l'assistance donnée pallie à la pauvreté en traitant ses symptômes, tandis que le système de Hambourg voulait empêcher sa formation.

---

18 ERICH BRAUN & FRANKLIN KOPITSCH éd. : *Zwangsläufig oder abwendbar ?* Hambourg 1990.

Building a Hero : Poverty and Rebellion between History and Folklore
—————— Carlo Baja Guarienti ——————

The usefulness of a historical point of view in the analysis of an urgent theme such as poverty is not merely to be found in the word – generally attributed to History – of "eternal possession" theorized by Thucydides: there are more specific reasons to be found in the study of popular mentality.

The permanence of attitudes, reactions, desires can be easily found in surprisingly different places and times: in Ireland at the end of the nineteenth century[1] as in sixteenth century Italy, for instance, during periods of economic crisis (periods that in some cases can be considered as an endemic state) people could often choose to support an outlaw by providing him chances to escape from the authorities, if they did not consider his violation of the estabilished rule as a breach of unwritten common laws. Places and times, perhaps far from each other, but united by objective conditions of difficulty and by similar feelings are also widespread in our contemporary world.

Therefore the attention to factors different from the ones based on economy or education and – generally – to elements that could hardly be studied through statistical data or quantitative history can help understand the ways that lead to the perception of facts and the relation between the community and the outside world: in practical human behaviour the impact of events on popular imagination has got an even greater relevance than the real facts we can subsequently reconstruct through the use of documents. If it is true – on one side – that the suggestive strength wielded by ballads and traditions on a human set has been well known for a long time,[2] on the other side it is perhaps possible (and certainly useful) to catch primary aspects of a people's life by the analysis of the ways in which historical events are processed.

---

1 J. M. SYNGE, *The Aran Islands*, Dublin 1907.
2 P. BURKE, *Popular Culture in Early Modern Europe*, London 1978.

The history of mountains is often a history of its own, ruled by a concept of time different from that of the plain: climbing along roads, scarce and inefficient until not long ago, meant getting away from the network of communication and exchanges that took place in larger cities. As described by Fernand Braudel,[3] the mountain is a territory that current civilizations, created in European capitals open to the outside world, struggle to reach. In this, the mountains can in some ways be compared to an island.

Due to their relative isolation and the delays in communication with the more lively areas of the territory (or thanks to these factors), the mountains often maintain social, economical and cultural models that have been superseded elsewhere. It is not coincidental that a good portion of our artistic wealth, including music, craftsmanship, legends and religious or magical practices, survives in valleys after it disappeared from the popular memory of the plains. Whoever is interested in tracking down what is left of the splendid and multifaceted cultural wealth that was born over the centuries from the syncretism among the different religions, literatures and historical events, will certainly find a more fertile ground where isolation allowed the necessary time for the expressive forms to consolidate and imprint themselves on common knowledge.

In view of this, mountain populations become a source of knowledge important to those trying to understand and analyse how historical events became part of the wealth shared by a specific community. And it is clearly wrong to think that the poverty or isolation of a human nucleus cannot generate valuable cultural forms.

Located at the foot of the Tusco-Emilian Apennine mountains which form the hinge between Northern and Central Italy, the cities of the now called Emilia Romagna region were in the first quarter of the sixteenth century part of a land upset by wars as Papal, French, Spanish armies and mercenaries from all over Europe crossed along the ancient routes that went from Milan to Bologna and Ferrara and then on to Florence and Rome. In particular, the cities of Modena

---

3 F. BRAUDEL, *La Méditerranée et le Monde méditerranéen à l'époque de Philippe II*, 2nd ed. Paris 1966, Vol. 1. See also P. BURKE, *Popular Culture* (as note 2).

and Reggio, that were forced to quarter and provision foreign soldiers to the detriment of the local population, were exhausted under the dominion of the Este family, constantly under pressure from Pope Julius II and his armies.

Instead of providing stability to the city, the taking of Reggio by the Papal armies in July 1512 reinvigorated a bloody feud between two noble families, the Bebbis and the Scaiolis. The old denominations of Guelph and Ghibelline, now emptied of their original meaning, served as a sign of distinction for the allies of the two families fighting for supremacy in the social corpus of the city.[4]

Among the followers of the Ghibelline Scaiolis, Domenico de' Bretti, a charismatic man of remarkable military capabilities, began to emerge. With his father, a wealthy innkeeper with political ambitions, and his fierce brother Vitale, Domenico was awarded the castle in Carpineti by Pope Julius II.[5] Carpineti, a small village in the Secchia river valley, located on the road connecting Reggio with the Este province of Garfagnana, was Domenico's homeland. The history of Carpineti is illustrative of the state of mind of the people living in these lands. A series of pleas to Pope Leo X, granted with the concessions of March 29th and October 10th, 1514, underlined how the inhabitants were "poor and exhausted from the long-lasting wars" and impoverished by the costs of maintaining foreign troops.[6] In the following years, the presence of mercenary troops, especially from other nations, in cities and countryside would be the cause of a never-ending series of pleas, encounters and measures of the central and local governments. Certainly, the sentiment of hostility toward foreigners and the clashes between the armies of Domenico de' Bretti and the mercenaries can be counted among the elements that fostered the entry of this character into popular imagination.

---

4 See now C. BAJA GUARIENTI, "Le "guerre civili" di Reggio: una faida fra guelfi e ghibellini all'inizio del XVI secolo," in G. BEBBI, *Reggio nel Cinquecento. Le guerre civili cittadine tra guelfi e ghibellini del secolo XVI*, ed. C. BAJA GUARIENTI, Reggio Emilia, Antiche Porte 2007, pp. 11–61.

5 Archivio di Stato di Reggio Emilia (ASRe), Registro di lettere e decreti, 10 September 1512 and 6 May 1513; ASRe, Carteggio degli Anziani, 15 October 1521.

6 A. BALLETTI, *Storia di Reggio nell'Emilia*, Reggio Emilia 1925, p. 281.

We do not know much about Domenico's youth. Born in the last quarter of the XVth century, Domenico obtained an education that was above what was generally available in a place so distant from the cultural centres of that time. He spoke good Italian and was able to maintain a personal correspondence with the local authorities. After all, his brother Vitale was his lieutenant in the army, while another brother, Alessandro, was a notary.

The earliest information we have about him is the chronicle of the murder of a rival in a market. This is traditionally held as Domenico's debut and it catapulted him from the life of a shepherd to that of an outlaw; however, confirmation to substantiate this episode has not yet emerged from official documents. It is therefore not possible to express an opinion on the tradition. What we know for certain is that since the beginning of his career Domenico was ready and willing to side with whomever requested his help. Member of the Ghibelline faction, he declared himself a loyal servant of the papal government: in the XVIth century the colours and violent chants of Guelphs and Ghibellines (so widespread and dangerous to require special laws)[7] had been emptied of their original meaning and were used by families and outlaws to justify hostility and alliances of a personal nature.[8]

During Mass in the cathedral of Reggio Emilia on June 25th, 1517, the papal Governor, Giovanni Gozzadini, who had openly sided with the Scaioli family, was stubbed to death along with 22 other people. The Bebbis presented the documentation (a series of papers between Gozzadini and the Scaiolis) that demonstrated the partiality of the highest papal authority in the city and supported the thesis of the massacre as restitution for the illegal acts of a corrupt officer.

To the city council's request for a new governor, Rome responded with the appointment of the illustrious humanist Francesco Guicciardini, who had already built for himself a reputation for impartiality and discipline when in Modena. Guicciardini took office in Reggio on July 8th and immediately had a taste of his future relationship with Domenico de' Bretti: on July 23th Domenico brought 400

---

7 ASRe, Gride, 2 March 1519.
8 F. Braudel, *La Méditerranée...* (as note 3), vol. 2.

men down the mountains all the way to the city gates. He then pulled back (probably because he realized the insufficiency of his troops) and later denied his intention to attack the city.

Starting from this episode, we have the richest source of information on the events of Domenico de' Bretti in Guicciardini's letters, which allow us to follow the course of the relationship between the humanist and the marauder forced to live in the same environment. In these letters, Domenico is portraited as a bloodthirsty and unreliable criminal, politically ambiguous in his relationship with the Este and always involved in conspiracies and plots. Certainly, this portrait is a relatively faithful representation of the situation and shows one of the many faces that Domenico has left to history. But we can also see how Guicciardini was not completely sincere in reporting his actions and thoughts.

During the year 1517, the *modus operandi* of Domenico and his followers emerged: raids against the mountain populations and incursions into the territories of Frignano in the province of Modena and Garfagnana. In February 1518,[9] Guicciardini sent an initial contingent of 25 soldiers to try to restore order in the district of Carpineti, without success. The governor then requested the appointment of an agent for the mountain territories as well as the intervention of 500 foot soldiers settled in the Northern part of Tuscany. Some sources tell us of an unfruitful trip to Rome by Domenico and others in order to request the substitution of Guicciardini with Alberto Pio, landlord of Carpi. In the meantime, as an extreme measure, Guicciardini requested that Cardinal de' Medici offer Domenico an assignment in Tuscany or Bologna to take him away from Carpineti.[10]

In those days, the so-called "war of the mountaineers" was being fought in the valleys between the territories of Reggio and Modena with the forces of Cato da Castagneto on one side and the troops of Domenico de' Bretti on the other. The heads of these two irregular militias, whose power was tolerated and sometimes supported by the authorities, had been fighting for a few years over a cause more

---

9 ASRe, Provvigioni, 8 February 1518.
10 F. GUICCIARDINI, Letter to Cardinal de' Medici, 24 August 1518.

personal than political. The kidnapping (perhaps consensual) of a girl – one of de' Bretti's relatives – by Cato da Castagneto aggravated the fight, making it into a true war fought with pitched battles, loots, and raids. The peace accord stipulated in March 1519 among the major players in the feud did not involve the heads of the two mountain factions. The two men continued their fight which led to their death in just a few years to come.

In July 1519, Francesco Guicciardini obtained leave to return to Florence and remain there until autumn, entrusting government tasks to a few loyal people. The official documentation about the activity of Domenico de' Bretti during this period is very fragmentary, but the chronicles ascribe to him an intense activity, especially against the increasingly frequent expeditions sent by the absent governor. Apparently, two expeditions were routed by the mountaineers while a third one, headed by the nobleman Antonmaria Fontanelli resulted in the destruction of de' Bretti's houses in Carpineti and the flight of the brothers into the woods.

In 1520, after more than two years of fighting, Guicciardini's requests were heard and Domenico de' Bretti was transferred out of Carpineti to the city of Bologna, under the command of a certain Captain Ramazzotto.

Given the little information we have, we can only conjecture about de' Bretti's stay in Bologna. In a letter dated December 13th, 1520, Alfonso d'Este, Duke of Ferrara, wrote Giacomo Tebaldi, his orator in Venice, that de' Bretti could not bear to hold a subordinate position and had returned to his homeland and violently recaptured the fortress of Carpineti. The documents[11] we have confirm that a few expeditions were sent against Domenico with the objective of taking the castle away from him, but without success. While the Duke ascribed Domenico's return from Bologna to his resistance to subservience, the tradition sees it as the sign of his homesickness. Even if we do not want to believe such a sentimental point of view, we must recognize that the role of ally and rescuer that Ramazzotto played later excludes the possibility that there could have been any significant

---

11 ASRe, Provvigioni, 10 December 1520.

clashes between the two men. We have to note that anecdotes and rumours started to flourish among his contemporaries: the rebellion, the refusal to obey authority and the call of the mountains are persistant aspects of a bandit's character. They are also types of behaviour that place the single outlaw in contrast to the community and his social class of origin.

The failure of the expeditions sent to recapture the fortress of Carpineti presented the Governor with a difficult choice: either the destruction of the castle with all its inhabitants or the route of diplomacy. Despite the fact that Guicciardini entertained the idea of sacrificing the fortress in order to get rid of its troublesome guest once and for all, diplomacy prevailed in the end. The negotiators, led by Marquis Lazzaro Malaspina, obtained the surrender with one condition: that the castle should not be delivered to the Governor and that the Governor would have to recall his troops. Guicciardini agreed, but then wrote his superiors complaining about the princely treatment accorded to the common brigand. He also complained about a new task assigned to Domenico in the region of Bologna.

On December 21st 1520, Guicciardini wrote to Cardinal de'Medici that from the nobleman Count Gaspare Sessi he had received the confession about a plot to have the governor killed Besides Count Sessi himself, the other hired killers were Roberto Messori (born in Reggio) and Domenico de' Bretti.

During that period the de' Bretti brothers were in Bologna working for bishop Bernardino Rossi. When they went back to Carpineti in January of 1521 a ban, the confiscation of all their assets and a reward of 200 ducats for their capture were waiting for them. In case of one of the brothers' death, the ban also provided for the transfer of all the assets to his assassin and some tax exemptions in the municipality of origin.[12] From this moment on, Domenico became a true "bandit" and found refuge in the woods along with his followers. On January 20th, Domenico tried to attack the fortress of Minozzo, important centre in the Apennine mountains, but without success. The habitants threatened to destroy the castle in order to prevent

---

12 ASRe, Gride e ordini manoscritti, without date (probably January 1521).

Domenico from taking it again. As a response to these events, Guicciardini sent foot soldiers and cavalry in order to hunt down the de' Bretti brothers. In the meantime, Guicciardini renewed the appointment of Alessandro Malaguzzi as governor of the Reggio Emilia mountain region, granting him authority to manage the operations.

It is during this period that Domenico de' Bretti sacked some villages using the tactics of rapid incursions, which were over before the government troops could intervene. His profound knowledge of the mountains and woods allowed the bandits to hide without ever being found. Furthermore, the soldiers that had been assigned to hunt the bandits down and who were colourfully nicknamed *ammazzatori* ("killers"), by the people of the mountains, caused a growing discontent, which sometimes manifested itself in support for the de' Bretti's gang.

This phase in Domenico's life is certainly the one which left the deepest mark in the popular imagination and which created the legend. Even though fairly short, this period of time is the repository of many stories related to the bandit. This is because the oral tradition places its characters in a time that can be stretched or shortened compared to the historical one in order to create proportions in keeping with the importance of the event; this process is similar to that of naive or childlike pictures where the major characters are represented on a bigger scale than the other characters. In the whole biography of Domenico popular tradition has chosen to emphasize the right part for the purpose to awaken feelings of sympathy: the escape from established authorities, the return to forests and mountains as an opposition to cities and palaces.

Even the environment in which Domenico lives is full of complex fascination: besides the mountain, the forest is the other protagonist of the bandit's exploits. The forest represents another limit to the progress or expansion of civilization, authority and law. It is another frontier which order can hardly conquer: the forest is the place where laws lose their value and where the world of rationality and order is questioned and often inverted. The forest is the place of transformation: from Actaeon – the Greek hunter punished for having seen the bath of the goddess Diana – forward there are numerous traditions that ascribe to the forest and its tutelary deities the power to transform the hunter into the prey. A popular French ballad, *La blanche biche*, narrates how a young woman transformed into a deer is eaten alive by her brother's dogs without him realizing the tragedy: in the forest the laws of the city lose their value, and hunter and prey exchange roles.

The same thing happens to the bandits who find refuge in the woods: even when convicted by the authorities, they become the repository of the laws of the forest. The call to a superior justice, the same appeared in the episode of the killing of the former governor, comes back in the words of the bandits themselves. In the eyes of the oppressed populations the bandit becomes through this process of legitimation an antagonist of the governor, but not necessarily the villain. Very often when the population had to choose between two sources of violence and power, it preferred to support the one deriving its legitimacy from an abstract and universal justice, rather than the one vested with police power. If, as Peter Burke[13] observed, it is true that in modern times the idealization of historical bandit figures is a phenomenon that is more widespread in Eastern Europe where the popular class is extremely poor and oppressed by feudal systems, it is also true in regions relatively more advanced (like the Este and Papal states in the XVIth century) where people look for their heroes among the outlaws. For these reasons and because of very ramified networks of kinship, the central authority often turns to foreign armies, in this case the "killers", who were unable to capture Domenico because of the protection afforded him by the environment and the people.[14]

The hunt lasted only a few weeks: in February Domenico appeared in front of the Governor and promised that he would leave the mountains in exchange for the ban's withdrawal. Guicciardini accepted the proposal and Domenico was sent for the third time to Bologna. In this context, we witness a minor historical episode that is indicative of the popular perception of the clash between the Governor and the

---

13 P. Burke, *Popular Culture* (as note 2).
14 See E. J. Hobsbawm, *Bandits*, London 1969 and R. P. Harrison, *Forests. The Shadow of Civilization*, Chicago 1992.

mountaineer. Having learnt that people were talking about a "peace agreement" between him and his adversary, Guicciardini wrote the following fiery words:

If I have pardoned Domenico and his followers his crimes, I have not made peace with him, as you do not make peace between a superior and a subject but you offer mercy and pardon; peace is between two equal parties. (...) These are terms that ruin one's reputation.

In the words of Guicciardini the core of the transformation is encapsulated that Domenico's character changes when moving from reality to perception: the governor fears that his "reputation" might be compromised and that the equilibrium between legitimate power and usurped power could disappear in favour of the latter. The humanist, who revealed himself as a careful interpreter of his people's role in the course of political events during his government in Modena, Reggio and Parma, did not ignore the danger that could stem from the mountain people's making a myth of the brigand. When a historical figure becomes a symbol, the magnitude of his role in community events is enlarged. We can further say that in the history of popular behaviour the perception of a character is often bigger than the real historical figure. As King Louis IX of France has had a significant role in French culture[15] by showing different aspects of the historical reality and the idealistic and hagiographic transposition, so bandits have crossed the threshold of their own actions by living a double life without being able to establish a predominancy of one of the two narrative lanes.

The year 1521 witnessed the region of Lombardy shaken by the prelude to wars. Local disagreements faded into the background: the Church state was recruiting troops to oppose the advance of the French army and the two most important military authorities, Vitello Vitelli and Prospero Colonna, were allocating their contingents to the different cities that would become theatres of war. On July 10th, 1521 Guicciardini was appointed General Commissioner of the Papal armies and in September Reggio was full of mercenaries recruited to

---

15 J. Le Goff, *St. Louis*, Paris 1996.

block the continuous incursions which pro-French troops undertook from the region of Parma.

On October 15th, the de' Brettis wrote a letter to the Elders of Reggio, the council that ruled the city together with the governor and the other officers, in which they put their troops at the government's disposal. The following text is interesting for it shows the image that the brothers wanted to give of themselves and the reasons for their actions. The de' Bretti brothers say "we are eager to do something that pleases the city to which we want to be good servants" and they specify that "all the wrong that we have done to the citizens of this city we did it against our will [...] to defend ourselves and live."

This concept of support to a cause and of service to the official authority by the representatives of an unofficial power can be found somewhere else: in Eastern Europe, for example, the *haiduc*, turbulent men that aggregated to create armed gangs, offered their services to local landlords and even central authorities while maintaining a parallel business of looting and robbery especially towards travellers.[16] The de' Bretti brothers were trying to create the same equilibrium by siding with the Papal state and at the same time robbing the merchants that travelled between the Emilia Romagna region and the Este region of Garfagnana.

The Garfagnana, a region in Tuscany enclosed by mountains, was a very tough land – under the dominion of the Este but squeezed by the states of the Pope, the Medici domains and the Republic of Lucca, it was constantly crossed by smugglers and its caves and canyons offered refuge to many bandits.[17] From 1522 to 1525, Ludovico Ariosto was appointed commissioner for the Garfagnana region, its highest office. Ariosto, the greatest Italian Renaissance epic poet, was characterized by an unremitting zeal for fulfilling his duties of office. In Ferrara, people hoped that he could bring order to the region.

---

16 E. J. HOBSBAWM, *Bandits* (as note 14).

17 G. C. MONTANARI, "Storie di banditi fra Modena e la Garfagnana nei secc. XV–XVI," and G. NESI, "I banditi dell'Ariosto e la politica ducale di assimilazione della Provincia di Garfagnana al sistema estense", both in *La Garfagnana dall'avvento degli Estensi alla devoluzione di Ferrara*, Congress Reports, Modena 2000.

As a matter of fact, during his mandate Ariosto kept asking to be removed from his job because he did not want to face the dangers and discomforts that came with his assignment in such an uncivilized region. Before his transfer Ariosto had the opportunity to exchange letters with Domenico de' Bretti and his followers. In November 1522 Ariosto communicated to Duke Alfonso I of Ferrara his opinion of Domenico:

He [a notary in the area] has tried many times to persuade me that Domenico is a good servant of Your Excellency. That he is a good servant or not, Your Excellency should know better than I do: I am not very sure of this good opinion of Domenico because the effects I saw in the past times seem opposite. But, having he more power in these lands than Your Excellency's officials, I don't think it would be wrong to show that we believe him to be more a friend than an enemy until God will arrange for us to be stronger than him.[18]

In these words we can understand more clearly than in any other place the most authentic meaning of Domenico's historical actions. On one hand, his attempt to serve two opposed masters shed light on the true nature of the bandit's political behaviour: a man of his time, Domenico tried to infiltrate the thick network of plots involving the different powers fighting for the supremacy in northern Italy. On the other hand, the fear that Ariosto expressed as to the relationship of the different powers is astonishing: as already mentioned, in the mountains and forests of the Apennines, it can happen that a bandit has more power than the Duke of Ferrara. By examining the real power of Domenico, who had an irregular army of 400 soldiers, we see that he had a following bigger that any other outlaw in his zone, but not big enough to undermine the sovereignty of the Este in that part of the Apennines. Ludovico Ariosto's words have to be interpreted as the expression of a popular opinion more than that of a historical fact.

In the summer of 1521, in the mountain territory of Modena, Domenico de' Bretti guided his troops against the eternal enemy Cato da Castagneto besieging him in the castle of Fanano. After the con-

---

18 ASMo, Letterati, Ludovico Ariosto to Alfonso d'Este, 25 November 1522.

quest of the castle, a massacre took place in which Cato was killed. On the way back, the de' Brettis were intercepted and only the intervention of Captain Ramazzotto with his Papal soldiers from Bologna could help the men. Meanwhile the war was spreading: between October and November the Papal armies and the imperial troops conquered Milan and Piacenza. The fall of Parma and the death of Pope Leo X followed soon after. The interim kingship put the army in a state of uncertainty mainly because of the interrupted payment of the troops' salaries. The siege by Federico Gonzaga almost drove Parma to surrender, but the population, headed by Guicciardini, rallied to resist the attack and the pro-French troops retreated.[19]

At the beginning of 1522 and in spite of the key role that Guicciardini played in this phase of the war the new Pope, the austere Flemish monk Adrian VI, had assigned the goverment of the city of Modena to Guido Rangone and that of Reggio to Alberto Pio. Parma was ruled by the Marquis of Mantova. The city of Reggio, already exhausted, was forced to house some of Prospero Colonna's troops that were coming back from Milan and some of the men of Giovanni de' Medici, known as Giovanni dalle Bande Nere. Meanwhile the news about cases of plague in the North increased the distrust of foreigners in general and soldiers in particular. At the request of the city council to send away the troops of Giovanni de' Medici, the Pope responded affirmatively, but the Duke of Milan declared that he could not move the troops without the consent of general Prospero Colonna.[20] Having established the futility of a second order from the Pope, a measure from the council allowed people from Reggio to carry weapons to defend themselves against the bullying of the mercenary troops.[21]

In the following months, Giovanni de' Medici's mercenaries fought against the troops of Domenico: Giovanni, father of the future Grand Duke of Florence Cosimo I, attributed to de' Bretti the inability to collect taxes from the population.

---

19 F. GUICCIARDINI to his brother Jacopo, 21 December 1521.
20 ASRe, Provvigioni, 27 August 1522 and 2 September 1522.
21 ASRe, Provvigioni, 21 October 1522.

In November 1522, Guicciardini was re-appointed to the go-vernment of Modena and Reggio even though the troops of Alberto Pio still occupied the citadel. At the beginning of the new year Do-menico's activity became so unrestrained as to lead the governor to an extreme measure: he secretely turned to his enemy, Duke of Ferrara, and asked him to help get rid of what he considered a thorn in his side. Duke Alfonso withheld his help and the plot was never executed, but the situation precipitated both for the city and for Domenico.

At the beginning of summer, Reggio was the prey of wide-spread riots. Some of Giovanni de' Medici's troops still infested the countryside to get back the credit they never collected and the homi-cide of a citizen convinced Guicciardini to ban the use of weapons by the citadel guards loyal to the Pios. The arrest of one of them sparked off fights between the people of Reggio and the troops. A letter from the council to the Pope offers a desolate picture of the city's condi-tions.[22]

In this climate of terror, the "war of the mountaineers" finally came to an end. The chronicles tell us that on July 5th, 1523, the troops of Domenico de' Bretti engaged those of Virgilio da Castagneto, brother of Cato, in the mountains of Modena. Some scholars have advanced the hypothesis that Duke Alfonso d'Este sent troops from the Garfagnana to support Virgilio da Castagneto and finally get rid of Domenico, but we have got no written documents to prove this theory.

The battle, which chronicles describe as long and bloody, en-ded with a one-on-one fight between the two men. From far away, one of Domenico's[23] men killed Virgilio with an arquebus shot. Gio-vanni da Castagneto, Virgilio's uncle and priest, then seriously injured Domenico in his throat. When they saw their leaders on the ground, the two armies quickly dispersed and the followers of Domenico de' Bretti loaded his body on a horse trying to reach the fortress of Cor-neto. On their way, they met Tebaldo Sessi and Antonio Pacchioni in a clearing that, according to some people, still carries the name

---

22 ASRe, Provvigioni, 23 June 1523.
23 His son in law Ugolino Giarola.

of "pian de Morott", "plain of Morotto" that was Domenico's nickname. In the past, the Sessi and Pacchioni families had been the object of sieges and attacks by the de' Brettis. The two men were bringing reinforcements to Virgilio da Castagneto from Reggio Emilia. When they met the men of de' Bretti, Tebaldo Sessi ran Domenico through with a sword while Antonio Pacchioni amputated Domenico's right hand and decapitated the body. The hand was then exposed as a warning to robbers and the head was sent as a gift to the Rangoni noble family that was an enemy of the Bretti party.

After this episode, a couplet started to go around the mountains of Reggio and Modena: the verses,[24] untranslatable because they are based on a *calembour* involving the names of the contenders, told the people to be happy for the death of both Domenico and Virgilio.

Francesco Guicciardini received the news with happiness, describing the event as a "holy thing" in a letter dated July 7th, 1523. Because rumours were circulating on his involvement in Domenico de' Bretti's death, Guicciardini decided not only to publicly deny, but also to explain his feelings towards the enemy:

"Whoever said that I tried to ruin Domenico is wrong, since I never did anything nor had such thoughts." [25] Nevertheless, Francesco Guicciardini admitted that Domenico's death would be very beneficial to the city of Reggio. His effort to find an agreement with the duke of Ferrara to quietly kill the bandit was something to forget.

Domenico's character immediately became a legend – numerous stories about him and his actions flourished and even in our days they continue to be told and generate interest among people. In the oral history as in the written one, Domenico shows a double personality. Some episodes portray him as a gentleman brigand: it is told that during an ambush to a group of travellers including Ludovico Ariosto, the bandit freed the poet, reciting some verses from the *Orlando Furioso* by heart. Instead, other legends describe him as a damned soul responsible for guarding cursed treasures. There is a third group of

---

24 *Allegramente, su, più alcun non piagna / ch'egli è potato il Moro e la Castagna.*
See G. Panciroli, *Guidi Panciroli J. U. D. patrii regiensis ac olim in patavino gymnasio lectoris celeberrimi rerum historicarum patriae suae libri octo*, Reggio Emilia 1877.
25 F. Guicciardini, Letter to Cesare Colombo, 16 July 1523.

stories hard to classify: anecdotes built on a historical background, but adding a florilegium of hardly verifiable details. In these tales Domenico is portrayed as a charismatic leader and adventurer: hard but fair, unyielding when dealing with traitors, but gentle when dealing with women. In the middle years of the nineteenth century a traveller, stopping in the birth place of the outlaw, heard the facts of Domenico's life in a version that cannot be described as historically false, but which shows traces of the ambiguous mark left by the bandit.[26] Not even centuries after his death, this character displays an unambiguous face; and we shall probably never be able to obtain a realistic portrait of this man because of the common sliding that historical events face during the centuries.[27]

His name is still enveloped in a shadow of fear and mystery and many people today know only his actions from a more romantic perspective. In order to write a comprehensive biography of this man one would have to dig deeper in the documents that are available in order to fill the gaps and correct the mistakes. However, one should not neglect the richness of legends that are still alive.

If it is true that events which really happened are the first step in a historic analysis, it is also true that the image handed down in the form of legend has sometimes an even bigger role than true facts. When it does not result in violent acts, the desire of self-affirmation of socially or economically disadvantaged people results in the creation of mythical figures: Robin Hood and the hidden Kings studied by Yves Marie Bercé hold the hopes and dreams of people waiting for justice and redemption. In some instances, history provides men suitable to be made into heroes. In other cases, characters that are anything but heroic become legend. In this perspective, according to an observation of Jorge Luis Borges,[28] the errors in the process of popular memorization can be seen as unavoidable forms of invention, necessarily involved in the elaboration of myths fitting to our deepest needs. As Eric J. Hobsbawm pointed out, when we lack heroes we recruit less suitable candidates. The paths of oral history and time will cure their shortcomings.

---

26 P. Fantuzzi, *Viaggi geografici* vol. III, Reggio Emilia 1999 [1858].

27 P. Burke, *Popular Culture* (as note 2).

28 J. L. Borges, Prologue to *El Matrero*, Buenos Aires 1970.

List of abbreviations
ASMo: Archivio di Stato di Modena
ASRe: Archivio di Stato di Reggio Emilia

Bibliography
ALEOTTI, A., *Storia della città e provincia di Reggio Emilia*, Bologna
    1984 [Reggio Emilia 1852].

BADINI, G. (Ed.), *Ludovico Ariosto: documenti, immagini, fortuna critica*,
    Rome 1992.

BADINI, G. (Ed.), *Ludovico Ariosto: il suo tempo, la sua terra, la sua gente*,
    Deputazione di Storia Patria per le Antiche Provincie
    Modenesi, 1974.

BAJA GUARIENTI, C., "Le "guerre civili" di Reggio: una faida fra guelfi e
    ghibellini all'inizio del XVI secolo," in G. BEBBI, *Reggio nel*
    Cinquecento. Le guerre civili cittadine tra guelfi e ghibellini del secolo
    XVI, ed. C. BAJA GUARIENTI, Reggio Emilia, Antiche Porte
    2007, pp. 11–61.

BALLETTI, A., *Storia di Reggio nell'Emilia*, Reggio Emilia 1925.

BELLOCCHI, U. (Ed.), *Reggio Emilia. Vicende e protagonisti*,
    Bologna 1970.

BRAUDEL, F., *La Méditerranée et le Monde méditerranéen à l'époque*
    de Philippe II, 2nd ed. I–II, Paris 1966.

BORGES, J. L., Prologue to *El Matrero*, Buenos Aires 1970.

BURKE, P., *Popular Culture in Early Modern Europe*, London 1978.

CAMPORI, C., "Di alcuni capi di fazioni nelle montagne di Modena,
    di Reggio e di Bologna nel secolo XVI," in *AMPM* VI,
    Modena 1872.

CAPPELLI, A., *Lettere di Ludovico Ariosto*, Milan 1887.

Carpineti medievale, Congress Reports, Carpineti (Reggio Emilia)
    25–26 September 1976, Reggio Emilia 1976.

CERLINI, A., *Storie e leggende dell'Appennino e del Po*, Milan 1939.

CHIESI, L., *Reggio nell'Emilia sotto i pontefici Giulio II, Leone X,*
    Adriano VI e Francesco Guicciardini governatore della città,
    Reggio Emilia 1892.

DAVOLIO, M.–PEZZAROSSA, F., *Leggende della Val d'Asta*, Reggio Emilia 1992.

Dizionario biografico degli italiani, vol. 14, Rome 1972.

FANTUZZI, P., *Viaggi geografici* vol. III, Reggio Emilia 1999 [1858].

FRESTA, A. (Ed.), *Ludovico Ariosto e Reggio Emilia*, Reggio Emilia 1989.

GINZBURG, C., *Il formaggio e i vermi. Il cosmo di un mugnaio del '500*, Turin 1999.

GRASSELLI, E., *Domenico d'Amorotto de Beretti da Carpineti nelle lotte fra Chiesa e Este*, Reggio Emilia 1993.

GUICCIARDINI, F., *Lettere*, Ed. by P. Jodogne, Rome 1986–2004.

HARRISON, R. P., *Forests. The Shadow of Civilization*, Chicago 1992.

HOBSBAWM, E. J., *Bandits*, London 1969.

LE GOFF, J., *Saint Louis*, Paris 1996.

LIVI, G., *Il Guicciardini e Domenico d'Amorotto*, Bologna 1879.

MANCONI, F. (Ed.), *Briganti mediterranei: secoli XV–XVI*, Rome 2003.

MEDICI, D., *Le cronache di Reggio*, Reggio Emilia 2002.

MILANI, F., *Minozzo negli sviluppi storici della pieve e podesteria*, Reggio Emilia 1938.

MONTANARI, G. C., *Storie frignanesi del '500*, Modena 2003.

MONTANARI, G. C., "Storie di banditi fra Modena e la Garfagnana nei secc. XV–XVI," in *La Garfagnana dall'avvento degli Estensi alla devoluzione di Ferrara*, Congress Reports, Modena 2000.

NESI, G., "I banditi dell'Ariosto e la politica ducale di assimilazione della Provincia di Garfagnana al sistema estense," in *La Garfagnana dall'avvento degli Estensi alla devoluzione di Ferrara*, Congress Reports, Modena 2000.

ORTALLI, G. (Ed.), *Bande armate, banditi, banditismo e repressione di giustizia negli stati europei di antico regime*, (Congress Reports, Venice 3–5 novembre 1985), Rome 1986.

PALUMBO, M., *Francesco Guicciardini*, Naples 1988.

PANCIROLI, G., *Guidi Panciroli J. U. D. patrii regiensis ac olim in patavino gymnasio lectoris celeberrimi rerum historicarum patriae suae libri octo*, Reggio Emilia 1877.

PIOMBI, G., *Superstizioni e leggende della montagna reggiana*,
    Reggio Emilia 1959.

RIDOLFI, R., *Vita di Francesco Guicciardini*, Milan 1982.

ROMBALDI, O., *Cinquecento reggiano*, Reggio Emilia 2001.

ROMBALDI, O., "La Garfagnana nello stato estense del Cinquecento,"
    in *La Garfagnana dall'avvento degli Estensi alla devoluzione
    di Ferrara*, Congress Reports, Modena 2000.

ROMBALDI, O., "La Comunità reggiana nello Stato estense nel secolo
    XV," in *Annuario 1965–1967 del Liceo-Ginnasio Statale 'L.
    Ariosto" di Reggio Emilia*, Reggio Emilia 1967.

SCHENETTI, M., *Carpineti: memorie e ricerche*, Modena 1974.

SFORZA, G., "Documenti inediti da servire alla vita di Ludovico
    Ariosto," in *Monumenti di storia patria delle Provincie Modenesi*,
    Modena 1926.

SILINGARDI, G., *Storia di Reggio Emilia*, Modena 1970.

STELLA, A., *Lettere di Ludovico Ariosto*, Milan 1965.

SYNGE, J. M., *The Aran Islands*, Dublin 1907.

TINCANI, A.–SCHENETTI, M., *Verabolo e Carpineti*, Modena 1974.

Una società violenta. Morte pubblica e brigantaggio,
    Manduria-Bari-Rome 1996.

VEZZANI, M., *Domenico d'Amorotto e la sua stirpe*, Reggio Emilia 1962.

VEZZANI, M., *Usanze, tradizioni e leggende dell'Appennino reggiano*,
    Reggio Emilia 1933.

VIGANÒ, G., *Il Medioevo delle Carpinete*, Correggio 1881.

Quart État, Lumpenproletariat et Quart Monde
──────── Tobias Teuscher ────────

Quart Etat, Lumpenprolétariat et Quart Monde : ce qu'apportent les révolutions européennes au combat de la grande pauvreté et de l'exclusion sociale et à la reconnaissance de la misère comme violation des droits de l'Homme.

I. Introduction

Considérer la grande pauvreté et son potentiel pour « humaniser l'Humanité » demeure aujourd'hui l'un des principaux enjeux théoriques de l'éthique sociale contemporaine dont les différentes approches telles que l'histoire, la philosophie, la sociologie, les sciences politiques et le droit nourrissent la poursuite des stratégies politiques à partir de la représentation sociale des personnes et familles les plus défavorisées. Durant 250 ans, Louis-Pierre Dufourny de Villiers (1738–1796), Karl Marx (1818–1883) et Joseph Wresinski (1917–1988) apportent quelques éléments de réponse à travers les notions de « Quart Etat », de « Lumpenprolétariat » et de « Quart Monde ». Les conceptions et les idées sociales qu'elles véhiculèrent demeurent stimulantes sur trois plans. D'abord, l'on est invité à examiner l'étendue des termes « pauvreté » et « exclusion sociale » pour mieux saisir l'objet de la lutte contre l'exclusion. Ensuite, il faudrait s'interroger sur le soutien financier destiné au combat de la misère des familles les plus défavorisées, ainsi que sur leur participation active à leur bien-être : personne n'est jamais dépourvu de ses facultés pour ne pas contribuer à son propre bien-être et à celui de son prochain. Enfin, la pauvreté étant désormais considérée par les organisations internationales en termes des droits de l'Homme, il convient de s'interroger sur l'origine de cette revendication des plus pauvres.

Dans ce contexte, le retour aux trois moments révolutionnaires qui ont marqué la civilisation européenne pourrait s'avérer utile. Dépassant le cadre de la réflexion anthropologique, les réponses à ces questions revisiteront les politiques sociales européennes dans le seul but de les rendre plus efficaces. Chacun des trois moments révolutionnaires européens – la Révolution française (1789), la révolution industrielle en Angleterre (et les révoltes de 1848) et la révolution culturelle au mois de mai 1968 un peu partout en Europe – négligea une partie de la population discriminée en raison de son potentiel révolutionnaire déficient dû à sa condition sociale. A travers l'histoire européenne le constat est accablant : « Le pauvre est celui qui de façon permanente ou temporaire se trouve dans une situation de faiblesse, de dépendance, d'humiliation caractérisée par la privation des moyens variables selon les époques et les sociétés, de puissance et de considération sociale : argent, relation, influence, pouvoir, science, qualification technique, honorabilité de la naissance, vigueur physique, capacité intellectuelle, liberté et dignité personnelle. Vivant au jour le jour, il n'a aucune chance de s'en sortir, sans l'aide d'autrui. »[1] Puisque le pouvoir revendicatif minimal du pauvre – formulé alors encore en termes d'appartenance sociale – ne lui permettait pas de se faire entendre par sa propre force, cette population fut exclue du progrès que la révolution était supposée apporter à tous. Sur le plan normatif, le Quatrième Ordre, le Lumpenprolétariat et le Quart Monde désignent une même population et forment ainsi autrement une triarchie européenne[2] qui se situe dans l'émergence du processus de la pensée sociale moderne, inaugurée par la rédaction des *Cahiers du Quatrième Ordre*[3] au moment de la Révolution française, et qui s'achève provisoirement au mois de mai 1968 dans la notion du Quart Monde. Construire la triarchie des révolutions européennes à travers la prise en considération des plus pauvres conduit à rassembler trois figures très différentes qui ont été exposées à l'intérêt scientifique d'une manière très différente.

1 MOLLAT, MICHEL, *Les pauvres au moyen âge*, Paris 1978, p.14.
2 Cf. HESS, MOSES, *Berlin, Paris, Londres. La triarchie européenne*, trad. Michel Espagne, Tusson (France), 1988.
3 DUFOURNY DE VILLIERS, LOUIS-PIERRE, *Cahiers du Quatrième Ordre, celui des pauvres Journaliers, des Infirmes, des Indigents, etc… l'ordre sacré des Infortunés, ou Correspondance Philanthropique entre les Infortunés, les Hommes sensibles et les Etats généraux pour suppléer au droit de députer directement aux Etats, qui appartiennent à tout Français, mais dont cet Ordre ne jouit pas encore,* n. 1, 25 Avril 1798 ; réimp. Paris 1967.

En quoi le recours à Dufourny de Villiers est-il important pour comprendre l'enjeu théorique présenté ici ? Lorsque les trois états se réunissent au moment de la Révolution française, Louis-Pierre Dufourny de Villiers, architecte de la ville de Paris, proteste contre l'exclusion des plus pauvres de ces assemblées qui rédigent les cahiers de doléances et élisent les électeurs des députés pour la réunion des Etats-Généraux de 1789. Les exclure, explique l'architecte de la ville de Paris, revient à nier leur capacité de penser et met en question leur condition humaine, car seuls les plus pauvres connaissent les effets de la misère sur leurs conditions de vie. Par conséquent, combattre la misère au moment révolutionnaire nécessite leur participation et leur représentation. Or, les plus pauvres ont été exclus des assemblées révolutionnaires. Même le Tiers Etat les ayant refusé, n'auraient-ils pas droit de former un « Quatrième Ordre », « l'Ordre des Infortunés » ? Ainsi, Louis-Pierre Dufourny de Villiers accuse le premier cet éloignement de la vie participative naissante. L'exclusion politique reflète celle vécue dans la vie sociale, le mépris, l'humiliation, l'oubli de ces populations abandonnées par la société dans leur misère. Il invite à se rapprocher des exclus, à les écouter et à rassembler des éléments d'information qui pourraient servir à « réveiller l'intérêt » que « tout citoyen » doit porter à leur sort qui n'est pas tolérable, à « resserrer les liens de la fraternité » et à permettre aux députés, élus aux Etats-Généraux, de mieux les représenter. C'est au nom du droit naturel d'exprimer sa pensée que L.-P. Dufourny considère cette exclusion des pauvres comme illégitime. Dufourny se voit ainsi attribué, selon Harvey Chisick, le rôle d'un des « premiers porte-parole de la démocratie », ayant un réel idéal de paix cherchant « à convaincre ses contemporains de la nécessité de répondre aux attentes des pauvres au sujet de leur subsistance, de leur travail et de leur admission à la participation politique ».

Il se demande alors comment « cet avocat de l'harmonie sociale, de la paix universelle devint un défenseur de la Terreur et dans quelle mesure cette vision morale est caractéristique de cette période ? » [4]

Les *Cahiers du Quatrième Ordre* furent rédigés par Louis-Pierre Dufourny de Villiers lors de la Révolution française et publiés sous le titre « Cahiers du quatrième ordre, celui des pauvres Journaliers, des Infirmes, des Indigents, etc., l'ordre sacré des Infortunés ; ou Correspondance Philanthropique entre les Infortunés, les Hommes sensibles, et les États généraux : pour suppléer au droit de députer directement aux États, qui appartient à tout François, mais dont cet ordre ne jouit pas encore, n° 1, 25 avril 1789 ». Revendiquer la jouissance des droits accordés à tout Français, tel fut l'objectif du cahier que l'auteur consacre aux mauvais pauvres ou à la canaille, pour se rappeler le vocabulaire d'alors.[5] « C'est de cette prétendue canaille que je me ferai gloire d'être le défendeur » écrit Dufourny de Villers[6] en réponse à la convocation des États généraux du 24 janvier 1789. Il est vrai, les plus pauvres, les journaliers, eurent leur place aux Etats généraux à travers le bas-clergé chargé de la représentation indirecte des plus pauvres. Le décret royal affirme en effet que : « Sa Majesté a tâché de remplir encore cet objet particulier de son inquiétude, en appelant aux Assemblées du Clergé tous les bons et utiles pasteurs qui s'occupent de près et journellement de l'indigence et de l'assistance du peuple, et qui connaissent plus intimement ses maux et ses appréhensions. » Par la revendication des droits directs et participatifs des plus pauvres au destin de la société, Dufourny de Villiers dépasse ses contemporains dans sa réflexion et dans son action. Grâce à la publication des *Cahiers du Quatrième Ordre*,

---

4 Chisick, Harvey, « An Intellectual Profile of a Jacobin activist. The Morality and Politics of Dufourny de Villiers (1789–1796) » ; dans : Adams, Christine, Conser, Jack R. & Graham, Lisa Jane, *Visions and Revisions of Eighteenth Century France*, Pennsylvania State University, PSU-Press, 1997 ; idem, *La Notion de Paix perpétuelle pendant la Révolution : la vision irénique de Dufourny de Villiers* ; Présentation au colloque Rousseau Montmorency II, dactylographiée, pp. 125, 129 ; cité par Paturle-Grenot, Michèle, *Dufourny de Villiers et les plus pauvres (1736–1796) : Vaincre l'exclusion au nom des Droits de l'Homme*, Thèse de doctorat, Université Paris VII, 10 décembre 2001, à paraître.

5 De Vos van Steenwijk, Alwine, *Comme l'oiseau sur la branche*, Paris 1986, pp. 37–41 et 55.

6 Dufourny de Villiers, *op. cit.* (note 3), p. 22.

il demande pour la première fois de reconnaître aux plus pauvres des droits politiques directs afin qu'ils deviennent eux aussi membres des Assemblées et puissent déléguer leurs représentants aux États généraux.

Le lien entre Dufourny de Villiers et Joseph Wresinski a été approfondie notamment lors du colloque international sur les plus pauvres dans la démocratie, intitulé « Du Quatrième Ordre au Quart Monde » et organisé à l'occasion du bicentenaire de la Révolution française par l'Université de Caen et le Mouvement international ATD Quart Monde.[7] Ensuite, Michèle Grenot a présenté au mois de décembre 2001 une thèse de doctorat intitulée « Louis-Pierre Dufourny de Villiers et les plus pauvres : Vaincre l'exclusion au nom des droits de l'Homme. »[8] Dès lors, cette présentation vise ici particulièrement le lien entre le Lumpenprolétariat et le Quart Monde.

La notion du Quart Monde est intimement liée à Joseph Wresinski, « un des meilleurs experts en Europe de la pauvreté ».[9] Ses parents ne précisèrent jamais où il vint au monde.[10] Tout au long de sa vie, il restera hanté par cette incapacité de connaître ses racines familiales.[11] Les années d'enfance et de jeunesse sont marquées par la violence, le manque d'argent et la honte, mais aussi par le courage de sa mère. Wresinski évoque des « chemins de la honte » lorsqu'il devait retourner chez l'épicière avec la bouteille d'huile de noix qui n'était pas remplie jusqu'à ras bord, pour qu'elle rajoute les gouttes payées. D'autres chemins de la honte encore le conduisaient chez la bouchère pour réclamer une meilleure qualité de viande de cheval reçue en ré-

---

7 REMOND, RENÉ et al., *Démocratie et pauvreté : du quatrième ordre au quart monde*, Paris 1991.

8 PATURLE-GRENOT, MICHÈLE, *Dufourny de Villiers et les plus pauvres*, (comme note 4).

9 COUVREUR, JEAN, « Un cas permanent et public de mauvaise conscience », dans : *Le Monde*, 1er juin 1966, p. 1 ; il écrit notamment : « Des sociologues tiennent cet ecclésiastique pour un des meilleurs experts en Europe de la pauvreté. »

10 DE VOS VAN STEENWIJK, ALWINE, *Père Joseph*, Paris, Editions Science et Service Quart Monde, 1989, p. 22.

11 WRESINSKI, JOSEPH, *Les pauvres sont l'Eglise, Entretiens avec Gilles Anouil*, préface de *Charles Ehlinger*, Paris 1983, pp. 6–7 (désormais cité PSE). Toutes les références aux écrits de Joseph Wresinski reprennent uniquement le titre cité ainsi que les indications bibliographiques sans toujours reprendre le nom de l'auteur.

compense des courses effectuées.[12] Plus tard, il reconnaîtra que la violence familiale était « la manière de laver des humiliations sans nombre que nous faisait subir notre extrême pauvreté ».[13]

Devenu apprenti pâtissier, Wresinski fréquente la Jeunesse Ouvrière Chrétienne. Il y apprend que « personne n'est jamais compétent ni pour la pauvreté ni pour la justice. Compétents, nous le devenons en acceptant les tâches qui nous sont confiées. (…) j'ai appris non seulement à observer mais à noter pour mieux comprendre ».[14] Nommé curé de campagne, il s'intéresse toujours aux plus démunis. Son évêque l'envoie comme aumônier dans le bidonville de Noisy-le-Grand en banlieue parisienne.[15] Il est désormais connu comme « prêtre qui vivait et agissait avec un crayon dans la main, qui notait et écrivait dans la précarité, le feu d'action, et sans la sécurité de l'ouvrage, qui accorda le temps qu'il faut pour réfléchir à fond et dire les choses, mais « qui n'a pas trop de temps » non plus parce que, suivant le mot de Vergniaud à la Convention, « le malheur n'en accorde pas » ».[16] Marie-Pierre Carretier témoigne de sa rencontre avec Wresinski : « Pour la première fois dans ma vie j'entendais quelqu'un parler différemment de l'aide aux plus démunis. Il disait que ces gens n'étaient pas ainsi qu'on les décrivait habituellement dans les rapports de sociologues ou articles de presse. Je m'exclamais parfois : « Mais enfin ! Pourquoi ces femmes font-elles tant d'enfants ? Et la pilule alors ! » J'espérais qu'il n'allait pas me sortir le discours catho grand teint sur les enfants que le Seigneur nous envoie. Je me disais aussi qu'il ne pouvait pas rétorquer que les gens pauvres ne connaissent pas la contraception. Non, il ne parlait pas non plus d'enfants désirés, mais il m'étonnait : « Chaque naissance est un nouvel espoir. Les parents se disent que pour celui-là,

---

12 *PSE*, pp. 10–11.

13 « A la maison, papa criait tout le temps. (…) Ce n'est que bien plus tard, à l'âge d'homme, en partageant la vie d'autres hommes comme lui, d'autres familles comme la nôtre, que j'ai compris que mon père était un homme humilié » *PSE*, p. 8.

14 Carretier, Marie-Pierre, *La misère est un péché. Biographie de Joseph Wresinski*, Paris 2000, p. 39.

15 Monfils, Thierry, *Le Père Joseph W. fondateur d'ATD Quart Monde. Sacerdoce et amour des pauvres*, Namur 1994, p. 39.

16 Cuny, G.B., « Introduction », dans : De Vos van Steenwijk, Alwine, *Joseph Wresinski -Ecrits et Paroles*, Tome 2, Paris 1994, pp. 18–19 (désormais cité EP 2).

ils feront tout ce qu'ils n'ont pas pu faire pour les autres et qu'on ne le leur enlèvera pas. Parce que, vous savez, on enlève leurs enfants aux pauvres. On les met dans des institutions. Oui, oui, encore aujourd'hui ! » Chaque fois, il me donnait une réponse à laquelle je ne m'attendais pas ».[17]

Nous rencontrons tout au long de ces pages le Mouvement international ATD (Aide à Toute Détresse) Quart Monde. Née en 1957, on pourrait caractériser ATD Quart Monde comme une organisation, présente dans des pays industrialisés d'Europe de l'Ouest, d'Amérique du Nord, plus tard d'Amérique Latine, d'Extrême Orient et d'Afrique. Organisation de solidarité et de partage avec des familles les plus rejetées et exclues du monde, ATD mène des programmes d'action et de recherche qui touchent à la petite enfance et à l'accès à la culture ainsi qu'à divers domaines comme la qualification professionnelle, le droit à la santé ou le logement. Ses actions en faveur de la participation sociale et citoyenne sont, surtout, appuyées par de grandes organisations internationales comme le Conseil de l'Europe ou l'ONU qui lui ont reconnu un statut consultatif. Cette approche démontre avant tout une organisation. Néanmoins, ATD Quart Monde a pris le nom de « Mouvement ». Dès lors, il convient de s'interroger sur ce qui fait sa particularité.

L'histoire d'ATD Quart Monde commence en 1956 au bidonville de Noisy-le-Grand. Ce camp fut créé, en 1954, à la demande de l'abbé Pierre, ancien député à l'Assemblée nationale, fondateur des « Compagnons d'Emmaüs ». Par les dons financiers qu'il récolta suite à un appel sur les ondes radiophoniques, le 31 janvier 1954, devenu historique pour le « sursaut de bonté » qu'il provoqua,[18] il pouvait acheter des terrains dont personne ne voulait, autour de la capitale, afin d'y construire des habitations à loyer modéré (H.L.M.). Ils ne pouvaient

---

17 CARRETIER, *op. cit.* (note 14), p. 13 (nous soulignons).

18 « Mes amis, aux secours ! Une femme vient de mourir gelée, cette nuit, à trois heures sur le trottoir du boulevard Sébastopol, serrant sur elle le papier pour lequel avant-hier on l'avait expulsé. Chaque nuit, ils sont plus de deux mille recroquevillés sous le gel, à la rue, sans toit et sans pain, plus d'un presque nus. Devant tant d'horreur, les cités d'urgence ce n'est même plus assez urgent. Il nous faut pour ce soir, et au plus tard pour demain, cinq mille couvertures, trois cents grandes tentes américaines, deux cents poêles... » ; LUNEL, PIERRE, *L'Abbé Pierre, l'insurgé de Dieu*, Paris 1989, pp. 254–255.

cependant pas accueillir immédiatement tous ceux qui arrivaient des quatre coins de l'Hexagone. Les transferts eurent lieu à Noisy-le-Grand, dans la banlieue est de Paris. En attendant que les habitations d'urgence soient construites, les familles passèrent d'abord une année dans des tentes de fortune, ensuite dans des abris de fibrociment, appelés IGLOOS à cause de leur forme arrondie et bien alignés en rang d'oignons. Toutefois, certaines familles y vivront pendant dix-huit ans. Dans l'opinion publique, « la population dérangeante » n'était plus à la rue. Le bidonville fut cependant ressenti comme « un cas permanent et public de mauvaise conscience », comme le titrait *Le Monde*.[19] L'étrange malaise que l'on éprouva dans le bidonville, observe le journaliste, était avant tout « une gêne, une honte pour notre condition d'homme de voir ainsi l'homme humilié, ravalé. » Car dans les bidonvilles, les familles « se sont vite fait remarquer par leur indigence et leur ignorance. Pour comble d'injustice, on leur reprochait leur manque d'hygiène, dans un camp où il n'y avait que quelques bornes-fontaines. (…) En somme, tout le monde accusait les familles des manques qui leur étaient infligés : manque de sens de la communauté, manque d'ordre, d'harmonie, de propreté. Si elles vivaient dans la boue, sous un toit en demi-lune, sur un sol battu, c'était de leur faute, elles se plaisaient ainsi et le voulaient bien. Les accuser de leur misère, les prendre pour « des cas sociaux », on pouvait le faire autant plus facilement qu'elles étaient dans l'impossibilité de justifier leur condition. Elles n'étaient pas des sans-logis comme les autres, mais pourquoi ? Elles ne pouvaient pas dire qu'elles étaient les victimes de la perte de vitesse de telle région, de telle branche d'activité ; elles n'étaient pas des personnes âgées, ni les sinistrés d'une catastrophe naturelle. Dans le registre des explications courantes de la misère en France, il ne restait que la maladie mentale, la déficience caractérielle et la mau-

---

19 Du 1ᵉʳ au 8 juin 1966, le journal *Le Monde* consacra une série d'articles de JEAN COUVREUR et PIERRE TREY sur les bidonvilles en banlieue parisienne, surtout celui de Noisy-le-Grand. « Un cas permanent et public de mauvaise conscience », 1ᵉʳ juin 1966, n° 6650, pp. 1 et 10 ; « Bidonvilles et sous-prolétariat urbain », 2 juin 1966, n° 6651, p. 9 ; « Pour sortir du cercle », 4 juin 1966, n° 6653, p. 15 ; « Pauvreté et déviances », 5 et 6 juin 1966, n° 6654, p. 8 ; « Une majorité d'émigrés vivent dans les cités de la misère autour de Paris », 7 juin 1966, n° 6655, p. 11 ; « Encore cinq hivers dans la boue ? », 8 juin 1966, n° 6656, p. 18.

vaise volonté. Elles furent toutes utilisées en même temps ».[20] De ce constat, le correspondant du *Monde* conclut que promouvoir des projets de relogement ou la destruction des bidonvilles ne suffit pas. La société devrait rétablir le dialogue entre les très pauvres et le reste de la Nation par des « rapports humains d'une qualité exceptionnelle ».[21]

Etre exceptionnel face à l'inacceptable, être capable de soutenir une population à être capable de comprendre sa situation, de l'expliquer et de la justifier pour permettre une action libératrice : Wresinski demanda aux bénévoles du bidonville de Noisy-le-Grand de « vouloir devenir excellents pour pouvoir faire des choses excellentes ». Ainsi se créa, sous l'impulsion des familles des bidonvilles, le volontariat ATD Quart Monde, d'abord sous le nom d' « Association européenne pour la culture ». Celle-ci fut aussitôt interdite par la Préfecture : l'administration s'est méfiée des plus démunis. D'autres personnes se portèrent garantes, notamment Geneviève de Gaulle-Anthonioz, nièce du Général de Gaulle. « Nul doute, dira-t-elle plus tard, l'expression que je lisais sur les visages de ces hommes et de ces femmes était celle que j'avais lue bien longtemps auparavant sur les visages de mes camarades de déportation, au camp de Ravensbrück. Je lisais l'humiliation et le désespoir d'un être humain qui lutte pour conserver sa dignité ». Suite à la rencontre du Père Joseph, elle quitta le cabinet du Ministre André Mal-raux à Paris et se vit confier, quelques années plus tard, la responsabilité de Présidente du Mouvement ATD Quart Monde en France et le restera jusqu'à sa mort en 2001.[22] De l'action communautaire naîtra le mouvement qui connaîtra de dénominations différentes. Par ces démarches, Wresinski voulut d'abord restituer à une population méprisée sa liberté de penser, de croire et de s'associer activement aux événements de la société qui l'entoure, mais aussi son accès au droit à l'identité, à l'information et au savoir.

Ensuite, le Lumpenprolétariat. Forgée au XIXe siècle dans le contexte de la révolution industrielle anglaise, la conception de Lumpenprolétariat demeure stimulante. Le terme et la catégorie se sont vite imposés : ils n'en étaient pas moins problématiques car le groupe

---

20 *PSE*, pp. 146–147.
21 Couvreur, Jean, « Pauvreté et déviances », *Le Monde*, 5 et 6 juin 1966, n° 6654, p. 8.
22 Glorion, Claire, *Geneviève de Gaulle-Anthonioz. Résistances*, Paris 1997, p. 76.

social ainsi désigné semblait d'emblée privée de statut, de fonction et de conscience propres. A la lettre du *Manifeste du parti communiste* (1848), texte commun le plus emblématique de Marx et d' Engels, le Lumpenprolétariat désigne le « pourrissement passif des couches les plus basses de la vieille société ». Il aurait dû, dès le départ, rejoindre les ambitions révolutionnaires du prolétariat. Or, « toutes ses conditions de son existence font qu'il sera plus disposé à se laisser acheter pour des machinations réactionnaires ».[23]

Au départ de la question du Lumpenprolétariat se retrouve la conception des classes et de la société chez Marx et Engels. C'est à la fin de l'introduction à la « Critique de la philosophie du droit de Hegel » que pour la première fois le jeune Marx évoque le concept de classe. Il attaque alors la faiblesse des aspirations révolutionnaires allemandes, principalement en raison du désaccord irrémédiable entre les exigences théoriques sur le plan philosophique et les réponses pratiques de la réalité. Seul remède à la solution des problèmes, la praxis entre en scène et conduira à une révolution allemande laquelle, toutefois, ne se voudra non pas aussi sanglante que le fut la Révolution française. En Allemagne, la révolution selon Marx sera de préférence partielle, purement philosophique et politique et « laisse subsister les piliers de la maison ». La force motrice de cette révolution douce est alors « une classe déterminée [qui] entreprend, à partir de leur situation particulière, l'émancipation générale de la société. Cette classe libère la société tout entière, mais à la seule condition que la société tout entière se trouve dans la situation de cette classe ; à la condition, par exemple, qu'elle possède ou puisse acquérir à sa guise argent et culture ». Marx précise encore l'impératif de faire coïncider les exigences et les droits de cette classe avec ceux de la société dont elle se fait le représentant général, car « c'est seulement au nom des droits généraux de la société qu'une classe particulière peut revendiquer la suprématie générale ». Cette classe, représentante générale de la société, puise sa force révolutionnaire dans la concentration de toutes les tares de la société dans un seul état ; « Il faut, précise Marx, qu'un ordre parti-

---

23 MARX & ENGELS, *Manifeste du Parti communiste*, Présentation et traduction par EMILE BOTTIGELLI (traduction de 1972 pour AUBIER), Paris 1998, pp. 86–87.

culier soit l'ordre du scandale universel, l'incarnation de la servitude universelle ; il faut qu'une sphère particulière de la société représente le crime notoire de toute la société, de sorte que de se libérer de cette sphère apparaisse comme l'universelle libération de soi ».[24] Deux ans plus tard, dans *l'Idéologie allemande*, Marx revient sur la valeur universelle de point de vue historique : « En effet, toute nouvelle classe qui prend la place d'une classe précédemment dominante est obligée, ne serait-ce pour parvenir à ses fins, de présenter ses intérêts comme l'intérêt commun de tous les membres de la société ; c'est-à-dire, pour parler idées, de prêter à ses pensées la forme de l'universalité, de les proclamer les seules raisonnables, les seules qui aient une valeur universelle. (…) Aussi, son triomphe profite-t-il à nombre d'individus des classes exclues du pouvoir, mais seulement dans la mesure où il leur permet de s'élever et d'entrer dans la classe dominante ».[25] Or, on sait quel agent révolutionnaire Marx avait désigné : le prolétariat.

Joseph Wresinski désigne le Quart Monde comme moteur d'humanité au centre d'un projet de société, révélateur de l'indivisibilité des droits de l'Homme : « Tout homme porte en lui une valeur fondamentale inaliénable qui fait sa dignité d'homme. Elle donne à chacun le même droit inaliénable d'agir librement pour son propre bien et pour celui des autres ».[26] Aux conditions comparables d'une même population s'appliquent, à 150 ans d'écart, deux interprétations proches dans leurs intentions premières mais influencées par une compréhension fort divergente de l'individu et de la conscience collective : aux trajectoires descendantes s'opposent des trajectoires montantes. Du Lumpenprolétariat au Quart Monde : entre ces notions mitoyennes se dessine un lien de continuité mais aussi une rupture qui mérite d'être tenue pour un objet digne d'intérêt scientifique. Le Quart Monde réhabilite la population autrefois désignée par le terme de Lumpenprolétariat et confirme, par l'action militante qui s'ensuit, la méthodologie pertinente jadis employée par Dufourny

---

24 MARX, KARL, « Critique de la philosophie de droit de Hegel » dans : MARX : *Œuvres complètes*, Tome 3 (philosophie), Paris, Gallimard NRF (Collection de la Pléiade), 1982, pp. 392–396.

25 MARX, KARL, « Idéologie allemande », dans : *Ibid.* (comme note 24), pp. 1082–1083.

26 Cf. *Le Quart Monde. Un peuple en marche*, (Igloos 122), Pierrelaye 1981, pp. 3–4.

de Villiers pour le Quatrième Ordre de la Révolution française avec les personnes qui le composèrent pour donner un visage et une identité, une parole et une conscience collective aux plus pauvres afin de permettre leur pleine reconnaissance sociale, politique et leur accès inconditionnel aux droits. C'est la présupposition de départ qui guide les réflexions dans cet article.

Quelques précautions s'avèrent toutefois utiles. Suggérer la réhabilitation du Lumpenprolétariat par le Quart Monde paraît naïf si l'on considère comme exclusif le lien entre Quatrième Ordre révolutionnaire et Quart Monde contemporain. Nul ne le conteste. La conception théorique du Lumpenprolétariat rappelle cependant que l'œuvre « polyphonique » de Karl Marx « a posé de bonnes questions, donné un certain nombre de réponses qu'il ne faut pas méconnaître, même s'ils ne valent plus et qu'elle appartient au passé, à notre passé malgré tout ».[27] Puisque le marxisme ne sert plus ouvertement de prétexte idéologique aux régimes totalitaires, un horizon pragmatique s'ouvre alors pour considérer le message marxien initial pour en apporter un éclairage novateur. Ce retour créatif à Marx nécessite également d'évacuer l'obsession de vouloir y trouver la réponse à toute question que la vie pose, car « beaucoup de questions décisives, telles que l'importance de règles éthiques universelles et des droits de l'homme pour l'action politique sont soit absentes, soit traitées de façon inadéquate dans ses écrits ».[28] Enfin, l'ambiguïté fondamentale de l'œuvre marxienne, origine de sa force libératrice, continue à alimenter les controverses de son inter-prétation. L'ambivalence dont le Lumpenprolétariat est exemplaire, nous le verrons, se nourrit du double positionnement de Marx à la fois en tant qu' homme de sciences et homme d'action : il a formulé une théorie de la société qu'il a cherchée à assortir d'une pratique, les deux aspects étant animés par des présuppositions d'ordre éthique.[29] S'interroger sur cette substance éthique chez Marx, c'est relancer la question sur la valeur que Marx

---

27 TOUBOUL, HERVÉ, *Marx, Engels et la question de l'individu*, Paris 2004, p. 8.

28 LÖWY, MICHEL, *La théorie de la révolution chez le jeune Marx*, Paris 1997, p. 11.

29 RUBEL, MAXIMILIEN, « Notes sur le prolétariat et sa mission », dans : le même, *Marx critique du marxisme*, Paris 2000, p. 285.

accorde, avant et après la rupture épistémologique, aux questions de l'individu ou de la révolution en général.[30]

Cette approche néglige éventuellement l'un ou l'autre aspect du problème dans sa lumière comme dans ses ombres. Simple dans son énoncé, la démonstration reste, là encore, complexe en raison du risque d'abandonner la position scientifique au profit d'un raisonnement militant. Mon propos vise, dans sa droiture, la place de l'Homme de la misère dans la société et son apport aux forces révolutionnaires, ou, pour reprendre la formule de Jean Tonglet,[31] sa capacité d'humaniser l'Humanité. Même si le XIXe siècle n'était pas réellement parvenu à prendre en charge la population de misère,[32] retrouverions-nous chez Marx cette « idée d'une autre politique et d'autres formes de la pensée faisant éclater la distribution institutionnelle des savoirs »[33] à l'instar de Dufourny de Villiers ou, à sa suite, de Joseph Wresinski ? A mi-chemin entre une somme érudite et l'entreprise de vulgarisation, la mise en perspective entre Dufourny de Villiers, Marx et Wresinski vise à reconstruire les mobiles qui ont conditionné jadis l'approche de la misère chez Marx, d'une part, et de Wresinski lui-même influencé par Dufourny de Villiers, d'autre part. Se dessine ainsi un dialogue entre Marx et Wresinski sur leurs conceptions de la société et les implications politiques, philosophiques et éthiques aujourd'hui.

Par conséquent, l'économie du présent article comprend deux parcours consacrés successivement au Lumpenprolétariat chez Karl Marx et Friedrich Engels (II) ainsi qu'au Quart Monde chez Joseph Wresinski, fondateur du Mouvement international ATD Quart Monde et instigateur de la journée mondiale du refus de la misère (III). Le quatrième chapitre traite de l'influence du concept du Quart Monde sur les politiques sociales menées au niveau européen, notamment par rapport à l'approche participative et le respect des droits de l'Homme.

---

30 Kouvélakis, Eugène, *Philosophie et révolution. De Kant à Marx*, Paris 2003.
31 Jean Tonglet est directeur de la revue *Quart Monde*, http://www.revue-quartmonde.org/
32 Gueslin, André, *Gens pauvres, pauvres gens dans la France du 19ᵉ siècle*, Paris 1998.
33 Touboul, *op. cit.* (note 27), p. 10.

II. Premier parcours : Du Lumpenprolétariat dans l'œuvre de Karl Marx

La lecture successive des 39 tomes de la « *Marx-Engels-Gesamt-ausgabe* » fait apparaître le vocable de Lumpenprolétariat à 52 occasions.[34] Le terme émerge avec des développements inégaux – en fonction du caractère politique, économique ou scientifique des écrits – dans *La situation des classes laborieuses en Angleterre* (1845), dans *l'Idéologie allemande* (1846), dans le *Manifeste du parti communiste* (1848) et dans les articles *La lutte des classes en France* publiés initialement dans les quatre numéros de la Nouvelle Gazette rhénane (1850) dont Marx était le rédacteur en chef. *Le 18 Brumaire de Louis-Bonaparte* (1852) de Karl Marx présente, avec *La lutte des classes*, un texte particulièrement intéressant pour notre propos au même titre que les *Grundrisse* (1859). Le 23ᵉ chapitre du livre premier du *Capital* (1867) vient clore l'inventaire. Friedrich Engels fit pour sa part référence au Lumpenprolétariat dans *La Campagne pour la constitution du Reich* (1850) et dans *La guerre des paysans en Allemagne en 1525* (1850). Mentionnons enfin quelques missives de Marx et d'Engels. La répartition géographique du Lumpenprolétariat amène le lecteur en Allemagne, à Naples, à Paris, à Bruxelles, à Vienne, dans la Rhénanie-Palatinat et, enfin, à Londres. Ce premier parcours réunit les fragments les plus significatifs de cette lecture qui révèlent la portée de ce vocable dans les œuvres de Marx et d'Engels (A). Ainsi sera mise en lumière l'incohérence apparente dans l'utilisation de ce concept, à laquelle je consacrerai un commentaire approfondi (B).

II.I. Le Lumpenprolétariat dans l'œuvre de Marx et Engels

C'est par la réflexion sur la théorie matérialiste dans l'*Idéologie allemande* (1845–1846) que le Lumpenprolétariat fait son entrée. Marx et Engels évoquent alors la concentration de la propriété foncière dans la Rome ancienne qui fit disparaître à peu près complètement la population libre : « L'esclavage restait la base de toute la produc-

---

34 MARX, KARL, & ENGELS, FRIEDRICH, *Werke*, (Marx-Engels-Gesamtausgabe (MEGA) des Instituts für Marxismus-Leninismus beim ZK der SED herausgegeben nach der vom Institut für Marxismus-Leninismus beim ZK der KPdSU besorgten Ausgabe in russischer Sprache, Unveränderter Nachdruck der ersten Auflage 1956–1968), 41 Bände, Berlin 1969 ff.

tion. Placés entre les hommes libres et les esclaves, les plébéiens ne s'élevèrent jamais au-dessus du niveau d'un Lumpenprolétariat, d'un sous-prolétariat ».[35] Ils y reviennent ultérieurement dans la troisième partie de l'*Idéologie allemande* consacrée à une critique de l'ouvrage de Max Stirner « *L'unique et sa propriété* ».

La parution du Manifeste du Parti communiste au mois de février 1848 introduit la lutte des classes comme principe directeur de l'Histoire. Ce texte officialise une « simplification moderne de l'opposition des classes »[36] qui aboutit dans l'opposition entre la bourgeoisie et le prolétariat. Ce dernier représente la seule classe réellement révolutionnaire,[37] toutes les autres classes étant conservatrices ou même réactionnaires dans leur obsession de préserver leur existence face à la bourgeoisie. Pour cette raison, le Lumpenprolétariat, « pourrissement passif des couches les plus basses de la vieille société », devrait être assimilé par une révolution dans le mouvement prolétarien, pourtant « toutes ses conditions d'existence font qu'il sera plus disposé à se laisser acheter pour des machinations réactionnaires ».[38]

Intervient en 1850 et en 1852 la publication d'une série de feuilletons initialement publiés dans la Nouvelle Gazette rhénane sous le titre des « *Luttes de classes en France* » et « *Le 18 Brumaire de Louis-Bonaparte* ». Textes d'une extraordinaire vitalité, d'une prodigieuse agilité et d'une redoutable méchanceté polémique, ils représentent les dernières rigolades et les ultimes plaisanteries de l'étudiant berlinois.[39] Mais ils constituent aussi le moment constitutif du concept sociologique du Lumpenprolétariat désormais décrit comme groupe empiriquement déterminé par les vingt-quatre bataillons de la Garde mobile dans le Paris révolutionnaire de 1848 constitués de la canaille : « C'est dans ses rangs que se recrutent les voleurs et les criminels de toute espèce, vivant des déchets de la société, individus sans travail déterminé,

---

35 MARX, « Idéologie allemande », *op.cit.*, (note 25), p. 1089.

36 BOTTIGELLI, EMILE, « Introduction », dans : *Manifeste du Parti communiste*, op.cit. (comme note 23), p. 59.

37 MARX & ENGELS, *Manifeste du Parti communiste*, op.cit. (note 23), p. 86.

38 *Ibid.*, p. 87.

39 PRUNIER, GÉRARD, « Avant-propos », dans : MARX, KARL, *Les luttes des classes en France et Le 18 Brumaire de Louis Bonaparte* (trad. : LÉON RÉMY et JULES MOLITOR), Paris 2001, pp. 12 et 15.

rôdeurs, gens sans feu et sans aveu, variant avec le degré de développement de la nation à laquelle ils appartiennent et ne démentant jamais le caractère des lazzaroni ».[40] Toutefois, Marx n'échappe pas à la contradiction. Le Lumpenprolétariat ne se distingue non seulement « par le bas » du prolétariat mais aussi par le haut de la bourgeoisie : « La canaille [Lumpenprolétariat] se trouve transportée dans les sphères supérieures de la société bourgeoise et fleurit dans l'aristocratie financière, dans ses moyens d'acquérir et dans ses jouissances ».[41]

Deux expériences révolutionnaires qu'a connues l'Allemagne, à savoir les insurrections paysannes de 1525 et la révolution de 1848, alimentent la pensée de Friedrich Engels dans *La Guerre des paysans en Allemagne* (1850). Lorsqu'en 1848 Marx et Engels arrivent en Allemagne, ils comprennent sans détour que le prolétariat ne peut s'y imposer aussi longtemps que persistent les structures sociales féodales. Par conséquent, la révolution de 1848 en Allemagne devrait d'abord cibler l'abolition des structures féodales au profit de la bourgeoisie dont la partie démocratique pourrait être soutenue par le prolétariat pour chasser l'aristocratie et la monarchie : « Le Lumpenprolétariat, cette lie d'individus dévoyés de toutes les classes, qui établit son quartier général dans les grandes villes est, de tous les alliés possibles, le pire. Cette racaille est absolument vénale et importune. Quand les ouvriers français écrivaient sur les maisons, à chaque révolution, l'inscription : « Mort aux voleurs ! » et qu'ils en fusillaient même plus d'un, ce n'était certes pas par enthousiasme pour la propriété, mais bien parce qu'ils savaient très justement qu'il fallait avant tout se débarrasser de cette bande ».[42]

Le combat du système féodal et l'instauration, intermédiaire, de la bourgeoisie rendit possible l'émancipation du prolétariat. Friedrich Engels en fait allusion dans la « *Guerre des paysans en Allemagne* » lorsqu'il analyse les conditions sociales et politiques de la guerre des paysans pour anticiper les luttes historiques à venir par la descrip-

---

40 MARX, KARL, *Les luttes des classes en France*, op. cit. (note 39), pp. 45–46.
41 *Ibid.*, p. 28.
42 ENGELS, FRIEDRICH, *La guerre des paysans en Allemagne*, (trad. : EMILIO BOTTIGELLI), Paris 1974, pp. 28–29.

tion des immaturités et des erreurs contemporaines :[43] « L'opposition plébéienne se composait des bourgeois déclassés et de la masse des citadins privés des droits civiques : les compagnons, les journaliers, et les nombreux éléments embryonnaires du Lumpenprolétariat, cette racaille que l'on trouve même aux degrés les plus bas du développement des villes. (…) La masse des gens sans gagne-pain bien défini ou sans domicile fixe était, précisément à cette époque, considérablement augmentée (…) »[44]

Ensuite, dans le *18 Brumaire*, Marx consacre le cinquième chapitre à une âpre description du Lumpenprolétariat qui se rencontre dans la « Société du dix décembre » : « Sous le prétexte de fonder une société de bienfaisance, on avait organisé en sections secrètes la canaille [Lumpenprolétariat] de Paris ; (…) Des roués en déconfiture, dont les moyens d'existence n'étaient pas moins douteux que l'origine, des bourgeois déclassés, corrompus, véritables chevaliers d'industrie, des soldats et des prisonniers libérés, des galériens en rupture de ban, des charlatans, des faiseurs de tours, des lazzaroni, des voleurs à la tire, des prestidigitateurs, des joueurs, des maquereaux, des tenanciers de bordels, des portefaix, des littérateurs, des joueurs d'orgue, des chiffonniers, des rémouleurs, des rétameurs, des mendiants, en un mot toute la masse confuse, irrégulière, flottante que les Français appellent la bohème (…) tous ses membres, à l'exemple de Bonaparte, éprouvaient le besoin de vivre aux dépens de la nation qui travaille ». [45]

Ces portraits essentiellement négatifs du Lumpenprolétariat conduisent au constat que rien à première vue ne lui désignait une mission historique quelconque. On se souvient cependant que Marx et Engels prévoient pour la classe opprimée le rôle libérateur de la société tout entière. Dès lors apparaissent des contradictions qui sont discutées dans la section suivante (II.II).

---

43 Bottigelli, Emilio, « Introduction »; dans : *op.cit.* (comme note 36), p. 13.
44 *Ibid.*, pp. 54–55.
45 Marx, Karl, *Le 18 Brumaire de Louis Bonaparte, op. cit.* (note 39), pp. 488–489.

II.II. Analyse du concept de Lumpenprolétariat

Plusieurs approches peuvent alimenter la discussion. Nous exposerons d'abord la dimension linguistique (1). Ensuite, nous présenterons quatre définitions possibles du Lumpenprolétariat dont il sera question (2), avant d'insister sur son rôle prétendument contre-révolutionnaire qu'accusent Marx et Engels (3).

II.II.I. Approche linguistique : Un germanisme malheureux moralement chargé

L'une des premières difficultés auxquelles l'on se heurte lors de l'interprétation du terme de Lumpenprolétariat, c'est qu'il constitue un germanisme malheureux prêtant à la confusion en raison de l'affiliation de deux noms propres que nous voudrions rapidement déchiffrer. En langue allemande ancienne, le nom '*Lumpen*' signifie, dans une première approche, des vêtements vieux ou usés au sens du mot français '*haillon*'. Cette interprétation, souvent reprise par les traductions françaises, ne perçoit cependant pas l'idée de Marx et Engels dans l'« *Idéologie allemande* » quand ils évoquent la vie dure des plébéiens de l'ancienne Rome. Il est plus probable que les auteurs allemands songeaient au synonyme de condition asociale, analogue à la deuxième interprétation : '*Lump*' au sens figuratif évoque précisément les pauvres journaliers, les infirmes et les indigents que jadis Louis-Pierre Dufourny de Villiers regroupa dans l'ordre sacré des Infortunés. Egalement dans cet esprit, le verbe réflexif '*lumpen*' désigne une manière de vivre difficile ou peu ordonnée, et cette connotation s'impose. Notons que dans leurs écrits anglais, les auteurs parlent aussi de *mob* et de *social slum*.

Marx et Engels projetèrent donc tout simplement au Lumpenprolétariat l'expression de cette perception négative dont était frappée la population que l'on appelle aujourd'hui le sous-prolétariat. La bourgeoisie détestait les pauvres en raison de leur mode de vie répugnant, et craignait une possible rébellion de leur part.[46] Ce mélange de haine et de mépris se manifeste également chez Marx et Engels

---

46 CHEVALIER, LOUIS, *Classes laborieuses et classes dangereuses à Paris pendant la première moitié du XIXe siècle*, (Librairie Générale Française, 1978) Paris 2002.

quand ils utilisent le mot Lumpenprolétariat par rapport à leurs agents révolutionnaires : ce qui leur a fait peur, c'est que le Lumpenprolétariat puisse trahir la révolution du prolétariat.

En outre, les mots *'prolétariat'* et *'lump'* charrient, dans le sociolecte allemand des classes supérieures, des fortes connotations moralistes qui n'échappent, dans l'espèce, à personne. Leur emploi est conditionné par la position sociale de ceux qui les emploient et il prend désormais une coloration moins fonctionnaliste que morale. La remarque gagne tout son sens à la lumière de la vie de Karl Marx : issu de la bourgeoisie rhénane aisée, il souffre sa vie durant de soucis financiers ; et le philosophe de la révolution prolétaire est ainsi susceptible d'être assimilé à son tour au Lumpenprolétariat pourtant désavoué, ce qui renforce l'excès verbal envers cette classe populaire.

II.II.II. Un concept à quatre définitions fort différentes

Marx et Engels utilisèrent le vocable de manières fort diverses et souvent contradictoires. Pour s'en rendre compte, il convient de souligner les différentes catégories d'usage que font de ce terme Marx et Engels dans leurs écrits. Au moins quatre définitions sont possibles : (a) le reliquat historique d'une société antérieure, (b) le groupe de dégénérés sociaux individuels, (c) la partie inférieure du prolétariat en général et (d) le Lumpenprolétariat comme catégorie en dehors du système économique. Au-delà des définitions précises, il existe une catégorie caractérisée par une grande variété de connotations (e).

(a) Dans une première acceptation, le Lumpenprolétariat apparaît comme le reliquat historique d'une société antérieure. Rappelons que, dans le *Manifeste*, le Lumpenprolétariat était décrit comme le pourrissement passif des couches les plus basses de la vieille société. Cette dernière étant entendue dans la dimension historique, le Lumpenprolétariat est alors compris comme le reliquat préindustriel d'une société industrielle. Par contre, la manière dont Engels envisage le Lumpenprolétariat dans « *La Guerre des paysans en Allemagne* » implique que ce degré pourrait également être conçu comme un passage de sociétés antérieures à d'autres stades historiques de développement : « Le Lumpenprolétariat constitue d'ailleurs un phénomène qu'on retrouve plus ou moins développé dans presque toutes les phases de la société passée. La masse des gens sans gagne-pain bien défini ou sans domicile fixe s'était, précisément à cette époque, considérablement augmentée par la décomposition du féodalisme dans une société où chaque profession, chaque sphère de la vie était retranchée derrière une multitude de privilèges. Dans tous les pays développés, jamais le nombre de vagabonds n'avait été aussi considérable que dans la première moitié du XVIe siècle ».[47]

En effet, dans l'*Idéologie allemande* on trouve encore cette définition déjà plus étonnante : « Les plébéiens placés entre les hommes libres et les esclaves ne parvinrent jamais à s'élever au-dessus de la condition du Lumpenprolétariat ». Précédemment, lorsqu'il s'agissait de la pègre prolétarienne contemporaine, le groupe que l'on définissait ainsi incluait la population la moins favorisée de la société : nomades, voleurs, mendiants, rôdeurs, prostituées, qui ne pouvaient espérer conquérir un emploi, privilège détenu par les vrais ouvriers regroupés dans le prolétariat. Or ici, les plébéiens appartiennent au '*Lumpen*', tout en se trouvant placés, en position intermédiaire, entre les hommes libres et les esclaves. Mais pas n'importe comment. En effet et selon une formulation qui pose d'autres problèmes par ailleurs, les esclaves, bien qu'ils forment « la grande masse productive de la population » ne participent pas à la lutte des classes mais servent « de piédestal passif aux combattants », la lutte des classes se déroulant « à l'intérieur d'une minorité privilégiée entre les libres citoyens riches et les libres citoyens pauvres ». La notion de plébéiens est intéressante, car ce groupe ne fait partie ni de la masse productive de la population (les esclaves) ni du groupe constitué par les classes en lutte (les hommes libres).

(b) Une deuxième approche désigne le Lumpenprolétariat comme un groupe de dégénérés sociaux individuels. Dans le passage cité du *18 Brumaire*, le terme était employé pour signifier un groupe hétérogène de déclassés : des roués en déconfiture, des bourgeois déclassés, corrompus, des chiffonniers, des mendiants. Bref, il s'agissait de toute la masse confuse, irrégulière, flottante de la bohème. Marx, au pied de la lettre, les perçoit de toute évidence comme une seule et même catégorie sociale indépendamment des différences d'origine et

---

47 ENGELS, FRIEDRICH, *La guerre des paysans*, op. cit. (note 42), pp. 54–55.

de position sociale. Les membres du groupe partagent l'expérience d'une déchéance sociale individuelle. Leurs styles de vie présentent également certaines similitudes. La référence à la bohème suggère même que ces individus forment une classe sociale. Il convient toutefois de signaler l'écart entre la bohème de Marx et celle d'un Henry Murger[48] ou d'un Honoré de Balzac. Ce dernier par exemple observe que « la bohème, qu'il faudrait appeler la Doctrine du boulevard des Italiens, se compose de jeunes gens tous âgés de plus de vingt ans, mais qui n'en ont pas trente, tous hommes de génie dans leur genre, peu connus encore, mais qui se feront connaître, et qui seront alors des gens fort distingués... La bohème n'a rien et vit de ce qu'elle a. L'Espérance est sa religion, la Foi en soi-même est son code, la Charité passe pour être son budget. Tous ces jeunes gens sont plus grands que leur malheur, au-dessous de la fortune, mais au-dessus du destin ».[49] Cette deuxième interprétation du Lumpenprolétariat ouvre la voie à une approche intéressante bien que très romantique. Il convient de soulever l'importance de la déchéance sociale individuelle divergente d'une appréciation selon laquelle il s'agit d'une continuation d'un segment social issu d'une société plus ancienne. Dans le premier cas, la culture du Lumpenprolétariat peut être perçue comme ayant fait l'objet d'une transmission de génération en génération ; dans le second cas, il s'agit d'une sous-culture, probablement de nature plus floue avec laquelle l'on n'entre pas en contact avant d'avoir atteint un certain âge.

(c) Ensuite, le Lumpenprolétariat peut également être appréhendé comme faisant partie du prolétariat général. Marx recourt, dans *La lutte des classes en France*, à une définition sociologique qui assimile le Lumpenprolétariat au prolétariat général. Avant ce passage, nous apprenons qu'il n'y a rien que la bourgeoisie puisse faire sinon « opposer une partie des prolétaires au reste du prolétariat ». Sans doute, le Lumpenprolétariat est ici sans ambiguïté pris comme une partie du

---

48 MURGER, HENRY, *Scènes de la vie de bohème*, (d'abord publié à Paris, M. Levy, 1886), Introduction et notes de LOÏC CHOTARD avec la collaboration de GRAHAM ROBB, Paris 1988.

49 DE BALZAC, HONORÉ, « Un prince de la bohème », dans : *Scènes de la vie parisienne*, Paris 1984, pp. 232–233.

prolétariat en général. Cette approche du terme de Lumpenprolétariat s'inscrit cependant en faux contre les définitions précédentes, ce qui ne tarde pas à laisser le lecteur attentif dans un état de perplexité étonnée. Formulé de cette manière, le concept perd sa valeur heuristique.

(d) Du point de vue économique, enfin, le Lumpenprolétariat peut être appréhendé par sa situation en dehors du système économique. Dans la première partie du *Capital*, Marx complique la compréhension lorsqu'il s'approche du Lumpenprolétariat en termes d'économie. Au chapitre 23 du *Capital*, il disserte sur les lois de l'accumulation et affirme qu'une surpopulation relative constitue un préalable à l'établissement du mode de production capitaliste, un nombre suffisant de travailleurs devant maintenir les salaires suffisamment bas pour permettre l'accumulation du capital. Dans la quatrième section de ce chapitre, toutefois, Marx évoque les diverses composantes de la surpopulation et montre comment certaines catégories sociales peuvent être classifiées comme des contingents de la réserve de l'industrie et d'autres comme des matériaux usés du processus de production (les malades, les éclopés, etc., « les laissés-pour-compte de la classe ouvrière »). Ces catégories sont encore impliquées dans l'économie et conservent encore certains liens, aussi délicats soient-ils, avec le processus d'accumulation du capital. Cependant le vrai Lumpenprolétariat réunissant vagabonds, criminels et prostituées n'a plus aucun lien avec ce processus. Le trait caractéristique du « vrai » Lumpenprolétariat consiste en ce que l'existence de ces individus n'est pas un préalable à la production capitaliste ; ce ne sont que des parasites.

Marx pousse encore plus loin cette complexité dans les *Grundrisse*, lorsqu'il attribue un sens plus large à cette classe de parasites que dans le *Capital* : tous les individus qui n'ont pas de fonction dans le processus de production relèvent du Lumpenprolétariat, y compris les personnes dont le statut social est élevé. D'un point de vue économique, cette interprétation semble être éminemment discutable, même si l'on ignore les références haineuses au Saint-Père et aux concierges. Les travaux du Prix Nobel de l'économie Gary Becker sur l'efficacité du secteur informel de l'économie au quotidien, qu'il désigne de *real world issues in your every day life*,[50] ont conduit à une prise de conscience qu'à leur manière, les personnes d'un statut social différent, en occurrence, chez Marx, les vagabonds et les criminels, peuvent apporter une contribution au processus économique au même titre que le repos du dimanche ou même « l'économie chabbatique » mise en lumière par Raphaël Draï.[51] L'affirmation de Marx ne pèse pas beaucoup plus du point de vue sociologique puisqu'il se contente de dire ce que le Lumpenprolétariat *ne doit pas* être. Et de nouveau, cette définition économique ne cadre pas avec les autres : la première définition inclut tous les individus qui jouent un rôle dans le processus de production (rétameurs, tâcherons), la seconde définition ne s'accorde pas avec la définition du *Capital* et la troisième définition présente le problème de considérer le Lumpenprolétariat comme une classe sociale, ce qui est incohérent dans la mesure où la population concernée ne joue pas de rôle dans le processus de production.

Reste un panaché d'autres définitions. Par souci d'exhaustivité, nous allons incorporer dans la dernière catégorie un certain nombre d'autres définitions qui ne sont pas suffisamment significatives pour être reprises dans des catégories séparées, au risque d'accentuer encore la négligence dont firent preuve Marx et Engels dans l'utilisation correcte de leur propre concept. Bien que Marx et Engels eussent en permanence usé du terme de Lumpenprolétariat en référence à des segments de la population urbaine, au terme du *18 Brumaire*, Marx n'hésite pas à critiquer l'Armée française laquelle « n'est plus la fleur de la jeunesse paysanne, c'est la fleur poussée dans le marécage de la canaille rurale ».[52] Lorsque dans tous les passages cités le Lumpenprolétariat renvoie à l'échelon le plus bas de la stratification sociale, Marx s'en prend, toujours dans le *18 Brumaire*, à l'aristocratie financière sous Louis-Philippe, c'est-à-dire « toute la science financière de cette canaille [Lumpenprolétariat], qu'on la considère en bas ou en haut de l'échelle sociale ».[53] Et lorsqu'il aborde le chapitre de

---

50 Becker, Gary, *The Economics of Life. From Baseball to Affirmative Action to Immigration, How Real-World Issues Affect Your Every Day Life*, New York 1997.
51 Draï, Raphaël, *L'économie chabbatique*, Paris 1998.
52 Marx, Karl, *Le 18 Brumaire*, *op. cit.* (note 39), p. 308.
53 *Ibid.*, p. 233.

l'accession au trône de Napoléon III, il dépeint avec beaucoup de réalisme l'entourage social du souverain. Il ne s'agit pas là d'un simple sarcasme de la part de Marx, ce qui ressort particulièrement bien d'un passage du *Rôle de la force dans l'histoire*, écrit entre 1887 et 1888, où Engels, croquant la noblesse prussienne comme « *Schmarotzeradel* » (décadente noblesse pourrie). Qu'il suffise à présent de préciser que Marx et Engels emploient le terme de manière figurative et non de façon analytique. La conclusion de ce premier parcours se chargera d'apporter la clarté nécessaire à l'interprétation de ces pièces disparates. Encore faut-il s'interroger sur les conséquences de l'incohérence conceptuelle. Que représenterait le Lumpenprolétariat au juste ? Selon la première définition (le Lumpenprolétariat comme reliquat d'une société antérieure), le terme renverrait au résidu d'un prolétariat ancien accumulé dans certaines grandes villes depuis des générations. La deuxième définition (un groupe de dégénérés sociaux individuels) pourrait correspondre aujourd'hui à ce que René Lenoir désignera plus tard comme les inadaptés,[54] désignation contre laquelle Joseph Wresinski s'oppose en proposant une appellation plus positive, celle du Quart Monde. Si l'on conçoit le Lumpenprolétariat comme un segment inférieur du prolétariat global (troisième définition), on peut penser aux travailleurs non qualifiés, notamment d'origine étrangère. La quatrième définition (celle issue du *Capital*), qui implique le « vrai » prolétariat, englobera les « vagabonds, criminels et prostituées ». Cette incohérence rend le terme de Lumpenprolétariat, du moins de la manière dont Marx et Engels l'exploitent, relativement inutilisable. Il ne renvoie pas à divers aspects d'une seule catégorie sociale, mais bien à des groupes de personnes complètement différents. Cette opinion a par ailleurs rencontré l'approbation de… Engels lui-même ! Quelques années plus tard, en effet, Engels songera à réécrire ce livre. Un projet qui ne se concrétisera jamais en faveur de la révision du *Capital* rédigé par son plus vieux collègue et compagnon. Trois mois avant sa mort, dans une lettre à Kautsky en date du 21 mai 1895, il admettra avoir commis « deux fautes considérables » dans *La Guerre des paysans en Allemagne* dont une concerne les « déclassés, occupant presque la place

---

54 LENOIR, RENÉ, *Les exclus, un Français sur dix*, Paris 1974.

des parias ». Il affirme qu'à la fin de la féodalité, c'est ce segment de la population qui a servi de réservoir à ce qui se développera ultérieurement comme prolétariat ; il s'agissait d'un « pré-prolétariat ». Et ce sont ces gens qui, de son point de vue, ont fait la révolution dans les faubourgs de Paris en 1789. Il leur attribue maintenant un rôle révolutionnaire et non un rôle réactionnaire. Retenons, pour clore ce premier parcours, que le Lumpenprolétariat représente un groupe intermédiaire dépourvu de toutes les déterminations propres à la théorie marxiste. Marx et Engels se soucient moins de précision terminologique que de justification idéologique des révolutions qu'ils préparent. Il s'agit, dans les écrits de Marx et Engels, d'un groupe fluctuant bien qu'empiriquement prouvé, incontestable mais néanmoins contesté, présent tout en étant absent : la conception de Lumpenprolétariat sert à montrer sans montrer mais en montrant tout de même.

III. Deuxième parcours : Joseph Wresinski et la notion du Quart Monde

En 1974, René Lenoir, Secrétaire d'État à l'action sociale de la République Française, publia un essai « *Les Exclus : Un Français sur dix* ». On n'y retrouve aucune allusion à Wresinski ni à la notion de Quart Monde. L'abbé Pierre, fondateur du Mouvement « Emmaüs », autre figure emblématique de la société française, est également absent de cet ouvrage. Cependant, le livre garde le mérite d'avoir rappelé à la société française la persistance de l'extrême pauvreté, car Lenoir témoigne précieusement de la façon dont le Gouvernement appréhendait la population des plus défavorisés : les Français les plus pauvres y sont catégorisés en inadaptés physiques (les personnes qui vivent avec un handicap physique), débiles mentaux et inadaptés sociaux. Alors que les débiles mentaux furent distingués selon leur quotient intellectuel en « débiles moyens », « débiles profonds » et « arriérés profonds »,[55] la catégorie des « inadaptés sociaux » fut encore affinée. Lenoir recense « cinq catégories d'importance analogue [qui] peuvent être isolées : – les malades mentaux (environ 300000), – les suicidaires (165000), – les alcooliques (environ 200000), – les délin-

---

55 *Ibid.*, p. 11.

quants adultes (260000), – les marginaux ou asociaux (150000), (…) les adultes refusant les règles de la société industrielle et organisés en petites communautés qui arrivent à subvenir à leurs besoins, les vagabonds, d'anciens délinquants ou d'anciennes prostituées n'ayant pas réussi à trouver du travail, et quelques milliers de familles logées dans des bidonvilles et qui vivent d'expédients ».[56] Bref, l'extrême pauvreté fut considérée comme une situation vécue de manière individuelle et négative, provoquée volontairement par un refus d'adaptation aux règles de la société ou par la délinquance de celui qui la subit. Force est de constater que la population qui vit dans les bidonvilles constitue une catégorie à part. L'ouvrage de Lenoir considère, avant toutes choses, les exclus comme une catégorie à part entière. Cet ensemble mérite d'exister puisque les individus qui la composent ont un point commun : l'inadaptation. Le mot « exclusion », y compris son ensemble dérivationnel, n'apparaît que quatre fois dans l'ensemble des pages. Comme le constate l'auteur, « Dire qu'une personne est inadaptée, marginale ou asociale, c'est constater simplement que, dans la société industrielle et urbanisée de la fin du vingtième siècle, cette personne, en raison d'une infirmité physique ou mentale, de son comportement psychologique ou de son absence de formation, est incapable de pourvoir à ses besoins, ou exige des soins constants, ou représente un danger pour autrui, ou se trouve ségréguée soit de son propre fait soit de celui de la collectivité ».[57]

Face à cette interprétation, Wresinski appréhenda l'extrême pauvreté à travers le peuple du Quart Monde, terminologie qui revint régulièrement dans ses écrits et ses paroles ; elle distingue la population la plus défavorisée partout dans le monde, jadis désignée par Marx comme le Lumpenprolétariat. Analyser l'apparition de cette notion et son contenu est l'objectif du dernier parcours.

Pour mieux saisir sa motivation et les réflexions qui l'amènent à la prise de conscience d'une identité collective de la misère, il est utile de rappeler brièvement les conditions que Wresinski a rencontrées dès son arrivée au camp des sans-logis qui deviendra bientôt le

---

56 *Ibid.*, p. 15.
57 *Ibid.*, p. 130.

bidonville de Noisy-le-Grand. Dans son entretien autobiographique avec Gilles Anouil, il témoigne : « Je suis arrivé le 14 juillet 1956 et sur ce plateau, (…) Devant ce vide, je me suis dit : autrefois, les sources d'eau, les croisements de route, un clocher, une industrie réunissaient les hommes. Ici, les familles sont rassemblées par la misère. C'était comme une inspiration. Je savais ne plus être en face d'une situation banale de pauvreté relative (comme on disait alors), de difficultés personnelles. J'avais affaire à une misère collective. D'emblée, j'ai senti que je me trouvais devant mon peuple. Cela ne s'explique pas, ce fut ainsi ».[58]

A ce moment, le terme de « Quart Monde » n'apparaît pas encore dans le vocabulaire de Wresinski ; il était précédé par la notion du peuple. Deux trajectoires peuvent être constatées. D'abord, l'émergence de la notion du peuple caractérisé par sa condition sous-prolétaire qui reflète l'aspect collectif de la misère. Ce processus se déroule entre le 14 juillet 1956 (arrivée de Wresinski dans le bidonville) et la publication du numéro de la revue Igloos : « *Un peuple parle* »[59] au printemps de 1968 (lorsque la société civile à travers l'Europe s'interroge sur sa finalité). Les familles des bidonvilles et des cités d'urgence participèrent à cette réflexion par le témoignage de leur vie et la revendication d'une justice et d'une équité (A). C'est ensuite la création de la notion Quart Monde qui couronna l'émergence de ce Peuple. Les « Cahiers de doléances », rédigés par les familles, font allusion à cette même action de Louis-Pierre Dufourny de Villiers lors de la Révolution française. Désormais, l'appellation Quart Monde symbolise une appellation militante, allant de pair avec le quart état révolutionnaire. Grâce à la publication d'une étude de Jean Labbens en 1969, intitulée « *Le Quart Monde. La condition sous-prolétaire* », cette notion fut pour la première fois utilisée publiquement. En 1982, elle rentre dans l'Encyclopédie Universalis (B). La dénomination de Quart Monde désigne désormais un Mouvement, « un peuple en marche ».

---

58 *PSE, op. cit.* (note 11), pp. 68–69.
59 *Igloos* 41–42, Pierrelaye 1968, 48 pp.

III.I. La notion du peuple chez Wresinski

Analyser l'émergence du « peuple » demande tout d'abord une conceptualisation de ce vocable. Il s'agit ensuite de synthétiser les éléments constitutifs du peuple tel qu'il s'utilise dans le discours wresinskien. La condition sous-prolétaire appelée jadis par Marx « Lumpenprolétariat », représentant le lien unificateur entre les individus qui composent le peuple, elle fera alors l'objet de la troisième partie.

L'étude d'Alain Pessin « *Le mythe du peuple et la société française du XIXᵉ siècle* »[60] démontre que le mythe du peuple est un fait collectif qui dépasse les formulations explicites du « populisme ». Pour systématiser l'émergence du mythe par les structures élémentaires du populisme, Pessin utilise la forme du quadrilatère et nomme les angles : Peuple, Exil, Guide et Etre. Deux axes, nommés Histoire (axe horizontal) et Parole (axe vertical), lient ces quatre points. Ensuite, il distingue six combinaisons désignées Absence (Peuple-Exil), Projet (Guide-Etre), Sujet (Peuple-Guide), Naissance (Peuple-Etre), Histoire (Exil-Etre) et Exil (Guide-Exil).[61] La relation Peuple – Exil est caractérisée par l'absence. Celle-ci naît par l'oubli, l'ignorance, et par une existence vaincue ou douloureuse. Dans « *Les Misérables* », Victor Hugo a démontré, que le problème de l'identification d'un peuple relève d'une importance surtout morale et sociale avant d'acquérir le statut de problème politique, métaphysique ou religieux.[62] Alain Pessin inverse l'ordre. Proche de la bipolarité de l'homogène et de l'hétérogène de Bataille, Pessin situe l'identification du peuple comme un problème d'ordre principalement politique car en l'absence de tout lien entre la société et le peuple, celui-ci n'arrive point à exprimer ses revendi-

---

60 PESSIN, ALAIN, *Le mythe du peuple et la société française du XIXᵉ siècle*, Paris 1992.

61 *Ibid.*, p. 228.

62 « Tant qu'il existera, par le fait des lois et des meurs, une damnation sociale créant artificiellement, en pleine civilisation, des enfers, et compliquant d'une fatalité humaine la destinée qui est divine ; tant que les trois problèmes du siècle, la dégradation de l'homme par le prolétariat, la déchéance de la femme par la faim, l'atrophie de l'enfant par la nuit, ne seront pas résolus; tant que, dans de certaines régions, l'asphyxie sociale sera possible ; en d'autres termes, et à un point de vue plus étendu encore, tant qu'il y aura sur la terre ignorance et misère, les livres de la nature de celui-ci pourront ne pas être inutiles. » dans : HUGO, VICTOR, *Les Misérables*, Tome 1, préface de CHARLES BAUDELAIRE, commentaire de BERNARD LEUILLIOT, Paris 1972, exergue.

cations politiques et sociales : « (…) le problème soulevé n'était pas d'abord celui du fardeau et de l'injustice, mais celui d'une coupure et d'une absence, d'un abandon. (…) Il y a constat d'un monde absent, d'un monde qui a cessé d'être atteint et concerné par les questions de justice et d'injustice ».[63]

L'existence oubliée consiste en une manière de vivre détachée de la société, enfermée dans une inculture (ou non-intégration) et privée d'éléments moralisateurs. Cette non-intégration est qualifiée d'exil, défini, quant à lui, par le manque matériel (le manque du nécessaire pour vivre), d'une part, et le manque spirituel (une place à l'écart de la société), d'autre part. A l'absence de vie s'ajoute l'incapacité de la société dite civilisée (bourgeoisie) de comprendre ce qu'est réellement la vie inculte. Cette incapacité conduit à l'ignorance. Celle-ci, ferme et explicite, renforce la polémique par laquelle se manifeste l'opposition entre la bourgeoisie et le peuple exilé. Ainsi, l'exil n'est plus une situation passagère mais persistante et prend forme dans l'opposition entre la bourgeoisie « victorieuse » et le peuple exilé « vaincu ». D'où émerge le destin d'une errance qui promet de se transformer en marche pour sa libération.

Ce bref détour par Pessin permet le cheminement envers la notion du Quart Monde. Nous pensons pouvoir assimiler la notion d'absence à ce que Wresinski appelle la condition sous-prolétarienne. Cette dernière se caractérise par le manque de tout travail stable et honnête, et unifie le peuple du Quart Monde. Encore faut-il reconstituer les étapes qui amènent Wresinski à prendre conscience du fait que les familles de Noisy-le-Grand font parti d'un peuple. Le processus qui mène à reconnaître la population du bidonville comme un peuple à part entière est animé par deux formes d'observation. D'une part, Wresinski observe le comportement des hommes, des femmes et des enfants du camp. Il choisit alors une compréhension orientée vers les aspects psychologiques individuels. A partir de 1963, on assiste à l'émergence d'une prise de conscience en raison de la solidarité du corps des volontaires avec les familles du camp. L'insistance paraîtra artificielle. Les sources permettent toutefois de constater que

---

63 PESSIN, *op. cit.* (note 60), p. 230.

Wresinski parle d'abord des enfants et des femmes, et s'interroge si les volontaires, qui commencent à le joindre, connaissent ces familles sans place ni rôle.[64]

Dès le début du Mouvement, Wresinski parle des familles au sens global,[65] même s'il « n'était pas un inconditionnel aveugle et euphorique de la famille ».[66] Il fut cependant convaincu que « la famille est le seul refuge pour l'homme quand tout manque (…). Dans la famille, il trouve son identité, (…) son ultime air de liberté. Même si leurs enfants leur sont arrachés, l'homme et la femme se réfèrent toujours aux êtres qu'ils ont procréés ».[67] Le camp de Noisy-le-Grand n'accueillit que des familles.[68] Wresinski accorda cependant une attention particulière aux mères,[69] « dernier rempart contre la misère ».[70] Sa mère lui avait appris que les femmes gardent leur énergie intérieure, leur fierté et leur distinction, quel que soit le degré de leur dénuement.[71] Même si « les femmes ne sont pas la solution à la misère [et] n'ont pas les remèdes entre les mains »,[72] elles restent le « pivot de la résistance à la misère » et incarnent l'aspiration des familles à vivre

---

64 « Pourquoi sommes-nous là et connaissons-nous ceux auprès de qui nous vivons ? », réunion de volontaires du 27 juillet 1961 ; dans : DE VOS VAN STEENWIJK, ALWINE, *Joseph Wresinski - Ecrits et Paroles*, Tome 1, Paris, Editions Quart Monde, 1992, p. 40 (désormais cité EP 1).

65 Cf : « Les enfants en milieu de misère », Réunion de volontaires du 4 avril 1962, *EP* 1, pp. 58–63. Voir aussi « Les familles sous-prolétaires sont des familles ouvrières », Dossiers de Pierrelaye, janvier 1983, côte d'archives 047 PA, pp. 1–2 ; « Quelle est la contribution des familles du Quart Monde à la construction de la paix », Dossiers de Pierrelaye, novembre/décembre 1985, côte d'archives 112 PA, pp. 7–8.

66 DE LA GORCE, FRANCINE, « Quand vivre en famille est un défi », *Revue Quart Monde*, 179, 2001, p. 12.

67 *PSE* (comme note 11), p. 16.

68 « Le Père Joseph et son peuple, mais de quel peuple s'agit-il ? », interview avec une journaliste, mars 1967, au Camp de Noisy-le-Grand ; *EP* 2, op. cit. (note 16), p. 26.

69 « Le volontariat d'aide à la détresse », extraits d'une réflexion du Père Joseph pour la revue Igloos, 15. 04. 1962 ; *EP* 1, op. cit. (note 64), p. 64.

70 « La femme, dernier rempart contre la misère », réunion des volontaires, mai 1962 ; *EP* 1, op. cit. (note 64), p. 81.

71 *PSE* op.cit. (note 11), p. 13.

72 « La femme, dernier rempart contre la misère », *art. cit* . (note 70), p. 87.

dans la dignité. Dans cette optique, l'action de Wresinski visait à renforcer l'honneur de chaque famille vis-à-vis des voisins par une action simple et concrète : la garde mutuelle des enfants.[73]

Sachant que c'est par son vocabulaire qu'une société manifeste son estime à l'égard des plus faibles de ses concitoyens,[74] Wresinski inventa le terme « familles sous-privilégiées ».[75] Ainsi, fit-il allusion au terme anglais *underprivileged families*, jugé plus juste par rapport au terme français *familles asociales*, et plus adapté par rapport au vocabulaire allemand qui connaît le mot *Problemfamilien*.[76] Ce choix de vocabulaire valorise les familles et ne leur rappelle pas constamment leurs défaites.[77] Or, faute de ne pas connaître cette population, la société fut incapable de la définir et de trouver des appellations justes.[78] Par conséquent, la société les écarta afin de conserver l'ordre établi.[79] Nous y reconnaissons facilement la caractéristique du Lumpenprolétariat marxien et l'hétérologie de Georges Bataille. Puisque les familles sous-privilégiées ne partagent pas l'héritage spirituel, culturel, social et matériel de la société qui les entoure et « ne réussissent pas à se conformer à l'ordre établi »,[80] la société ne prend en considération que l'aspect psychologique pour lui attribuer une origine psycho-pathologique.[81]

Wresinski demanda cependant de ne pas ignorer ni l'itinéraire personnel ni les entraves dans le développement des personnes en grande pauvreté.[82] Il observa que les causes de la souffrance psychologique en milieu de pauvreté – inhérente au développement personnel

---

73 « Grégarité et solitude », réunion des volontaires, mai 1962 ; *EP* 1, op. cit. (note 64), p. 112.

74 « Une mentalité scientifique », Réunion du Groupe d'Etude de travailleurs sociaux et volontaires, automne 1962, *EP* 1, *op. cit.* (note 64), p. 134.

75 « La famille sous-privilégiée », réunion des volontaires, mai 1962 ; *EP* 1, op. cit. (note 64), p. 91.

76 Problemfamilien = familles à problèmes (traduction littérale).

77 « Respecter le passé et croire en l'avenir », réunion d'un groupe d'Etude de travailleurs sociaux et de volontaires, le 12 janvier 1963; *EP* 1, op. cit. (note 64), p. 147.

78 « La souffrance psychologique que provoque la misère », réunion de volontaires, mai 1962 ; *EP* 1, op. cit. (note 64), p. 97.

79 « La famille sous privilégiée », *op. cit.* (note 75), p. 92.

80 *Ibid.*, pp. 91 ss.

81 « La souffrance psychologique que provoque la misère », *op. cit.* (note 78), p. 98.

82 *Loc. Cit.*

dès l'âge de la petite enfance – demeurent dans l'exclusion culturelle, mais également « dans la malnutrition, dans l'ignorance des mamans qui ne savent pas quelle est la bonne nourriture pour les tout-petits, dans leur manque d'argent et leur manque de savoir-faire, dans toutes ces années d'une enfance passée dans l'insécurité et les ruptures constantes. C'est ainsi que naît cette sorte d'inconséquence, ce manque de maîtrise de soi ».[83] Wresinski observa que, faute de ne pas avoir appris à connaître un monde bienveillant, l'enfant pauvre devenu adulte, « ne voit devant lui que des étrangers ».[84] La souffrance sociale qui en résulte, dévoilée au moment du glissement à l'intérieur du continuum, pour employer les termes de Bataille, réside dans la révélation « de ne pas être comme les autres, de ne pas avoir ce que d'autres possèdent ».[85] L'incohérence due au chômage ou aux retards d'allocations familiales amène les individus à perdre le sens d'autres responsabilités envers leur famille ou leurs voisins. « Cette privation constante de choses qui donnent des habitudes et permettent des relations avec les autres, finit par faire que les gens ne pensent pas de la même manière que ceux qui font partie de la cité des hommes. Ils n'ont plus la même dimension sentimentale, psychologique ou intellectuelle, ils n'ont plus la même dimension spirituelle ».[86]

Ainsi l'absence de culture et de sentiment d'appartenance[87] renforce les souffrances psychologiques et sociales.[88] Les familles sous-privilégiées « n'ont pas joui des privilèges des autres, spécialement du privilège de la reconnaissance de leur dignité, de leur droit à la fierté, donc au respect ».[89] Ce dernier devient l'outil principal pour soutenir les familles. S'adressant aux travailleurs sociaux, en janvier 1963, il projeta le respect des familles en grande pauvreté comme étant

---

83 *Ibid.*, pp. 103 s.

84 *Ibid.*, p. 98.

85 « Le malheur toujours à fleur de peau de se sentir inférieur », réunion des volontaires, septembre 1962 ; *EP* 1, op. cit. (note 64), p. 123.

86 « L'âme du bidonville. Une population qui a peur et qui fuit », soirée d'information, 1963, deuxième partie; *EP* 1, op. cit. (note 64), p. 158.

87 « Le développement communautaire », *Igloos*, 57–58, 1970, p. 34.

88 DE GAULEJAC, VINCENT, « Honte et dignité » ; dans : HAROCHE, CLAUDIN, VATIN, JEAN-CLAUDE, *La considération*, Paris 1998, p. 188.

89 « Le Père Joseph et son peuple, mais de quel peuple s'agit-il ? », *op. cit.* (note 68), p. 28.

une responsabilité majeure qui les valorise réciproquement. Ainsi, la promotion du respect des familles les plus pauvres deviendra tâche de la société entière,[90] afin d'éviter la souffrance sociale. Celle-ci naît « lorsque l'individu ne peut pas, ou ne peut plus, être ce qu'il voudrait être. C'est le cas lorsqu'il est contraint d'occuper une place sociale qui l'invalide, le disqualifie, l'instrumentalise ou le déconsidère ».[91]

« Dans ce rassemblement provoqué par la misère, chacun, au fond, est un isolé ».[92] La situation d'extrême pauvreté dans laquelle vécurent les familles « appauvrit les relations et les personnalités ».[93] Wresinski observa que « les familles n'ont pas les moyens de bâtir quelque chose ensemble. Elles ont pourtant besoin les unes les autres ; elles ont besoin de se cacher, chacune derrière les autres ».[94] Ainsi naquît entre les familles un lien social, nourri par le sentiment de culpabilité. Cette sanction, provoquée par le regard d'autrui,[95] fut considérée comme étant « l'élément le plus important de la solitude des hommes ».[96] Pour échapper à la sanction d'autrui, l'individu tente à se cacher. « Il coupe même et recoupe sans cesse les contacts inévitables avec ceux de son groupe, avec ses voisins. Aucun intérêt positif, aucun projet durable ne le lie à eux. (…) Même quand il se tapit dans son coin et qu'il fait le mort, ils sont là qui par leur présence le déshonorent. Car il le sait trop bien, le seul fait de vivre dans un tel milieu est déshonorant. Le groupe, son groupe est une chose déshonorante, et il ne peut pas se reconnaître en lui. Il a besoin de lui, car c'est le seul milieu où il puisse se sentir une certaine aisance et même se croire un peu de supériorité. C'est le seul groupe aussi à l'aider à survivre avec les siens, grâce à ce tissu de menus services qui sous-tend la vie des pauvres gens et les porte à travers les moments les plus dramatiques. Mais son sentiment envers ses voisins sera toujours ambigu et il ne cessera pas de dire du mal d'eux. (…) Chacun doit se justifier pour lui-

---

90 « Respecter le passé et croire en l'avenir », *op. cit.* (note 77), p. 147.
91 DE GAULEJAC, VINCENT, *art. cit.* (note 88), p. 190.
92 « Grégarité et solitude », *op. cit.* (note 73), p. 109.
93 *Ibid.*, p. 107.
94 *Ibid.*, p. 108.
95 GEREMEK, BRONISLAW, *La potence ou la pitié. L'Europe et les pauvres du Moyen Âge à nos jours*, trad. J. ARNOLD-MORICET, Paris 1987, pp. 12 ss.
96 « Grégarité et solitude », *op. cit.* (note 73), p. 109.

même et les justifications qu'on se donne, on ne peut pas les donner pour les autres ».[97]

Or, dans le bidonville, les familles ne purent pratiquement pas se dissimuler et furent, par conséquent, exposées sans cesse au regard des autres.[98] Afin de garder l'intimité familiale, et par là, leur dignité, les plus pauvres s'enferment davantage. La solitude qui en résulte conduisit à « l'isolement qui vient du désengagement, de l'indifférence que les personnes finissent par se porter ».[99] Wresinski n'en déduisit cependant pas une insensibilisation des familles, car ceci aurait ignoré leur souffrance pourtant révélatrice du besoin de se soutenir entre elles. La solution que Wresinski envisagea consistait en une transformation du camp à partir de l'intérieur. Or, aux yeux des pouvoirs publics, « la population n'[était] pas capable de se remettre debout ou de réussir quoi que ce soit ».[100] Pour prouver leur capacité, il lui fallait trouver les moyens d'intégrer les familles de la société et ne pas les laisser vivre isolées.

Contre l'isolation (l'exil chez Pessin, l'hétérogène chez Bataille ou Spencer), Wresinski accorda au bidonville une force créatrice d'identité pour deux raisons. D'abord, le bidonville – appréhendé comme étant l'espace public accordé par la société aux plus pauvres – réveilla le besoin d'une *terre natale*[101] propre aux plus pauvres. Ensuite, la solidarité et l'engagement du Volontariat conduisit à la naissance d'une *Communauté de destin*, intrinsèque à la vie du bidonville. Les travaux de Jean Labbens démontrent, en effet, que bien que les cités d'urgence ou de transit donnèrent un logement à titre provisoire pendant la rénovation du tissu urbain, elles prirent la fonction d'un filtre : « Destinées à héberger pour un temps, à faciliter le transit vers des logements plus modernes, plus sains, plus adéquats, mais aussi plus coûteux, elles ont éliminé progressivement tous ceux qui pouvaient

---

97 « Préface », dans : LABBENS, JEAN, *Le Quart Monde, la condition sous-prolétarienne*, Pierrelaye 1969, pp. 17–18.

98 *Ibid.*, p. 110.

99 *Ibid.*, p. 109.

100 « Le sous-prolétariat demande une politique », réunion de volontaires, janvier 1967, *EP* 1, op. cit. (note 64), pp. 546 et 547.

101 « Rendre aux exclus une terre natale », réunion de volontaires autour du Professeur Christian DEBUYST, 8 décembre 1962 ; *EP* 1, op. cit. (note 64), p. 139.

prétendre à de tels logements ; elles ont bien dû garder les autres, devenir les logis permanents de ceux qui n'arrivent pas à être admis dans les moins coûteuses des habitations que notre société considère comme normales ».[102]

Le bidonville fut l'abri des familles qui, trop démunies, ne pouvaient jamais obtenir un logement dans la région parisienne. Alors que l'opinion publique pensait qu'il s'agissait « simplement de ruraux déracinés de leur terre », la population du camp de Noisy-le-Grand se composait « de familles déracinées de leurs pays »[103] détachées à la fois de leur pays d'origine et de la société qui les entourait à nouveau. A partir de cette réalité, Wresinski mena une réflexion sur l'importance de l'espace public occupé par les plus pauvres. La *terre natale* eut un triple intérêt. D'une part, les exclus y trouvèrent une sécurité intérieure, ce qu'il appela le jardin secret ; et elle permit, d'autre part, d'expérimenter un modèle valable de société, ce qui donna finalement aux familles la possibilité d'échanger des valeurs réelles à égalité avec d'autres familles. L'exemple d'un bidonville de Toulouse explique l'importance de cet aspect dans la pensée wresinskienne. Ce bidonville fut « un terrain entouré d'un mur de près de trois mètres. Au pied de ce mur, à l'entrée de ce terrain, il y avait un gendarme montant la garde. (…) Mais il s'agissait simplement de gens qui vivaient là, dans des cahutes de bois, dans de vieux camions ou de vieux cars. De ces gens qui vivaient ainsi, la ville de Toulouse s'était préservée en les séparant de l'ensemble par un poste de police ».[104]

Face à cette situation, une *terre natale* procure un climat de confiance et permet de retrouver le « (…) jardin secret que chacun porte en soi, (…) où nous demeurons nous-mêmes, où personne d'autre ne peut rentrer facilement (…) et où chacun (…) est une personne qui a encore des valeurs ».[105] Or, du fait même de leur exclusion, les pauvres vivent là où la société leur accorde un terrain auquel ils ne

---

102 LABBENS, JEAN, *Le Quart Monde, la condition sous-prolétarienne* (note 97), pp. 120 s.
103 « La souffrance psychologique que provoque la misère », *op. cit.* (note 78), p. 101.
104 « L'âme du bidonville. Une population évincée des biens qui lui étaient dévolus », *op. cit.* (note 86), p. 154.
105 « Rendre aux exclus une terre natale », *op. cit.* (note 101), p. 140.

sont pas habitués.[106] Déracinés de là où ils ont grandi, ils perdent les repères de leur enfance. La « société modèle »[107] expérimentée dans le bidonville de Noisy-le-Grand se caractérisait par la participation active des familles à la vie du camp. Ceci leur permettait, de manière intrinsèque, de se retrouver à égalité avec les membres de la société. Ainsi, les capacités d'une famille se développaient avec les capacités de la population.[108] L'expérience vécue à l'intérieur du bidonville amena Wresinski à percevoir le monde de la misère comme un monde à part entière, habité par une population en état de ségrégation sociale.[109] Il qualifia le bidonville comme « un monde, comme un groupe absent à lui-même. (…) Le bidonville est comme une grande catastrophe où, seule, la misère unit les hommes, un monde extérieur au monde, mais aussi extérieur à lui-même, en dehors de la vie qui l'entoure, mais aussi sans vie propre, sans vie communale et sociale ».[110] Wresinski insista sur la dépendance qui marque le monde de la misère, mais il introduisit la notion du destin : « Le plus grave est qu'il s'agit d'un monde dépendant des autres. Sa destinée est aux mains des autres, alors qu'il n'a pas d'amis. Il forme un groupe qui n'a pas de destinée à lui, pas de marche de vie dont il puisse être certain ».[111]

L'importance de pouvoir maîtriser son destin amena Wresinski au concept de la Communauté de destin. Celle-ci « est fondée sur la conscience que, même réunie dans la misère, elle peut et doit servir les autres, faire en sorte que les autres partagent le bonheur d'être réunis ».[112] Les plus pauvres, privés d'une Histoire propre, n'ont pas conscience d'appartenir à un groupe quelconque. C'est pour cette raison précise que « dans l'ATD Quart Monde, tout un chacun se fait, d'abord, historien. Le Sous-prolétariat lui-même y cherche son

---

106 *Ibid.*, p. 139.

107 *Ibid.*, p. 140.

108 *Ibid.*, p. 142.

109 « L'âme du bidonville. Une population évincée des biens qui lui étaient dévolus », *op. cit.* (note 86), p. 154.

110 « L'âme du bidonville. Une population qui a peur et qui fuit », *op. cit.* (note 86), p. 165.

111 *Ibid.*, p. 165 (nous soulignons).

112 « La communauté pauvre », réunion de volontaires, 3 octobre 1963 ; *EP* 1, op. cit. (note 64), p. 193.

histoire, tout le corps des militants permanents sont tenus à approfondir toujours plus l'histoire passée et présente des plus pauvres dans le monde, de leurs combats, de ceux qui ont lutté avec eux et pour eux ».[113] Anne-Marie Rabier s'interrogea à raison : « Comment être fier de son histoire lorsque tout le monde la juge insignifiante, voire méprisable ? »[114] Par conséquent, le développement communautaire passe dans un premier temps par le réveil de la volonté d'appartenir à une histoire commune. La participation active des habitants du bidonville à la valorisation matérielle et culturelle de leur milieu en fut un aspect. Ensuite, le développement de la confiance dans la capacité des familles leur permit de maîtriser leur avenir. « Les familles peuvent prendre conscience que d'autres sont aussi malheureux ou qu'ils sont même plus malheureux ».[115] La mise en œuvre des deux aspects fut animée par la dynamique du volontariat Quart Monde. Censés soutenir la participation des familles au développement communautaire, les volontaires procurent en même temps une stabilité au sein de cette communauté. L'instabilité que constata Wresinski vint du fait que les familles « n'ont pas seulement les idées des familles des bidonvilles, [elles] ont aussi des idées du monde qui les entoure ».[116] De cette situation ambiguë résulte l'instabilité et l'ambivalence qui furent équilibrées par un pôle sûr et stable. La participation active, créatrice d'identité, se manifesta dans le Foyer des femmes où furent développés les principes de la vie communautaire. La *Communauté de destin* sera achevée lorsque les familles sous-privilégiées « accepteront de donner aux autres et d'accueillir plus pauvre qu'eux »[117] pour devenir « source de promotion pour la société ».[118]

---

113 De Vos van Steenwijk, Alwine, « Le sous-prolétariat dans le monde ouvrier : qui est porte-parole de qui ? », Dossiers de Pierrelaye, décembre 1982, côte d'archives 045 PA.
114 Rabier, Anne-Marie & Picquet, Guy, *Soleil interdit ou deux siècles d'exclusion d'un peuple* (Igloos 96, 1977), p. 10.
115 « La communauté pauvre », *op. cit.* (note 112), p. 192.
116 *Ibid.*, p. 189.
117 *Ibid.*, p. 192.
118 « La communauté des pauvres, source de promotion pour la société », réunion préparatoire au second colloque sur les « Familles inadaptées » à l'Unesco, 14 octobre 1963, *EP* 1, op. cit. (note 64), p. 204.

Cette réalité ne suffit pourtant pas à prétendre que la misère revient à un seul problème socio-psychologique. En posant la question de savoir si le même cumul de problèmes pourrait provoquer la misère dans une famille aisée,[119] Wresinski plaça la vie des familles rassemblées au camp dans un contexte aussi bien économique qu'historique. En effet, la situation économique des plus pauvres fut peu favorable à leur équilibre social et psychique. Lorsque le déséquilibre social put être maîtrisé par l'action communautaire dans le camp, l'insécurité économique aggrava leur situation. « C'est l'insécurité économique qui renforce et rend invivable le mal psychologique ».[120] Par cette observation, Wresinski mit en lumière la condition sous-prolétaire des familles du camp. Elle caractérise dans la pensée de Wresinski ce que Pessin appelle l'absence.

Nous devons nous arrêter un instant devant le tableau imposant que brosse Alwine de Vos van Steenwijk dans son étude « *La provocation sous-prolétarienne* ». Celle-ci fut la première entièrement consacrée à la condition de vie du sous-prolétariat en France des années 1960 : « … Dans les cas les plus favorables, les travailleurs sous-prolétaires se trouvent embauchés dans les petites entreprises marginales, les branches d'industrie en perte de vitesse, celles qui ne peuvent subsister qu'en payant les plus bas salaires, parfois en se dérobant à l'obligation d'inscrire leur personnel à la Sécurité Sociale. (…) Les conditions du travail y sont pénibles et malsaines. La main-d'œuvre est sans qualification, et très mobile. Toute forme de sécurité de l'emploi fait défaut. Pour ne citer qu'un exemple, nous y avons vu des mères de familles rester debout 8 ou 10 heures par jour, sur leurs jambes enflées et marquées, dans de vastes locaux bruyants et non chauffés, à nettoyer du poisson, à mettre en conserve, les mains rougies et gercées, plongées dans l'eau froide. Elles peuvent y être congédiées, sous des prétextes divers, d'un jour à l'autre. (…) Mais, c'est sans doute dans le secteur tertiaire que les travailleurs sous-prolétaires trouvent leurs occupations les plus habituelles. (…) Au mieux, ils assument les tâches les plus répugnantes. (…) Ils gagnent leur vie dans les abattoirs

---

119 « La souffrance psychologique que provoque la misère », *op. cit.* (note 78), pp. 98–99.
120 *Ibid.*, p. 99.

vétustes, souvent comme gardiens ou nettoyeurs de nuit. Il montent nos marchés à l'aube, en balayant les déchets en fin de matinée (pour les ramener à la table familiale bien souvent) on les trouve encore au fond des navires de la marine marchande, à nettoyer les caves dans la vapeur de produits chimiques néfastes aux yeux, à la peau et aux poumons. (…) C'est cela et bien d'autres choses encore, le travail de ce peuple accusé de paresse : occupations ténébreuses, irrégulières, souvent beaucoup plus lourde pour la faible santé, humiliante, parfois inavouable, toujours interchangeable et sans sécurité du lendemain, (…) condamné à l'inactivité honteuse, sans jamais rapporter aux siens de quoi vivre vraiment, ni pouvoir espérer une quelconque améliora- tion, un quelconque avancement dans l'avenir ».[121]

Xavier Godinot affine cette analyse à l'instar de l'auteur pré- cité, et met en lumière la dégradation de l'état du chômage des sous- prolétaires du chômage intermittent au chômage chronique. Il distin- gue les parcours stables (emplois stables, savoir-faire, bonne santé, marginalité dans l'entreprise en raison du manque de représentation corporatiste), des passages intermittents (emplois précaires, pro- blèmes de santé, impasses dans les tentatives d'insertion) et des itiné- raires épisodiques (emplois précaires, très mauvaise santé, difficultés relationnelles, problèmes avec la justice).[122] Pour Wresinski, « le com- bat des sous-prolétaires n'est pas pour n'importe quel combat, pour n'importe quel emploi et songer que n'importe quelle occupation ferait l'affaire des chômeurs de plus longue durée, c'est leur faire in- jure. Eux en ressentent à la fois l'humiliation et l'inefficacité. Les petits emplois condamnés à disparaître dans la modernisation, ne présen- tent qu'un sursis au chômage. Les sous-prolétaires le savent depuis longtemps ». Dès lors, cet engagement sous-prolétaire devient non seulement un combat pour un emploi stable, mais également une lutte pour la sécurité et la modernité ainsi qu'une lutte pour le droit à la parole.[123] Face à cette réalité, quelles furent les alternatives ?

---

121 DE VOS VAN STEENWIJK, A., *La provocation sous-prolétarienne*, Pierrelaye 1972.

122 GODINOT, XAVIER, *Les travailleurs sous-prolétaires face aux mutations de l'emploi*, Paris 1985, pp. 22–46.

123 « La lutte des sous-prolétaires dans l'appartenance au monde du travail », Dossiers de Pierrelaye, juin/juillet 1983, côte d'archives 063 PA, pp. 1–4.

Pour résumer Wresinski, les sous-prolétaires doivent passer par la dure vie des ouvriers pour sortir de la misère,[124] car le travail est à la fois un combat de l'homme pour sa libération[125] et une lutte pour la dignité.[126] L'importance, pour le travailleur, se manifeste dans sa reconnaissance et son intégration.[127] En posant la question de savoir si le même cumul de problèmes chez les familles les plus pauvres pourrait provoquer la misère dans une famille aisée,[128] Wresinski place la vie des familles sous-prolétaires dans un contexte aussi bien économique qu'historique. En effet, la situation économique des plus pauvres fut peu favorable à leur équilibre social et psychique. Lorsque le déséquilibre social a pu être maîtrisé par l'action communautaire dans le camp, l'insécurité économique aggrava leur situation. « C'est l'insécurité économique qui renforce et rend invivable le mal psychologique ».[129] Leur faible instruction scolaire ainsi que leur faiblesse physique amène les jeunes déshérités à se voir offrir « des places de travail sans avenir, (…) d'apprenti facilement dédaigné et mal rémunéré ».[130] Une fois devenus travailleurs, ils exécutent les tâches « que d'autres refusent dans le service des pompes funèbres ».[131] Ainsi, ils ne connaissent pas la fierté d'appartenir à une catégorie professionnelle honorée.[132] C'est pour cette raison que, « pour sortir de la misère, les

---

124 « Pour sortir de la misère, les sous-prolétaires doivent passer par la dure vie des ouvriers », réunion de volontaires, août 1963 ; *EP* 1, op. cit. (note 64), pp. 219–223.
125 « Le travail, une lutte de l'homme pour sa libération », séminaire de réflexion en soirée sur le travail, du 7 au 11 mars 1966, réunion du 7 mars 1966 ; *EP* 1, op. cit. (note 64), pp. 418–423.
126 « Le travail, une lutte pour la dignité », séminaire de réflexion en soirée sur le travail, du 7 au 11 mars 1966, réunion du 8 mars 1966 ; *EP* 1, op. cit. (note 64), pp. 424–428.
127 « L'importance, pour le travailleur, d'être reconnu et intégré », réunion de volontaires, 27.12.1966 ; *EP* 1, op. cit. (note 64), pp. 490–493 ; « Nous sommes des travailleurs », Dossiers de Pierrelaye, novembre 1982, côte d'archives 042 PA.
128 « La souffrance psychologique que provoque la misère », *op. cit.*, (note 78), pp. 98–99.
129 *Ibid.*
130 ATD Science et Service, « Un peuple parle. Cahiers de doléances, rédigés aux mois de mai et juin 1968 par les habitants de bidonvilles et de cités d'urgence de Stains, Mulhouse, Orly, Créteil, Reims, La Courneuve, Saint-Denis, Toulon, Noisy-le-Grand, etc. », *Igloos* 41–42, 1968, p. 40.
131 *Ibid.*, p. 42.
132 « L'âme du bidonville : une population évincée des biens qui lui étaient dévolus », *op. cit.* (note 86), p. 160.

sous-prolétaires doivent passer par la dure vie des ouvriers ».[133] Mais la précarité de leur travail, « la santé précaire sans moyen d'accès aux services médicaux, l'absence des moyens matériels et culturels nécessaires au développement psychomoteur et intellectuel, le faible éveil de l'intelligence et par conséquent l'impossibilité de bâtir sa pensée et de dominer les problèmes de l'existence, (…) l'impossibilité de développer les notions temporelles et de là de planifier sa vie sont des causes pour lesquelles les travailleurs sous-prolétaires ne sont pas intégrés dans les luttes syndicales : certains ouvriers se défendent seuls, d'autres se regroupent, mais il y a les autres, ceux qui ne savent pas se défendre, ceux que personne ne défend et que personne ne défendra jamais ».[134] Wresinski parla plus tard de l'absence de culture et d'appartenance.[135] Dans le monde du travail, les familles sous-privilégiées « n'ont pas joui des privilèges des autres, spécialement du privilège de la reconnaissance de leur dignité, de leur droit à la fierté, donc au respect ».[136] « Tous ne sont pas sans métiers alors que tous sont réduits à un état de manœuvre. De manœuvres sur le plan professionnel mais aussi sur le plan économique en général, sur le plan social, politique et religieux. Des manœuvres en tout, une catégorie d'hommes qui n'ont aucun droit et qui ne peuvent pas se défendre ».[137]

III.II. Du Quatrième Ordre au Quart Monde

Le terme de Quart Monde fut créé en 1969, pour donner un titre à l'étude de Jean Labbens sur le sous-prolétariat français. Cette étude fut censée appuyer les « Cahiers de doléances » rédigés par les familles des cités d'urgence et des bidonvilles. Il convient d'insister sur le fait que Jean Labbens lui-même n'applique cette terminologie

---

133 « Pour sortir de la misère, les sous-prolétaires doivent passer par la dure vie des ouvriers », *op. cit.* (note 124), p. 219.

134 « Pourquoi sommes-nous là et connaissons-nous ceux auprès de qui nous vivons ? », (note 64), p. 42.

135 « Le développement communautaire », *Igloos*, 57–58, 1970, p. 34.

136 « Le Père Joseph et son peuple, mais de quel peuple s'agit-il ? », *op. cit.* (note 68), p. 28.

137 « L'âme du bidonville. Une population qui a peur et qui fuit », *op. cit.* (note 86), p. 165.

nulle part. Il évoque des mal-logés,[138] de la population du camp,[139] parle d'une ou de population(s) déshéritée(s) et marginale(s)[140] et fait allusion aux « enfants des cités ».[141] Cette attitude prouve que le concept de Quart Monde dans les termes de Wresinski demeure au début ignoré par les sciences sociales universitaires. La trajectoire de cette terminologie n'est pas aussi lente que celle du *Peuple*. N'est-il pas plus difficile de se rendre compte d'une situation et de la décrire, que de lui assigner un nom propre ? Comme en témoigne Jean Tonglet : « Au cours de la même période, un ami du Père Joseph découvre à la Bibliothèque Nationale les « Cahiers du quatrième ordre », évoquant un quart état à la Révolution française. Immédiatement, le père Joseph s'en empare et subvertit le terme quart-monde (sociologique, descriptif d'un état) en un Quart Monde, héritier du quart état, mouvement de libération des plus pauvres, symbole de fierté ».[142]

Comment cette compréhension de la démarche active se retrouve-t-elle dans la connotation de Quart Monde d'aujourd'hui ? Selon Francine de la Gorce, la création du terme de Quart Monde était nécessaire puisque Wresinski ne fut pas satisfait du terme du sous-prolétariat. Ce dernier avait une connotation « trop marxiste ». Elle souligne l'héritage du Quatrième Ordre révolutionnaire pour le Quart Monde : « A y bien regarder, écrit elle, c'est la même lignée. Il y a une lignée de la noblesse, une lignée bourgeoise, et aussi une lignée de misérables, de pauvres gens ».[143] Pour Xavier Godinot, le lien entre le Quatrième Ordre et le Quart Monde est le suivant : « Ces familles de travailleurs très défavorisés sont les héritiers du « Quatrième Ordre », celui des pauvres journaliers, des indigents, qui tenta en vain de se faire représenter aux États Généraux de 1789 aux côtés des trois autres Ordres. Ils sont issus de ce « lumpenprolétariat » du 19e siècle,

---

138 LABBENS, J., *op. cit.* (comme note 97), p. 51.

139 *Ibid.*, p. 55.

140 *Ibid.*, pp. 89, 107, 157.

141 *Ibid.*, p. 167.

142 Correspondance avec Monsieur JEAN TONGLET, volontaire permanent ATD Quart Monde.

143 DE LA GORCE, FRANCINE, *Un peuple se lève : Noisy le Grand 1963–1968*, Paris 1995, p. 310.

sans gagne-pain bien défini, sans domicile fixe pour certains. D'où les appellations de « sous-prolétariat » et de « Quart Monde » ».[144]

Le concept de Wresinski mérite toute attention, car le terme de Quart Monde est devenu une notion militante. Dans la préface à l'étude de Jean Labbens, Wresinski met en lumière que le Quart Monde accuse la société de « forfaiture ».[145] Pour ensuite mobiliser, « Il faut mettre fin à la condition prolétarienne » et la « faire éclater ».[146] Louis Join-Lambert, auteur de l'article « Quart Monde » dans l'Encyclopaedia Universalis, insiste sur le fait que « le terme désigne moins une réalité nouvelle qu'une nouvelle façon de regarder la pauvreté et le sous-prolétariat ».[147] Dès lors, cette notion comporte trois aspects. C'est d'abord la réorientation du regard de la population et le rappel de l'existence d'une couche de population extrêmement pauvre dans les pays développés, alors que la société ne regardait, auparavant, que la pauvreté dans les pays en voie de développement, appelés Tiers Monde. C'est ensuite la dénomination d'une population défavorisée, car inadaptée aux normes sociales, nommée « cas sociaux ».

Enfin, la notion permet à cette population de s'identifier comme acteur de la société : « Le terme « Quart Monde » (…) désigne de moins en moins un milieu, en ce qu'il est passif et exclu. Il désigne au contraire ce que ce milieu recèle d'expérience d'injustice et d'espoir de justice, d'expérience du besoin et de compréhension des besoins, d'expérience d'exclusion et de capacité de participer comme partenaire social à l'élaboration d'une société démocratique. (…) Le terme « Quart Monde » s'adresse aujourd'hui au Quart Monde lui-même. Et lorsque les sous-prolétaires disent « nous du Quart Monde », il ne s'agit pas d'une population cible de la gestion administrative, mais plutôt d'un peuple qui a une cause, celle qu'il partage avec tous les exclus et tous les humiliés du monde ».[148]

---

144 GODINOT, XAVIER, *Les travailleurs sous-prolétaires face aux mutations de l'emploi*, (note 122), p. 13.
145 « Préface » ; dans : LABBENS, *op. cit.* (note 97), p. 6.
146 *Ibid.*, p. 30.
147 JOIN-LAMBERT, L., « Quart Monde », *Universalia 1981. Les événements, les hommes, les problèmes en 1980*, Paris 1981, pp. 341–442, (ici p. 341).
148 *Ibid.*, p. 342.

Le vocable « Quart Monde » reste un terme politique qui a un rôle d'étiquette et signifie le progrès et l'avenir. Comme le rappelle Wresinski, « si on n'arrive pas à donner et à conserver au mot une densité émotionnelle, politique ou religieuse, (…) l'appellation « Quart Monde » devient une marque. C'est pourquoi le terme Quart Monde est un terme qui doit être utilisé à bon escient et dans des circonstances qui le valorisent ».[149]

Aujourd'hui nous constatons que le terme n'a pas trouvé son entrée dans la littérature scientifique ou politique. Les institutions européennes n'utilisent pas ce terme. Une quête de la base EUR-LEX constate l'absence de ce terme dans les textes législatifs ou dans les communications de la Commission européenne. Les parlementaires européens se montrèrent plus apte à utiliser ce terme. Il s'avère toutefois être le cas qu'ils n'aient pas bien compris de quoi il s'agit. Les neuf questions écrites enregistrées depuis le 1er janvier 1960 portent toutes sur l'aide alimentaire.[150] L'enseignement social de l'Eglise catholique reprend la notion du Quart Monde pour la première fois en 1987, dans l'encyclique de Jean-Paul II « *Sollicitudo rei socialis* » : « On parle de plusieurs mondes à l'intérieur de notre monde unique : premier monde, deuxième monde, tiers-monde voire quart-monde ». La note de bas de page assignée à cette phrase n'interprète la notion quart-monde que dans ses deux acceptations descriptives : « L'expression Quart Monde est employée non seulement occasionnellement pour désigner les pays dits moins avancés (PMA), mais aussi et surtout pour désigner

---

149 « Quart Monde, Ghetto ou dynamique ? », Dossiers de Pierrelaye, février/mars 1979, côte d'archives 006 PA n° 13, p. 1.
150 E-1346/85, DURY, Raymonde, JO C-078, p. 17 ; E-1414/85, GLINNE, Ernest, JO C-078, p. 17 ; E-2740/86 ; VERNIMMEN, Willy, JO C-261, p. 34 ; E-2840/86, HAPPART, José, DURY, Raymonde, REMACLE, Marcel, JO C-292 p. 023 ; H-0378/87 (B2-0810/87 ; sous-division 33), WURTZ, Francis, JO annexe débat 355 ; E-0163/88, ANDRE-LEONARD, Anne, C-110, p. 002 ; H-0261/89, (B3-°217/89 ; sous-division 23), NICHOLSON, James, JO annexe débat 381 ; O-0053/90, HEREDIA, Ramirez, DE DIOS, Juan, (E-0949/90) ; H-0923/90 (B3-1504/90 ; sous-division 98) JO annexe débat 394 ; H-0905/90 (B3-1504/90), DURY, Raymonde, JO annexe débat 394 ; O-0306/90, LANGER, Alexander et al., (E-0089/91) ; O-0374/90, BARROS-MOURA, Jose, E-0659/91 ; O-0375/90, BARROS-MOURA, Jose, E-0660/91.

les secteurs de grande ou d'extrême pauvreté des pays à moyen ou haut revenu ».[151]

IV. Troisième parcours : L'identité, la participation active et le respect des droits de l'Homme prise en considération par les institutions européennes et internationales

À l'occasion de la Journée internationale de l'éradication de la pauvreté[152] en 2001, le Parlement européen (P.E.) réuni en séance plénière vota la résolution « Nations Unies : Journée mondiale du refus de la misère ».[153] Le texte considère que « la misère constitue une violation des droits de l'homme et une atteinte insupportable à la dignité humaine » et souligne l'importance de la lutte contre la misère comme « élément primordial de la paix dans le monde et du développement durable ». Les députés européens demandent ensuite que soit posée, sur le parvis du Parlement européen à Bruxelles, une dalle en l'honneur des victimes de la misère,[154] à l'instar de celle du Trocadéro à Paris.[155] Ainsi, l'assemblée européenne fit sienne le postulat du

---

151 JEAN-PAUL II, « Sollicitudo rei socialis (Personne humaine et développement) » ; dans : *Documentation catholique*, Paris, 6 mars 1988, n° 1957, p. 238, § 14 et note 31.

152 Par sa résolution 47/197 du 22 décembre 1992, l'Assemblée générale des Nations Unies déclara le 17 octobre « Journée internationale pour l'élimination de la pauvreté ». Ainsi fut officialisée une journée célébrée depuis le 17 octobre 1987 à l'initiative du Père Joseph Wresinski et du Mouvement international ATD Quart Monde. À l'occasion du 10ᵉ anniversaire de l'adoption de cette résolution, la *Revue Quart Monde* a consacré son numéro 183 (août 2002) au « Le 17 octobre : un pacte pour l'avenir » (Éditions Quart Monde, Paris, 2002).

153 Séance du jeudi 4 octobre 2001. *J.O.C.E.* C 87 E, p. 253, du 11 avril 2002.
http://www.europateam.cc.cec/eur-lex/pri/fr/oj/dat/2002/ce087/ce08720020411fr02530255.pdf

154 La « Dalle en l'honneur des victimes de la misère » fut gravée le 17 octobre 1987 sur le marbre du « parvis des libertés et des droits de l'homme » (Trocadéro) à Paris. Depuis, 25 répliques furent inaugurées à travers le monde. On en trouve, entre autres, à Genève dans le Hall du Bureau international du Travail, au Conseil de l'Europe à Strasbourg, à New York au jardin des Nations Unies et à Rome au pied de la basilique Saint Jean de Latran (cathédrale de Rome). Le 29 mai 2002, une réplique de la dalle fut inaugurée au Parlement européen.

155 Parlement européen, « Nations unies : Journée mondiale du refus de la misère », Résolution commune B5-0616, 0619, 0635, 0644 et 0654/2001, considérant B, considérant C et point 11.

Père Joseph Wresinski, fondateur du Mouvement international ATD Quart Monde : « Là où les hommes sont condamnés à vivre dans la misère, les droits de l'homme sont violés. »

Nous envisageons d'étudier dans ce dernier parcours les notions de droits fondamentaux et de grande pauvreté dans les rapports annuels de l'Union européenne (UE) depuis 1993. L'intérêt porté à cette question se justifie notamment par le constat que le propos envisagé ici est récurrent depuis le premier rapport bien qu'au niveau communautaire son contexte juridique demeure imprécis. Cette ambiguïté rend nécessaire de différencier l'argumentation sur le plan du droit communautaire et l'appréciation de ce même problème en termes politiques (première partie).

L'accent sera placé sur la perception de la grande pauvreté comme violation des droits de l'homme, selon la philosophie du Père Joseph Wresinski. La raison de cette approche réside dans le fait que le Parlement européen lui-même s'est orienté de manière explicite vers l'expérience du fondateur du Mouvement international ATD Quart Monde. Or, il est exceptionnel qu'une institution européenne se réfère dans ses prises de position à l'expérience d'une personne, à sa philosophie ou à son action politique.

Trois remarques méritent d'être faites à ce stade. Premièrement, cette définition fait apparaître à la fois la similitude et l'écart entre les situations de pauvreté et celles d'extrême pauvreté. Elles semblent être dues aux mêmes causes, mais être différentes selon la répétition, l'intensité et la durée. Wresinski souligne l'enchaînement entre la pauvreté et l'extrême pauvreté, par la persistance de multiples formes d'insécurité sur de longues périodes, parfois plusieurs générations, susceptible de contribuer à l'amplification d'une situation de pauvreté. Deuxièmement, la définition de la grande pauvreté sous l'angle des droits de l'homme peut s'appliquer aujourd'hui aussi bien aux pays riches qu'aux pays en voie de développement. Troisièmement, la grande pauvreté apparaît comme le résultat des relations intersociétales (par rapport aux obligations et responsabilités professionnelles, familiales et sociales ainsi qu'à la jouissance des droits fondamentaux). Par conséquent, elle doit être considérée dans sa dimension politique. Les mécanismes qui régissent les rapports sociaux concernent cependant le droit dont la forme la plus achevée est celle de l'État de droit qui s'adapte, lui, à l'évolution dynamique anthropologique de la société.

Suivant cette logique, dans sa première résolution en 1993, le Parlement européen répondit au souci de ne pas protéger les droits de l'homme pour eux-mêmes mais estime, en revanche, « que la codification des droits économiques, sociaux et culturels n'est pas suffisante en elle-même et – le processus de paupérisation ayant des causes structurelles – qu'elle doit s'accompagner de la mise en place d'actions soutenues, qui soient aisément accessibles aux personnes les plus défavorisées et permettent d'agir à la racine du problème ».[156] La question se pose cependant de savoir comment la notion de droits fondamentaux ou de droits de l'homme est définie au niveau communautaire.

Dans un premier temps, ni le juge ni le législateur n'a défini de façon explicite la portée des droits fondamentaux ou des droits de l'homme. La politique active des droits de l'homme dans l'Union européenne, comme la lutte contre la pauvreté et l'exclusion sociale, furent tardivement déclarées objectifs communautaires. Ceci ne surprend pas, compte tenu des objectifs à l'origine de l'intégration européenne : unir les peuples européens en créant d'abord entre eux une solidarité de fait. Celle-ci s'est manifestée à travers l'inclusion des droits et devoirs économiques au droit communautaire naissant. Inscrits dans le Traité de Rome, les droits sociaux protégèrent les travailleurs transfrontaliers européens dans l'exercice de leurs activités économiques et sociales.

Le lien entre la grande pauvreté et les droits de l'homme apparaît clairement pour la première fois lorsque le Parlement européen publie, en janvier 1993, son premier rapport annuel sur le respect des droits de l'homme dans la Communauté européenne.

Il convient toutefois de signaler que le Parlement traita des droits économiques et sociaux quatre ans plus tôt, lorsqu'il élabora sa Déclaration des droits et libertés fondamentaux. Dans un document de travail, la députée espagnole Concépcio Ferrer i Casals évoqua

---

156 *Résolution sur le respect des droits de l'homme dans la Communauté européenne*, Rapport annuel du Parlement européen, Rés. A3-0025/93, Doc PE 170.288, 11 mars 1993, § 27.

alors la nécessité d'un droit commun à la sécurité sociale censé « protéger l'individu des conséquences de divers événements généralement qualifiés de risques sociaux ». Cette mesure, prévue pour garantir l'établissement et la libre circulation des travailleurs à l'intérieur du marché commun, devrait permettre de résorber la disparité entre les régimes de sécurité sociale des travailleurs salariés et de leur famille pour « arriver à une conception globale de la sécurité sociale, de l'assistance médicale et de la protection de la santé, que tous les régimes constitutionnels régissent encore de façon séparée. »[157]

La résolution de 1993 sur le respect des droits de l'homme dans la Communauté étudie de manière particulièrement approfondie le lien entre la grande pauvreté et les droits de l'homme, même si l'avis de la Commission des affaires sociales et de l'emploi sur ce rapport restreint son appréciation « pour les indigents, [au] droit à l'assistance publique ».[158] Le catalogue des droits retenus dans la résolution s'ouvre par une section intitulée « Pauvreté et droits économiques, sociaux et culturels » (§§ 23 à 31). Avec 8 pages, le mémorandum explicatif concernant cette section constitue de loin la partie la plus importante de l'ensemble du rapport. Elle constate d'abord que la pauvreté « limite, de fait, l'exercice de droits fondamentaux », et souligne l'indivisibilité des droits : « Les droits économiques, sociaux et culturels, qui sont reconnus au niveau international comme des droits fondamentaux, ce qui signifie que la jouissance effective de ces droits doit être reconnue et assurée à toute personne, devraient, nonobstant leur caractère souvent programmatoire, bénéficier d'un niveau de protection semblable à celui des droits civils et politiques, du fait de l'indivisibilité et de l'interdépendance de l'ensemble des droits de l'homme et des libertés fondamentales ».[159] Le rapport insiste ensuite sur les causes structurelles du processus de paupérisation auxquelles

---

157 PARLEMENT EUROPÉEN, *rapport De Gucht*, A2-3/89/B, Annexe : Document de travail sur les droits économiques et sociaux, 7 octobre 1988, pp. 53–55.

158 PARLEMENT EUROPÉEN, *Résolution sur le respect des droits de l'homme dans la Communauté européenne*, Rapport annuel du Parlement européen, Rés. A3-0025/93, Doc PE 170.288, 11 mars 1993.

159 Résolution A3-0025/93 et 0025/903/compl., point 24. Il y aura par la suite toujours une allusion à cette fonction : *rapport Pailler* (1996) point 3.

la codification des droits économiques, sociaux et culturels ne saurait apporter une réponse suffisante en elle-même (§ 27). Les élus européens estiment en outre « qu'une pleine participation des personnes défavorisées à l'élaboration, au suivi et à l'évaluation des actions qui leur sont destinées serait un gage supplémentaire d'efficacité et de pertinence » (§ 28). Le Parlement européen demande, en outre, « en s'associant aux efforts de tous ceux qui, dans la Communauté et dans le monde, refusent la violation des droits de l'homme que constitue la pauvreté, que l'Assemblée générale des Nations Unies proclame le 17 octobre « Journée mondiale du refus de la misère » » (§ 31).

Le deuxième rapport annuel sur le respect des droits de l'homme dans l'Union européenne (1993)[160] fonde le chapitre relatif à la pauvreté (§§ 59 à 68) sur le constat que « la pauvreté constitue le problème le plus important auquel l'UE est confrontée en matière de droits de l'homme ». La promotion de l'emploi devient l'instrument approprié de lutte contre la pauvreté et l'exclusion sociale : « l'obtention d'un emploi convenable assorti d'un salaire raisonnable et de conditions de travail décentes » constitue la condition sine qua non pour jouir des droits de l'homme et pour sortir de la pauvreté. En effet, « la lutte contre le chômage débouche automatiquement sur la lutte contre la pauvreté et l'exclusion sociale. Les personnes lourdement endettées, en butte à des conditions insalubres de logement ou même sans logis, vivant souvent dans un monde obscur de villes où les conditions de vie exercent un effet déshumanisant, constituent autant d'exemples de groupes qui ont été coupés et exclus du courant majoritaire de la société. »

On y retrouve alors les deux éléments de la définition de la précarité économique et sociale et de la grande pauvreté avancée par J. Wresinski. L'aspect de symbolique politique s'y retrouve également, car le Parlement européen « confirme à nouveau son appui à toutes les personnes qui, à l'intérieur de la Communauté et dans le monde, refusent en actes d'accepter cette violation des droits de la personne qu'est la pauvreté » (§ 61) et « réaffirme que des mesures concrètes

---

160 PARLEMENT EUROPÉEN (Commission des libertés publiques et des affaires intérieures), *Deuxième rapport annuel sur le respect des droits de l'homme dans l'Union européenne* (1993), A4-0076/95, PE 211.779/déf.

de lutte contre la pauvreté et l'exclusion sociale sont indispensables et qu'elles doivent être conçues, menées et évaluées en partenariat avec les personnes et familles les plus défavorisées » (§ 64).

Quant à la résolution de l'année 1994, on constatera brièvement qu'elle ne fut pas aussi explicite que les résolutions précédentes.[161] Soulignons toutefois que son § 99 mentionne que « l'éducation constitue un droit qui ne doit pas se laisser guider par des intérêts économiques, mais par la formation des personnes, d'où la nécessité d'une éducation qui soit libre, gratuite et universelle ». Ce droit s'appliquerait, selon le paragraphe en question, aux enfants des rues ainsi qu'aux enfants des demandeurs d'asile et des réfugiés.[162] On peut encore signaler le choix du terme de « plus pauvres », car le Parlement « rappelle que les femmes représentent 70 % des plus pauvres, au niveau mondial comme européen, et qu'un effort particulier doit être fait pour le respect et le développement de leurs droits sociaux et économiques. »[163]

La résolution sur l'année 1995 est la première à citer le nom du Père Joseph Wresinski. En effet, l'assemblée européenne, après avoir estimé que « la pauvreté et l'exclusion sont indignes de sociétés démocratiques et prospères » (§ 107), « fait sien l'appel du père J. Wresinski, fondateur d'ATD Quart Monde, selon lequel 'l'esclavage a été aboli, la misère peut l'être aussi' » (§108).[164] À notre connaissance, ce fut la première fois dans l'Histoire du Parlement européen que celui-ci se réfère à une seule personne. Cette remarque est d'autant plus pertinente compte tenu du fait que la résolution du Parlement européen ne mentionne pas Wresinski dans sa fonction antérieure qui fut celle de rapporteur au Conseil économique et social. Par convention, les résolutions se basent sur des instruments internationaux, des textes émanant d'autres institutions européennes et sur ses propres résolutions.

---

161 Parlement européen, *Résolution sur le respect des droits de l'homme dans l'Union européenne en 1993*, INI/1994/2138, Rés. A4-0223/96, Doc. PE 252.048, 17.09.1996.

162 Parlement européen, *Résolution sur le respect des droits de l'homme dans l'Union européenne (1994)*, Rés. A4-0223/96, Doc. PE 252.048, 17.09.1996, § 99.

163 *Ibid.*, § 108.

164 Parlement européen, *Résolution sur le respect des droits de l'homme dans l'Union européenne (1995)*, Rés. A4-0112/97, 08.04.1997, § 107.

Il convient toutefois de signaler que l'intitulé de la section était « Droits économiques et sociaux et droit à la sécurité sociale » et que, dès lors, l'appréhension du lien entre la pauvreté et les droits de l'homme n'allait pas de soi. Encore est-il que le Parlement européen « estime que la pauvreté et l'exclusion sont indignes de sociétés démocratiques et prospères » (§ 113).

Le rapport relatif à l'année 1996 est particulièrement intéressant. Premièrement, il encourage les institutions européennes à collaborer avec les ONG (Organisations non gouvernementales, note de la rédaction) engagées dans la lutte contre la grande pauvreté. Afin de promouvoir la collaboration entre les institutions européennes et les associations actives dans le domaine, le Parlement européen se déclare prêt à « faire de la lutte contre l'exclusion sociale et contre la pauvreté une priorité politique, et, avec la participation des ONG concernées, à développer des politiques holistiques cohérentes visant à combattre ces phénomènes » (§ 48). L'importance des associations sera encore soulignée lorsque le Parlement européen « invite les États membres à adopter et à mettre en œuvre, en étroite collaboration avec les associations humanitaires, des lois de prévention et de lutte contre l'exclusion qui concerneraient notamment l'accès au travail, à la santé, aux prestations sociales, au logement, à l'éducation, à la justice » (§ 54). Deuxièmement, il cite le Père Joseph Wresinski et la Présidente nationale du Mouvement ATD Quart Monde en France, Madame Geneviève de Gaulle-Anthonioz, dans le mémorandum explicatif. Le nom du Père Joseph apparaît dans l'introduction, à l'exposé des motifs : « Votre rapporteur rappelle également que le père Joseph Wresinski, le fondateur d'ATD Quart Monde, soulignait avec force que la pauvreté constituait une des principales atteintes aux droits de l'homme : « Là où les hommes sont condamnés à vivre dans la misère, les droits de l'homme sont violés. S'unir pour les faire respecter est un devoir sacré » ».[165] Le troisième chapitre consacré aux explications relatives aux « Droits économiques, sociaux et culturels » contient une section sur la pauvreté. Le paragraphe suivant s'y trouve : « Geneviève de Gaulle-

---

165 PARLEMENT EUROPÉEN, *Rapport annuel sur le respect des droits de l'homme dans l'Union européenne (1996)*, A4-0034/98, Doc. PE 224.436/déf. 28.01. 1998, p. 23.

Anthonioz, qui a succédé au père Wresinski à la présidence d'ATD Quart-Monde, a fait remarquer : L'écart est devenu encore plus grand entre ceux qui ont et ceux qui n'ont pas, entre les riches et les pauvres pour parler clair. Nous sommes là en face d'une évolution inquiétante des sociétés, de l'utilisation des progrès techniques, de la productivité dont beaucoup d'hommes et de femmes ne bénéficient pas. Avant, pour prendre une image, quelques wagons se faisaient toujours décrocher de la locomotive porteuse de progrès. Aujourd'hui, davantage de wagons se font décrocher depuis que la locomotive est devenue un TGV (train de grande vitesse, note de la rédaction). »[166]

Le rapport relatif aux années 1998–1999 concrétise non seulement les droits sociaux, énoncés dans un chapitre intitulé « Protection des droits économiques, sociaux et culturels » (§§ 61–65), mais il consacre aussi un chapitre aux seuls droits de l'enfant, dans la partie intitulée « Lutte contre la violence sociale. » Peu avant que la Charte des droits fondamentaux de l'Union européenne ne soit signée, le Parlement « insiste pour que les droits sociaux et économiques figurent explicitement parmi les droits fondamentaux reconnus par la future Charte des droits fondamentaux. » Son § 67 réitère le constat que « la pauvreté et l'exclusion qui en est le corollaire sont indignes d'une société démocratique et développée. » Pour permettre aux personnes les plus défavorisées leur participation effective à la vie en société, les députés européens demandent que le législateur national « reconnaisse aux plus pauvres le droit de s'entraider et de s'associer car les personnes qui participent à une activité bénévole, au sein d'une association, ne peuvent subir de sanction financière, comme cela se pratique dans certains pays de l'Union européenne, où le militantisme associatif se voit soumis à des autorisations ou pénalisé. »

Par conséquent, les députés demandent que « le droit à une vie décente, c'est-à-dire à une protection sociale adéquate (qui mette à l'abri d'une grande pauvreté (financière)), à un logement, à des soins de santé appropriés, à un enseignement correct ainsi qu'à la culture, figure explicitement dans la Charte des droits fondamentaux » (§ 68). Enfin, les États membres sont priés de mettre en œuvre « une straté-

---

166 *Ibid.*, p. 30.

gie volontariste de lutte contre l'extrême pauvreté qui frappe particulièrement les sans-emploi, les femmes, les sans-logis, les sans-papiers et qui discrédite nos sociétés. » Le Parlement « estime que cette stratégie doit être fondée sur l'accès effectif pour tous à l'ensemble des droits fondamentaux et doit être conçue, mise en œuvre et évaluée en commun avec les populations concernées » (§ 69).

Le rapport 2000, dans sa partie relative à la protection sociale, se consacre plus particulièrement aux soins de santé, et demande « la garantie d'accès de chacun, et en particulier des personnes disposant de faibles revenus, à des soins de santé de qualité à un prix abordable » (§ 108). Quant à la lutte contre l'exclusion, le rapporteur insiste notamment pour « garantir la satisfaction des besoins matériels élémentaires des personnes en situation d'extrême pauvreté ». Selon le rapporteur, l'absence de logement représente « l'un des facteurs majeurs d'exclusion. »

C'est pourquoi « des politiques nécessaires à l'offre de logements décents à ceux qui ne disposent pas de ressources suffisantes, ainsi que la réhabilitation des quartiers dégradés par la promotion d'une architecture de qualité » doivent être encouragées (§ 112). Le rapport se prononce enfin contre « la sanction des pratiques qui les marginalise et la poursuite déterminée de la stratégie de réduction de la grande pauvreté dans l'UE » (§ 111). Dans l'exposé des motifs du rapport se retrouve la contribution du Mouvement international ATD Quart Monde, qui s'appuie sur l'expérience quotidienne des plus pauvres : « Enfin il conviendrait d'être vigilant, comme le signale ATD Quart Monde, eu égard à certaines législations (B, NL) qui imposent aux chômeurs d'accepter quelque travail que ce soit sinon, les allocations sociales leur sont supprimées, ce qui est excessif dans le cas de familles monoparentales ou d'emplois proposés très éloignés du domicile. À l'inverse, toujours selon cette ONG, dans certains pays, le seul fait de travailler bénévolement au bénéfice d'une association fait courir le risque de perte des allocations. »

En effet, l'exposé des motifs se nourrit des expériences d'ATD Quart Monde : « Mais autant sinon plus que les données objectives, l'état psychologique où se trouvent les personnes souffrant de grande pauvreté est alarmant. Le minimum dont bénéficient ces personnes leur permet juste de survivre mais peu à peu les marginalise. De plus, l'octroi de ces subventions est souvent accompagné de tracasseries administratives, d'où un sentiment d'humiliation qu'alimente l'attitude généralement négative que la société européenne porte sur ses exclus. L'humiliation peut aller jusqu'à la privation du droit au respect de la vie privée (d'après ATD Quart Monde, une loi de 1998 aux Pays Bas relative à l'assainissement des dettes des personnes pauvres très endettées prévoit la désignation par le juge d'un tuteur qui dispose non seulement de tout pouvoir sur le revenu mais aussi du droit d'ouvrir la correspondance de l'intéressé). »

Quel est l'incidence de ces rapports et résolutions, compte tenu de la distinction faite entre l'approche juridique et l'approche politique ? Il s'agit de savoir dans quelle mesure le Parlement européen peut se constituer « veilleur de conscience » par rapport aux autres institutions européennes, par sa capacité à dissocier la problématique de la grande pauvreté en tant que violation des droits de l'homme du contexte de la politique sociale européenne, interdépendante de la logique du marché commun.

V. Perspectives

À cet égard, la résolution citée en introduction « Nations Unies : Journée mondiale du refus de la misère »[167] souligne que le « rôle messianique » attribué au Parlement européen en ce qui concerne la défense des droits de l'homme dans les pays tiers pourra s'étendre à la qualification de la grande pauvreté comme violation des droits fondamentaux dans l'Union. Deux aspects méritent d'être relevés à cet égard.

L'aspect symbolique, d'abord. Cette résolution est la première du Parlement européen consacrée au 17 octobre. Elle se réfère, dès l'introduction, sur le fond et sur la forme, à l'engagement d'un citoyen et à son action civique, en l'occurrence le Père Joseph Wresinski et le Mouvement international ATD Quart Monde qu'il a fondé. Deux demandes de l'assemblée européenne soulignent le caractère militant

---

167 Séance du jeudi 4 octobre 2001. *J.O.C.E.* C 87 E, p. 253, du 11 avril 2002.
http://www.europateam.cc.cec/eur-lex/pri/fr/oj/dat/2002/ce087/ce08720020411fr02530255.pdf

de ce texte : d'une part, instaurer le 17 octobre comme « Journée européenne du refus de la misère » et, d'autre part, poser « sur le parvis du Parlement européen à Bruxelles, une dalle en l'honneur des victimes de la misère, à l'instar de celle posée sur le parvis du Trocadéro à Paris, du Conseil de l'Europe à Strasbourg, du Reichstag à Berlin, de la Basilique Saint-Jean du Latran à Rome et de l'ONU à New York. »

Le deuxième aspect se situe sur le plan politique. Le titre de la résolution européenne se distingue de la résolution initiale de l'ONU par un changement de vocabulaire. Rappelons que la formule de l'ONU fait allusion à l'éradication de la pauvreté alors que le Parlement européen a choisi de parler du refus de la misère. Il semble évident que la première résolution accorde une prédominance aux aspects plutôt techniques de l'éradication de la pauvreté, ce qui convient certainement plus au caractère mondial de l'assemblée générale de l'ONU.

La résolution européenne fait, quant à elle, appel à l'engagement citoyen pour refuser la misère et souligne « qu'il est nécessaire de mieux connaître les interdépendances entre les politiques économiques, sociales, environnementales, culturelles et éducatives. » Le Parlement européen réclame en outre le renforcement de la coopération avec les organisations non gouvernementales et du dialogue nord-sud. Les élus demandent non seulement « aux institutions européennes de se prononcer clairement en faveur d'un partenariat avec les associations de lutte contre la misère, et de donner aux politiques sociales une priorité égale à celle donnée aux politiques économiques. » Ils demandent également « à la Commission, au Conseil, au Comité économique et social européen et à sa commission de l'emploi et des affaires sociales d'effectuer chaque 17 octobre une évaluation publique des politiques communautaires en matière de lutte contre la pauvreté et l'exclusion sociale, conduite en collaboration avec des acteurs sociaux, en particulier ceux qui donnent la parole aux plus pauvres. »

Dès lors, refuser la misère passe par le développement de véritables stratégies qui permettent d'assurer le recours aux meilleures pratiques afin que tous aient un accès égal aux droits fondamentaux comme l'éducation, le logement, les soins de santé, ainsi qu'à la culture et à un emploi durable. Ces politiques devront être mises en œuvre dans le cadre de plans nationaux pour l'inclusion/insertion sociale et donner la priorité aux personnes les plus vulnérables. En corollaire, la demande d'améliorer le suivi des actions entreprises dans ces domaines. Pour ce faire, le Parlement européen demande d'arrêter d'un commun accord des indicateurs qualitatifs en matière de la lutte contre l'exclusion sociale.

Enfin, on constate que « la notion selon laquelle les droits de l'homme, et en fait l'état de droit, ont pour fonction principale de protéger le faible contre le fort ne relève pas d'une quelconque sentimentalité. Elle est le produit d'une époque historique au cours de laquelle l'égalité de traitement et l'égalité des chances sont désormais perçues... comme un bien inconditionnel, et de la reconnaissance généralisée qu'il n'est pas possible de réaliser l'égalité simplement en la proclamant mais seulement par le nivellement vers le haut des inégalités héritées et systémiques qui font que certains acteurs de la société sont trop faibles pour faire usage de leurs droits et que d'autres sont suffisamment forts pour étouffer leurs aspirations ».[168] On constate aisément que le Parlement européen, sur le plan politique, prend une position importante en la matière vis-à-vis des autres institutions de l'Union.

VI. Conclusion

Karl Marx ne pouvait être sensible à la dimension de l'action telle que la conçut Joseph Wresinski à travers le volontariat Quart Monde. Marx se situait lui-même trop près de cette conception qui fait du travail l'essence de l'homme alors qu'il n'était pas insensible à la réalité impitoyable de la vie ouvrière à Manchester. Le travail représente cet espace de sociabilité où l'*Homo faber* se découvre et se réalise lui-même. Or, le Lumpenprolétariat, aussi bien que le Quart Monde, sont exclus du monde du travail. Pour Bataille, le « Lumpen », qui, à la différence d'un prolétariat organisé, ne représente rien, serait un hétérogène dont la libération entraînerait la désintégration de toutes les structures assurant l'homogénéité de l'édifice social.

---

168 SEDLEY, S., « Human Rights : a Twenty-First Century Agenda », *Public Law*, 1995, p. 399.

Il semblerait que la thèse de la réhabilitation du Lumpenprolétariat par le Quart Monde se trouve confirmée, en raison de la perception du Quart Monde comme classe sociale avec un pouvoir revendicatif qui fait de lui un véritable partenaire politique : « Le terme « Quart Monde » (…) désigne de moins en moins un milieu, en ce qu'il est passif et exclu. Il désigne au contraire ce que ce milieu recèle d'expérience d'injustice et d'espoir de justice, d'expérience du besoin et de compréhension des besoins, d'expérience d'exclusion et de capacité de participer comme partenaire social à l'élaboration d'une société démocratique. (…) Le terme « Quart Monde » s'adresse aujourd'hui au Quart Monde lui-même. Et lorsque les sous-prolétaires disent « nous du Quart Monde », il ne s'agit pas d'une population cible de la gestion administrative, mais plutôt d'un peuple qui a une cause, celle qu'il partage avec tous les exclus et tous les humiliés du monde ».

Soulignons, pour conclure, le rôle des plus pauvres comme partenaire actif à l'élaboration d'une société démocratique. La pensée politique de Joseph Wresinski propose, en effet, un renforcement de la démocratie à travers la réorientation de l'activité humaine : « L'important est l'homme. Plus l'homme est abandonné, méprisé, écrasé, plus il est précieux ». Par conséquent, plus l'homme est précieux, plus il doit contribuer au bien-être de sa famille et de l'humanité toute entière. Or, l'absence de toutes les sécurités de base, comme le travail, le logement, la santé, les ressources ou l'éducation, met en effet en cause la participation du Quart Monde à la démocratie. Dans la pensée de Wresinski, le travail est un facteur essentiel d'égalité entre les citoyens : « Ce qui rend libre, ce n'est pas le travail mais c'est la dignité qu'il confère. »[169] Or la réalité au plus bas de l'échelle sociale est caractérisée par la modestie de l'emploi, appelée *condition sous-prolétarienne*. Celle-ci devint le lien unificateur du Quart Monde, à l'instar du Lumpenprolétariat de la révolution industrielle en Angleterre. Avec les hommes et femmes concernés, Wresinski affirme qu'ils étaient des travailleurs et voulaient être reconnus comme tels. Ils attirèrent l'attention publique sur l'existence d'une couche de population qui n'avait jamais pu entrer dans la société industrielle. Par cette démonstration, il rap-

---

169 « Editorial », *Igloos*, 93–94, 1978.

pela à la société que la porte à l'exclusion sociale était restée ouverte. Dès lors, il convient de concevoir la vie active de tous dans le sens d'un partage égalitaire, aussi bien de l'activité culturelle et sociale que l'activité proprement économique. Ce projet pourrait aider à mettre en œuvre aujourd'hui le principe hétérologique de Georges Bataille. Cette action, où se rejoignent l'apprentissage civique et la vie de travail, la découverte de la culture et de nouveaux engagements sociaux, mène, selon nous, à une réorientation de l'activité humaine. Au centre de cette notion se trouve l'idée d'offrir à tout citoyen toujours plus de chances égales d'être créatif et utile au profit de la société toute entière. Ce que je propose de retenir de Wresinski, c'est qu'il a davantage insisté que Marx sur le fait que tous les groupes et toutes les personnes, y comprises celles du sous-prolétariat, avaient des talents et des capacités, aussi pour leur propre émancipation, mais que pour cela il fallait les accompagner avec des autorisations sociales qui pouvaient les représenter et les aider à se mettre en action, en route ; le rôle des organisations étaient là un peu comme celui des pédagogues.

Le Quatrième Ordre, le Lumpenprolétariat, le Quart Monde : ces trois notions évoquent le destin de la contrebasse selon Patrick Süskind.[170] Dans cette pièce, l'orchestre symbolise par sa stricte hiérarchie la société humaine elle-même hiérarchisée. Georges Bataille en trouvera le signe de l'homogénéité sociétale. La contrebasse, le Quasimodo de l'orchestre, plus embarrassante qu'instrument véritable, trouve sa place tout au fond de l'orchestre. Mais elle possède une puissance dont aucun compositeur ne peut se passer et sans laquelle aucun auditeur ne peut apprécier la musique. Cela nous conduit enfin au théorème de la « misère de position » dont parle Pierre Bourdieu dans *La misère du monde*. La mission historique du Quart Monde est désormais de donner une représentation juste du cosmos social et de rappeler que tout au bas de l'échelle sociale perdure une classe méconnue pour sa puissance de choc capable d'humaniser l'humanité.

---

170 SÜSKIND, PATRICK, *La contrebasse*, trad. BERNARD LORTHOLARY, Paris 1992.

Pauvreté et droits de l'homme
Mascha L. Join-Lambert

Contrairement à ce que l'on pourrait d'abord penser, la pauvreté affecte bel et bien les droits fondamentaux. En effet, le recours aux droits fondamentaux dans la lutte contre la pauvreté pourrait se compliquer à l'avenir.

Allant à l'encontre d'une étude superficielle du problème, un état de pauvreté prolongé constitue indubitablement une atteinte non seulement à l'exercice des libertés et droits fondamentaux civils et politiques d'une personne, mais aussi à leur simple reconnaissance.

Prendre conscience de cela rapproche aussi en Europe le débat sur la pauvreté de celui sur les droits de l'homme. Cela engage également à aborder les préoccupations de la lutte contre la pauvreté ainsi que de la protection des droits de l'homme, non pas comme des questions universitaires ou législatives, mais plutôt à les rendre accessibles à des groupes de personnes et de population, dont les chances d'épanouissement s'en trouvent affectées.

Parallèlement, l'observation des évolutions politiques et scientifiques soulève des questions quant à l'avenir de l'idée des droits de l'homme telle qu'elle prévaut depuis 1948. La multiplication des responsables entre société civile et nationale implique des chances mais aussi des dangers pour la protection des droits fondamentaux, car l'opposabilité des droits de l'homme d'un point de vue social, économique et culturel ne constitue pas un acquis. La reconnaissance universelle du concept ainsi que le rôle dévolu traditionnellement aux droits de l'homme, ne s'appuient que sur une base chancelante.

I.   La pauvreté affecte les droits fondamentaux d'une personne

I.I.   Une pauvreté prolongée altère l'exercice des libertés, des droits et devoirs fondamentaux

I.I.I. Au premier abord la situation matérielle d'une personnen'affecte en aucun point ni la reconnaissance ni l'exercice des ses droits politiques et civils

L'estimation selon laquelle « la démocratie et les droits de l'homme ne coûtent rien », c'est-à-dire qu'ils sont en vigueur indépendamment de la situation économique d'une population, prévalut jusqu'à l'élaboration des textes internationaux assurant la protection des droits économiques et sociaux[1] dans le respect effectif des droits de l'homme, et s'impose encore aujourd'hui, malgré le préambule de la Déclaration de 1948, qui confère aux droits fondamentaux le rôle de rempart contre « la terreur et la misère ».

Cette estimation idéaliste mérite notre attention du fait qu'elle se réfère à la dignité inaliénable de l'homme, qui puiserait suffisamment d'énergie dans cette prise de conscience pour pouvoir affirmer sa personnalité, même dans des situations défavorables.

Les droits et libertés civils acquièrent et préservèrent une prépondérance par rapport aux droits économiques, sociaux et culturels, s'expliquant par la difficulté de fournir une définition adéquate, permettant de rendre opposables ces derniers. Par quels moyens déterminer l'engagement culturel par exemple ? Il en résulterait des catégories dont les limites confondues ne serviraient à personne. De même le débat en Europe sur le rapport entre le principe de la liberté de contrat et le droit à un emploi n'est toujours pas clos.

I.I.II. En y regardant de plus près, il apparaît qu'un appauvrissement persistant, et portant atteinte aux besoins élémentaires des citoyens, entrave l'exercice de leurs libertés et droits fondamentaux

La recherche sur la pauvreté dans plusieurs disciplines répond à une ancienne[2] revendication de droits fondamentaux économiques et sociaux : sans condition de vie sûre et reconnue, l'exercice de droits, de libertés (et de devoirs) civils est compromis, par exemple, il ne peut y avoir de formation scolaire réussie sans logement salubre, pas de droit de vote sans adresse, et sans habits présentables pas d'exercice

---

1 Pacte social européen 1961 ; convention ONU sur les droits économiques et sociaux1966 (ECOSOC).
2 Des exemples : Comité de Salut Public, Paris 1793 ; Discussion sur la juridiction fédérale, Suisse, 1848 ; BETTINA VON ARNIM, *Armenbuch*, Frankfurt am Main 1969.

de ses droits à la liberté de pensée et de religion, ce qui présuppose d'ailleurs l'appartenance aux groupes sociaux en question, etc.

I.II. Un état de pauvreté prolongé constitue une violation des droits de l'homme

I.II.I. La mise en pratique des droits fondamentaux pour les citoyens en grande difficulté sociale est confrontée à plusieurs problèmes :

- méconnaissance de la haute importance des intérêts et des droits fondamentaux de ces derniers,
- la mise en œuvre de contrôle de la pauvreté,
- la privation concrète du droit à la protection et aux droits fondamentaux.

Plus la régression ou la descente sociale durera et moins une jeune personne participera activement à la société, plus le mépris de soi-même ainsi que de son entourage croîtront. La conscience de la « dignité » devient d'avantage un stigmate de l'échec qu'une source de motivation. Leur environnement rabaisse les « ratés », de telle façon que ces derniers poursuivent sur la même voie. La pauvreté durable et la marginalisation sociale de groupes et de personnes entraînent finalement des violations, des atteintes aux droits de l'homme.

Des exemples emplissent les médias, mais ne sont guère interprétés comme des atteintes aux droits de l'homme.

I.II.II. La lutte contre la pauvreté fait partie de la protection et du soutien des droits de l'homme

Notamment grâce aux efforts de l'ATD Quart Monde International[3] la pauvreté, réapparue en Europe de l'Ouest dans les an-

---

3 Père JOSEPH WRESINSKI, *Les plus pauvres, révélateurs de l'indivisibilité des droits de l'homme*, Paris 1998 ; colloque « Familles du Quart Monde et Droits de l'Homme » organisé par le Mouvement A.T.D. Quart Monde, en collaboration avec la direction des Droits de l'Homme au Conseil de l'Europe, Strasbourg 1981.

3a A. DESPOUY, *Extreme Armut und Menschenrechte*, UNO-Menschenrechtskommission, Genf 1995 ; *Arbeiten zur revidierten Sozialcharta des Europarates, zur Charta der Grundrechte für die Verfassung der EU* ; Straßburg/Brüssel 1998–2002.

nées 80, était accompagnée de la question du respect des droits de l'homme. De vastes monographies et des statistiques alimentèrent le concept « d'interdépendance » de l'exercice des droits et libertés civi-lo-politiques d'une part et des droits économiques, sociaux et culturels d'autre part.

Il se transforma en un concept « d'indivisibilité » de tous les droits de l'homme et se répercuta tant dans les travaux de la charte sociale du Conseil de l'Europe qu'au sein de la Commission des droits de l'homme de l'ONU et des travaux préliminaires d'une constitution pour l'Union Européenne.[3a]

Dans le but de mettre en pratique les possibilités d'interprétation ainsi acquises, en France par exemple, des ONG comme ATD Quart Monde et Amnesty International travaillent ensemble. Il s'agit, en plus d'efforts pour disposer de cas types à soumettre à la commission des droits de l'homme à Strasbourg, de la formation de l'opinion pu-blique, de la formation complémentaire ainsi que de l'interconnexion de militants et de personnes concernées.[4]

Des observations montrent que justement dans des situations extrêmes les gens sont dépendants et n'acceptent d'aide et de recon-naissance que de leur propre entourage.

L'objectif de ces dites institutions éducatives populaires (Uni-versités Populaires du Quart Monde) consiste à faire prendre con-science de cette réciprocité et à soutenir leur prestation éthique. Ce programme de perfectionnement repose sur l'expérience des « plus pauvres en tant que pionniers des droits de l'homme ». Leur action sur le terrain est interprétée avec l'aide du concept des droits de l'homme ; dans un même temps cela renforce une conscience des droits de l'homme, ce qui favorise la capacité des citoyens à dialoguer et à con-tester la façon dont le problème de la pauvreté est abordé.

Les efforts dans la lutte contre la pauvreté, durables en Europe, confirment[5] le fait que, c'est dans des situations extrêmes que cette capacité éthique de reconnaissance mutuelle de leur dignité égale doit

---

4 Journal « Résistances », depuis 2004, ATD Quart-Monde/Amnesty International, Paris; « Universités Populaires du Quart-Monde », ATD-Quart-Monde International.
5 Des expériences dans les camps de concentration européens sous la dictature nazie, voir par exemple G. DE GAULLE-ANTHONIOZ, *Le secret de l'espérance*, Paris 2001.

être mise à l'épreuve. Il est du devoir de la société des pays membres du Conseil Européen, à fortiori de l'Union Européenne, d'entretenir cette capacité du mieux qu'ils le peuvent.

II. Le concept des droits de l'homme pourrait à l'avenir dévier de la référence universelle en vigueur

Entretenir la capacité de reconnaissance mutuelle d'une dignité égale apparaît d'autant plus justifiée que la conception traditionnelle des droits de l'homme pourrait à l'avenir être considérablement remise en question.[6]

II.I. La multiplication des responsables constitue une chance, mais elle présente également des dangers

II.I.I. La perception croissante de l'indivisibilité des droits de l'homme va de pair avec la volonté de mettre au point de nouvelles formes de leur opposabilité contre toute forme d'abus de pouvoir

À travers la reconnaissance d'une responsabilité personnelle de chacun, concrétisée par la mise en place d'un tribunal international (en 1998), face aux atteintes aux droits de l'homme endurées par d'autres, que ce soit en temps de paix ou même en période de guerre civile, une porte s'ouvre, offrant une perspective possible de respect des droits de l'homme dans tous les secteurs de la société.

La responsabilité dans la vie économique est particulièrement variable. Les nouvelles formes d'opposabilité des droits sociaux dans le cadre de la charte sociale du Conseil Européen et l'institution d'un code antidiscriminatoire de l'Union Européenne illustrent la volonté de s'assurer, dans l'action de chaque citoyen, du respect des droits de son partenaire.

---

6 M. BORGHI, P. MEYER-BISCH (éd.), *Société civile et indivisibilité des droits de l'homme*, Editions Universitaires, Fribourg (CH), 2000 ; H. P. SCHNEIDER, « Vom Recht, das mit uns geboren ist », *Frankfurter Allgemeine Zeitung*, 19. Mai 2005.

II.I.II. La condamnation des violations horizontales des droits de l'homme peut également mettre un individu dans l'incapacité d'agir

Le combat contre l'arbitraire, les exactions entre citoyens, particulièrement dans l'exercice de leur responsabilité militaire, politique ou économique, aussi louable soit-il, il faut malgré tout reconnaître qu'une condamnation conséquente empiétant sur la liberté de contrat des acteurs, ne sert l'esprit des droits de l'homme que sous certaines conditions.

L'histoire des efforts entrepris contre la discrimination de minorités sociales montre qu'une protection juridique améliorée ne remédie que très lentement à des préjugés et types de comportement profondément ancrés, et qu'au contraire elle peut même engendrer leur durcissement. Des personnes et des familles dans la pauvreté renonce précisément pour ces raisons à faire valoir leurs droits.

La condamnation se doit d'aller de pair avec une rencontre vécue et une « éducation aux droits de l'homme » de tous les acteurs, sinon elle sera contre-productive, banalisera les droits de l'homme et fera des sociétés des zones de combat au lieu d'endroits de tolérance et de conciliation. Le danger d'une formalisation de la notion des droits de l'homme se dessine.

Ainsi apparaît la condamnation des violations horizontales des droits de l'homme comme une condition nécessaire mais pas suffisante à la lutte contre la marginalisation de personnes ou de groupes menacés par la pauvreté.

II.II. L'acceptation universelle du concept apparaît encore plus incertaine que l'avenir de l'opposabilité des droits de l'homme [7]

Outre les progrès importants faits dans la protection améliorée des personnes, des familles et des groupes en proie à l'arbitraire militaire, économique, politique et administrative, il faut considérer les transformations éventuellement susceptibles d'effriter le consensus en vigueur sur la place des droits de l'homme.

---

7 Voir à ce propos FRANÇOIS JULLIEN, « Universels, les droits de l'homme ? » *Le Monde diplomatique* février 2008, pp. 24–25.

II.II.I. « L'individu » perd de ses contours

Le concept de l'individu doué de raison et de conscience, auquel (l'unicité en tant que créature de Dieu et) une volonté libre confère une dignité inaliénable, s'abrite derrière les textes internationaux. Ce concept est cependant contesté :

Le concept non seulement des droits de l'individu mais aussi du groupe ayant la primauté sur l'individu progresse depuis longtemps. Issu des cultures du Moyen- et Extrême-Orient, il progresse d'autant plus que les pays les représentant à l'ONU gagnent en influence. Le concept « imposé par l'Occident », toujours à la base de la Déclaration générale des droits de l'homme de 1948 ainsi que de tous les textes consécutifs, se penchera plus clairement sur d'autres pensées et devra s'imposer dans de nouveaux contextes. Une méditation sur le concept de la dignité inaliénable et égale pour tous, s'inscrit dans une défense aussi claire.

Les enseignements du caractère conditionnel psychosocial de la « libre volonté », l'exploration des fonctions du corps et de l'esprit humains dans son maintien artificiel et sa programmabilité, la découverte des activités biologico-chimiques du cerveau, tout cela rend aujourd'hui la dignité de l'individu, au « début » et à la « fin » de sa vie, difficilement concevable. Dans une large mesure, allant avec une raréfaction des ressources vitales, on recourra à la possibilité technique croissante de disposer de l'homme.

De même, nouvellement sous couvert de nécessité, l'individu pourra être instrumentalisé dans toutes les phases de sa vie. Cela sera justifié comme le fut l'Eugénisme dans le passé, du moins l'aide ou respectivement la négligence consciente de certains groupes de la population sera tolérée.

II.II.II. La notion de « dignité égale de tous les hommes » pourrait perdre de sa valeur universelle

Pour cette raison il est concevable que le consensus sur la mise en pratique et l'opposabilité des droits de l'homme faiblisse même en Occident. Ainsi, de même que des expériences historiques se reproduiront, cela s'opérera aux dépens des personnes, des familles et des groupes les plus défavorisés socialement, même si parallèlement on maintient le débat sur les droits de l'homme.

Car le dénominateur commun le plus infime soit-il au sein de l'ONU et de l'opinion publique mondiale pourrait être une éthique, qui s'appuie sur la protection des droits de l'homme « plus faible » et s'applique à la légitimation du pouvoir sous toutes ses formes.

L'abandon de la notion de « dignité égale des hommes » et son opposabilité à l'avenir en revanche d'un accord universel minimum sur les droits de l'homme n'est pas sans risques. De même, des dangers résident dans l'évolution vers une démocratie médiatisée et simplificatrice ainsi que dans la transformation de valeurs sociales de la solidarité vers l'individualisme égoïste.

Par contre, se développe une conscience plus forte tant des facteurs de pauvreté et de la nécessité de la lutte contre elle au service des droits de l'homme, que des tendances de répression des violations horizontales des droits de l'homme.

Conclusion

Pour que les droits de l'homme soient durables, non seulement en tant que discours, mais aussi en tant que mise en pratique d'une référence éthique valable pour tous, leur conception doit satisfaire tant à l'accent mis sur l'individu qu'à la connaissance de ses limites. Mais il ne s'agit pas là de compromis dans la confrontation « droits de l'individu contre droits de la collectivité ». Il est plutôt question d'éviter l'erreur de considérer l'un ou l'autre comme les valeurs absolues des droits de l'homme.

La reconnaissance de la « dignité égale » de tous les hommes ne saura être préservée que si les droits de l'homme n'apparaissent pas comme une fin en soi, mais comme l'expression de l'aspiration des hommes vers des forces intellectuelles et religieuses qui leur confèrent leur dignité. C'est alors que les droits de l'homme deviennent « les droits des autres », et c'est uniquement de cette manière qu'un rassemblement face au malheur et à la misère des hommes, dans l'intention justement de faire respecter les droits de l'homme, devient un « devoir sacré ».[8]

En d'autres termes, la reconnaissance des droits de l'individu ne pourra être garantie que par la reconnaissance de la réciprocité de ces droits : libre à moi d'exercer la « dignité égale » de l'autre de façon créative, et inversement. Dans son interprétation actuelle la référence aux droits de l'homme cessera probablement d'être la source d'un consensus éthique mondial. Mais elle survivra sous une forme qu'il nous incombe d'inventer, laquelle impliquera les citoyens de façon plus active que jusqu'à présent. Car les personnes vivant dans le malheur et le mépris ont besoin d'une instance rendant publique leur humanité, de même que les sociétés recherchent des instances afin de satisfaire à leurs besoins de charité et de solidarité.

---

8 Sur l'initiative du Père Joseph Wresinski et du Parlement Européen, une « dalle en l'honneur des victimes de la misère » fut posée sur le parvis du Trocadéro à Paris le 17 octobre 1987.

Conclusions and Perspectives
Thomas Riis

For several reasons, scholars have not only neglected the historical dimension in their efforts to find remedies against poverty, but they have also denied the usefulness of diachronic statistical research into the economic and social situation of lower social categories. Consequently, only the short term causes of poverty were taken into account. Thus, there is a considerable risk that the measures of poor relief treat only the symptoms of poverty and not its causes.

The scope of the Exploratory Workshop was to bring together leading scholars in poverty research and to invite them to discuss the possibilities of an interdisciplinary approach to poverty and its relief, taking in account both the hereditary nature of poverty and the definition of famine as the last stage of malnutrition. Unfortunately, it proved extremely difficult to find speakers on every planned subject; in these cases, short communications were presented, summing up the state of research in the field.

The definition of poverty constituted a major concern of the workshop; many scholars argue that it is methodologically impossible to compare facts given in different countries or societies. Nevertheless, comparative approaches to other historical topics have been extremely productive for many years. On the other hand, as already mentioned in the Preface, contemporary definitions of poverty are insufficient from a methodological point of view.

In his study of the building accounts of the bridge over the Rhône at Lyons 1501–1502, Richard Gascon defined the poverty line as the necessity of a family to spend at least half the available income on bread. Studies of poor households in England and Germany in the eighteenth and nineteenth centuries appear to confirm Gascon's definition, but with a slight modification. Thus the poverty line can be defined as the necessity of a family to spend at least half the available income on bread and its substitutes (potatoes, beans, noodles, rice).

Also as far as housing is concerned a poverty line can be established. As an adult lying on the ground covers about two metres, four square metres can be considered the minimal surface available for an adult. Actually, this was the measure adopted by the British administration in Northern Germany and by the municipal government of Kiel immediately after 1945.

Thus the workshop succeeded in discovering two definitions of the poverty line which can be used in the study of poverty, today as well as in the past.[1]

From different angles the degrees of poverty were studied in four papers. On the basis of a documentation from eighteenth-early nineteenth century rural Norway Sølvi Sogner could show that the widely spread mental image of the poor and numerous family must be corrected. On the contrary, she discovered a tendency of later marriages and consequently smaller households where conditions were modest; samples from parishes in Sweden, Denmark and Germany show the same trend.[2] Moreover, her results are confirmed by my own study of the population of Copenhagen about the middle of the seventeenth century.[3]

In her paper, Marion Kobelt-Groch asks the question whether or not women were touched by poverty to a higher degree than men. In several towns of fifteenth-sixteenth century Europe (Basel, Strasbourg, Toledo, Luzern) women constituted more than two thirds of the poor, and at Schaffhausen they formed three fourths in the first half of the nineteenth century. When we realize that even today unemployment is more widely spread among women than among men (see table), we must recognize gender as a cause of poverty or at least as an aggravating factor. Why it was so, must be left to future research.

---

1 THOMAS RIIS: "Communication: la définition de la pauvreté"
2 SØLVI SOGNER: "Size of Families. Are Children Poor People's Riches?"
3 THOMAS RIIS: *Should Auld Acquaintance Be Forgot... Scottish-Danish Relations c. 1450–1707*, II, Odense 1988, pp. 21–28.

Gender Ratios of Unemployment 1994

	Women		Men	
Greece	13	72.2 %	5	27.8 %
Italy	17	68.0 %	8	32.0 %
Spain	30	61.2 %	19	38.8 %
European Community	13	59.1 %	9	40.9 %

Source: KOBELT-GROCH, Des hommes pauvres, p. 26.

In his paper, Giovanni Ricci investigates the most elusive group of poor people, namely the so-called shamefaced poor (*pauvres honteux, poveri vergognosi*).[4] Generally, they had known "better days", but only for craftsmen or other persons accustomed to manual work, this could remedy their situation. For the destitute aristocrat, manual labour would be degrading; discreet aid, an occasional theft or prostitution were to the aristocrat more acceptable than manual work. In the discussion it was stressed that the status of shamefaced poor would be a transitory phase, which would hardly last for more than two generations. Either you would succeed in regaining your social status or you would lose it for good. This conclusion appears to be valid for the Middle Ages, the Modern Period and for contemporary society alike.

Already in the 1970s, the hypothesis of hereditary poverty was formulated, but the study in question was hardly considered by scholars. Basing himself on the rich archives of Early Modern Aberdeen and Lyons Torsten Fischer investigated over 15,000 poor persons.[5] The hypothesis of hereditary poverty can be confirmed, but in spite of assistance from the public relief system, this did not allow families to break the vicious circle of poverty. Only when the individual had efficient and solid networks at his or her disposal, it would be possible to break the circle. Again the importance of the network is underlined; also the shamefaced poor depended upon good networks in order to regain the lost social status.

---

4 GIOVANNI RICCI: "Les pauvres honteux, ou l'anomalie légalisée."
5 TORSTEN FISCHER: "Crossing the Poverty Line or Can Poverty Be Considered Hereditary?". The paper forms a summary of Dr Fischer's thesis *Y-a-t-il une fatalité d'hérédité dans la pauvreté? Dans l'Europe moderne: les cas d'Aberdeen et de Lyon*, Stuttgart 2006 (Beihefte Vierteljahrschrift für Sozial- und Wirtschaftsgeschichte 187).

The second section of the workshop discussed the causes of poverty. In her comparative paper on unemployment in Britain and France Noel Whiteside[6] underlines that our current notion of unemployment reflects a special type of work: life-long employment in the same enterprise or authority. However, this system is breaking up: where half a century ago married wives were expected to take care of household and children as unwaged domestic workers, rising divorce rates have forced married women into the labour market. On the other hand, numbers of older workers (adult males between 55 and 65 years of age) have been discharged in the late twentieth century, but they were seldom classified as unemployed but as sick or in early retirement. Thus, unemployment is a relative concept. However, Professor Whiteside discovers that contemporary employment patterns are reminiscent of those of earlier centuries. Moreover, since the end of World War II the cost of the labour market risk has been transferred from the employers to the state and from there to the employees themselves, with an increased risk of poverty as a result.

That excessive taxation coupled with dishonest financial administration could increase poverty to an intolerable degree is demonstrated by Matteo Provasi in his case study of the fiscal administration of Ferrara 1565–1575.[7] Also economic fluctuations can ruin people; Germany immediately after World War I is a classic example, the monetary troubles of the Reich prior to 1622 (with its repercussions on the Danish and Milanese economies) are another. Illness must also be considered a cause of poverty and both in fifteenth century Florence and Kiel at the end of the twentieth century the break-up of families is equally important as a cause of poverty.[8]

Earthquakes, tsunamis and their effects are studied by Emanuela Guidoboni and James Jackson in Iran since the 1960s and

6 NOEL WHITESIDE: "Constructing Unemployment: Britain and France in Historical Perspective."
7 MATTEO PROVASI: "Popular Unrest, Bread Riot, Legitimism. Power and Poverty in Ferrara under Este Rule."
8 THOMAS RIIS: "Communication II: Les causes de la pauvreté : maladies et conjonctures."

in Southern Italy for the last two centuries.[9] Subventions by the state to the reconstruction of damaged settlements could give a stagnating regional economy a needed impetus;[10] otherwise, if reconstruction lasted for a longer period, the disaster could have unfortunate long-term effects like loss of know-how and economic relations with the outer world.

For the younger sons of poor peasants in countries like Switzerland or Scotland, war could give them their daily bread, if they enrolled as mercenaries. Further, producers of arms were able to make considerable fortunes. For the civilian population, however, the presence of undisciplined soldiers with their acts of plunder, destruction, and rape was dreaded and often meant the ruin of individuals and the community. Sometimes, the effects of war initiated a chain reaction: if the horses were requisitioned in the region of Liège, the coal mines could not work with unemployment and poverty as a result. With many examples from the region corresponding to present-day Belgium, René Leboutte demonstrates the double face of war.[11]

That technical innovations were met with protest, is a commonplace of the industrial revolution; especially the textile industry was early mechanized, thus making great numbers of workmen redundant. Also in contemporary society the increasing use of machines and the spread of information technology reduce the number of jobs available. As these are mostly those where less qualifications are required, the new technologies generate poverty, as the persons formerly employed will mainly be unable to find a new employment corresponding to their skills. Finally, huge numbers of the population have not got the qualifications necessary to use the information technology.[12] Also today, the invention of new technologies must be considered a cause of poverty.

---

9 EMANUELA GUIDOBONI & JAMES JACKSON: "Seismic Disasters and Poverty: Some Data and Reflections on Past and Current Trends."

10 This was the case of the reconstruction after the Sicilian earthquake of 1693, see F. BOSCHI et alii: *Catalogo dei forti terremoti in Italia 461 a.C.–1980*, Bologna (CD-Rom) 1994.

11 RENÉ LEBOUTTE: "Guerre et pauvreté."

12 THOMAS RIIS: "New Technologies as a Cause of Poverty."

If the information technology risks to polarize contemporary society, we find the same tendency in the lifestyle industry. To a decent life belong holidays in the right place, convenient hobbies and signed clothes. As in certain branches the production exceeds the real needs, aggressive publicity endeavours to increase the needs, the automobile industry is an obvious example. Standards of life rise, and only one income does not allow the family to keep up with its friends and colleagues. Increasingly large sections of society realize that they will never get access to the world described by publicity; thus also here, society is polarized, more psychologically speaking than in actual economic terms. However, the sense of privation can become so strong that society explodes, as we saw it in the suburbs of Paris in 2005.[13]

The third and last section of the workshop dealt with poor relief and with the perception of poverty. In his study of Early Modern poor relief Jean-Pierre Gutton[14] stressed that our contemporary notion of efficiency does not necessarily correspond to that of the past. The medieval system of individual almsgiving had proven less satisfactory, but the measures adopted in the first half of the sixteenth century did not abolish begging. Since 1580 the poor were increasingly concentrated in institutions, where they were set to work, a measure adopted already about 1400 in Northern Italy.[15] If the saving of the poors' souls was still a matter of concern in the late sixteenth as well as in the seventeenth century, the mercantilistic ideas claimed all hands to be active; the manufacture was the appropriate place, where the poor could be put to work. Only in the eighteenth century people realized that an efficient poor relief required the involvement of the state; Montesquieu went so far as to consider it a duty of the state to take care of the well-being of its citizens.[16]

---

13 THOMAS RIIS: "Les niveaux de vie et la "société de consommation"".
14 JEAN-PIERRE GUTTON: "Les institutions charitables de l'Europe moderne et la question de leur efficacité."
15 BRONISLAW GEREMEK: "Renfermement des pauvres en Italie (XIVᵉ–XVIIᵉ siècles). Remarques préliminaires," in : *Mélanges en l'honneur de Fernand Braudel* I, Toulouse 1973, pp. 205–217.
16 *De l'Esprit des Lois* (1748) livre XXIII, chapitre XXIX.

However, it must be recognized that very often manufactures worked with a deficit; it was rather improbable that a beggar could be taken from the street and after a short training appear as a skilled worker of silks. Under Friedrich Wilhelm I (1713–1740) the wool manufactures of Berlin were successful; they used the wool of the region, the workers lived already at Berlin, and the produced cloth had a guaranteed outlet, as it was sold to the army to be used for uniforms. An interesting feature of Early Modern poor relief is the creation of cheap credit since the fifteenth century (the Monti di Pietà, in Northern Europe savings banks). As today most savings banks have acquired a status as ordinary banks, the charitable credit institute disappeared, but the need for it is still there.[17]

In his analysis of the historical facts connected with the role of Domenico de' Bretti between 1512 and his death in 1523 Carlo Baja Guarienti confronts them with written and oral tradition. Soon after his death, de' Bretti became a legend, portrayed as a charismatic leader, hard but fair, an Italian Robin Hood. In de' Bretti the economically and socially disadvantaged people saw a mythical figure, who would make justice triumph in the end.[18]

Tobias Teuscher investigates the perception of the poor since the French Revolution, beginning with Dufourny de Villiers who qualified them as the Fourth Estate (*Quart État, Quatrième ordre*); in spite of the right belonging to every Frenchman to be represented in the Estates, this did not pertain to the poor. According to Karl Marx, the poor formed a subproletariate (*Lumpenproletariat*), but his definitions of it are far from unambiguous, if not to say contradictory. Directly inspired by the concept of the poor as the Fourth Estate formulated by Dufourny de Villiers, Father Joseph Wresinski who since the 1950s until his death in 1988 fought for the dignity and rights of the poor saw them as the Fourth World.[19]

---

17 THOMAS RIIS: Communication IV: Les réactions de la société à la pauvreté"

18 CARLO BAJA GUARIENTI: "Building a Hero: Poverty and Rebellion between History and Folklore."

19 TOBIAS TEUSCHER: "Quart Etat, Lumpenproletariat et Quart Monde: ce qu'apportent les révolutions européennes au combat de la grande pauvreté et de l'exclusion sociale et à la reconnaissance de la misère comme violation des droits de l'homme"

Herself a member of the movement (Mouvement ATD-Quart Monde) founded by Father Joseph Wresinski, Madame Join-Lambert pleads for the recognition of misery as a violation of human rights.[20]

The workshop has increased our knowledge in several fields:

I. Poverty has been defined in a way that appears to allow comparisons between contemporary poverty and that of the past.

II. Physical poverty (e.g. famine) is only the final critical phase of a long development.[21]

III. It must be taken for granted that gender is a cause of poverty, which is not necessarily true for large families, as poor people tend to marry late and to get less children.

IV. The shame-faced poor will be able to keep their social status for one or two generations after their economic decline; as their network is still intact, they can succeed in regaining their social status.

V. Poverty must be considered as hereditary in certain families; in spite of public or private assistance they are seldom able to break the vicious circle of poverty, first of all, because they lack an efficient network.

VI. Contemporary society is exposed to the risk of polarization (and of the reduction of the middle class) because of the expansion of information technology and of the increasing standard of life.

VII. Poverty must be seen as a violation of human rights.

From these acquisitions it becomes clear that contemporary poor relief treats mainly the symptoms and not the illness; in order to do this, the historical aspect of poverty must necessarily be considered, as only thus the causes of poverty can be identified. The recognition of this fact must be seen as a precondition for the formulation

---

20 MASCHA L. JOIN-LAMBERT: "Pauvreté et droits de l'homme."

21 AMRITA RANGASAMI: "The Masking of Famine: The Role of the Bureaucracy," in: *Famine and Society* ed. JEAN FLOUD & AMRITA RANGASAMI, New Delhi 1993, pp. 53–64.

of a new social policy. However, discussion during the workshop showed us that poverty is perceived very differently from one region of the World to the next. Before the final conference can be organized in order to discuss a new approach to social policy, a workshop ought to discuss the related questions of the perception of poverty and of the reasons why gender must be seen as a cause of poverty. Five zones should be specially studied as they must be considered to represent characteristic attitudes:

I.   Britain (with the USA and Australia)
II. Continental Europe (Western Europe as well as the former socialist countries)
III Africa
IV. Asia (especially India, China or Japan)
V.   Latin America.

The papers read to the workshop shall be published and will serve as a basis for the final conference dealing with social policy.

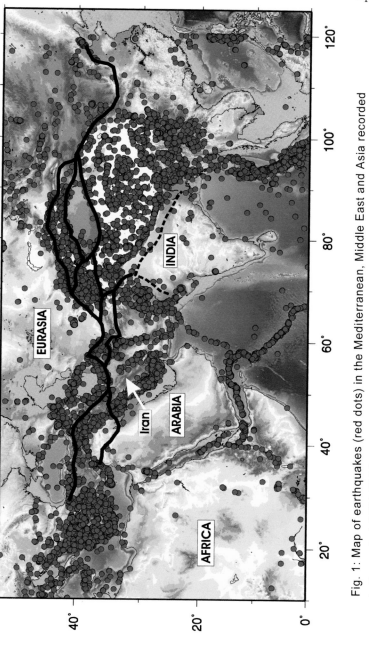

Fig. 1: Map of earthquakes (red dots) in the Mediterranean, Middle East and Asia recorded in the period 1964-2002.

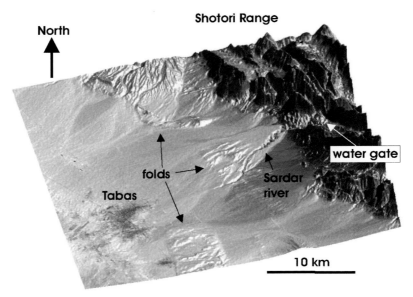

Fig. 2: Perspective view from the south of the desert oasis at Tabas, formed by draping an ASTER satellite over digital topography. The outwash surfaces from the mountain are interrupted by folds, through which drainage, like the Sardar river, incises. The folds are above buried blind thrusts, which moved in the 1978 earthquake, destroying Tabas, but incision ceases as soon as the river has crossed the SW front of the fold (Image courtesy of J. Hollingsworth).

Fig. 3b: View over the modern megacity of Tehran, adjacent to the Alborz range front, which is bounded by a known active thrust fault. The city has between 10-12 million daytime inhabitants.

Fig. 3a: View over part of the old inhabited region of Bam, destroyed in the 2003 earthquake. In this part of the town, construction was of adobe sun-dried brick and was completely destroyed.

351

Fig. 4: Perspective view looking north over Tehran, formed by draping a satellite image over a digital topographic model.

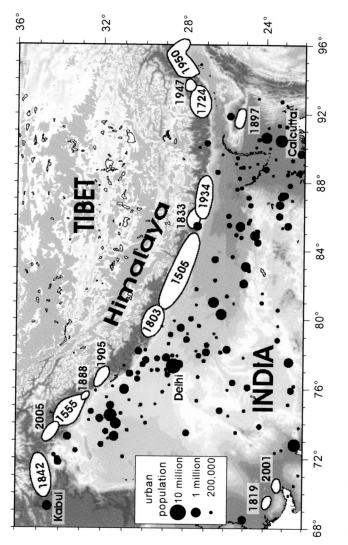

Fig. 5: White areas with dates are the sites of large earthquakes along the Himalayan range front between 1500 and 2005. Also shown are significant population centres in the region, many of which are vulnerable to future repeats of these past earthquakes (data from Bilham, 2004).

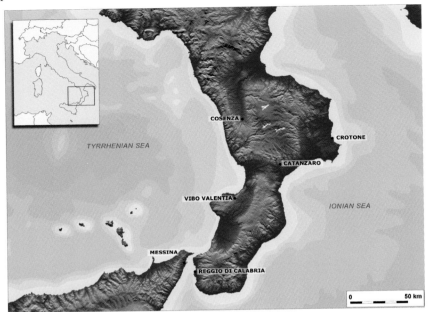

Fig. 6: Main towns of the Calabria region (Italy).

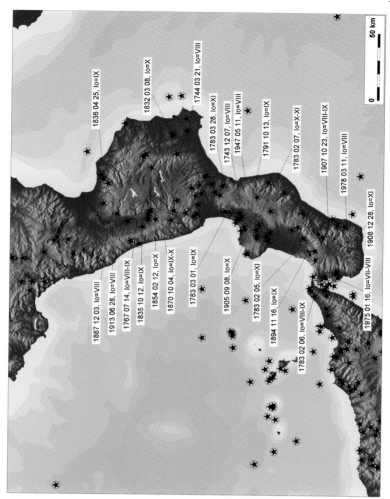

Fig. 7: The epicentres of the strongest earthquakes of Calabria from the 17th to the 20th century (these total 152 events). In red, the epicentres of the earthquakes mentioned in this text.

Labels on map:
1836 04 25, Io=IX
1832 03 08, Io=X
1744 03 21, Io=VIII
1783 03 28, Io=XI
1743 12 07, Io=VIII
1947 05 11, Io=VIII
1791 10 13, Io=IX
1783 02 07, Io=X-XI
1907 10 23, Io=VIII-IX
1978 03 11, Io=VIII
1908 12 28, Io=XI
1887 12 03, Io=VIII
1913 06 28, Io=VIII
1767 07 14, Io=VIII-IX
1835 10 12, Io=IX
1854 02 12, Io=X
1870 10 04, Io=IX-X
1783 03 01, Io=IX
1905 09 08, Io=X
1783 02 05, Io=XI
1894 11 16, Io=IX
1783 02 06, Io=VIII-IX
1975 01 16, Io=VII-VIII

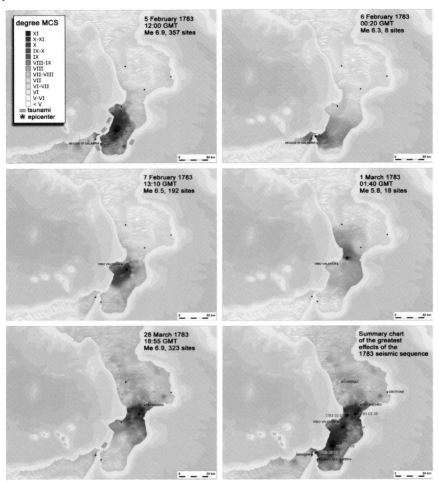

Fig. 8: Effects of five strong earthquakes occurring in Calabria between 5th February and 28th March 1783. The last map on the right portrays the cumulative effects of the previous shocks.

Fig. 9: Three of the 70 tables drawn by Pompeo Schiantarelli and Ignazio Stile (1784) to represent the impressive effects in the natural environment of the earthquakes in Calabria in 1783:
a) cracks and gaps at Gerocarne;
b) new lakes close to Polistena;
c) hydro-geological effects at Terranova.

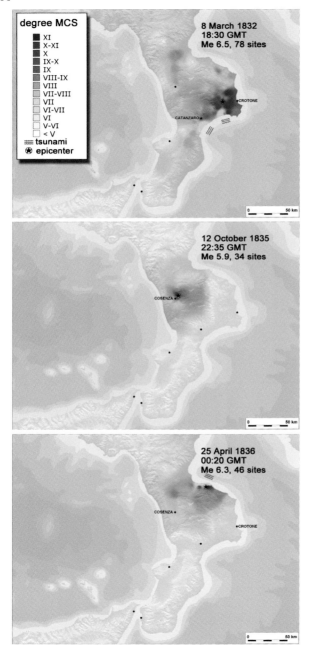

Fig. 10: Effects of the earthquakes of 1832, 1835, 1836.

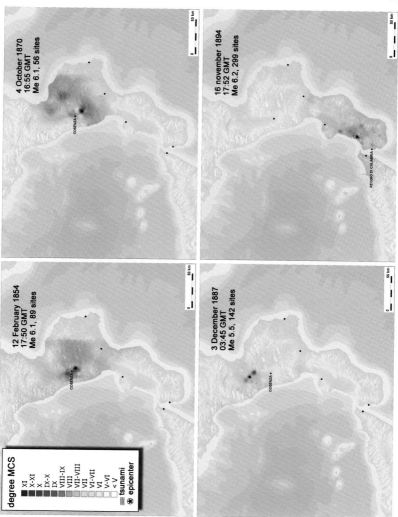

Fig. 11: Effects of the earthquakes of 1854, 1870, 1887, 1894.

359

Fig. 12: Effects of the earthquake of 1894 in
three municipalities of the province of Reggio di Calabria
a) Bagnara Calabra; b) Sant'Eufemia; c) Seminara
(from Sieberg, Archives at Jena)

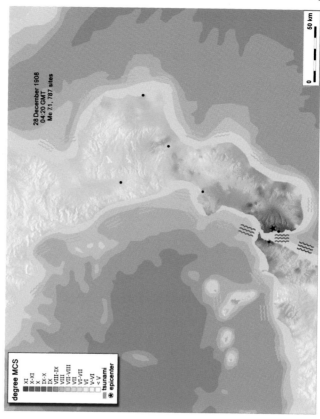

Fig. 14: Effects of the earthquake of 1908 and the tsunami.

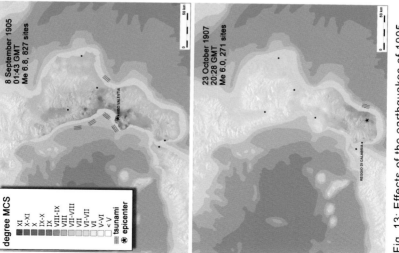

Fig. 13: Effects of the earthquakes of 1905 and 1907.

361

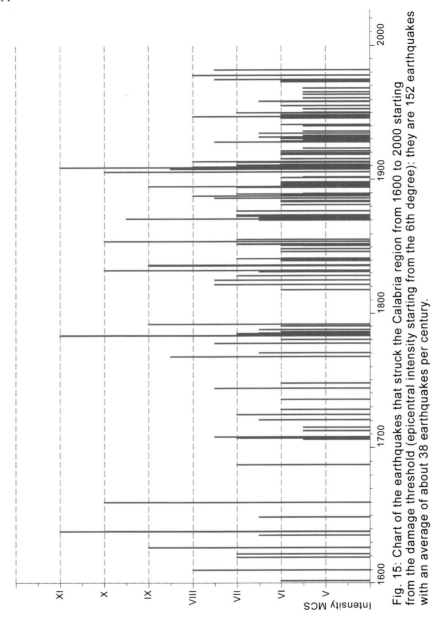

Fig. 15: Chart of the earthquakes that struck the Calabria region from 1600 to 2000 starting from the damage threshold (epicentral intensity starting from the 6th degree): they are 152 earthquakes with an average of about 38 earthquakes per century.

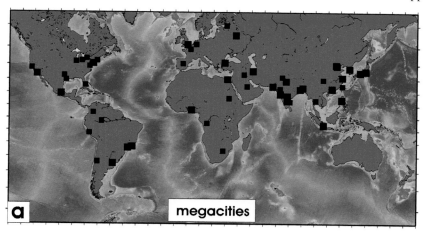

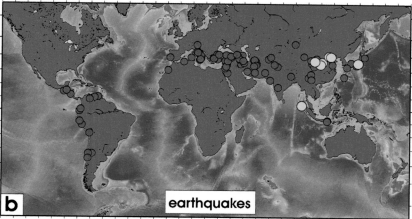

Fig. 16
(a) Cities with a population of more than 5 million (small squares)
or 10 million (large squares).
(b) Earthquakes of the past 1,000 years known to have killed more
than 10,000 (red dots) or 100,000 (yellow dots) people:
113 earthquakes altogether; 34 of these earthquakes have
occurred in the past 100 years

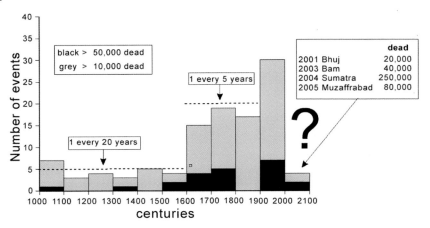

Fig. 17: Histogram of the 113 earthquakes mapped in Fig. 16
killing more than 10,000 (grey) or 50,000 (black) people
per century over the last 1000 years. Until about 1600 they
averaged about one every 20 years, increasing to nearly
one every 5 years between 1600-1900. This century we have
had nearly one every year.

List of Authors

Dr. Carlo Baja Guarienti
Viale Monte Grappa 25
I-42100 Reggio Emilia
Italy
carlo.bg@libero.it

Dr. Torsten Fischer
Rüdesheimer Strasse 20,
D-53175 Bonn
Germany
torsten_kiel@yahoo.de

Prof. Dr. Jean-Pierre Gutton
72, boulevard des Belges
F-69006 Lyon
France

Madame Mascha Join-Lambert
Haus Neudorf e.V.
West-Ost-Forum für Europas Gemeinschaft
Friedenfelde
D-17268 Gerswalde
Germany
atd.vierte-welt@t-online.de

Dr. Marion Kobelt-Groch
Bergstrasse 4
D-23669 Timmendorfer Strand
Germany
kobelt-groch@web.de

Prof. Dr. René Leboutte
Université du Luxembourg
Campus Limpertsberg
Département d'Histoire
162A, avenue de la Faïencerie
L-1511 Luxembourg
rene.leboutte@uni.lu

Dr. Matteo Provasi
Dipartimento di Scienze Umane
Università degli Studi di Ferrara
Via Savonarola 27
I-44100 Ferrara
Italy
iperteo@supereva.it

Prof. Dr. Giovanni Ricci
Dipartimento di Scienze Umane
Università degli Studi di Ferrara
Via Savonarola 27
I-44100 Ferrara
Italy
rcc@unife.it

Prof. Dr. Thomas Riis
Historisches Seminar
Olshausenstrasse 40
D-24098 Kiel
Germany
th.riis@email.uni-kiel.de

Prof. Dr. Sølvi Sogner
Department of History
Box 1008
N-0316 Blindern
Norway
ssogner@mail.hf.uio.no

Tobias Teuscher
55, rue Saint-Alphonse
B-1210 Bruxelles (St Josse)
Belgique
tobias.teuscher@ulb.ac.be

Prof. Dr. Noël Whiteside
Department of Sociology
University of Warwick
Coventry CV4 7AL
England
N.Whiteside@warwick.ac.uk